*Joint International
Business Ventures
In Developing Countries*

Joint International Business Ventures In Developing Countries

Case Studies and Analysis of Recent Trends

WOLFGANG G. FRIEDMANN
& JEAN-PIERRE BÉGUIN

With the collaboration of
James Peterson and Alain Pellet

Columbia University Press
New York and London · 1971

The preparation of this book
was made possible by funds made available
to the International Legal Research Program
from a grant made to Columbia University by
the Ford Foundation.

PREFACE

In 1956, the undersigned began to direct a Columbia University research project on joint international business ventures between developed and developing countries, in which he was subsequently joined by Mr. George Kalmanoff. The project was concluded five years later, with the publication of a book [1] that contained a considerable number of case studies of joint ventures as well as a general analysis of the types, problems, and prospects of this new and increasingly important form of foreign investment in developing countries. In the mid-fifties, such joint ventures—although a familiar phenomenon between business enterprises of developed countries—were still experimental, haphazard, and, quite frequently, unsuccessful. On the one hand, business enterprises of the Western world were accustomed to complete control of their investment in the undeveloped world, which, except for the politically sovereign but economically dependent countries of Latin America, meant almost entirely colonial possessions or protectorates. Moreover, they found it very difficult to adjust themselves to sharing, let alone abandoning, complete control of their foreign branches or subsidiaries, or to enter into new ventures on a basis very different from that of their previous operations. On the other hand, in the immediate post-war period, the newly independent states of Asia came slowly and painfully to the insight that political and legal sovereignty over their natural resources and industrial development by themselves were no substitute for the lack of capital, skill, and know-how, for which they still had largely to rely on the more developed countries. The 1961 book was an attempt to analyze the experiences as well as the problems and prospects of joint ventures, in the conviction that this type of association was bound to become an increasingly important form of business association between the industrially developed countries of the Western world and the rapidly growing number of newly independent and economically backward states.

1. *Joint International Business Ventures,* W. Friedmann and G. Kalmanoff (eds.), Columbia University Press, New York and London (1961).

In the intervening years, the joint international business venture has become the predominant form of foreign investment in developing countries. Whether by way of special legislation, by policy directives, or as a condition of a concession granted by the host government to a foreign investor, some equity participation by public or private interests of the host country is now the normal pattern. It has been adopted more and more, not only by the Asian but by the newer African states, while the growing economic nationalism of the Latin American states accounts for the increasing use of joint ventures as an alternative or a preliminary to outright nationalization. Joint venturing has spread from manufacturing to raw materials, such as copper, iron ore, and oil. Joint ventures between foreign-private entrepreneurs and the governments of the developing countries, or public development corporations, have greatly increased. Many of the most important joint ventures are now multipartite rather than bipartite. The associations of foreign consortia with host governments are often supported by major loans from international and national public aid and development institutions.

In view of the greatly increased economic and political significance of joint ventures, the growing variety of joint venture patterns, and the need to analyze the experiences and problems encountered, it was decided in 1967 to supplement the 1961 book by a further study that would incorporate the new experiences. The United Nations Industrial Development Organization (UNIDO), which had been asked to undertake a project on joint ventures in manufacturing, has made a financial contribution to the Columbia project and has circulated condensed versions prepared by UNIDO of some of the case studies. The responsibility for the present book is, however, exclusively that of the undersigned.

The present study is not a new edition of the 1961 book. It is a follow-up study, based on major case studies as well as a survey of the policies of one of the most important of the developing countries, India, with regard to joint ventures, and a separate study—prepared by Mr. Béguin—on the problem of control. Except for the revised case studies of Merck of India, Agip, and Mannesman-Sümerbank, earlier versions of which were published in the 1961 book, the case studies are new and they are considerably more detailed than those of the earlier book. They have been chosen so as to represent the greatest possible variety of types of joint ventures. They therefore include multipartite as well as bipartite ventures, associations between private partners as well as several between private investors and governments or government corporations. American, British, Canadian, Dutch, French, German, Italian, Swedish, and Swiss enterprises representing the industrially developed countries; and African, Asian, and Latin American enterprises representing countries of the developing world, are included in the case studies. A variety of processes—from electronics and steel tubes, food products, and other consumer goods, to the extraction of copper, iron ore, and oil—have been selected. At the same time an effort has been made to represent the most important patterns of joint ventures, especially in the distribution of equities and the different forms of multipartite associations.

Needless to say, the cases chosen are selective, designed to represent the most important types rather than even a fraction of the actual number of joint ventures now abundant throughout the world. The field investigations have been mainly undertaken by Jean-Pierre Béguin, and the case studies involving Canadian participation have been prepared by James Peterson. The Fives Lille-Cail study has been prepared by Alain Pellet, Assistant at the Faculté de Droit de Paris. My research assistant, Michael Kaprelian, has been of great help in the final preparation of the manuscript for publication. The index has been prepared by Martin L. Friedmann.

There is no reason to modify basically the general analysis attempted in the 1961 book on *Joint International Business Ventures*. However, the introductory chapter of the present book attempts to reappraise the problem, in the light of more recent developments. The more extensive and up-to-date case studies contained in the present study should help to broaden the understanding of this matter, and assist the growing number of enterprises engaged in foreign investment decisions in the appreciation of the modalities, the benefits, and the risks of joint international business ventures.

Wolfgang Friedmann

ACKNOWLEDGMENTS

The authors wish to express their gratitude to the various government agencies and business enterprises which have generously supplied and checked the data contained in the studies collected in the present volume. It should be stressed, however, that any evaluations, criticisms and appraisals contained either in the case studies or in the concluding observations are entirely the responsibility of the authors, and not of the informants.

The authors and publisher also wish to thank the following for permission to reprint certain materials included in this book from the books and periodicals listed below:

Trustees of Columbia University, for permission to reprint from J. Meyhen, W. Friedmann, and K. Weg, "Joint Ventures Revisited," 1 *Columbia Journal of World Business* 19 (1966).

Columbia University Press, for permission to reprint from W. Friedmann and G. Kalmanoff, *Joint International Business Ventures* (1961).

The Division of Research, Harvard Business School, for permission to reprint from E. R. Barlow, *Management of Foreign Manufacturing Subsidiaries* (1953).

Richard D. Irwin, Inc., for permission to reprint from C. Kindleberger, *International Economics* (1963).

Unilever Ltd., for permission to reprint from Hamengkubuwono IX, "Indonesia Plans a Brighter Future," *Progress: The Unilever Quarterly* (no. 2, 1968); Sir A. Smith, "Catching the Wind of Change: The Redeployment of the United Africa Company," *Progress: The Unilever Quarterly* (no. 1, 1965).

CONTENTS

Joint International
Business Ventures
In Developing Countries

I: SOME GENERAL
OBSERVATIONS

Foreign Investment and Joint Ventures in Developing Countries

It should be stressed at the outset that many of the basic problems of contemporary foreign investments in developing countries are independent of the particular legal and business form chosen for the investment, and they are therefore shared by joint international business ventures with other forms of investment, where the ownership may be entirely either in national or in foreign hands. Problems of association between investors from the developed world and the developing countries derive essentially from the need to combine the minimum business attractiveness for corporations which have many alternative profitable forms of investment, with the integration of the investment in the general and economic plans of the host country. It is not the purpose of the present book to discuss these wider problems in depth.[1]

Suffice it to say that any foreign investment in a developing country—be it the transformation of an existing former investment or the creation of a new enterprise—must seek and achieve a sat-

1. Among the many contemporary discussions of this problem we may mention the following: B. Higgins, *Economic Development*, New York, W. W. Norton (Revised ed. 1968); R. F. Mikesell (ed.), *U.S. Private and Government Investment Abroad*, Eugene, University of Oregon (1962); A. Maddison, *Foreign Skills and Technical Assistance in Economic Development*, OECD Development Center (1965); *Investment and Development: The Role of Private Investment in Developing Countries*, London Overseas Development Institute (1965); and W. Friedmann and R. Pugh (eds.), *Legal Aspects of Foreign Investment*, London, Stevens & Sons (1959).

isfactory compromise between the purposes and aspirations of the host country on one part and of the foreign investor on the other part.

The host country will strive for the following objectives:

1. The joint venture must be integrated in the national economic development plan. This means that it will generally—either in accordance with the condition of the form of an investment law or the specific terms laid down in the concession agreement or instrument of approval—be assigned a certain priority in the national development plan. This is normally done by making the allocation of foreign exchange, the importation of foreign materials, the repatriation of capital, profits, salaries, etc., dependent upon the value assigned to the enterprise in the national development plan.

2. Since all developing countries are chronically short of investment capital, and particularly of foreign exchange, the capital contribution brought by the foreign investor in the form of cash, machinery, or other assets will be an important factor.

3. The training of local skills, from the general management and scientific expertise to skilled labor, constitutes generally one of the highest priorities in the host government's decision. This implies a training scheme and the gradual replacement of foreign personnel by nationals.

4. An important factor is the extent to which the foreign investment will strengthen the national economy of the host country by development of productive facilities that will reduce the need for foreign imports (import substitutions), or lay the foundations for an export industry.

5. Large scale foreign investment will generally be linked with social development purposes, such as the construction of "infrastructure" facilities (railways, harbors, roads); of educational facilities (training establishments, schools); and other social services (hospitals, welfare centers).

The foreign investor will seek:

1. A return on his investment that will justify the investment decision from a commercial point of view and, therefore, often be somewhat higher than that expected from a corresponding investment in a developed country.

2. Some legal guarantee of the security of his investment. This may consist of certain assurances against nationalization, contained either in the relevant investment code or in the specific investment

agreement. Since the guarantor is usually a government, the foreign investor will, whenever possible, seek to buttress the arrangements by an arbitration agreement, either within the framework of the World Bank sponsored Convention for the Settlement of Investment Disputes, or by specific arbitration agreement.

3. To compensate for what is generally regarded as a heightened risk of investment, the foreign investor will normally seek and obtain certain privileges with regard to taxation, repatriation, earnings, and capital, and, more controversially, assurances against the granting of licenses for competitive enterprises.

All these, and many other factors, arise whether the enterprise in question is wholly foreign-owned, wholly nationally owned, or a joint venture. The intensity of cooperation between foreign and local interests is by no means always proportionate to the sharing of equities. Critics of the joint venture have often pointed out that a wholly foreign-owned subsidiary which makes a maximum use of local skills and personnel, which avoids discrepancies in the remuneration and standard of living between foreign and local personnel, which uses local materials, services, and institutions to the greatest possible extent, and which is generally guided by an understanding of the country, its people, and its purposes, can be a much more successful experiment in partnership than a joint venture that is merely a financial device.

Nevertheless, the joint capital venture, i.e. an enterprise in which two or more parties, representing one or several developed and one or several developing countries, share the financial risks and the decision-making through joint equity participation in a common enterprise, has more and more become the most important form of foreign investment in the developing countries of Africa, Asia, and Latin America.[2]

2. The case studies collected for the present volume are confined to joint ventures between the developing countries of these three continents and the Western world. In recent years, various members of the Soviet group of socialist countries have begun to form joint ventures in the developing world. These joint ventures will obviously vary, in certain respects, from those characteristic of the Western type of joint venture, and they may well deserve a special study in the future. See also, on the special position of Yugoslavia, where enterprises enjoy autonomy and recent legislation encourages foreign investment: W. Friedmann and L. Mates (eds.), *Joint Business Ventures Between Yugoslav Enterprises and Foreign Firms*, Belgrade, Kultura (1968).

The reasons for the growing frequency and importance of the joint capital venture, as they were formulated in our earlier study,[3] still hold good:

1. In a significant proportion of cases, there is an absolute business advantage in the association of local capital with the enterprise. The foreign investor may be short of capital, or he may be unwilling to bear the entire risk alone.

2. Closely allied are cases in which availability of the best local entrepreneurial or managerial talent is linked with local participation.

3. The acceptance of a joint venture is sometimes the only alternative to desisting from or abandoning an existing enterprise by a foreign investor. A joint venture may be "forced" upon a foreign investor, either through legislative requirements for local participation, or by administrative measures which make the granting of the necessary licenses and currency allocations contingent upon jointness. Such forced ventures are generally disliked by the foreign investor because they hamper his freedom of decision and movement. It is all the more important for the foreign investor to appreciate the non-economic factors which, in the great majority of the less developed countries, create the psychological pressure for jointness. Such understanding will eliminate the less desirable alternative of a forced joint venture.

4. To many of the governments and peoples of the less developed countries, partnership in the full sense, that is, jointness in ownership, control, and responsibility, is a symbol of equality.

5. Such symbols are important, regardless of the immediate business aspects, because they help to reduce deeply ingrained suspicions of foreign economic domination. Whether such suspicions are justified in a particular case or not, they are a real and an important aspect of that national sensitiveness which characterizes many emancipated peoples who were formerly held in a state of political or economic dependency.

6. Overwhelmingly, the new nations want economic development. In the world of today, they will get support from either the Western or the Communist world. The joint venture is a vehicle, though not the only one, for helping these aspirations and for influencing the course they will take.

Attitudes of Host Governments towards Joint Ventures

For an up-to-date evaluation of attitudes of developing countries towards joint ventures, we have made a survey of official policy and

3. W. Friedmann and G. Kalmanoff, *Joint International Business Ventures*, New York, Columbia University Press, pp. 261–62 (1961).

private attitudes towards joint ventures, as adopted in the largest of the developing countries, India. It should however be borne in mind that the term "developing country" comprises a vast number of countries which are in very differential stages of development. Certain common elements apply to all of them, and they may be summarized as follows. First, there is a wide gap between the actual standard of living of the great majority of the population, and the minimum aspirations—expressed in terms of nutrition, housing, education, and other basic aspects of life. Second, underdeveloped nations lack means of economic diversification. This implies, generally, a predominantly static and agricultural economy, and dependence on the export of a single primary staple commodity, such as coffee, cocoa, cotton, palm oil, or sugar.[4] Third, a chronic shortage of indigenous capital for economic and particularly industrial development entails far-reaching dependence on public development aid and private investment from abroad. Fourth, all these discrepancies are reinforced by the low level of general educational standards, administrative capabilities, technological and scientific training, and the availability of such skills. Within this general framework there are, however, enormous differences between countries such as India or Brazil, which have a considerable background of managerial, scientific, and technological training, as well as considerable commercial experience and sophisticated indigenous enterprises, and some of the small, new independent states of Africa or the West Indies, which have made a sudden transition from tribal and static communities to the aspirations of modern states.

Such differences are bound to influence greatly the attitudes towards joint ventures. As far as capital supplies are concerned, a country like India—which has such major industrial concerns as Tata, Birla, Delhi Cloth and General Mills, as well as a large number of smaller Indian entrepreneurs—can aspire to a far greater

4. While a self-contained agricultural economy normally entails a low though stable standard of living, dependence on export of a primary commodity has, especially during the last fifteen years, meant sharp fluctuations in national income and depressed prices, which contrast starkly with the constantly rising costs of industrial products. This increases the gap between the developed countries which export industrial products and the developing countries, which do not have the capital, the technological know-how, or the organizations to compete with the more advanced countries. See the Report of the Commission on International Development, *Partners in Development*, New York, Praeger, Ch. 2 (1969).

share of private national participation in the transformation of old, or the formation of new business ventures, than many of the new African states, which lack indigenous capital and, therefore, must to a far greater extent depend on the participation of government financed development corporations. Similar differences exist with regard to managerial, scientific, and technological skills. As our India study shows, the Indian Government in 1968 established a governmental Foreign Investment Board which is responsible for all matters relating to foreign private investment and joint ventures and is presided over by a senior official of the Finance Ministry. And while the Indian Government, unlike many other states, has adhered to the principle of establishing policy guidelines rather than issuing investment laws, the new guidelines laid down in 1968 distinguish between three categories of enterprises involving foreign participation, i.e.:

(a) those where foreign investment may be permitted without restrictions,

(b) where foreign technical collaboration, but no foreign investment, may be permitted, and

(c) where no foreign collaboration, either financial or technical, is permitted at all.

New, wholly foreign-owned investment, as well as enterprises of strategic importance and those where Indian managerial and technical skills are adequate, belong to the last category in which joint ventures are excluded in principle. The guidelines with regard to the other two categories are described in more detail in our India study. Generally, the guidelines, as administered by the Foreign Investment Board, strongly encourage the formation of equity joint ventures where considerable foreign exchange and sophisticated techniques are needed, i.e. "in the developing fields of chemicals, fertilizers, electronics, specialized kinds of steel making, other metals, machine tools, earth moving equipment and shipbuilding." Within these general guidelines, considerable discretion remains. As is the case in all developing countries, whether they have issued special investment laws or not, the authorization of any foreign investment is a matter of administrative decision by the appropriate government board of authority. As our specific India case studies show—covering such various fields as the manufacture of pharmaceuticals, fertilizer production, cotton, engineering products, and general merchandizing— the participation of both Indian public and private investors in joint ventures has steadily increased. This is illustrated by the decreasing share of the Swiss firm of Volkart in Voltas, matched by a corresponding increase of the Indian participations, which now include the government-owned Life Insurance Corporation, the Unit Trust of India, and shares held by the Indian public. Similarly, in the Coromandel fertilizer venture, the public and some financial Indian institutions, together with a minor participation by the Indian promoter, hold a majority of the shares. In the Merck pharmaceutical venture, a somewhat older enterprise, the American firm has hitherto retained a majority participation.

Most of the less developed countries—among which are a majority of the new African states—still lack sufficient indigenous capital and skill to be able to insist on local participation to the same extent. Insofar as there is African equity participation, it is predominantly that of government-owned corporations. Thus, in the Ghana Textile Printing Company the Ghana Industrial Holding Corporation holds 51 percent of the shares. In the West African Portland Cement Company, which operates in Western Nigeria, 51 percent of the capital of £8 million is held by the Unilever-controlled United Africa Company, and the remaining 49 percent by the government-owned Western Nigeria Development Corporation. In the most interesting of the joint ventures formed by the French Fives Lille Cail (FLC) company, which manufactures and exports industrial equipment, FLC holds 51 percent and the Factory Workers Union of North-east Brazil 49 percent. This is an unusual partnership between a foreign industrial company and the workers' organization of an underdeveloped region. Our study of the Société Industrielle et Agricole du Niari (Sian) shows that the various governments of the French speaking, and formerly French controlled, African states that participate in the operations of this group, generally hold a minority of the shares, while most of the equity as well as the additional loan capital is contributed by private French financing consortia, such as the Compagnie Financière pour l'Outre-Mer (Cofimer), or government agencies, such as the Fonds d'Aide et de Coopération (FAC), or the Caisse Centrale de Coopération Economique (CCCE). African joint manufacturing ventures generally require relatively modest financial investments, since they operate mainly in the sphere of processing of agricultural produce or light consumer products. A very different picture is shown in the giant multipartite Liberian American Swedish Minerals Company (Lamco) venture in Liberia. Here the Government of Liberia is a 50 percent partner in the equity venture. But this might give a deceptive impression of the magnitude of the Liberian Government's participation. The joint equity venture between the Government of Liberia and the foreign consortium, capitalized at $2 million, is but a minute part of the total capital investment, which is close to $300 million. The remainder of the capital is, as our study shows, supplied by the contractual participation of Bethlehem Steel, as well as by major loans of German and United States aid agencies, in addition to some private capital sources. Moreover, the Government of Liberia has paid for its equity share not in cash but by the concession granted to the joint venture to exploit minerals in its territory. In other words, it has conceded certain aspects of its sovereign control over the natural resources within its territory, in return for its equity participation.

Different techniques of increasing the national share in once wholly foreign-owned major operations in the field of natural mineral resources and public utilities are demonstrated in two of our Latin American case studies. Increasingly, Latin American governments, which, for many decades, have to a large extent been controlled by foreign economic interests, are proceeding toward the nationalization of basic industries and natural resources, often through an intermediate stage, i.e. joint ventures with national majority control. The Brazilian Light and Power Company, a Canadian holding and management company for utility subsidiaries which commenced operations in Brazil in 1899, owns assets in various Central and South American countries totalling more than $1.1 billion. In Brazil its operations have included all the major public utilities, including tramways, gas and electricity, and telephones. In 1966, after years of complicated negotiations, Brazilian sold all its telephone utilities to the Federal Government for just under $100 million, payable over a twenty-year period. However, as is shown in detail in the case study, most of the proceeds have to be reinvested by Brazilian in a variety of enterprises, none of them in the field of public utilities. As of the summer of 1969 seven of these new enterprises, all involving a minority participation by Brazilian, had been formed. If this process continues, both with regard to Brazilian and to other foreign investors, it will mean that Brazil will gradually acquire the ownership of its basic industries and utilities and minimize the expenditure of foreign exchange involved in the repatriation of the sales price; the technique is that of agreeing—under the open or veiled threat of nationalization on confiscatory terms—with the foreign company on a reinvestment of most of the proceeds, as a minority shareholder, in a variety of enterprises. These enterprises will be designed to develop various manufacturing processes and skills in fields other than those of natural resources and basic utilities.

Equally significant is the conversion, since 1964, of the Sociedad Minera El Teniente S.A., formerly wholly owned by the U. S. Kennecott Corporation, into a joint venture in which the Copper Corporation, a Chilean agency, holds 51 percent of the shares. Although this greatly increases the share of the Chilean Government in the exploitation of one of its most important resources, copper, it has paid only a minor part of the sales price of $80 million in cash. Moreover, the cash payments, capital and interest, have been returned to Chile as a loan repayable over a period of twenty years.

Whether this conversion of a formerly foreign-owned operation into a joint venture in which the Chilean Government holds a majority is a more or less permanent or merely a transitory solution remains to be seen. The other big American company operating in Chile, Anaconda, which did not make an agreement corresponding to Kennecott's, was quite recently compelled (by the threat of outright nationalization) to agree to an immediate conversion of its Chilean enterprise into a 49 percent holding. The other 51 percent was transferred to the Chilean Government with the remaining interests of Anaconda to be purchased sometime during the period 1973–1981. Whether parallel legislation will also nationalize the 49 percent interest of Kennecott in El Teniente with the Chilean Government is likely to depend on political rather than on economic factors. As parallel developments in other Latin American countries as well as in Africa show, there is a growing tide of nationalism, the main target of which are foreign investments in natural resources, and political emotions may well prevail over considerations of efficiency and economic advantages.[5]

What is clear from these various examples is the growing tendency of developing countries—depending to some extent, though not entirely, on the state of their own technological, industrial, and financial resources—to reduce the area of foreign-owned investment. In this

5. In August, 1969, Zambia followed the Chilean example by acquiring—in the form of nationalization decrees—a 51 percent interest in the foreign-owned copper companies, and offering compensation at "book value" (and payable out of future profits) for the expropriated shares. Zambia also offered new mining concessions for a period of 25 years. In October, 1970, the newly elected Allende government declared its intention to fully nationalize all foreign mining interests. See further, *infra*, p. 97.

process the joint venture is the chosen instrument. Depending on political developments, and on the degree of harmony achieved between the partners, it will be a permanent or a transitory feature in the transformation of the relations between the developed and developing countries.

Attitudes of Foreign Investors towards Joint Ventures

There has been a gradual but distinct change in the outlook of foreign investors from the Western world—principally the limited number of multinational corporations with worldwide investments and interests—towards joint ventures in developing countries. As our 1961 publication showed, the great majority of Western enterprises —where they did not prefer liquidation of their interests to any form of joint venture—accepted them reluctantly. The case studies collected in the present volume—which include surveys of the general joint venture policies of such giant multinational enterprises as Unilever, Philips, and Nestlé's—show that a majority of Western corporations have come to adopt a much more flexible attitude, and that they have in principle accepted the necessity and importance of joint ventures in developing countries as a fact of life. Certain corporations, notably the big American motor car manufacturers such as General Motors or Ford Motors, still refuse to enter into joint ventures, even in developed countries, as a matter of principle. General Motors has refused to make even limited offerings of shares in its highly successful Australian Holden manufacturing enterprise to the Australian public; and Ford, some years ago, during a severe United States balance of payment crisis, bought out the British minority shareholders of the British Ford Motor Company in order to gain full control. Even if one can rationalize such attitudes by the desire to retain liberty in the transfer of manufacturing from one country to another (e.g. from Britain to Germany), it must be admitted that these policies are not always based on rational considerations, but on tradition or prejudice. It is noteworthy that the giant multinational IBM Corporation, which dominates the international computer market, and has been generally taken to be foremost among the enterprises that wish to retain complete control over both the technology and the marketing of their products, has specifically stated [6] that it

6. See *infra*, pp. 218–21.

adopts a flexible attitude toward joint ventures and will examine each situation on its merits.

That this is now the predominant attitude of international investors is due not so much to enthusiasm as to the recognition of the fact that the developing countries are determined to gain an increasing measure of control over their industrial development, sometimes at the cost of economic rationality, and that, therefore, the joint venture is often the only alternative to complete exclusion from the country concerned or, where an existing enterprise is in question, to nationalization on usually unfavorable terms. If, in the light of this situation, more and more Western enterprises have accepted joint ventures—including associations with governments as well as with private enterprise—this is due to a careful weighing of the advantages and disadvantages. Such multinational enterprises as Unilever, Nestlé's, Merck, or Mannesmann obviously need worldwide outlets for their standardized products. The decision to accept joint ventures —increasingly even in minority positions—is due to the calculation that, on balance, the association with the development of countries such as India, Nigeria, or the five republics of the Central American Common Market offers the only chance of participation in new and expanding markets for their products.

Majority or Minority Participation

In our earlier study,[7] we noted that there was still general hostility to the acceptance of minority participations by Western and in particular by American investors, but that a change in attitude was beginning to become perceptible. We summed up the reasons for the growing proportion of foreign minority participations in joint ventures in developing countries as follows:

1. Local legislation may stipulate a stated minimum majority to be held by nationals in certain industries or services. The alternative for the foreign investor is either to accept a minority interest or to stay out.

2. National prestige factors may account for strong pressure to reduce a foreign interest to a minority holding, at times resulting in specific legislation to that effect. This is notably so in air transport, where national prestige is strongly involved. Foreign firms such as Pan American Airways, which once dominated Latin American air transportation, have

7. Friedmann and Kalmanoff, *op. cit. supra* note 3, at pp. 266–68.

gradually come to accept a minority interest (usually one-third) in many cases.

3. Some firms, in industries particularly suitable to joint venturing such as chemical products, draw a distinction between specialty products (a patented drug) and a general production line (plastics). For specialties they will insist on majority control, but for general products they are prepared to accept a minority interest.

4. Experience has shown that the apparent disadvantage of a minority interest is, in many services and industries, countered by the continuing advantage of know-how and technological superiority.

5. The apparent minority interest, say of 49 percent or even 33⅓ percent, can mean effective majority control if the local holdings are scattered among many participants. It is only where the foreign investor accepts a minority participation with one local investor that he faces possible majorization.

In the course of our inquiry it was pointed out by some experienced Western investors that to hold a substantial minority interest in a foreign enterprise has compensating advantages. In many of the less developed countries, the foreign investor is apt to be looked upon with greater suspicion than the domestic investor in the conduct of his operations. As a minority shareholder, the foreign investor escapes the responsibilities for the often complex and cumbrous procedure of minority protection. As long as the foreign investor is needed because of his capital investment, his managerial experience, and his technological know-how, he is not likely to suffer from the position of a minority stockholder, and he is not subject to the accusation of dominating the enterprise at the expense of the minority holders. A foreign minority participation will usually classify the joint enterprise as "national" and thus save it from general legislative or administrative measures directed at foreign enterprises. It is largely for this reason that some of the largest enterprises of the United States have accepted minority positions in joint ventures. . . .[8]

There is no reason to modify that presentation in any way. The case studies collected in the present volume show that the great majority of enterprises still prefer majority control where they can get it, but that they are increasingly ready to accept minority participation where this is required, either by legislation or by over-riding policy considerations. The governments of the developing countries —whether in the capacity of partners or licensing authorities—are often quite content to accept a national minority participation because this means a correspondingly smaller capital investment, and a proportionately larger influx of foreign capital investment and for-

8. *Id.* at pp. 267–68.

eign exchange. As we have seen, many local majority participations are made possible only by the host government paying in the form of a concession to utilize its natural resources, or by borrowing, in one form or another, from the foreign investor or from a foreign or international lending agency, most of the capital that it requires for its own investment. A generation, perhaps even a decade ago, few American or European enterprises would have accepted such a solution. That they do so now is due to the increasing determination of the developing countries to reduce or eliminate foreign economic control, at least in vital sectors of the economy, and the growing collective political weight which they exercise in the United Nations, in the U. N. Conference on Trade and Development (UNCTAD), in the Organization of Petroleum Exporting Countries (OPEC), and in other international organizations. This corresponds, on the part of the developed countries, to the growing recognition of the limitations of physical and economic power. Big power diplomacy or military pressure may still be used by the super powers in countries considered to be in the immediate sphere of influence and security—as the actions of the U.S.S.R. in East Germany, Hungary, and Czechoslovakia, and the interventions of the U.S.A. in Guatemala, the Dominican Republic, and the Cuban missile crisis have shown. But no less significant is the fact that the United States—deeply influenced by the costly experience of the Vietnam war, which has shown the limitations of military and technological superiority—does not dispatch its navy or air force to stop the seizure of American trawlers within the self-proclaimed 200 mile zones of Peru and Ecuador, and is reluctant to use economic sanctions against the confiscation of U.S. oil properties in Peru. There are also signs that the U.S.S.R. may be unwilling to repeat or extend its brutal intervention in Czechoslovakia. The sheer magnitude and destructiveness of the military power enjoyed by the super-powers reveals its limitations. This has its definite effects on the balance of economic power. The United States, let alone Britain or the other Western powers, is increasingly reluctant to use its military superiority or even the power of economic retaliation towards the smaller states. It is doubtful whether even the economic reprisals and trade boycott applied by the United States against Castro's Cuba, a few years ago, would be repeated today. Hence private investors cannot count, as they could have a century ago, on the intervention of their governments, and they must make the best economic accommodation with the host country that is possible in the circumstances. This means the increasing acceptance of minority participations, of associations with governments or government-owned development corporations, or, in a number of cases, fifty-fifty partnerships. This is well illustrated by the policy statements made to us by the giant Dutch electronics enterprise of Philips and the British-Dutch Unilever concern. Philips, like the rest, prefers to have as large a majority as possible, but often accepts 50 percent or minority participation. It minimizes the risks of flexibility by formulating various arrangements concerning control over the planning and operations of the enterprise and the sales policy for its trademark-protected products. The Swiss firm of Volkart goes even further. In India it has, since 1954, pursued a systematic policy of gradual reduction of its equity participation, in proportion to an increase of Indian participation. On the other hand, Unilever policy is "one of preference for majority participations. . . . When Unilever is in a minority position it seeks management control" (which it can obtain by concluding a management contract with the local partner). The Unilever Group also accepts fifty-fifty joint ventures in some cases. We have already referred to the evolution in Brazilian Light & Power, which—under pressure from the Brazilian Government—is reinvesting the proceeds of the sales of its telephone assets in Brazil in minority participation in a number of smaller joint ventures. It may be predicted that government pressure for local majority control will increase, but that a crisis point will be reached when the foreign investor feels that he can no longer exercise adequate control over the efficiency of management and the commercial standards associated with its brand products. Minority participation by itself does not necessarily produce such a state of affairs; but it may presage a policy of complete nationalization of the foreign interests.

Control and Management

At first sight, it would seem that the measure of control exercised over the enterprise by the different partners is automatically determined by their equity holdings. This, however, is clearly not the case. There are a variety of factors that may divorce the degree of control and management exercised by the various partners from the size of equity holdings. The first of these is familiar to students of the modern corporation: where voting shares are scattered among a large number of individual or small corporate shareholders, the principal shareholder can effectively control the operations of the enterprise even without a majority interest. This applies to international joint ventures, where a part of the shares has been distributed to various investors (as, for example, in the case of Voltas or Prolacsa). A second factor that is very important in international joint venturing is the degree of activity of the various partners. In many cases—and the Lamco venture would be a pertinent illustration—the local shareholder or shareholders are essentially recipients of the dividends, or they confine themselves to periodic representation on general board meetings while leaving the effective management in the hands of the foreign partners. In the case of Lamco, both the Liberian and the foreign participants have delegated the technical and commercial management to one of the major participants, Grängesberg. Where technical expertise and know-how and the continuous supply and modernization of processes is a decisive factor, a foreign partner is apt to exercise a control not commensurate with the extent of his share of holdings. This is likely to apply to such processes as the manufacture of synthetic fibres, various chemical and pharmaceutical materials, electronics and aircraft. But for this very reason the governments of developing countries, as partners or as licensors, insist on adequate training schemes, not only for skilled labor but also at the scientific and managerial level. As the reservoir of native personnel able to fill the executive and scientific positions increases, foreign managerial control will decline, even in the diminishing number of cases where the foreign investor still operates wholly-owned subsidiaries. In a number of cases, representation on the board is strictly proportionate to the equity holdings, but the foreign investor, even as a minority shareholder, has control over the day to day management, which is in the hands of a management committee. This may, of course, lead to conflicts between the Management Committee and the Executive Board, and the use of this device is likely to decline as the business experience, and the managerial and technical skills of the developing countries increase.

What is more important than the precise distribution of equities or management arrangements, is identity of outlook and objectives between the partners.[9] Nevertheless, in many cases, the question of majority or minority participation is essentially a symbol rather than a reflection of the actual degree of control exercised over the operations of the enterprise.

9. See further, on this point, *infra*, pp. 409–11.

Partnerships with Governments

In our earlier book [10] we ventured to criticize the then prevailing attitude toward joint ventures with governments in the following terms:

The question of direct participation by the government or a government-owned corporation in a capital-importing country is still viewed differently in many Western business circles—definitely unfavorably in the United States. Our case studies include successful joint ventures between foreign private enterprises and local governmental enterprises, such as a government bank or a national development corporation. In countries where private entrepreneur capital is scarce or lacking, such partnership —at least during a long transitional period—should be welcomed as guaranteeing a higher level of responsibility and long-term vision than an association between an experienced foreign enterprise and an inexperienced, often speculative-minded local partner. On the whole, European entrepreneurs accept such association pragmatically, judging it on the merits of the situation. United States entrepreneurs are still inclined to reject any such association as inherently evil, as a token of socialism, and unacceptable to a free enterprise economy. It may be—and indeed, it must be hoped—that, with a growing insight into the great variety of conditions prevailing in the less developed countries, such *a priori* prejudices, characteristic of a domestic-oriented rather than of an international outlook, will gradually give way to a more experimental and pragmatic approach. Objections are slightly less pronounced where the foreign government partner is not a government department as such but a semi-autonomous governmental corporation with separate legal personality, budget, and business experience. Some of these, like the Nacional Financiera of Mexico, the Corporación de Fomento of Chile, the Instituto de Fomento Industrial of Colombia and the Sümerbank of Turkey have established a fine record of stimulating industry, often by initial capital association with a foreign enterprise. In some cases, these development corporations have subsequently disposed of all or part of their holdings to the public.

Be that as it may, it cannot be denied that in some of the least developed countries, the only alternative to initial participation by the government is no local participation at all. Quite often (in Ghana, for example) the government is content with a relatively small minority participation, if it is in association with an experienced and a responsible foreign enterprise, such as the Unilever concern. Outside of the Soviet Bloc, few

10. Friedmann and Kalmanoff, *op. cit. supra* note 3, at pp. 272–73.

people today see the panacea in a wholly government-controlled and government-operated economy. But there is hardly any country, even in the industrially developed world, and most emphatically in the less developed world, where a mixed economy is not, at least for a long transitional period, a necessary concomitant of planned economic development. That countries like India, Pakistan, Mexico, or Nigeria—to name but a few representative examples—must base the general tempo and direction of their economic development on long-term plans and governmental participation in enterprises and seek to find a reasonable balance between ambitions and resources is today no longer seriously denied in Washington any more than in London, Paris, New Delhi, or Accra. The proper degree of public participation in industrial development is a delicate matter, to be judged in the light of a mixture of political and economic conditions.

Subsequent developments appear to have borne out this critique. The number and importance of joint ventures with governments has markedly increased, due in part to the desire of many governments in developing countries to participate directly in important economic developments, especially in the field of public utilities and natural resources, and in part to the recognition by foreign investors that in many of the developing countries, especially the newer and poorer ones, public participation and capital is the only responsible form of partnership that can be found. In *Joint International Business Ventures* we gave an account of the Mannesmann-Sümerbank joint venture in the manufacture of seamless steel tubes in Turkey. The present volume contains a revised and up-dated account of this venture, which has continued to develop and prosper. But in addition, we have a number of new case studies reporting on recent joint ventures between Western private enterprises and governments of developing countries. In an agreement between Philips and the Indonesian Government for the manufacture of radios, television sets, and electric bulbs, of March 1968, Philips has a 60 percent share and the Indonesian Government a 40 percent share. We have already noted the transformation of the formerly wholly foreign-owned copper operations of Kennecott—now followed by Anaconda—into joint ventures with the Chilean Government, which has acquired 51 percent of the shares. But this, like other recent moves towards the nationalization of natural resources, is not an entirely voluntary partnership. Part of the complex structure of the giant multipartite Lamco enterprise consists of a joint equity venture between the Government of Liberia and the Liberian Iron Ore Limited, a multinational consortium, in which each of the partners controls 50 percent of the stock. This is paralleled by a contractural joint venture between the Liberian American Swedish Minerals Company (Lamco) and the Bethlehem Steel Corporation. In the various multipartite enterprises reported in this volume, public development corporations participate jointly with private, national and foreign interests. Thus, in the Coromandel Fertilizer enterprise, the Andhra Pradesh Industrial Development Corporation, the Industrial Finance Corporation of India, and the government-owned Life Insurance Corporation of India participate together with the Industrial Credit and Investment Corporation of India—a joint stock company—and other shareholders. In Prolacsa, the Nestlé venture in the Central American Common Market, the principal Nicaraguan partner is a public development corporation, Instituto de Fomento Nacional (Infonac). In Africa, the participation of a public development corporation in major ventures is, at least at the present stage of the capital market, almost inevitable. Like private partners, some of the governmental participants are better than others. The record of public development corporations is uneven, and some of them have unquestionably been used as political tools. Some are corrupt. On the other hand the role played in the development of their respective national economies by such institutions as the Brazilian Banco Nacional do Desenvolvimento Economico, the Chilean Corporación de Fomento, the Mexican Nacional Financiera, or the Uganda Development Corporation is beyond question. Even those who, like the Chairman of the United Africa Company, are skeptical of government participation in other than infrastructure activities—mainly on the ground that the decision-making process is more cumbrous—admit the inevitability of partnership with government institutions in Africa (and the same reasons apply to most of the other developing countries). The problem of bureaucratic interference by the responsible minister must be met by conferring far-reaching autonomy and decision-making power on a government development corporation.[11]

In this respect, as in others, the need is—as we suggested in our earlier volume—to get away from rigid ideological preconceptions on either side. Participation of governments in business enterprises is today a fact of life in the great majority of countries, and by no

11. See for a fuller discussion of this problem W. Friedmann and J. F. Garner (eds.), *Government Enterprise*, London, Stevens & Sons, pp. 325–33 (1970).

means only undeveloped countries.[12] It is bound to be reflected in the field of joint international business ventures.

The Extension of Joint Ventures to New Fields

In our earlier study [13] we observed that joint equity ventures are generally "appropriate to a standardized product with a continuous market" and that they are particularly widespread "in the manufacture of such products as chemicals, drugs, plastic, bicycle tubes, diesel trucks and radio equipment." It remains true that for non-continuous projects such as the construction of steel mill, a harbour, a road system, a joint equity venture is generally less suitable than a contractual arrangement which deals with the provision of finance, technical services, equipment, personnel, and other relevant matters.

However, joint venturing has in recent years been extended to fields from which it was formerly excluded, notably in the exploitation of minerals and other raw materials. We have already referred to the participations of the Chilean Government in the formerly wholly-owned American copper enterprises, and of the Liberian Government in the exploitation of iron ore in the Nimba Mountain by the Lamco consortium. The most remarkable development is the introduction of joint venturing in the oil industry.[14] The state-owned Italian Ente Nazionale Idrocarburi (ENI) has been a pioneer in this development. Our case study deals with the operations of the ENI subsidiary Agip in Iran. In 1957 Agip and the National Iranian Oil Company, (Nioc) a government corporation, established Sirip, a joint Italo-Iranian company in which each partner holds 50 percent of the shares. The object of this company is the exploration and production of liquid and gaseous hydrocarbons. In 1965 this equity joint venture was supplemented by a contractual joint venture between the Nioc on the one part and a consortium consisting of Agip, the American oil company Phillips, and the Indian Oil and Natural Gas Commission on the other part. As in the 1957 agreement, both parties participate equally in the joint structure. But the second venture,

12. Britain, France, and even more strongly, Italy, are among the industrially developed countries of the Western world in which publicly-owned enterprises control major sectors of the economy. See the relevant articles in Friedmann and Garner, *ibid.*

13. Friedmann and Kalmanoff, *op. cit. supra* note 3, at p. 264.

14. See generally, on this matter, Mughraby, *Permanent Sovereignty Over Oil Resources,* Beirut, Middle East Research & Publishing Center (1966).

unlike the first, did not result in the formation of an Iranian commercial company with a corresponding distribution of equities. There is, however, no reason why equity ventures should not be formed in the field of raw materials as much as in manufacturing.

Multipartite Ventures

One of the most significant developments since the publication of our earlier book has been the growth of multipartite and multinational ventures. This has usually been a function of the magnitude of the enterprise in question, and of the consequent need for capital supplied on a scale that exceeds the resources of any one party, even resources of giant corporations. The Volta River Development consortium—on which we report briefly—is one such venture. Its objective is the generation of cheap electric power from the Volta River, coupled with the extraction of bauxite and the production of aluminum through the Volta Aluminium Company, a private Ghanian company in which two major American aluminum producers pooled equities. Massive loans are provided by various national and international lending agencies. In the Lamco project, on which we report in detail, the foreign partners of the Liberian Government include the American Bethlehem Steel Corporation and an international consortium dominated by a group of Swedish companies, with American and Canadian participation. The major part of the investment capital is provided by loans from a United States and a German public aid development institution, as well as by private banks. Fria, concerned with the extraction of bauxite and the manufacture of alumina in Guinea, is an international consortium in which the major shareholders are the French company Péchiney and the United States Olin Mathieson Corporation, with minor participations of British, German, and Swiss companies. The Government of Guinea itself is not yet a shareholder, but its equity participation is a distinct possibility in the foreseeable future. Meanwhile, it has entered into an equity joint venture with another group of foreign aluminum companies.

The Adela Investment Company (Atlantic Community Development Group for Latin America), incorporated in 1964 in Luxembourg, constitutes a different kind of multipartite consortium. This is a private investment company, with an authorized capital of $40 million, whose shareholders include more than 140 industrial companies, banks, and financial institutions, from 16 different countries, i.e. the United States, Canada, and Japan, as well as a number of West European countries. It is the objective of Adela to, inter alia, "invest its own capital and other available resources in private enterprises which contribute significantly to the economic and social progress of individual Latin American countries or regions." [15] Most of these investments will, in contemporary conditions, be in joint ventures.

Characteristically, the multipartite joint ventures will comprise various companies of one or, more frequently, of several nationalities specialized and expert in the field of operations, as well as—in the case of Lamco—a proportion of publicly distributed shares. They will generally have a participation by the host country, and its capital resources will be supplemented by national or international public lending agencies. While the World Bank itself does not engage in joint equity ventures, its subsidiary, the International Finance Corporation, is specifically empowered to make equity investments and does so to an increasing extent.

In certain respects, the multipartite and multinational elements inevitably complicate the decision-making and administrative procedures. This is often countered by conferring the management on one of the parties. In the case of Lamco the day-to-day management is in the hands of the Swedish Grängesberg Company.

Depending on political developments, and especially a further liquidation of the cold war, it is not inconceivable that at some time in the future Western private and public investors might join with Soviet or other Socialist state corporations in joint multipartite ventures in developing countries.

Contractual Joint Ventures

An important recent development in international business associations has been the increasing use of the contractual joint venture. This is not to be confused with the long-term contract by which a foreign firm or consortium undertakes a major operation in a developing country such as the construction of a harbour, a bridge, a railroad system, or a steel mill. In these cases—of which the steel mill construction undertaken in India by British and German consortia

15. From "General Information," a pamphlet published by Adela in March 1967.

and the USSR are illustrations—the foreign contractor undertakes some long-time but non-recurrent operation for a fee. Where the venture is of major financial dimensions, this is often supported by public credit financing, usually on the part of the government whose national obtains the contract. While this kind of operation necessitates a great deal of cooperation, on the financial, technical and managerial levels, it is not a joint venture in which the partners share the risks. The contractual joint venture, as it is described in more detail in our chapter on "The Control of Joint Ventures," is by contrast a risk-sharing venture but one in which no joint enterprise with separate personality is formed, in which the partners hold equity shares proportionate to their investment. It corresponds more closely to what is called a joint venture in American law, i.e., "a special combination of one or more persons, where, in some specific venture, a profit is jointly sought without any actual partnership or corporate designation." [16] The increasing use of this type of joint venture in international relations is to some extent due to nationalistic disinclination against foreign co-ownership of national enterprises, especially in the field of natural resources. Sometimes it is due to incompatibilities of the legal systems. The contractual joint venture of 1969 between Iran and five Western European firms is in the former category. The institution of joint contractual—but not of equity—ventures with foreign interests in the Yugoslav legislation of 1967 is in the latter. While Yugoslavia now strongly favors foreign investment, its legislation and policy based on enterprise autonomy and workers' self-determination has been held to prohibit equity joint ventures with foreign interests.[17]

The equity joint venture is likely to remain the predominant form of continuous association between developing countries and foreign investors. But the contractual joint venture is likely to be increasingly utilized, especially in the joint exploitation of natural resources where the desire for total national control is particularly strong.

A General Appraisal

In our earlier study [18] we observed that "[t]he joint venture is an important symbol of the changing relationship between the developed

16. *Tompkins, v. Commission of Internal Revenue,* 97 F.2d 396 (4th Cir. 1938).

17. For a critique of this view, see Friedmann and Mates, *op. cit. supra* note 2, at pp. 39–40.

18. Friedmann and Kalmanoff, *op cit. supra* note 3, at p. 265.

and less developed countries, but it cannot be regarded as a panacea. It is a device to be adopted, rejected, or modified after a sober consideration of the many legal, psychological, and technical factors prevailing in a given situation. Confidence between the partners will overcome the most difficult obstacles; lack of confidence will destroy the most perfect devices." As a major negative factor, we mentioned disparity of outlook between the foreign and local partners: [19]

. . . In joint ventures between industrially developed countries, such as the United States, Britain, West Germany, the Netherlands, Italy, or Sweden, there is a certain community not only of tradition and of scientific, technical, and legal standards, but there has also been more experience with responsible investment practices and legal supervision, although such standards have often evolved only after disastrous experiences with unscrupulous speculators. In many of the less developed countries, this stage has not yet been reached in the business environment. Power and wealth are often concentrated in relatively few hands, and they are not matched by a corresponding sense of responsibility. The partner from the industrialized country, usually a large corporation with worldwide interests and long experience, generally takes a long-term view of profits, placing the development of the enterprise before quick dividends. Tax considerations may provide an additional incentive to reinvest in a developing foreign enterprise.

Inflationary conditions may produce the reverse situation: The local partner will want to leave his investment in the enterprise where it is relatively inflation-proof, while the foreign investor will be anxious to take out his earnings before devaluation decimates them.

A similar note is struck by Dr. Pieter Kuin, a member of the Board of Unilever and Chairman of the ICC Commission on International Investments and Economic Development, in his introduction to a report of that Commission on International Joint Business Ventures in Developing Countries: [20]

. . . The rising tide of national independence and self-reliance in developing countries has created a desire for even more active participation by local people in this process. Shares in the capital and profits of foreign business have sometimes been claimed too readily, without much consideration for mutual performance. But gradually a more mature idea of partnership is taking shape, in which the partners share risks as well as benefits.

Joint ventures in production are one way of meeting this need for part-

19. *Id.*
20. United States Conference on Trade and Development, TD/B/NGO/9, 20 January, 1969, p. 2.

nership. Like other forms of co-operation they are in themselves neither good nor bad. Their value depends entirely on the degree to which they meet each partner's requirements. Only successful and mutually satisfactory joint ventures serve the cause of world economic development. Contrary to what some enthusiasts seem to believe, joint ventures are not a panacea for progress in the promotion of this cause. Certain conditions must be fulfilled. For private ventures, there must be a local business community from which partners can be recruited. Their industrial and trading traditions must not be caused by incomprehensible behaviour. For any joint venture—with private partners or government agencies— to be successful, the host country should also have at least the beginnings of a managerial class. Without this, a disproportionate number of expatriate managers will prevent the new company from looking like a real joint enterprise. The government and the administration in the host country should in principle be sympathetic, understand the requirements of modern enterprises and be reasonably equipped to meet these. If a government agency is the local partner, it should be fairly free from day-to-day politics.

This is a sober and realistic appraisal of the place of the joint international business venture in contemporary conditions of economic development. It contrasts with the following expression, by Kenneth Weg, Senior Associate Editor of *Business International,* of a more negative point of view, as it was typical until a few years ago of many American business enterprises:

. . . Even though joint ventures may currently be in vogue, many firms with extensive international commitments are becoming increasingly dissatisfied with this approach to international business. The case against joint ventures in the less-developed countries rests on two major points: the presence of a local partner contributes to (1) day-to-day operational problems and policy conflicts, and (2) lack of managerial flexibility in adjusting to new market and investment requirements and opportunities.

Companies with a policy of establishing wholly owned subsidiaries whenever possible have been more fortunate in planning for rationalized operations in both industrialized and less-developed regions. For example, IBM World Trade Corp. has had a conscious policy of 100% ownership ever since it began moving into foreign markets. Today, IBM is an outstanding example of an international corporation in which full-line assembly plants tend to disappear in favor of a very few world production centers for a given product or component.[21]

21. "Joint Ventures Revisited: A World Business Symposium," *Columbia Journal of World Business,* Vol. 1, p. 19, at 23, 25 (1968). As our case study

In rebutting certain statements made by the U.S. State Department and AID in favor of joint ventures, Mr. Weg observed:

The rebuttal is obvious: a wholly owned subsidiary offers all these possibilities, and may even be a better training vehicle since it does not encounter internal opposition to advanced management techniques, as is often the case in joint ventures. In addition, if the growth of the new managerial class follows traditional patterns, many local nationals trained in the wholly owned subsidiary will undoubtedly set out on their own and establish competitive enterprises or ancillary product companies with the know-how they have assimilated.

As far as economic theory is concerned, two factors should be considered. First, a wholly owned venture may make a greater contribution to economic development because of greater efficiency and less internal conflict; second, it may be a fallacy to think that the joint venture will offer more direct material benefits to the public, since in the majority of cases it is the already wealthy and established investor who becomes the joint-venture partner or shareholder.[22]

Mr. Weg, however, declared himself in favor of regional development corporations—which have played an important role in some recent multilateral joint ventures, such as Prolacsa.

. . . What is required is acceptance both by the people and the governments of the new nations and by foreign investors of the need for regional development corporations in which all parties would participate. These regional companies would offer their shareholders profits resulting from total *regional* operations, thereby helping to break down the nationalistic barriers to development, and coordinating production planning on a multinational basis for the most efficient and competitive operations.[23]

On the latter point, there will be general agreement. But the competition argument is highly questionable. In many developing countries there is, at present, no room for more than one enterprise, e.g. in the manufacture of trucks, nylon, or radio equipment, and competition would simply be a waste of precious new materials and foreign exchange. Nor is Mr. Weg's reasoning entirely consistent. For the reason why some giant multinational corporations, such as General Motors or IBM, are not favorable to joint ventures, is their wish to maintain complete technological and managerial control, and to coor-

of IBM shows, IBM is not, or is no longer, opposed to joint ventures in principle, although it has avoided them until now. See *infra*, pp. 218–21.

22. *Ibid*. at 27.
23. *Ibid*. at 29.

dinate their operations on a worldwide goal. This is an anti-competitive factor.

The recent observations of C.D. Michaelson. President of the Metal Mining Division of Kennecott Copper Corporation, reflect a more positive approach to both the necessity and the desirability of joint ventures:

> I am convinced that joint ventures are the most promising approach for American enterprise abroad. They are not a tentative and uneasy accommodation between national aspirations and the interests of private foreign capital. Rather, they are a formalized convergence of interests, whereby the work that you and I perform is intertwined with the other tasks that nations must pursue—if they are to achieve a state of decent self-sustenance. I am persuaded that, in the long run, this is not only one way for American corporations to operate profitably abroad, but that for many it may be the *only* way.
>
> Beyond that, it is a way for you and me to work to elevate the conditions of our fellow men. I think we would all take great personal satisfaction from the knowledge that we were enlisted in the quest for economic advancement and human nobility. It was expressed with eloquence by President Eduardo Frei, when he announced the historic agreement on El Teniente to the people of Chile and told them, "economic facts are little able to express themselves to man and his hopes. But in what I deliver to my country today are more than figures; it is the solid feeling of our great march and a new banner of confidence in our advance towards a future of dignity and justice." [24]

Evidently complete control over all foreign subsidiaries, as it prevailed generally until the Second World War, simplifies matters for the mother company. But such an approach totally ignores the political and psychological realities of the post-war world, and, in particular, the worldwide rebellion against complete foreign economic control. This rebellion is not confined to the new countries but extends to some of the old countries of Western Europe. The policies of France under de Gaulle illustrate the extent to which political considerations are apt to prevail over economic rationality. For U.S.

24. 1969 D. C. Jackling Award Lecture by C. D. Michaelson, President of Metal Mining Division of Kennecott Cooper Corporation. "Joint Mining Ventures Abroad: New Concepts for a New Era," February 19, 1969. The validity of these observations is not impaired by the fact that, in Chile, the joint venture experiment of Kennecott is likely to give way to full nationalization by the Allende government, which succeeded the Frei government in October, 1970.

corporations—which represent by far the greatest concentration of economic power in international business relations—the question is whether to assert such power, at the risk of an ultimate political confrontation, or to seek an accommodation between their immediate business interests and the aspirations of the country in which they operate. The former course is feasible in the long run only if the business enterprise can count on the political—and ultimately the military—support of its government. This used to be so in the pre-1914 world, and continued to some extent as long as the major powers still had colonial or quasi-colonial empires. This situation plainly no longer prevails. Where the United States has intervened by force in the post-war world, as in the Guatemalan, Dominican, and Cuban situations, it has done so primarily for political reasons, not for the protection of economic investment. And the colossal expenditure of men and resources in the Vietnam war can only in the most distorted perspective be ascribed to economic rather than political and strategic reasons. It is fortunate that the great majority of the U.S. and other Western enterprises have, however, reluctantly come to appreciate these realities and, therefore, are closer to the attitudes outlined by Dr. Kuin and Mr. Michaelson than to those expressed by Mr. Weg. In business, as in politics, the distinction between statesmanship and tactical accommodation lies in the ability to foresee developments and to take decisions that will anticipate problems rather than to make last-minute responses to direct pressures. Perhaps the difference is illustrated in the different responses made by the two major U.S. producers of copper in Chile, to the demands for greater Chilean participation by the left-wing, non-Communist Frei Government. The Kennecott Corporation in 1964 agreed to a conversion of its wholly-owned operations into a 49 percent participation with the remainder being held by the Chilean Government. This was coupled with various loan arrangements which have been discribed in our case study. The Anaconda Corporation, which did not make a corresponding arrangement, was compelled in 1969 to agree to a similar 51-49 joint venture, coupled with an agreement by the Chilean Government to purchase the remaining 49 percent between 1973 and 1981. It is of course possible that strong nationalist pressures may lead to a similar demand on Kennecott. But it is probable that the earlier response of Kennecott to the relatively moderate demands of the Chilean Government saved it from the kind of pressure that five years later was exerted upon Anaconda. There is, of course, no assurance that the Kennecott agreement may not be superseded by a new wave of intensive and radical nationalism, despite the contractual guarantees given in the 1964 Basic Agreement and the 1967 Decree. The legal force of international engagements is still limited and they are apt to be superseded by strong internal political pressures. Nevertheless, it is evident that, on a worldwide scale, the graduated response to the growing claims of developing countries for an increasing share of control over their resources and industrial development, by a variety of joint venture agreements, has been the major factor in the peaceful transformation of an era of international business relations characterized by the complete economic political and legal dominance of the foreign investor, to one in which the poorer countries claim a larger share of wealth as well as a greater degree of participation.

In our 1961 book we posed the question whether the joint venture was likely to be a permanent or a transient phenomenon in the evolution of relations between the developed countries of the West and the developing world. The answer we gave to this question would appear to be equally applicable nearly a decade later:

From the point of view of the less developed countries, the joint venture serves three essential purposes: 1) it stimulates the engagement of responsible local capital in productive enterprises; 2) it helps to develop a nucleus of experienced managerial personnel in the public and in the private sectors, in proportion to the participation of public authorities and private capital in joint ventures; 3) it helps to advance the training of native labor and technicians.

As the less developed countries advance in these respects, their need for joint ventures is likely to decline. Some of our most experienced collaborators from the less developed countries have pointed out that it is advisable for foreign investors to begin their enterprises in the form of joint ventures from the outset rather than later on as a belated concession or as a result of pressure. They believe that local enterprises will eventually exploit a growing proportion of industrial production without the participation of foreigners, unless the foreigners are associated with the enterprises from the start.

It is not possible to estimate with any degree of precision how many joint ventures now existing or developing are likely to endure. Probably many of them will, in the course of years, give way to entirely locally-owned and managed enterprises as a result of organic developments or of legislative or administrative pressure. It is also likely that the most successful joint ventures will endure because the sharing of risk capital often will be an advantage to both parties; successful partnership association will be advantageous to both sides in the intricate network of business decisions, public relations, and social adaptation that constitute so characteristic a feature of the joint venture; and the human associations formed through joint endeavors in critical periods of development may endure beyond the period of immediate necessity.[25]

The experience of the intervening years has greatly increased the number, variety, and significance of joint ventures between developed and developing countries, and it has underlined the importance of this device in this highly sensitive and important area of international relations. In the long run, its future will be determined by political developments, and above all by the answer to the fateful question whether cooperation or conflict will prevail between the minority of rich and the majority of poor nations of the world.

25. Friedmann and Kalmanoff, *op. cit. supra* note 3, at pp. 262–63.

*Equity and Contractual Ventures
between Government Corporations and
an International Consortium*

II: OIL PRODUCTION IN IRAN

Ente Nazionale Idrocarburi

Organization. The Ente Nazionale Idrocarburi (National Hydro-carbons Agency, hereafter referred to as ENI) was established by a law of February 10, 1953.[1] It is a state-owned holding corporation for the oil and natural gas industry. Under its charter, its role is to promote and implement ventures of national interest in the field of petroleum. In 1967, Parliament amended ENI's objectives, extending them to the chemical and nuclear industries.

The Board of Directors of ENI, including the chairman, is appointed by the Prime Minister. The directors serve three-year terms and may be reappointed. The economic policy of the agency, and consequently that of the controlled companies, is laid down by a special committee of ministers. The balance sheet of ENI must be approved by the Ministers of Finance, Treasury, and Industry and Trade. Net profit must be distributed in the following way: 20 percent to the ordinary reserve fund; 15 percent for the promotion of scientific and technical research; and 65 percent to the state.

ENI has a capital endowment fund, which was supplied by the Italian Government. It operates through three main companies; their Italian and foreign subsidiaries number about 140. It may purchase stock in corporations, dispose of the assets it is not interested in retaining, and reorganize the controlled companies into homogeneous groups. ENI's operating companies were incorporated and operate under the civil code, in the same way as privately-owned companies with which they must compete on the market.

1. On ENI and Sirip, see: W. G. Friedmann and G. Kalmanoff, *Joint International Business Ventures,* New York and London, Columbia University Press, pp. 500–23 (1961).

In a strictly legal sense, ENI is in the position of a majority stockholder and, therefore, its influence on the operating companies is formally expressed through participation in the meetings for the election of the directors and auditors. ENI's intervention in the affiliated companies takes the form of a program of co-ordination of the group's investments. Moreover, the whole ENI Group benefits from the scientific and technical research that is carried out in a complex of laboratories located at San Donato Milanese, near Milan.

Although the ENI operating companies, as private corporations, do not enjoy any particular privileges as compared to normal private enterprises, their parent organization, as a public entity, enjoys preferred treatment and certain tax benefits. In addition, ENI's bond issues are exempt from all present and future taxes, whereas similar issues by private companies are subject to a tax on capital and a tax on returns.

ENI has played a major role in the growth of the Italian economy. First of all, it has provided industry with increasing amounts of natural gas and petroleum products at favorable prices, thus removing one of the major obstacles to expansion, i.e. energy supply problems. Moreover, it has carried out a number of industrial projects, in some cases on a large scale, in the country's depressed areas, thus creating a nucleus for industrialization, e.g. at Gela (Sicily) and Pisticci (Lucania). Through the end of 1967 ENI had invested over 500,000 million lira in Southern Italy.[2]

The management of the agency has consistently examined Italy's economic growth problems against the background of a world economy which is increasingly affected by the policy of the Afro-Asian countries. This outlook has undoubtedly influenced the expansion of ENI's activities in over twenty African and Asian countries in line with the general trend of the oil industry. The companies of the ENI Group, taking advantage of the experience acquired in their manifold activities in Italy, launched into ventures abroad, ranging from oil and gas exploration and production to the construction of refineries and pipelines and to the distribution of oil products. Within the framework of its objectives, ENI decided to turn to the exploration of oil resources abroad as a means of supplementing Italian resources.

The ENI companies' foreign activities have been mostly centered in a number of developing countries in Africa, the Middle East, the

2. 10,000 lira represent about 16 dollars.

Far East, and Latin America. Nevertheless, the group now tends to do business in an increasing number of countries. Some of these activities are carried out directly by ENI affiliates operating as contractors for third parties. In other cases, activities are carried out by joint business ventures in which ENI affiliates have substantial holdings.

Enrico Mattei, the first President of ENI, who was killed in an airplane crash in October 1962, played a decisive role in the group's expansion. Under his guidance and in the period of a few years, ENI became one of Italy's largest industrial groups. He foresaw the role of Afro-Asian countries, with which he made operating arrangements based on new formulas.

In the course of a few years, ENI has become an integrated oil group of multinational standing. Between 1954 and 1967 its sales rose from 190,000 million lira to 1,100,000 million lira and the number of personnel from 15,800 to over 59,000.

Operations of ENI's Subsidiaries. ENI has three main operating companies (Agip, SNAM, and Anic), with three larger subsidiaries (SNAM Progetti, Nuovo Pignone and Lanerossi).

Assienda Generale Italiana Petroli (Agip), which will be described in greater detail below, handles petroleum exploration and production and the marketing of petroleum products. Oil and gas exploration is ENI's main activity, with which all of its other operations are linked by means of the group's integrated structure. After its considerable discoveries in the Po Valley, Agip extended exploration and production to central and southern Italy and Sicily. It is also carrying out exploration in Tunisia, Libya, the U. A. R., Nigeria, Iran, and Saudi Arabia. In the North Sea, in certain permit areas in the Persian Gulf and in Abu Dhabi it is operating in association with other companies. Sizeable oil or gas fields have been found in the U. A. R., Iran, Tunisia, Nigeria, and in the North Sea. Furthermore, Agip is the foremost petroleum products marketer in Italy. Its modern sales network consists of over 5,000 roadside outlets, of which over 1,100 are service stations. A chain of 37 ultramodern motels, and two tourist centers are linked with the network. Through subsidiaries, Agip is also marketing in several European countries and in over 20 African countries.

SNAM deals with oil and gas transport and natural gas distribution. In view of the European countries' growing oil requirements and Italy's role as a link between these countries and the Middle East, SNAM laid down the Central Europe Pipeline connecting the port of Genoa with Ingolstadt in the Federal Republic of Germany and Aigle in Switzerland. Transports of oil and gas to Italy from the producing countries are carried out by the group's ever-growing fleet.

Anic is in charge of refining, chemicals, and textiles. The ENI Group has an interest in 11 refineries, 5 of them in Italy (among which is the important refinery and petrochemical works of Gela, Sicily). The others are located at Ingolstadt (Federal Republic of Germany), Bizerta (Tunisia), Mohammedia (Morocco), Tema (Ghana), Dar es Salaam (Tanzania), and Moanda (Congo—Kinshasa). ENI has built refineries abroad to provide independent supplies for its distribution networks. This is in accordance with the principle of integration that is typical of the group's operational structure. For the manufacture of chemicals, Anic has plants in Ravenna (fertilizers and synthetic rubber), Gela (nitrogenous and complex fertilizers, plastics and other chemicals), and Pisticci (acrylic and polyamide fibres, methanol).

SNAM Progetti handles project engineering, the erection of refineries and petrochemical plants, nuclear projects, drilling, thermoelectric power stations, etc. for the group companies and outside firms. In the nuclear field, ENI built the first Italian nuclear power station at Latina, which was transferred to ENEL when the electric industry was nationalized. The two other larger subsidiaries are Nuovo Pignone, which is engaged in mechanical engineering, and Lanerossi, which was previously a private textile group and which was taken over at a time when it was going through a difficult period.

Agip Mineraria

The Company. Agip Mineraria was established in Milan on May 30, 1953, as a joint stock company. It has a fully-paid capital of 100 billion lira. The shares are not listed on the stock exchange, and the stock is wholly owned by ENI. As has already been mentioned, Agip is active in the field of exploration, prospecting, drilling, and production of gaseous and liquid hydrocarbons.

In recent years, ENI's requirements for oil and natural gas have considerably increased. For several reasons, the group has consistently followed a policy tending to the diversification of its supply sources. First, although the Italian deposits are still an important source of supply, it is unlikely that future discoveries on the national territory and in the continental shelf will be able to satisfy its growing requirements. Second, the risk of failure in mineral exploration is so great that it is increasingly necessary to find and develop new sources of supply in association with several partners. Third, the political situation in various countries where exploration and production is carried out has in recent years constituted an additional risk factor: the closure of the Suez Canal, the Middle East crisis, and the Nigerian war have all seriously impeded Agip's operations.

As a result of the policy towards geographic diversification of supply, about 80 percent of the Agip's total investments were, as of December 31, 1967, made abroad.

Location	*Amount*
	(millions of lira)
Investments in Italy	13,270.4
Investments abroad:	
Europe	18,020.8
Africa and Mediterranean	16,632.1
Asia	626.1
The Americas	15,253.7
Total of investments abroad	50,532.7
Total of investments	63,803.1

Operations. In 1967, the supply of crude oil for the ENI Group stood at 15.11 million tons, an increase of 10.5 percent as compared with 1966. Of this quantity, 24.3 percent was crude oil produced by Agip and its associated companies, and 75.7 percent was bought from third parties. Of the crude oil, 78.7 percent was destined for refining in Italy, 16.8 percent for refining abroad, and 4.5 percent was sold to outside buyers.

In addition to Italy, the main countries and areas where Agip and its associated companies conduct exploration activities are Tunisia, the U. A. R., Iran, Nigeria, Libya, the North Sea, Morocco, Abu Dhabi, Saudi Arabia, the U. S. A., Madagascar, Congo (Brazzaville), Tanzania, Argentina, and Indonesia. The main countries, in addition to Italy again, where Agip and its associated companies produce crude oil are Tunisia, the U. A. R., and Iran.

The relative importance of each country as a supply source may vary substantially from one year to another. New permits are constantly negotiated in order to further the policy towards the diversification of supply sources.

Société Irano-Italienne des Pétroles

Formation. A basic collaboration agreement between Agip and the National Iranian Oil Company (Nioc), a company established in 1951 by the Iranian Government, was signed in Teheran on August 3, 1957, by Mr. Abdullah Entezam, Chairman of Nioc, and by Mr. Enrico Mattei, Chairman of Agip.

The Société Irano-Italienne des Pétroles (Sirip), a joint Italo-Iranian company, was established on September 8, 1957. The capital of this company was subscribed in equal parts by the two partners, both government-owned corporations: Agip on the Italian side, and Nioc on the Iranian side. The object of this joint company is to explore and produce liquid and gaseous hydrocarbons in three specific areas of Iran.

The shares are registered: they can be freely transferred only to the companies controlled by either partner. The stockholder who wishes to dispose of all or part of his shares is required to offer to the other stockholders an option in proportion to their holding. In any event, where the option is not taken up, the seller may not transfer his share to third parties without the unanimous consent of the Board of Directors. In the case of an increase in the capital stock, the new shares must be subscribed by the old stockholders in proportion to the respective holdings.

The agreement is to remain in force for 25 years from the date on which the sale of petroleum has begun. The parties will have the possibility to extend the agreement for a maximum of three five-year periods.

Management. Sirip is managed by a board of six directors who serve four-year terms. The parity of shareholding of both groups is reflected in the composition of the board: half of the directors are appointed by Nioc and half by Agip. The office of Chairman of the Board is to be filled by a director appointed by Nioc, and that of Deputy Chairman by a director appointed by Agip. The Managing Director, who is also General Manager, is appointed by Agip. The approval of at least four directors is required for the validity of the board's decision. The Technical Managers of Sirip are appointed by the Managing Director from among personnel designated by Agip.

Among other obligations, Agip committed itself to draw up exploration plans, at its own expense and after consultation with Nioc, and to carry out such plans. It also agreed to bear in full Nioc's share for expenditure incurred in exploration work should the exploration prove unsuccessful. Furthermore, it assumed the obligation to spend a minimum sum of $22 million during the exploration period. Twelve years after the agreement was concluded, Sirip was left only with the land where commercially exploitable deposits had been discovered, as provided in the agreement.

Sirip is required to refund to Agip the aforementioned expenditures and capital costs in connection therewith only in the event that exploration work has led to the discovery, on the basis of internationally recognized standards, of commercially recoverable oil reserves. Fifty percent of the amount credited to Agip by Sirip as refunds for exploration work is paid to Nioc. After the discovery of an oil deposit sufficient to warrant commercial exploitation, Sirip bears any expenditure to be incurred for the purposes of developing and working the deposit.

Sirip grants to Nioc and Agip the "right of first refusal" on any quantity of petroleum available for sale. If neither Nioc nor Agip is prepared to purchase the oil at conditions acceptable to Sirip, then Sirip is free to sell it to other purchasers at no less favorable conditions.

Sirip publishes and notifies Nioc and Agip of "posted prices," these being the prices at which crude oil of given qualities and densities is generally offered for sale by Sirip to all buyers at each export point. Said posted prices are to be the current Persian Gulf area prices for products of similar qualities and densities.

Iranian Taxation and Profit Sharing. One-half of net profits (gross income less operating expenses in Iran and abroad including overhead, depreciation, and losses as provided under the Income Tax Act, 1949) are paid to Iran as taxes and royalties and the other half to Agip and Nioc in equal parts. Therefore, in effect, 75 percent of Sirip profits goes to the Iranian Government, and 25 percent is paid to Agip. Depreciation is computed at an annual average of 14 percent.

The agreement that resulted in the establishment of Sirip constituted an innovation, if not a revolution, in the pattern of relationship between petroleum concession holders and host countries. The old system of concessions issued against a 50-50 sharing of the profits gave way to the system of a joint company in which the host country is an equal partner in terms of financial contribution and representation on the Board of Directors, the profits being split 75-25 in favor of the host country.

Settlement of Disputes. Any dispute may be submitted to a joint conciliation committee, composed of four members, two for each party, to be responsible for seeking a mutually acceptable solution to the dispute. The conciliation committee, after hearing the parties or their representatives, renders its decision within three months of the date on which the dispute was submitted. The committee's decision is binding on the parties only if it is unanimous.

Any dispute on the interpretation, application, or execution of the basic agreement, including the validity of the conciliation clause, is decided by an arbitration panel of three referees, two being appointed by the parties (one each), and the third, who acts as chairman, appointed by the first two referees. In case the latter fails to agree on the appointment of the third referee, the chairman is designated, at the request of either party, by the Chief Justice of the Geneva Cantonal Tribunal.

The arbitration panel sits in Geneva. Procedural rules are laid down by the parties or, failing action from the parties, by the law of the country where the arbitration takes places.

Evaluation. Sirip represents one of the most important Italian oil ventures abroad. In the late fifties, however, the initiative taken by Agip was, both in Italy and abroad, the object of much heated debate and comment. In Italy, which was still suffering from an inadequate supply of capital for its own needs, doubts were expressed as to whether the heavy financial effort Agip had undertaken was advisable. Abroad, the circles most directly interested raised as the main objection the fact that Agip had offered to Iran conditions that seemed very favorable to that country, breaking with the fifty-fifty profit sharing principle and endangering the traditional balance of relations between oil countries and concessionary oil companies.

Agip's executives answered Italian criticism by arguing that the principal benefit that Italy derived from the agreement with Nioc lay in the possibility of participating in exploration activities in one of the world's most promising oil regions and of obtaining direct sources of oil supply. Criticism from international oil companies was countered by the argument that the Agip proposals were in keeping with the general requirements established by Iran in the Petroleum Act of 1957. The agreement accordingly revolutionized the system of mere concessions to foreign companies by initiating the active participation of Iran in the development of its oil resources. The formula accepted for the first time by Agip was accepted in agreements subsequently signed by Nioc with other foreign oil companies. This indicates that the formula was still advantageous to the oil companies concerned.

The study of the subsequent evolution of oil agreements will show that actually the "revolutionary" Sirip formula was only one step in the course of a consistent and well-reflected policy.

Nioc-Agip / Phillips / India Joint Structure

THE JOINT VENTURE STRUCTURE

The Agreements Proposed by Nioc. The Petroleum Act of July 31, 1957, provides for two kinds of association with foreign oil interests: the equity joint venture, which implies the creation of a joint stock company, e.g. Sirip, or the contractual joint venture, which is a form of business cooperation quite popular in the U. S. A.

In the early sixties, the Iranian Government opened international tenders for the allocation of several new oil areas. The government aimed at the formation of contractual joint ventures, because it regarded this type of association as a means of ensuring a greater participation by Nioc in oil operations. Concrete agreement proposals were accordingly submitted to the competing foreign companies.

Before the opening of international tenders, Nioc had carried out seismic prospection checks in some areas and had ascertained the existence of certain structures. It was decided that the granting of licenses for the more promising surfaces would be conditional on the payment of a cash bonus. The draft agreements mentioned that a bonus would have to be paid, but no exact figure was mentioned.

In international business transactions between developed and developing countries, the agreements are generally prepared by the lawyers of foreign corporations rather than by those of developing countries. In Iran, the oil agreement proposals that were submitted to the foreign competing companies in the early sixties had been entirely prepared and drafted by the lawyers of Nioc, which constitutes a noteworthy evolution.

The Association between Agip, Phillips and ONGC (India). Agip, Phillips (the American oil corporation), and the Oil and Natural Gas Commission of India (ONGC) decided to join together in an informal association, in order to obtain the right of exploration and operation in one of the more promising areas submitted to the international tender. As Agip was Nioc's only foreign partner in Sirip, one might wonder why the Italian company decided this time to associate with other foreign interests.

In the late fifties and in the early sixties, Agip developed its general policy of diversifying the risk of oil exploration. As the company was spreading its operations, it became increasingly necessary to share with others the mineral risk and the financial burden, which are considerable. In 1957, Agip committed itself to spend a minimum of $22 million in Sirip oil exploration. As will be seen below, in 1965, Agip, Phillips, and ONGC undertook to spend a minimum of $48 million in mining explorations. Quite frequently, the considerable funds thus spent on exploration prove to be fruitless. Whereas the political risk is certainly not negligible in oil operations, the mineral risk and cost were the main reasons that induced Agip to associate with other foreign interests.

In 1957, the oil companies were still very individualistic. A few cases of heavy losses, however, brought about a fundamental change of attitude. Hence, when Agip started to apply its new policy, it discovered that other foreign companies were likewise seeking partners. The scope for association appeared to be rapidly increasing.

The association of several foreign companies is not necessarily an advantage in the competition for concessions in Iran. Shell, which was tendering alone, managed to conclude an important contract. In its final choice, the Iranian Government makes no discrimination between a single company or an association of several corporations. It is true, however, that the establishment of the Oil and Natural Gas Commission of India has opened up the vast Indian market to the distribution of Iranian oil. This fact was certainly an incentive for Nioc to consider favorably the bid of the tripartite association.

The Joint Venture Agreement of 1965. The three foreign companies held negotiations with Nioc between 1961 and 1965. In the agreement of January 17, 1965, a "joint structure" was created for offshore exploration and operational activities in certain parts of District I of the Persian Gulf. The foreign corporations agreed to pay to Nioc a cash bonus of $34 million.

The agreement established a contractual joint venture between the first party (Nioc) and the second party (Agip, Phillips and ONGC), who share in costs, expenses, and production. Article 2 (paragraphs 1 and 2) of the agreement reads as follows:

First Party and Second Party do hereby mutually enter into a Joint Structure relationship, which as contemplated by the Petroleum Act, does not constitute a separate juridical personality. . . .
Except as otherwise stated herein and in the Petroleum Act, the Par-

ties hereto shall participate equally in and under said Joint Structure Relationship.

Accordingly, the four entities participate in the joint structure as follows:

First Party	50 percent Nioc
Second Party	50 percent foreign interests
Agip	one third
Phillips	one third
ONGC	one third

The legal structure is the first basic difference between the 1957 and the 1965 agreements. Whereas the former brought about the formation of an Iranian joint stock company (Sirip), the latter established a contractual joint venture (or, according to the term used in the agreement, "joint structure.").

Second Party may not transfer its interest in the joint structure without the prior written approval of First Party, which before granting the approval shall obtain the confirmation of the Council of Ministers and approval of the legislature. Nioc's consent is unnecessary only when the interest is sold to any company or companies controlling Second Party or to any company or companies controlled by Second Party. Although any stockholder of Sirip is denied the right to transfer his share to third parties without the unanimous consent of the Board of Directors, the 1965 agreement does not restrict in any way Nioc's right of transfer.

The 1965 agreement shall remain in force for 25 years from the date of commencement of commercial production. The parties will have the possibility to extend the agreement for a maximum of three five-year periods. On this matter, there is no difference between the agreement of 1957 and that of 1965.

Applicable Law. The law to be applied to the interpretation and the execution of a contract is frequently a matter of argument in oil negotiations. The 1965 agreement does contain a clause on applicable law. Article 43 reads as follows:

1. This Agreement is made pursuant to the Petroleum Act and in respect of any matter where this Agreement is silent, the provisions of the Petroleum Act shall apply.

2. The provisions of the Mining Act of 1957 shall not be applicable to this Agreement, and any other laws and regulations which may be wholly

or partially inconsistent with the provisions of this Agreement shall to the extent of any such inconsistency be of no effect in respect of the provisions of this Agreement.

This clause does not state which law would be applied if both the agreement and the Petroleum Act were found to be silent on any point of doubt or controversy. In particular, it is not clear according to which law any problem in the relations between the joint venture partners should be interpreted. Italian law recognizes the *associazione in partecipazione,* but this form of association differs from the contractual joint venture.[3] Indian law does not allow for this form of business organization. On the other hand, U.S. corporations often form joint ventures for operations on the home market. Nevertheless, an express reference to American law would not have been fully consistent with the fact that the agreement was to be concluded and executed in Iran.

Consequently, it is likely that should the agreement and the Petroleum Act both be silent on any point of doubt or controversy, Iranian law would be applied. Such an application would be practically feasible because Iranian law on commercial and oil business matters is elaborate. Because of this, it is likely that the application of local law would not be objected to by the foreign companies. It might also be assumed that the general principles of law recognized by civilized nations would be used as a subsidiary source. These companies might be less ready to accept the application of local law in some other countries where commercial and petroleum laws are not as elaborately developed.

THE CONSEQUENCES DERIVING FROM THE LEGAL STRUCTURE

The Direct Ownership of Production. Contrary to the case of Sirip, the production of the joint structure is not owned by a joint stock company but is owned directly by the partners. Article 23 (paragraphs 1 and 3) of the agreement reads as follows:

1. Petroleum produced from the Area shall be owned at the well-head 50 percent by First Party and 50 percent by Second Party.
2. First Party, Second Party and their customers may freely export Petroleum from Iran without the necessity of a license or other special formalities.

3. See Art. 2549–2554 CCI (1942).

The basic difference in legal structure between the 1957 and 1965 agreements has been caused mainly by the Iranian Government's determination to directly own part of the oil production. Direct ownership represents for the government a significant means of asserting its permanent sovereignty over its oil resources and contributing to national prestige. In the 1965 agreement, the relations between the government and foreign companies remain those of a conceding authority and of concessionaries, but the direct ownership by the government of part of the production introduces a subtle but significant change in these relations. This change was confirmed by the ulterior evolution of Iranian oil agreements.

By law, ENI is committed to provide the energy supply for the Italian market. Consequently, Agip regards as an advantage the direct ownership of a part of the production, which to a certain extent can be determined in advance and which can be exported at the company's will. The 1957 agreement provides that if neither Nioc nor Agip is prepared to purchase the oil at conditions acceptable to Sirip, then the company is free to sell it to other purchasers at conditions no less favorable to itself; theoretically, this clause represents for Agip an element of uncertainty that is not present in the 1965 agreement. It is true, however, that if Sirip were to make sales at good prices to third parties, its stockholders would benefit from such transactions indirectly, upon receipt of dividends.

Likewise, direct ownership represents for the Oil and Natural Gas Commission a guaranteed supply for the Indian market.

Direct ownership has a different meaning for Phillips. An American corporation investing abroad may obtain considerable fiscal advantages in the U. S. A. if it can prove to the fiscal authorities that it has the direct ownership of its part of the production. Fiscal considerations are a powerful incentive for U.S. oil corporations seeking the formation of contractual joint ventures rather than of joint stock companies. When proof of direct ownership is established, the American company is entitled to deduct the expenses corresponding to the intangibles (costs of sterile research, know-how, etc.) from the taxable account in the year of occurrence. Moreover, the company is also entitled to the depletion allowance, which is a kind of fiscal compensation for the fact that the deposits deplete each year. The depletion allowance represents a deduction of 22 percent from the taxable profit of the company in the U.S.A., provided such deduction does not exceed 50 percent of the gross profit.

Fiscal considerations were not essential to ENI. From a purely fiscal point of view, the contractual joint venture was not more advantageous or less advantageous than a joint stock company.

The Flexibility of the Contractual Joint Venture. Except insofar as it is specifically excluded, Iranian company law applies to any joint oil stock company such as Sirip. Because Sirip is an Iranian company, it is subject to all the controls that a state exercises on its own nationals. In the case of a joint structure, the ties with the local legal system are looser. Almost any rule may be adopted in the contract at the parties' will. Contractual joint ventures are usually a more flexible form of cooperation than equity joint ventures.

For instance, in a company the meetings of the general assembly of shareholders or of the board of directors have to be organized according to the rules of company law. In the case of a contractual joint venture, the basic agreement may contain flexible rules as to when and how the partners or the executives should meet.

Different rules also apply to the sharing of profits. In the case of a company, the profit and loss accounts are made at the end of the year. Later, the general assembly of shareholders has to examine the accounts and the dividend proposals of the board of directors. Part of the profits may be allocated to the ordinary and extraordinary reserves. Usually, the shareholders receive what is left as dividends a year after the productive and commercial operations have brought about profits. In a contractual joint venture, the partners do not need to comply with such formalities and they benefit immediately from the result of productive and commercial operations.

In any specific case, the respective advantages and disadvantages of a contractual or an equity joint venture have to be weighed carefully, but in the negotiations preceding the 1965 agreement the flexibility of the joint structure appeared to offer significant advantages.

IRANIAN TAXATION AND PROFIT SHARING

Principles. The profit sharing between the government and foreign interests provides the second basic difference between the agreements of August 3, 1957, and January 17, 1965.

As has already been mentioned, the net profits of Sirip are paid as to one half to Iran as corporate taxes and royalties, and as to the other half to Agip and Nioc in equal parts. Therefore, the split is 75-25 in favor of the government.

The 1965 agreement provides that the joint structure relationship of the parties does not entail any tax obligation. Nioc and each foreign company are separately subjected to taxation and have to draw up separate balance sheets.

Tax Calculation. This mode of calculation brings about a split that is even more favorable to the government, that is, about 80-85 percent for the government. Each entity has to pay a tax of 50 percent on profits, which is not more than the corporate tax paid by Sirip. The gross receipts, however, are not calculated on the basis of the market price, but on the basis of the posted price which is an artificial one higher than the market price. At present, the posted price bears no fixed relation to the market price, but the former is about 30 percent higher than the latter. The posted price is not, however, completely arbitrary. It is adapted from time to time according to the variations of the market price, but these adaptations are neither automatic, nor immediate, nor necessarily proportional: it is a procedure determined by agreement between the partners. In case of disagreement, the problem could be referred to arbitration, but the partners would certainly prefer to settle the divergence by bargaining or conciliation.

Each entity multiplies the number of barrels that it has received by the posted price. From this amount, the entity is entitled to subtract its costs, expenses, and any charges incurred in the oil operations. Moreover, each of the entities comprising Second Party is entitled to further deductions in respect of depreciation of the bonuses paid to First Party and of exploration or other expenditures.[4]

Fiscal Guarantee. First Party and each of the entities comprising Second Party are subject to taxation in accordance with the Iranian income tax laws "as they may prevail from time to time." [5] Although the 1965 agreement was the object of negotiations between the government and the foreign companies, the basic draft was prepared by Nioc. Iran has thus asserted one of its sovereign rights, i.e. the right to levy taxes on nationals and foreigners and, more significantly, the right to change them whenever it sees fit.

Nevertheless, the 1965 agreement contains a guarantee of nondiscrimination which is laid down in Article 30, paragraph 2:

The Government of Iran guarantees that First Party, each of the entities comprising Second Party and any Trading Company shall not be

4. The deductions for exploration or other expenditure will be described in greater detail on pp. 48–50.

5. Article 30, paragraph 1.

subject to rates of income tax or other provisions governing net income which are less favorable than those to which other companies, engaged in similar operations in Iran, which together produce or cause to be produced more than 50 percent of Iranian crude oil are subject.

As several Iranian oil agreements contain a similar guarantee of nondiscrimination, any fiscal change would have to be general in character. Moreover, other agreements contain a guarantee of stability as to the level of taxes. Consequently, the foreign companies that signed the 1965 agreement feel that through the clause of nondiscrimination they are indirectly protected by the guarantee of tax stability that was expressly granted to others.

MANAGEMENT

Iranian Marine International Oil Company. The partners have formed an operating corporation, the Iranian Marine International Oil Company, which is commonly called Iminoco. This corporation is an Iranian nonprofit joint stock company, which has no balance sheet and is not subject to taxation. Nioc, Agip, Phillips, and ONGC have all a share in the capital, in proportion to the respective participations which they have in the joint structure. Iminoco has an initial authorized capital of 2,520,000 rials.[6]

As a nonprofit operating corporation, Iminoco does not modify the contractual nature of the joint venture between First Party and Second Party. During the exploratory operations, it acts as agent of Second Party only. During the phases of development and commercial production, Iminoco acts as agent of both parties. If any question arose on the rights and the duties included in this agent function, it is likely, as has already been observed concerning the relations of the joint venture partners, that Iranian law would be applied.

The Board of Directors of Iminoco meets about once every three months. Half of its members are nominated by First Party and half by Second Party. The Chairman of the Board is nominated by First Party, while the Vice-Chairman and the Managing Director are chosen by Second Party. The board plays an important role in the management of the oil operations. In particular, it is responsible for the preparation of the budget.

The production program for each year is prepared by Iminoco at

6. One U.S. dollar is equal to 75 rials.

least six months before the end of the preceding year. On the basis of the budget, the company requests the necessary funds from First Party and from each entity comprising Second Party, all of which receive quarterly the invoices corresponding to expenses actually sustained.

Without any special difficulty, the parties have agreed on accounting principles similar to those generally recognized in the oil industry. First and Second Parties each furnish one half of any type of the currencies necessary for the operations of Iminoco. The principal books and accounts of Iminoco or Second Party are kept in U.S. dollars.

Agip, Phillips, and ONGC are each jointly and severally responsible for all the obligations pertaining to mineral operations, especially the exploratory operations. For instance, if one of these companies failed to provide its share of the minimum expense for exploration, the other two companies would have to make up the difference. Such a joint responsibility does not apply to the payment of taxes.

Day-to-day Management. The Managing Director is nominated by agreement between the three foreign entities. At present, the Managing Director is a person nominated by Agip; he is likely to remain in this post during the phases of exploration and development. At the end of these periods, it will be for the Board of Directors to appoint the Managing Director during the phase of commercial production. Possibly it will adopt a rotating system between the three foreign entities.

As in all Iranian oil contracts, the 1965 agreement gives preference, whenever possible, to the employment of Iranian personnel. Article 13, paragraphs 5 and 6, states the commitment of the parties:

5. To minimise the employment of foreign personnel by ensuring so far as reasonably practicable that foreign personnel are engaged only to occupy posts for which Iminoco and, where applicable, Second Party do not find available Iranians having the requisite qualifications and experience;

6. To prepare plans and programmes for industrial and technical training and education, and to co-operate in their execution with a view to ensuring the gradual and progressive reduction of foreign personnel in such manner that upon expiry of ten years from the Effective Date the number of foreign nationals employed by Iminoco shall not exceed two percent of the total staff employed by it, and the top executive positions occupied by non-Iranians shall not exceed 49 percent of the total executive positions available. . . .

Actually, the exploration period on the one hand, and the development and commercial production on the other, present different personnel requirements. During the phase of exploration, most of the qualified jobs are bound to be occupied by foreigners. Technicians from Agip, Phillips, and ONGC, as well as from Nioc, have thus been employed by Iminoco. At the end of the exploration period, Nioc might ask that more nationals be employed in qualified jobs and senior posts. As the relations between Nioc and the foreign entities are excellent, no special difficulty is anticipated. But in any case, the day-to-day management will always remain under the responsibility of the Managing Director.

Preference will also be given to equipment and supplies made in Iran when the local articles can be acquired at no less favorable conditions than for similar foreign articles. It appears, however, that the bulk of equipment and machinery will still have to be purchased abroad. Imports of equipment and machinery are effected without import licenses or duties.

Management Efficiency. The corporate form of doing business provides an adequate frame for an integrated managerial organization. It has sometimes been contended that in comparison, a non-equity or contractual joint venture is hampered in its activities by the difficulty of reconciling this legal structure with a strong and efficient management.

It is therefore interesting to note that hitherto the management of Iminoco has been working no less efficiently than Sirip's management. Iminoco is only a nonprofit operating company, whereas Sirip is an extensive corporate organization that to a certain extent pursues a business life of its own. Nevertheless, the Managing Director of Iminoco enjoys powers similar to those of the Managing Director of Sirip. In a joint structure, the partners are free to grant a large delegation of powers to the Managing Director and to the other executives.

Whereas a company usually has at its disposal a certain amount of working capital and some ordinary and extraordinary reserves, in principle the management of a contractual joint venture cannot exceed the precise budgetary limits that have been convened between the partners in any given year. In practice, however, the budget may be planned so as to leave a sufficient margin of financial freedom to the management. Moreover, the rules of the agency contract could be applied in any case of emergency. Accordingly, Iminoco, as agent for the parties, would be entitled to take, in case of an emergency, any initiative it would deem necessary. As any agent, it would have to observe the diligence proper to an agent and to notify immediately these extraordinary measures to the parties for their approval.

In conclusion, the legal structure established by the 1965 agreement is not expected to hamper the efficiency of management, although it is not denied that in certain exceptional circumstances it could be an obstacle.

EXPLORATION, DEVELOPMENT AND COMMERCIAL PRODUCTION

Exploration. Second Party is in charge of all exploratory operations and carries the entire burden of the expenses of exploration. Moreover, during this period, Iminoco acts as agent of Second Party only.

Second Party has committed itself to spend a minimum of $48 million as exploratory expenses over twelve years. The foreign companies have delivered to Nioc a letter of guarantee from a bank for $24 million, which represent their minimum exploration obligation for the first four years. After discovery of petroleum in commercial quantities, Second Party may elect to fulfill all or part of its outstanding expenditure obligations by spending for the joint structure account a stated amount on operations other than exploration. First Party contributes one half of all the costs which are not exploratory expenses.

No taxes are paid during the exploration and development periods. During the phase of commercial production, each of the entities comprising Second Party may subtract, from its gross receipts for each taxation period, exploration expenditure incurred by it equal to one fifteenth of that expenditure (that is, a total depreciation of fifteen years) or $0.10 for each barrel of oil produced and saved, whichever is greater.

Development. During the period of development, the joint structure still records no earnings, but Nioc participates in the operations and the expenses.[7] From then onwards, Iminoco is an agent for both First Party and Second Party.

If and when Nioc requires, the foreign companies will, in addition to their own share, also provide Nioc's 50 percent share of all the ex-

---

7. In the spring of 1969, the joint structure was entering in the period of development.

penditure required for development and exploitation of commercial fields until the date of commencement of commercial production. First Party would then have to pay to Second Party an interest equal to the rate of discount of the Federal Reserve Bank of U.S.A. plus 1.5 percent. Reimbursement of the expenditure (in U.S. dollars) would have to be made in sixteen equal semiannual instalments, as from six months after the date of commencement of commercial production.

Each of the foreign companies may subtract from its gross receipts during each taxation period an amount for depreciation, at a rate of ten percent per annum of all expenditure incurred by it on operations of development as well as on those of commercial production.

Commercial Production and Internal Sales. As from the date of commencement of commercial production, the parties jointly assume the responsibility for all expenditure subsequent to that date required for all petroleum operations.

The parties have agreed on an internal arrangement that allows for flexibility in the allocation of the production. This arrangement has been laid down in the Article 22, paragraph 1:

Iminoco shall bring to the notice of First and Second Parties its estimate of production. . . . Each Party may take from Iminoco one half of the quantity available for export and may purchase any part of the other half to the extent that the other Party may not elect to take the quantity available to it.

When one party buys from the other party, the purchase price is equal to the total of the cost by barrel plus half the difference between the posted price and the cost. Here is a theoretical example of what is known as the half-way price: [8]

Barrel cost	$1.00
Posted price	$1.80
Half-way price	$1.40

When the cost of production increases, the half-way price also increases:

Barrel cost	$1.10
Posted price	$1.80
Half-way price	$1.45

8. The figures which are indicated here are purely imaginary and are only chosen to illustrate the mode of calculation of the half-way price.

This means that the purchasing party, which had already to assume increased costs on the production side, has also to sustain a higher half-way price in the internal selling arrangement. Consequently, although the profit of the seller is reduced, the system of the half-way price in itself does not provide a sufficient incentive for any one party to buy from the other.

In some ways, the joint structure between Nioc and the three foreign companies is like a cooperative of consumers, but the half-way price system shows that in other ways there are some differences.

SETTLEMENT OF DISPUTES

Deadlock. Sirip, which has been active for more than a decade, has at no time experienced any deadlock between the two equal shareholders, Nioc and Agip. The very possibility of a deadlock and its consequences has always induced the partners to aim at compromise. Moreover, the positions taken by each party usually are not so far apart that they cannot be brought together by hard bargaining and constant adjustment to changing circumstances.

Similarly, First Party and Second Party have equal participations in the joint structure. In this case also, the partners try to seek a compromise whenever a divergence of opinion arises, thus avoiding any deadlock.

De Facto *Arbitration.* The statutes of Iminoco provide that each shareholder deposit in a designated Swiss bank a number of shares equal to 1 percent of the capital. The bank is entrusted with a mandate for the entire existence of the joint structure. In case of deadlock—but only in such a situation—the bank is empowered to vote the shares it holds in the General Assembly of Shareholders. The decision of the bank becomes the decision of Iminoco and is irrevocable. A similar system had been provided in Sirip's statutes.

This procedure has a limited scope of application because it can be used only in relation with the questions that concern the activities of Iminoco and that are dealt with by the company's General Assembly. It cannot be used for the solution of a dispute arising out of the interpretation or execution of the 1965 agreement.

Conciliation. If any dispute arises out of the execution or interpretation of the 1965 agreements the parties may agree that the matter shall be referred to a mixed conciliation committee composed of four members, two nominated by each party, whose duty shall be to seek a solution. The conciliation committee, after having heard the representatives of the parties, shall give a ruling within three months from the date on which the dispute was submitted. The ruling, in order to be binding, must be unanimous.

This conciliation clause is nearly identical to that which had been provided in the case of Sirip.

International Arbitration. In the absence or the failure of conciliation, the sole method of settling a dispute is international arbitration. Any dispute shall be settled by an arbitration board consisting of three arbitrators. Each of the parties shall appoint an arbitrator and the two arbitrators shall appoint an umpire who shall be the President of the Arbitration Board. If the two arbitrators cannot agree on the person of the umpire, the latter shall, if the parties do not otherwise agree, be appointed, at the request of either party, by the President or judge of equal rank of the highest court of Denmark. In the case of Sirip, the same function was entrusted to the Chief Justice of the Geneva Cantonal Tribunal.[9]

If one of the parties does not appoint its arbitrator, or does not advise the other party of the appointment made by it, the other party shall have the right to apply to the President or equal judge of the highest court of Denmark to appoint a sole arbitrator.

The place and procedure of arbitration shall be determined by the parties. In case of failure to reach agreement, such place and procedure shall be determined by the sole arbitrator or by the umpire, as the case may be. In this respect, the 1965 agreement differs from the 1957 agreement which provides that the arbitration panel shall sit in Geneva and that procedural rules shall be laid down by the parties or, lacking action from the parties, by the law of the country where the arbitration takes place.

The provisions of the Joint Structure Agreement relating to arbitration shall continue in force notwithstanding the termination of the agreement.

If the party liable to execute a final decision or award given in accordance with the 1965 agreement fails to comply therewith, the party in favor of which the decision or award has been given shall be entitled to seek the termination of the agreement by a decision of an arbitration board or sole arbitrator.

9. See above, p. 35.

Evaluation and Prospects

Iranian Policy. In the mid-sixties, several oil agreements were concluded between Nioc and various foreign companies. Although the modalities vary from one case to another, the same basic principles can be found in all of these agreements.

These principles have been applied in the agreements concluded in other countries as well. In 1967, a 50-50 association between Phillips and Agip formed a contractual joint venture with the General Petroleum and Mineral Organization (Petromin), which is the Saudi-Arabian equivalent of Nioc. The participation of Petromin in the joint venture varies between 30 percent and 50 percent, according to the level of production. The joint venture operates through a nonprofit corporation. For fiscal purposes, the gross receipts are calculated on the basis of the posted price. The agreement grants to the parties a guarantee of nondiscrimination, but stipulates that fiscal rates may vary from time to time.

All these similarities point to a general tendency of the oil producing countries to assert their sovereign rights generally, and their permanent sovereignty over oil resources in particular. The comparison between the agreements of 1957 (Sirip) and 1965 (the "Joint Structure") has revealed two major differences that derive from this tendency: first, where a contractual joint venture is adopted instead of an equity joint venture, each partner owns directly a part of the production; second, the profit sharing between the government and foreign interests is more favorable to the state in the second agreement.

It should be emphasized that although the basic principles of government policy are consistently insisted upon in Iranian oil negotiations, each agreement is the result of bargaining and has its own balance of economic benefits.

The Sirip formula was judged revolutionary in 1957 and the Joint Structure Agreement of 1965 appeared to innovate boldly in many ways. In the government's thinking, however, the permanent sovereignty of Iran over its oil resources can be translated into reality only by a long-term and progressive policy. This attitude was confirmed by the general evolution subsequent to the 1965 agreement, and especially by the agreement of March 3, 1969.

The Agreement of March 3, 1969. This agreement was signed between Nioc and five West European firms for the exploration and exploitation of oil in South Iran, near the Persian Gulf. The firms are France's Entreprise de Recherches et d'Activitées Pétrolières (ERAP), Italy's Agip, Spain's Espanoil, Belgium's Petrofina, and Austria's Oesterr. Mineraloelverwaltung.

The essential feature of the agreement is that no oil concession is granted to the foreign companies. Nioc is the titular holder of the concession. The foreign companies function as mere contractors for Nioc, during a period of eight years. They execute the mineral operations and provide Nioc with the funds necessary to cover the expenses. Each year, these funds are consolidated as loans. Their reimbursement is dependent upon the discovery of commercial deposits.

In cases of commercial production, the foreign companies will be entitled to a remuneration consisting of guaranteed purchases of definite oil quantities. As part of the compensation for services rendered, these quantities will be sold at prices advantageous to the foreign companies. These companies will thus acquire ownership of a part of the production by purchase, instead of a direct ownership as is the case with the 1965 agreement.

In March 1969, this service contract system was a new formula for Agip, but not for the Middle East. In 1968, the French company ERAP had already concluded a service contract in Iran and another in Iraq. The 1969 agreement was the third Middle East service contract. This formula has, however, been popular for some time in Latin America (e.g. Venezuela) and in Indonesia.

The service contract formula is another means for Arabian countries to assert their permanent sovereignty over their oil resources. The government agency that is the titular holder of the concession has the direct ownership of 100 percent of the oil production. The concession relationship, which in the past has usually characterized the cooperation between governments and foreign companies, is replaced, in the service contract formula, by purely contractual relations.

From Agip's point of view, the service contract formula is not likely to differ in practical effect from the previous Iranian agreements. The guarantee of definite oil quantities satisfies ENI's desire to provide the Italian market with energy supply. As far as taxes and profit sharing are concerned, the financial equilibrium of the 1969 agreement does not differ fundamentally from the financial equilibrium reached in the 1965 agreement.

It is no accident that no U. S. corporation is involved in the 1969 Agreement. The service contract formula appears to involve some disadvantages for American corporations, as the absence of direct ownership deprives them of considerable fiscal deductions in the U.S.A. It should be noted, however, that tax considerations are not necessarily paramount in a service-contract arrangement.

It is interesting to note that, at the same time as the Iranian state tightens its hold on its oil resources, the oil agreements increasingly resemble genuine civil law contracts.

The Solidarity of OPEC Countries. In recent years, the Member States of the Organization of Petroleum Exporting Countries have tended to present a unified front in all oil negotiations in order to assert their sovereign rights.

This solidarity has undoubtedly increased the bargaining power of the OPEC countries. In some instances, they have derived substantial advantages from it. Thus, Libya promulgated a new Petroleum Law on November 20, 1965. The concession agreements that had been concluded before the promulgation of the law contained a guarantee of status stability.[10] Consequently, the new law could not apply automatically to the old concessionaires. The Lybian Government asked these companies to comply voluntarily with the provisions of the new law. At that time, OPEC declared that no member of the organization would grant a concession to any foreign company operating in Libya that would not accept the 1965 Petroleum Law of Libya. All foreign companies accepted the new law.

The importance of the solidarity between OPEC countries should not be overestimated. The attitude towards foreign investment sometimes differs substantially from one Arabian government to another. As has already been mentioned, moreover, each contract has its own economic equilibrium, which is the result of direct bargaining between the producing country and foreign interests. It remains true, however, that the solidarity between OPEC countries has become a significant factor in oil negotiations.

10. This meant that taxes, for instance, could be changed only with the agreement of the foreign concessionaires.

III: IRON ORE MINING IN LIBERIA

Liberia

Geography. Liberia was discovered in the fifteenth century by the Portuguese. It is situated in the southwestern corner of the West African Coast, within the tropical rain forest belt. The Liberian Government has estimated the area of Liberia to be about 43,000 square miles, or approximately the area of the state of Ohio in the U.S.A.

Liberia is bounded by the Republic of Guinea to the north, the Ivory Coast Republic to the east, Sierra Leone to the west and the Atlantic Ocean to the south.

Population. It is difficult to estimate precisely the size of Liberia's population. The results of the first national census conducted in 1962, however, indicated that the population of Liberia exceeded 1,000,000 and the population of Monrovia, the capital of Liberia and its principal city, was approximately 82,000.

The majority of the population is constituted by a number of African tribes. These are often in opposition to the Americano-Liberians (approximately 50,000), who are the ruling class and who live mainly along the coast.

Government and Institutions. In 1822, the American Society of Colonization, which was founded in 1816, began sending freed Negro slaves into Liberia, although this met with the hostility of the native population. In 1847 Liberia became an independent republic, which in 1848 was recognized by all the most important powers of that time, with the notable exception of the United States, which waited until 1862. From the beginning, relations between the Americano-Liberians and the indigenous population have been very strained.

The Constitution of Liberia is modeled on that of the United States. However, only citizens paying personal taxes may vote. The United States dollar, together with a subsidiary Liberian coin, is legal tender in Liberia. The official language is English.

William Vacanarat Shadrach Tubman was born in 1895. A practicing lawyer, he became a Senator in 1923, Justice of the Supreme Court in 1937, President in 1943, and has since been repeatedly re-elected to this post. In 1944, Liberia entered the war on the side of the Allies, and at that time became an important strategic position for the Americans. After the war, Tubman relied very much on American aid and on foreign corporations for the economic development of his country. An advocate of Pan-Africanism, he participated in the Conference of Bandung (1955) and the Conference of Accra (1958). He also organized the Pan-African Conferences of Monrovia (1959 and 1961), in which he proposed the economic union of the Western African countries.

It is not easy to forecast Liberia's future. Looking back in the past, one should bear in mind that at the beginning of President Tubman's career, Liberia was at a very early stage of economic development. The President succeeded in ensuring political stability and in attracting foreign investments, and has managed to achieve a more balanced economy. But it is still as if the country outside Monrovia has little knowledge of the twentieth century. Moreover, the friction that exists between the indigenous tribes and the Americano-Liberians (always a sensitive problem), could one day result in violent clashes.

Natural Resources and Economic Policy. There is, as yet, very little industrialization in Liberia. The largest sectors of the economy are mining and agriculture. Coffee, cocoa, diamonds, and gold are important products, but the main resources remain rubber and iron ore.

A subsidiary of Firestone Tire and Rubber Company has operated in Liberia since 1926, and in 1964 B. F. Goodrich brought a substantial Liberian plant into production. In 1953, the government levied a 25 percent tax on Firestone profits. For a long time rubber was by far the leading Liberian export.

The first company to exploit iron ore in Liberia was the Liberian Mining Company. In 1962, the National Iron Ore Company—of which 50 percent belongs to the Liberian Government—also commenced production and shipment of iron ore. In 1963, Lamco started productive and commercial operations. By 1961 iron ore had replaced rubber as Liberia's leading export.

The development of mineral resources was made possible by Liberia's favorable attitude towards foreign investment. In January 1964, in his Fifth Inaugural Address, President Tubman reaffirmed his administrative "open door" policy towards foreign investment. Under this policy, enunciated shortly after President Tubman was first elected to the Presidency in 1944, foreign capital was invited to Liberia on a partnership or joint-participation basis with the government. Foreign investors were assured fair treatment as well as full recognition and enforcement of their contractual and other rights.

One should also mention Liberia's important fleet: most of the ships belong to foreigners, who register their ships in Liberia for tax purposes.

Liberia is of great strategic interest to the United States, which also controls a large proportion of its external trade. The economic problems of Liberia are very serious; the nation's load of debts has grown even heavier in recent years, yet the government hopes that American economic aid will help to solve these problems.

Formation of Lamco

Early History. In 1953, a concession on an area in the northern part of Liberia was granted by the government to the United African American Corporation (UAAC), a group of American and Canadian interests, which later became the International African American Corporation (IAAC). In 1955, the Nimba orebody was discovered. It soon became apparent that considerable financial resources would be required to exploit this adequately, yet the IAAC was not able to sustain such a financial load. At that time, however, Grängesberg of Sweden showed a growing interest in the venture, and discussions and negotiations culminated, in 1959–1961, in a series of important agreements.

Mining Concession Agreement of 1960. The parties to the Mining Concession Agreement of 1960 are the Government of the Republic of Liberia, the Liberian American-Swedish Minerals Company (Lamco), and Bethlehem Steel Corporation (which is now represented in Liberia by its wholly-owned subsidiary, Liberia Bethehem Iron Mines Company, or Libeth). The agreement of 1960 has superseded the agreement that had previously been concluded with the UAAC.

According to Article 4 of the agreement, the mining concession includes:

(a) the exclusive right and privilege within the Concession Areas to explore for, drill, develop, extract, strip, mine, process (including beneficiate, agglomerate or otherwise treat), manufacture, transport, load, ship, sell and export the following ores, minerals and substances, and products derived therefrom: iron ore, iron bearing material, manganese, bauxite, columbite, mica, oil and natural gas. . . .

The exclusive character of the concession should be noted. Lamco holds a 75 percent undivided interest, and Bethlehem disposes over a 25 percent undivided interest in the concession and in the entire project. The obligations of the concessionaires are joint and not several. Nevertheless, any liability with respect to obligations undertaken by Lamco alone is solely the liability of Lamco. Furthermore, unless amended by agreement between them, the liability of Lamco with respect to any other obligation is limited to 75 percent thereof and the liability of Bethlehem with respect to any such other obligation is limited to 25 percent thereof.

As Bethlehem holds a 25 percent share and Lamco a 75 percent share, not only in the concession but in the entire project, all property of the mine (machines, equipment, etc.) belongs to the concessionaires in the same proportions. Whereas Lamco has a 75 percent right in this property, the shareholders of the company have only an indirect right in them.

Upon the termination of the concession, all subsurface mineral rights and all roads, railroads, airstrips, harbors, and docks constructed by the concessionaires together or by either one of them, shall become the property of the government. All machinery, equipment, etc. shall remain the property of the concessionaires or of either of them, and may be freely withdrawn, exported, or sold, except that the government shall be given the right of first refusal to purchase from the concessionaires any of such assets located in Liberia. It appears, therefore, that in case of liquidation, the government would receive half of Lamco's share of the equipment, machines, and other assets, or of the corresponding value.[1]

Among other things, the agreement guarantees the free repatriation of capital, dividends, and interests. The concession expires on November 18, 2023, but extensions are possible by agreement of the participants.

Joint Venture Agreement of 1960. The Joint Venture Agreement of

1. At the end of 1968, Lamco's interest in property and equipment in the concession area was worth more than $190 million.

1960 established a nonequity or contractual joint venture between Lamco and Bethlehem, and the concession was granted to this joint venture (Lamco Joint Venture). The nature and composition of Lamco will be described below.

Bethlehem is the second largest producer of steel in the United States. The American corporation did not wish to be fully linked with the whole venture, but, on the other hand, aimed at something more than a mere long-term contract. A contractual joint venture was chosen as a convenient way of giving Bethlehem advantageous terms for the iron ore it needed, while allowing it to contribute to the expenses of the venture.

There is no partnership or fiduciary relationship between the participants in the Lamco Joint Venture. This has been emphasized in the agreements for fiscal and liability reasons.

There has been no specification as to the law to be applied in cases where any differences in the interpretation or implementation of the agreement may arise. Because Liberian law does not exist in this field of economic concessions, it is likely that general concepts developed by American and English courts would be applied.

The Joint Venture Agreement will terminate upon expiration of the Concession Agreement.

Lamco. Lamco was incorporated in 1953 and is a Liberian corporation. It is an equity joint venture between the Liberian Government and the Liberian Iron Ore Limited (Lio), which will be described below. The capital of Lamco is divided into Class A and Class B stock. No right of first refusal has been provided for. The Liberian Government owns the Class A stock, which corresponds to 50 percent of the capital. These A shares entitle the government to have five members on the Board of Directors. The government paid for its shares by making the mineral resources available.

Lio owns the Class B stock, that is, the remaining 50 percent. It is entitled to designate six members on the Board of Directors. Lio paid for its shares in cash. It seems that Lamco would not have obtained the concession in the first place if the foreign interests had been aiming at operating on a solo basis; this would have been contrary to the official policy of joint participation between the government and foreign interests, the so-called "Tubman formula."

Lio. Lio was incorporated in 1958 and is a Canadian corporation. It is controlled largely by the Swedish Syndicate, which will be described below. About a quarter of the shares are in the hands of the public. Lio has shareholders in many countries, a large majority of whom are Americans, Canadians, Swedes, or Liberians. In agreement with the Liberian Government, Lio offered shares to the local public. At present, there are over 2,000 Liberian shareholders out of a total of approximately 5,000. Nevertheless, only about 3 percent of the shares are owned by Liberian citizens. This shows that the savings capacity of the Liberian people is somewhat limited, or alternatively, it might mean that Liberian savings do in fact exist, but are invested in other assets.

Swedish Syndicate. The Syndicate was created in 1958 and is a corporate juridical entity organized under the laws of Sweden. It consists of six Swedish companies, each of which has acted as a supplier of goods and services in the development of the Nimba project:

Sentab, Skånska Cement, Iföverken   participation of 4/28
Atlas Copco and Nordströms Linbanor participation of 9/28
Grängesberg   participation of 15/28

At the beginning, Grängesberg did not have the absolute majority in the Syndicate. But subsequently one of the partners of the Skånska Group sold its share to Grängesberg, which thus acquired the absolute majority in the Syndicate and the ultimate control of Lio.

Grängesberg. Grängesberg is one of the largest business enterprises in Sweden. Formed in 1896 to acquire and administer a group of railway companies and the iron ore mine at Grängesberg, its activities now comprise, in addition to the mining of ore in Sweden and Liberia, mineral prospecting in various parts of the world, ship owning (ships totalling approximately 730,000 tons dead weight), railway and port operation, production of iron ore and steel, steel construction and related engineering, hydroelectric power production, and other subsidiary activities. Mr. Erland Waldenström is Chief Executive of Grängesberg.

Productive and Commercial Operations. The high grade iron ore deposits exploited by the joint venture are situated in the Nimba Mountain region of northern Liberia. The joint venture had to build roads, install a port on the coast at Buchanan, and establish a 165-mile single track railroad between Yekepa in the Nimba Mountains and Buchanan.

Productive operations started in May 1963, and commercial operations began a short time later, in July. In the first half of 1968, the pelletizing and washing plants were completed and came into operation. These new plants were financed with borrowed funds to the extent of approximately $47,000,000 and from Lamco's retained earnings to the extent of approximately $4,400,000. At present the mines have an annual productive capacity of 10 million tons, including 2 million pellets. If one includes expansion, the venture represents a basic investment of more than $275 million. The joint venture is now one of the largest producers of high-grade iron ore in the world.

Taxation

Taxation of Bethlehem. A separate agreement between the Liberian Government and Bethlehem provides for an income tax of 50 percent of the net income from Bethlehem's 25 percent interest under the Concession Agreement. Bethlehem is entitled to an allowance for depreciation and has a choice as to the method of computing the allowance. The creditors and shareholders of Bethlehem are not subject to any tax for interest or dividend paid by Bethlehem on the disposition of the ore. In recent years the Liberian Government has received a substantial income from taxes paid by Bethlehem.

Lamco's Tax Exemption. Article 9 of the Concession Agreement provides that:

Since the Government is to receive 50 percent of the annual net profits of Lamco by reason of its ownership of 1,000,000 shares of the Class A Stock of Lamco, neither Lamco nor any contractor or subcontractor of Lamco or the Concessionaires for harbor, railroad, railroad roadbed, tracklaying, or other railroad, port or harbor construction (not including suppliers of materials), nor any manager of Lamco or of the Concessionaires nor any lenders to Lamco, nor any trustee for such lenders, shall be subject to the payment to the Government of any royalties (. . . . .), or of any export duties whatever, or of any income or other taxes of any kind whatever, levied by the Government or any subdivision or agency thereof in respect of activities connected with the Concession. . . .

The agreement thus explicitly establishes Lamco's tax exemption, conceded by the government in recognition of the substantial dividends it receives from the company. In 1965, 1966, 1967, and 1968 these dividends have each year exceeded $3 million.

Financing

Sharing in the Costs. As has already been mentioned, Bethlehem has to contribute 25 percent of the costs of the venture. Hitherto it has always provided the necessary funds from its own sources.

Pursuant to a Financial Advisory Agreement concluded in 1959, the Stockholms Enskilda Bank has been appointed exclusive financial advisor to Lio and Lamco, offering them professional guidance over their financing programs and other financial matters. In rendering its services it may retain such consultants and advisors outside its own organization as it may see fit to select. It receives remuneration from Lamco and Lio for its services on a reasonable and customary basis and is reimbursed for normal out-of-pocket expenses. Marc. Wallenberg, Sr., President of Lio and Chairman of the Board of Lamco, is chairman and a shareholder of the bank and is a trustee of a foundation that is a substantial shareholder of the bank.

Lamco has several sources of funds:

Sale of shares to Lio: $1 million;

Advances by the Swedish Syndicate and IAAC: $10.25 million;

"Entrance fee" paid by Bethlehem: $4.5 million;

Cash generated from sales of Lamco's share of the ore: $10.59 million have been thus budgeted.

Nevertheless, an important part of Lamco's share has been financed by the following credit agreements concluded in 1961:

Loan from the Swedish Syndicate: $38 million;

Loan from the Export-Import Bank of Washington: $30 million;

Loan from the Kreditanstalt für Wiederaufbau of Germany: approximately $52 million;

Loan from the First National City Bank of New York: $5.7 million.

On December 31, 1968, Lamco's long-term debt amounted to $152,217,000, of which $10,036,000 represented current maturities. Lamco was formed with an equity capital of $2 million, being divided equally between the Liberian Government and Lio. Including reserves and capital obligations that do not bear interest, the capital amounted at the end of 1968 to $27,831,000. Even so, the ratio of loan capital to equity capital seems quite high, and this is a distinctive feature of Lamco. The reason is, of course, that the resources needed for the financing of the enterprise are of unusual magnitude. Interest payments, naturally, will affect the cost of production of the iron ore for some time. But as the principals are gradually repaid, the cost of iron ore will become more competitive and the ratio of loan capital to equity capital will become more balanced. This, of course, would no longer be true if Lamco had to conclude new credit agreements.

Purchase of Equipment. Because of Lamco's borrowings from the Export-Import Bank of Washington and because of Bethlehem's desire to comply with the guidelines published by the United States Government regarding investments abroad by U.S. companies, a substantial proportion of the expenditure for equipment and machinery was incurred within the United States. This is an interesting example of the growing influence that lenders have in the shaping of an industrial or mining venture. The remaining equipment was purchased in various European countries, on the basis of competitive bidding.

Further Monetary Requirements. If more money were needed for further expansion, it would be possible to conclude new credit agreements. It is also possible that Lio's capital could be increased. On the other hand, it would be difficult to increase the capital of Lamco because it is uncertain whether the Liberian Government could find the money necessary to finance its share of the increase. A major and simpler means of financing expansion, however, is by the reinvestment of profits.

Management

Lamco's Board of Directors. As already mentioned above, Lio is entitled to 6 seats, and the Liberian Government to 5 seats on the board. In answer to the question why the Liberian Government is in a minority position on the board while having an equal participation in the capital, a Lamco executive explained that it is really irrelevant whether the government has 1 or 5 seats. It is better to count positions than actual seats. Lio would never take a long-term position against the government. It is argued that in every situation there can be a deadlock between the powers in presence, and that the possibility of conflict is not dependent upon the respective number of seats on the Board of Directors. Asked if Lio could have agreed to a 5-to-5 situation, the same executive answered that although he did not know exactly how Lio would have reacted, he personally could not conceive of any reason why this could not have been adopted.

Although the board has only 11 members, all those in positions of importance with Lamco attend the meetings. In all, 25 to 30 persons manage the venture: according to Lamco's management, it is this that permits the venture to be run efficiently.

Liberian Government and Management. Foreign corporations frequently refuse to enter upon a joint venture with a government or a government corporation of a developing country, because they anticipate constant interference in the management of the company by government officials. Hitherto there has hardly been any interference from governmental quarters with the venture. This is mainly because, to date, the government seems satisfied that the enterprise is being run efficiently.

Whereas this is true for the technical, financial, and commercial management of the venture, when it comes to the question of the joint venture's social contribution to the country the government's ideas do not altogether coincide with those of the management.

Day-to-day Management. Under a Management Contract of 1960 between the Swedish Syndicate, Lamco, and Bethlehem, Grängesberg —as the delegate of the Swedish Syndicate—is employed as Manager to supervise and direct further exploration within the concession areas, the location and development of mines, required construction, the mining, production, and transportation from mine to harbor of iron ore, and the general operations and management of the joint venture.

Grängesberg now receives a fee at the rate of 7½ cents per ton of ore produced and delivered to Lamco or Bethlehem at stockpile in Buchanan. In order to carry out its management responsibilities, the Manager has established a Liberia Division, under the direction of one of its Vice-Presidents, and has incorporated a Liberian subsidiary, Lamco J.V. Operating Company. The Stockholm office of Grängesberg's Liberia Division is in charge of long-range planning, major purchasing, personnel recruitment, and general administrative activities for the joint venture. The Operating Company conducts all mining, railroad and harbor operations of the joint venture in Liberia, carries on technical planning and local labor recruitment, and administers the communities of the joint venture at Yekepa and Buchanan.

The Liberia Division has to deal with general personnel recruitment, whereas the Operating Company is concerned with hiring local labor. As to senior personnel, Grängesberg fixes remuneration after consultation with the two partners. As to local labor salaries, Grängesberg is required to respect the agreements concluded with the National Mine Workers' Union. In any case, its activities are open for inspection when the budget is presented for examination at the shareholders' General Assembly. This example shows that, although Grängesberg is invested with broad powers in its capacity of manager, its activities are constantly checked by the participants in the venture.

The manager may not assign its rights, interests, and obligations under the Management Agreement without the consent of both partners, that is, Lamco and Bethlehem.

The Technical Committee, which provides for co-operation and consultation between Lamco, the manager, and Bethlehem, deserves a final mention. It provides its members with the possibility of discussing matters of importance perhaps more freely than in an open debate. The Technical Committee used to meet quite regularly at the beginning, but has done so less frequently during the last few years.

Lamco and Bethlehem supply funds to the manager every month, in accordance with an overall financial plan which they have approved. The manager prepares the monthly and annual budgets.

In the development of the Nimba project, Bethlehem contributed expert advice on technical matters, especially regarding the pelletizing plant, as Grängesberg had no experience in this field. Bethlehem also supervised the work performed in the United States by contractors and suppliers for the pelletizing and washing plants. In general, however, it has no important responsibilities in management or technical matters. Hitherto there have been no causes for conflict between Grängesberg and Bethlehem over technical or other issues.

Financial Policy

Discretion of the Board. The Board of Directors can, at its own discretion, allocate a proportion of the profits to the reserves. This power gives the board a great flexibility in the management of the venture. An outsider, however, bearing in mind that foreign interests are in a majority position on the board, may wonder whether this discretion is in the best interests of Liberia.

The exploitation of mineral deposits has always involved long-term planning, expansion, and considerable financial resources. Consequently, the foreign managers of Lamco have been aiming primarily at expansion and have taken a very long-term view of the venture. Substantial reserves have been constituted, so as to finance expansion at least partially. Both in 1967 and 1968, the amount of the annual reinvestment program has been in the neighborhood of $5 to 6 million. Total reserves at the end of 1968 were $8,475,000, of which $6,190,000 were required under the various credit agreements and $2,285,000 were free reserves.

The alternative course would be to pay larger dividends to the government and to ask it for capital contributions in return, once a specific expansion has been decided upon by the three partners of the Lamco venture. But in view of the huge financial burden that lies upon most governments in developing countries, it is doubtful whether a government would always have available the amount of money required.

Although many conjectures can be made at this point, it is problematical whether this situation should be regarded as a possible source of conflict in the future. Not receiving any money from Lamco in the form of taxes, the government is probably anxious to obtain from the company as much money as possible through dividends. Even if it accepts the policy of expansion and reinvestment, its imperative need for funds may force upon it a pressing concern for more short-term benefits.

Advance Dividend Payments. In 1959 there were no earnings, as productive and commercial operations were not yet under way. Nevertheless, at that time, Lamco had already authorized the payment of the sum of $250,000 per year to the Liberian Government, payable monthly commencing April 9, 1959, as an advance against future dividends.

A 1965 agreement between Lamco and the government, with the consent of Lio, provided for quarterly advance dividend payments to the government, as holder of the Class A shares, of up to 50 cents per ton of Lamco ore produced and shipped from Liberia out of the net profits of Lamco as computed under the Concession Agreement. Lamco's obligation to make such advance dividend payments is not cumulative from year to year. To the extent that profits are available after such payments to the government, Lio, as the holder of the Class B shares, receives equalizing payments on a cumulative basis. Any remaining profits are distributed to Lamco stockholders by the declaration of dividends.

The first $1,083,333 of such dividends owing to the government were offset against advance payments on account of future dividends made by Lamco to the government at the rate of $250,000 per year before the production of ore commenced.

There has been no problem hitherto over this because there has always been a profit of more than $1 per ton of ore. In fact, at the request of the government, Lamco has paid it (and also Lio) 55 cents per ton in respect of each of the years 1966 and 1967 and 60 cents per ton in respect of 1968. The advantages of the system are that the government enjoys a regular return, while the management knows at any time exactly where it is. Legally, the shares held by the government are common shares. In fact, they are the equivalent of preference shares insofar as dividends are concerned, while obviously they would have no preference on liquidation.

Sales

Lamco's Sales. Whereas Bethlehem uses for its own purposes the 25 percent share of the ore it receives, Lamco sells its 75 percent share to various purchasers. In 1959 Lamco and Grängesberg concluded a sales agency agreement. Grängesberg acts as exclusive selling agent for Lamco's share of the ore mined by the joint venture. Grängesberg receives a sales commission on such a share at the rate of 2 percent of the net invoice price, f.o.b. loading port, Liberia, of the first 5,000,000 tons and 1 percent of such price of any ore over 5,000,000 tons sold in each calendar year.

Grängesberg employs the Stockholm office of its Liberia Division and the services of Malmexport AB. in performing its functions as sales agent for Lamco. Malmexport is owned 50 percent by Grängesberg and 50 percent by Luossavaara-Kiirunovaara A.B. (LKAB), a Swedish corporation, 95.7 percent of which is owned by the Swedish Government, and 4.3 percent by Grängesberg. Malmexport, the largest purveyor of iron ore in European markets, has sales offices organized as subsidiary companies in Germany, Belgium, and the United Kingdom through which it maintains contact with European ore markets.

Grängesberg owns and operates a fleet of ore carriers which in the past have been used mainly for the transportation of Grängesberg and LKAB ore sold on a c.i.f. basis.

Sales Contracts. Lamco's aim is, of course, to conclude as many long-term contracts as possible for the sale of the ore. Of all the contracts concluded by Lamco through its sales agent, Grängesberg, only the so-called "Ruhr-contract," however, is truly a long-term contract. On July 14, 1960, Lamco entered into a contract with thirteen major producers of pig iron in West Germany. Each buyer has agreed to purchase a specified tonnage of Nimba iron ore, such tonnages aggregating approximately 6,400,000 tons for all of the buyers over the period 1963 through 1965 and 2,500,000 tons in respect of each year thereafter through 1979. Basically the price is a formula price based upon the operating expenses of the project, a portion of the debt service, and other factors. Amortization of the long-term debts of Lamco will cause the formula price to decrease as time goes on. Because of this, the price is in principle fixed for several years in advance. Nevertheless, Lamco recognizes that changes in the conditions of the world market for iron ore may from time to time lead to discussions, resulting in modifications of the terms of the contracts. The result is that the price is, in fact, renegotiated every year.

Other contracts have been concluded with Belgian, Italian, and French firms. In recent years, Lamco has also negotiated and concluded substantial contracts with Japanese, U.K., and U.S. corporations.

The World Situation of Iron Ore. Today's iron ore market is undergoing a slump, and is characterized by a high degree of competition, an ample supply, and a high rate of technological change. In eleven years the price of iron ore has been cut by half. Many new important deposits have been discovered in Gabon, Australia, South America, and India. The situation is further complicated for Lamco by the fact that the major steel producers have usually their own iron ore deposits. Bethlehem Steel, for instance, only required from Lamco marginal additional surpluses. As a consequence of this situation, Lamco's operating results for 1967 showed, in comparison with 1966, a reduction in sales and profits. However, the trend was favorable again in 1968.

Mining operations have always to be evaluated in a long-term perspective. The world supply of iron ore is abundant, but the demand is also increasing. Lamco's iron ore is very competitive because of low production cost and high quality. Also, the washing and pelletizing plants now permit the production of diversified and higher quality ranges of iron ores. Consequently, Lamco's management is confident that the company's economic situation will progressively improve over the next few years. The conclusion of substantial Japanese contracts was already a step in this direction.

Social Contribution to Liberia

As has already been mentioned, the government has so far avoided interfering in the management of the enterprise, but has very definite ideas nevertheless as to the social contribution Lamco could make to Liberia. The management of Lamco has always recognized its obligations in this respect. Consequently, the divergences that from time to time appear do not concern the principle of this obligation, but rather its modalities.

Some 40 percent of the total project investment of $275 million represents infrastructure development. Each year, moreover, a minor, but not negligible proportion of the operating budget is devoted to education, training, medical, and other community services.

Education and Labor. About 10,000 people were employed during the construction program of Lamco. As of late 1968, the staff consisted of 759 employees, of whom 169 were Liberians. At the same time the labor force numbered 3,454. Approximately 85 percent of those employed by the joint venture were Liberian citizens, and some 22 nationalities were represented among the remaining 15 percent.

There is an international school in which the teachers are Swedish, British, and French. For the time being few Liberians attend this school. Education through elementary grades, however, is provided for the immediate members of the family of every employee. As to this educational school, the following episode illustrates the kind of social and psychological problems which foreign enterprises have to face in an unfamiliar environment. In 1966 many children suddenly appeared who were not the sons or daughters of the venture's employees. Facing this great influx, Lamco's management felt the time had come to limit attendance at the school. They then discovered that many of these children were wards.[2] On the board of Lamco the government of Liberia made it known that it would be a mistake to send these children away. It is a very strong tradition in Liberia that the community takes responsibility for wards, a tradition which the management of Lamco finally decided to respect.

Night schools are operated for the benefit of adults. There are also correspondence courses. For the time being, the students enrolled in these courses learn mainly to read and write. Perhaps at some point in the future the school will also start to provide for secondary levels.

As to the development of professional skills, on-the-job training is an internal and important part of the operations. But there is also a vocational school at Yekepa, where, for instance, 65 Liberians have

2. The term "ward" is used here in the sense of any child who comes or is brought under the roof of a particular family: it may be the son or daughter of a poor relative from another part of the country; it may be no blood relationship at all, but the child of a friend or business associate; or it may be the child of the father by another woman who may be considered a second or third wife or may have no defined relationship to the man.

been trained to become workshop supervisors and foremen in the washing and pelletizing plants. The vocational school was not initiated by Lamco; it is a governmental project, which was conceived during an official visit of President Tubman to Sweden. It is, however, operated by Grängesberg.

The workers and employees are affiliated to a union. The labor situation has not always been untroubled. In February 1965 the workers went on a wildcat strike, then on a general strike. In June 1965 a two-year collective bargaining agreement was signed with the union. Just over a year later, in July 1966, there was a one-week strike which was followed, in June 1967, by a new two-year contract concluded with the union. These strikes were certainly motivated by demands for higher wages, but significant aspects of Liberian and union politics were also involved. The labor situation has remained favorable throughout 1968, and there have been no strikes.

Community Facilities. Lamco has devoted special attention to medical care. Nimba and Buchanan each have their own hospital; the doctors are expatriates, whereas the nurses all come from the area. Nimba also has a clinic, which mainly runs a maternity ward as well as providing treatment for an eye disease that is prevalent in the region. The clinic is open not only to the workers and employees of Lamco, but also to all other inhabitants in the area.

Lamco has also established various facilities essential to the sound operation of the enterprise and to the life of the community: airports; power generation and transmission facilities; water supply and sewage farms; repair shops; housing; commissaries; churches; a theater-assembly hall; and a Workers' Recreation Center in Yekepa.

In 1967, Radio Lamco, the first company-owned and -operated radio station on the west coast of Africa, with studios in Yekepa, Nimba, and Buchanan, offered the management the means of communicating with the employees in some local languages as well as in English and Swedish. The new station carries educational programs, news about the company, and news of what is happening in Liberia and abroad. Radio Lamco relays some programs of the Liberian Broadcasting Corporation, ELBC, and presents a weekly roundup of international news. This innovation met with a favorable reaction. The radio is one of Lamco's community services that is of interest not only to the employees and workers of the company, but to the entire community of the area.

Railway and Harbor. The basis of this contribution is to be found in an obligation assumed by the joint venture in Article 4 of the Concession Agreement, which reads as follows:

The Concessionaires agree that a reasonable amount of commercial traffic will be accommodated for hire by any railroad or port constructed and operated by them in accordance with the foregoing rights and privileges, but the Concessionaires shall not be compellable to accept for transportation for others any iron ore or iron bearing material, nor shall the operation by the Concessionaires of a railroad or of a port constitute them a common carrier or public authority or company engaged in operation of public character. It is understood that the primary and essential purpose of the railroad and the port is the transportation and export of iron ore under this mining concession and that use of the railroad and of the port for other commercial traffic must not be burdensome for the Concessionaires and must not interfere with such purpose.

Although both the government and the foreign interests try to apply the spirit rather than the letter of this article, its phrasing should be remembered in order to understand some of the current discussions between the parties. Lamco's management regards the work carried out on the railway and the harbor as one of the joint venture's major contributions to the country. In a way, the money devoted to these projects replaces dividends.[3] If these amounts had not been employed for this purpose, higher dividends would have been declared.

Railway. From the main track Buchanan-Nimba, the joint venture is building now a single track railway to rubber plantations and a single track to timber plantations. These will allow the rubber exploited by American companies and the timber exploited by private Liberian companies to be transported from the plantations to the port. The joint venture will be free to fix the schedules of the trains, provided, of course, it takes the wishes of the rubber and timber companies into account as much as possible.

At the Nimba end, the railway is very near the Guinean border. In 1966 the joint venture and the governments of Guinea and Liberia came to an agreement that a certain amount of commercial traffic between the two countries would be directed through this railroad. It should be noted that in the Guinean area near the Liberian border the economy is almost entirely agricultural.

3. Reference here is made only to the incidental benefits provided by the railroad and the harbor. Obviously, the construction of the facilities was necessary to the whole project and as such did not reduce dividends.

The agreement has not yet been implemented for two reasons. There is, first of all, a problem of communication. While there is a road from Nimba to the border, after the border there is no communication for a distance of 25 miles before the first collecting point. The Guineans plan to bring their products by trucks, and intend, consequently, to build a highway; this may take a long time. Even when the highway is completed, it seems likely that the traffic would be relatively slight, and only increasing slowly; this accommodation, therefore, seems unlikely to hinder the joint venture's operations.

There is a second difficulty, as Liberia and Guinea agreed that the agreement would not go into effect until the harbor problem had been settled.

Harbor. The government decided to set up a National Port Authority (NPA), which would supervise all ports throughout the country. At present the two main ports are located in Monrovia and Buchanan. As the NPA is to be a public agency, a statute was enacted in order to regulate its activities. There is, however, some uncertainty as to the implementation of the idea. Although seven members of the NPA have now been named and an executive director has been appointed, this new group has not yet focused on the port of Buchanan. Lamco's management sees some risks in this governmental project and is determined to preserve the satisfactory running of the venture's operations.

No matter of principle is involved, as management is quite willing to fulfill this aspect of its social obligations to the country. The Concession Agreement protects the joint venture's rights. Also the government officials recognize that they do not have the necessary personnel to manage the harbor. Three governmental departments are involved: the Department of Commerce and Industry, the Secretary of the Treasury, and the Department of National Planning and Economics. The Secretary of the Treasury is on the board of Lamco and the Secretary of the Department of National Planning attends all board meetings—but it is President Tubman who takes the basic governmental decisions.

Lamco's management relies on the Concession Agreement, but aims to conclude a more elaborate agreement with the NPA. The company feels the need to fix the reciprocal obligations of the parties, and is especially anxious to preserve the right to plan the harbor's expansion. Because of the interests involved, a compromise seems likely, but some time may pass before such a compromise can be reached.

Disputes and Arbitration

No procedure for conciliation has been provided for, but the Concession Agreement, the Joint Venture Agreement, and the Management Agreement each have an arbitration clause. In addition, the Joint Venture Agreement provides for the cases of default by one of the partners.

Concession Agreement. Any dispute with respect to the interpretation or application of the Concession Agreement between the Liberian Government and Lamco and Bethlehem or either of them, which cannot be settled by mutual agreement, is required to be submitted to arbitration. Each side selects one arbitrator. Such arbitrators, or, failing agreement, the President of the International Chamber of Commerce (ICC), select the third arbitrator. The arbitral court shall meet in Monrovia, unless the parties or the arbitrators unanimously agree on some other place. The clause does not provide for the case of one of the parties failing to nominate an arbitrator: it was probably considered to be inappropriate to have a third party designate an arbitrator for a sovereign nation.

Joint Venture Agreement. The clause here is similar to that of the Concession Agreement. The Joint Venture Agreement, however, stipulates that if either participant fails to nominate an arbitrator, the President of the ICC shall appoint the second arbitrator. The arbitration clause of the Management Agreement is almost identical to that of the Joint Venture Agreement.

The agreement has also a rather elaborate clause concerning the case of default of one of the partners. It will be sufficient for the purpose of this study to describe the principle of the clause, without entering further upon its details. In the event of certain defaults (for instance, financial ones), the non-defaulting participant may require Grängesberg to decline to make deliveries of ore to the defaulting participant and may, under certain circumstances, purchase the interest of the defaulting participant in the joint venture. The defaulting participant has the right to require the non-defaulting participant to retransfer to it the interest under the various agreements, but only under some specified conditions and during a limited space of time.

The default clause can, of course, apply to either partner. One should bear in mind, however, that Bethlehem had financed its share of the costs from internal funds, while Lamco concluded substantial long-term loans. It was, therefore, Bethlehem that insisted on including this clause. There has been no cause to apply it, however, since Lamco has hitherto always honored its debts.

Results and Prospects

Results. Lamco has now a total annual productive capacity of at least 10 million tons of ore. It is able to produce washed fines, washed lumpy ore and pellets, and to improve through the washing process the physical characteristics of its run-of-mine ore. If it is economical and profitable to do so, and after consultation with the government, Lamco and Bethlehem could create further processing and manufacturing facilities in Liberia. At one point the government was interested in constructing a steel mill, and feasibility studies were carried out; contacts were made with other African governments but no agreement could be reached. In addition, President Tubman feels that mining investments in Liberia could well lead to the establishment of Liberian service businesses.

Lamco represents an interesting form of cooperation between foreign and local interests. The legal structure was made to measure, so as to fit in with the wishes and the requirements of the various partners. At the top of this structure, the contractual joint venture allows Bethlehem to be much more than a mere buyer, without becoming tied like an equity partner. Lamco itself is an equity joint venture, which permits the Liberian Government to implement the "Tubman formula" of joint participation and to derive dividends from the venture.

The structure also ensures what seems to be one of the essential conditions of success in a joint venture, namely a unified management. At board level the government does not interfere in basic policy decisions, and the day-to-day management is in the hands of Grängesberg. Also the venture is managed by a limited number of executives, who know each other very well and meet together frequently. All this allows for an efficient management and a minimum of friction.

Problems. One of Lamco's main problems is the world situation of iron ore. Consequently, Lamco's success is dependent not only on its technical or financial management, but also to a large extent on its ability to sell in the depressed world markets. As has already been mentioned, since the conclusion of new contracts Lamco's prospects for the next few years look brighter. The solid financial basis of the venture should allow it to withstand temporary setbacks. Even with adverse market conditions Lamco has hitherto been able to maintain a reasonable profit margin.

It is possible that Lamco may have to face another difficulty. Many governments of developing countries try to combine the financial satisfactions of the tax collector with those of the shareholder. It is possible that the Liberian Government might be tempted to do the same, especially in view of its heavy external debt. Nevertheless, the tax exemption is explicitly guaranteed in the Concession Agreement. As an alternative the government may try to obtain from Lamco's Board of Directors a more liberal policy with regard to the distribution of profits. Naturally, as expansion is one of the primary goals of Lamco's management, the board is unlikely to relax its conservative dividend policy without a struggle. Nevertheless, a joint venture has often to be adapted to changing circumstances—it should not be a rigid construction. Although it is difficult to make forecasts in this respect, it seems that in the case of Lamco any change in the tax situation or in the dividend policy would result rather from negotiations and bargaining with the government than from a unilateral move.

Hitherto relations with the government have been satisfactory. Even in the discussions relative to Lamco's social contribution (especially the problem of the harbor), a compromise seems likely. But this capacity of the parties to compromise is made possible because of the personality of President Tubman, who is in favor of foreign investment. After Tubman, future policy and prospects for foreign investors are likely to be much more problematical.

Lamco and Liberia. Before the coming of the mining companies, the Liberian economy was to a large extent dominated by the rubber companies. The symbol of this domination was Firestone. It would be reasonable to suppose that the rubber companies might not have regarded the arrival of these newcomers without resentment.

The internal equilibrium of the country has certainly been affected by these new investments, but not necessarily to the detriment of the rubber companies. It is true, for instance, that labor costs have risen since that time, and that, as a consequence, the production costs of all companies have been affected. On the other hand, the government in the past was always tempted to turn to the rubber companies whenever it needed funds; now that the government has several sources of income, the pressure on the rubber companies is unlikely to increase. Moreover, Liberia can no longer be described as a gigantic Firestone plantation, and this certainly has important economic, but also psychological consequences. Finally, relations between Lamco and the rubber companies have so far been excellent, as is shown by the fact that Lamco's railway is used by the latter. Many foreign corporations now show at least adequate social consciousness when they come to settle in a developing country. Whether they come on a joint venture or on a wholly-owned basis, they often establish satisfactory infrastructure installations and suitable community services. A distinctive feature of Lamco in this respect is that some of its achievements are of interest not only to its own workers and employees but to the whole population of the area: this is true, for instance, of the clinic and the radio. Similarly, some of its infrastructure developments, such as the harbor and the railway, are of use not only to Lamco but to other companies also.

In the long run Lamco's social contribution may prove to be its finest guarantee against adverse internal developments.

Venture between a Government Corporation and a Multinational Corporation

IV: COPPER MINING IN CHILE

Kennecott

In 1915, three companies that exploited copper in the U.S.A. (Western States and Alaska) and in Chile, combined to form the Kennecott Copper Corporation. Kennecott has now moved into its second half-century by vigorously expanding within and beyond its traditional copper role.

Copper Activities. Copper has dominated Kennecott's first half-century and today it produces more of this metal in the United States than any other company. Copper is durable and is an excellent conductor of electricity and heat. These basic characteristics have led to the employment of the metal for a broad variety of uses and has resulted in a steady, long-term increase in demand. Consumption in the United States has now reached such dimensions that the country has become a net importer of copper and, as such, has reversed its export role of many decades.

Kennecott is increasing capacity in response to this demand. The company operates four large open-pit mines, which are located near Salt Lake City, Utah (the Bingham Canyon mine is the largest copper producer in the U.S.A.); Hurley, New Mexico; Hayden, Arizona; and Ely, Nevada. The mining methods employed in these open pits are essentially the same and are typical of the techniques used to mine large, low-grade ore deposits at or near the surface.

Deeper ores, overlain or cut through by large masses of barren waste rock, are usually mined by underground methods, which are more costly than open-pit mining. Consequently, profitable underground mining is usually dependent upon a higher grade of ore. Kennecott's major production from underground ore deposits comes from the El Teniente mine located 50 miles southeast of Santiago, in the

O'Higgins Province, Chile. On the steep slopes of the Andes, some 7,000 feet above sea level, is Sewell, the site of El Teniente. This mine was first investigated in 1903 by an engineer, William Braden. It is now the world's largest underground copper mine and is managed by Kennecott's subsidiary, the Braden Copper Company, which was formed in 1904. The mine contains over 300 miles of tunnels, shafts, and levels. Ore from this mine contains about 1.8 percent copper and is mined by a system known as "block caving." Blocks of ore weighing up to 2 million tons each are undercut to induce caving and are drawn off uniformly through a system of chutes and passes to the rail-haulage levels below. Here the ore is drawn from the passes into rail-cars and hauled to the concentrator ore bins located near the tunnel entrance.

Kennecott's copper operations include a wholly-owned fabricating subsidiary, the Chase Brass & Copper Company, a leading producer of copper tubes, copper, and brass rods, and copper and brass sheet for the industries, offices, and homes of America.

Copper's Future. Two events are likely to bring about a decrease in copper consumption for the near future. First, during the second half of 1967 and the first quarter of 1968, a nationwide strike cut U.S. copper production; higher prices and unavailability of copper during the long shutdown encouraged significant substitution of other materials. Second, it is hoped that the Vietnam War will end in the foreseeable future. In that case, the copper needs of the U.S. military forces will be considerably reduced.

Nevertheless, long-term growth in copper consumption is forecast. Noncommunist consumption of newly-mined copper in the coming years is expected to grow at an average annual rate in excess of 4 percent. Consumption in the early seventies is expected to reach approximately 6¼ million tons, as compared to about 4¾ million tons in the mid-sixties. This optimistic forecast is based on the fact that copper is the best conductor of electricity, at a time when electric power generation is growing rapidly, thus taxing the supply of copper and many other basic materials. Another reason for the growth of copper demand is the economic development of emerging nations in Africa, the Far East, and Latin America.

To meet the anticipated increase in consumption, noncommunist copper mine capacity, based on announced consumption, is expected to total 6½ million tons in the early seventies, that is, one third more than in the mid-sixties. Major expansions are now under way in the United States, Canada, Chile, and Peru. There is a great potential for future expanded production in Chile, Peru, Zambia, and the Congo, which now supply 40 percent of the noncommunist copper production.

Meanwhile, exploration for new deposits in the United States continues at a greatly accelerated pace. An important potential for additional copper production lies in fracturing deep, low-grade, buried copper deposits with nuclear explosives and extracting the copper by in-place leaching methods. As part of the Atomic Energy Commission's Plowshare Program to investigate and develop peaceful uses for nuclear explosives, the U.S. Atomic Energy Commission and Kennecott have designed an experiment to determine the feasibility of this technique at a Kennecott deposit near Safford, Arizona.

For many years, there has been a trend towards the substitution of other materials for copper, yet demand has risen steadily in spite of this evolution. As in the past, copper has lost ground for certain uses, but has gained measurably in others, such as in air-conditioning equipment. Its overall growth continues to increase as a result of new uses and applications. A prime example is the utilization of copper in the building of desalination plants.

Other Activities. Kennecott is more than a copper company; it is also the country's second largest producer of gold and molybdenum, as well as an important producer of silver, zinc, lead, titanium, iron, columbium, selenium, rhenium, palladium, and platinum. In recent years, the company has increased its productive capacity of these metals.

On March 29, 1968, Kennecott entered a new field of production by acquiring the Peabody Coal Company. Peabody pioneered the long-term contracting of coal production to supply electric utilities and this market has become the mainstay of a revived coal industry. Forecasts indicate continued demand for coal in the utilities and in other markets.

Finally, Kennecott has a financial interest in a large phosphate deposit in North Carolina.

Profile in Figures. Kennecott is a public company, which has some 82,000 shareholders. About 30,000 employees work for the company and its subsidiaries in 36 states of the U.S.A. and 14 other countries.

Kennecott's total assets have more than doubled in 20 years and now exceed one billion dollars. Approximately 11 percent of the net current assets and approximately 23 percent of all assets shown in the 1967 consolidated balance sheet are located outside the United States. Net income derived from foreign sources represents normally 30 percent of the company's consolidated net income. Kennecott's foreign assets are located principally in Chile and Canada.

In 1967, Kennecott changed the basis of its consolidated financial statements so as to include subsidiaries in which it had invested more than 50 percent of the capital. Previously, only wholly-owned subsidiaries had been included in the consolidated financial statements. It was felt that this new method of reporting would give a more accurate picture of the financial results of Kennecott's diversified operations.

Chile

Profile. A Republic since 1821, Chile is surrounded by Peru and Bolivia in the north, Argentina in the east, and the Pacific Ocean in the west. Covering 741,767 square kilometers, the country forms a long belt along the Pacific Ocean. It can be divided into three distinctive areas: the desert of Atacama in the north with its copper mines; the Great Valley in the center, ideal for agriculture; the forests and the rolling uplands of the south where sheep are reared. The areas of Chile complement each other and communicate by means of an important coasting trade. Chile's trade with foreign countries was greatly facilitated by the opening of the Panama Canal and the construction of the transandean railway.

In 1966, Chile had 8,750,000 Spanish-speaking inhabitants, a quarter of whom (2,270,700) lived in the important capital of Santiago. The other main cities are much smaller: Valparaíso (278,000 inhabitants); Concepción (170,000 inhabitants); Viña del Mar (131,500 inhabitants). As the agricultural sector is not very important, 70 percent of the population lives in the cities. The annual rate of the population increase is slightly above 2 percent, which nevertheless is one of the lowest rates in Latin America. Since 1958, both the birth rate and the death rate have decreased.

The average individual income is relatively high by Latin American standards. Chilean society is characterized by a great inequality, although this disequilibrium is less pronounced than in the other Latin American countries, (with the exception of Uruguay). As a middle class is slowly developing, there is hope for a more balanced society.

Recent History. In 1958, the hard-won victory of the Independent candidate, Alessandri, over the Socialist Party member, Allende, underlined the serious problems of the country, such as inflation and widespread unemployment. With the assistance of the United States, Alessandri undertook the reorganization of the economy and the implementation of an austerity program. The economy, however, which greatly depends on copper sales, remained in a critical state. The new monetary unit, the escudo, in 1960 alone lost two thirds of its value.[1]

This economic situation went far to maintain the acute social tension that came out into the open during the presidential elections of 1964. In order to neutralize the progress of the marxist Popular Action Front, the bulk of the centrist and right-wing electorate voted for the candidate of the Christian Democratic Party, Eduardo Frei, who defeated Allende. The congressional elections of March 1965 brought about a new victory for Frei and his Party. In January 1967, however, the alliance of the right wing and of the left wing in the Senate successfully opposed the trip that Frei was planning to make to the United States. The municipal elections of April 1967 and the parliamentary election of March 1969 showed a decline in the votes for the Christian Democratic Party.

Frei's program has been based upon the principle of the "Revolution in Freedom." The government has tried to bring about structural reforms, such as agrarian reform and the participation of the Chilean state in copper exploitation. Although the workers' standard of living has improved, the government has had to face growing opposition from the left wing and also from inside the ruling party. In February and March 1966, the copper miners' strikes took on an insurrectional character. A general strike in November 1967 led to bloody incidents in Santiago.

In foreign affairs, Chile has been a strong supporter of the Latin American Common Market. The government has also sought economic assistance from a variety of sources in order to counterbalance U.S. aid, which, however, has so far remained predominant.

The Economy. The Chilean economy has been dominated by the exploitation of its main mineral resource, copper. Other mineral resources are iron ore, gold, silver, coal, and oil. Iron ore production has considerably increased since 1958. Oil production too has more than doubled between 1958 and 1966 and is now sufficient to supply half the country's needs.

1. At present, one dollar is worth about 10 escudos.

The nature and volume of agricultural production have not varied greatly. As a result of the population increase, Chile imports increasing quantities of food products. In recent years, fishing has developed rapidly and anchovies have supplied fish-flour factories. Nevertheless, the agricultural sector as a whole employs only 25 percent of the active population and constitutes only a small part of the Gross National Product.

Because 4.3 percent of landowners own more than 80 percent of the cultivated area, the government began in 1962–1963 to introduce an agrarian reform. From February 1967 onwards, the Frei regime renewed its efforts to implement the reform. Until now, however, the latifundia have largely survived. Too often, the small tenant (*inquilino*) has neither the financial means nor the technical knowledge necessary for progress.

The manufacturing industry, which is sustained by the steel industry of Huachipato, has developed especially in metallurgy and textiles. However, manufactured articles still constitute half of the imports.

As in many Latin American countries, "galloping inflation" has been a very serious problem. In recent years, however, the annual rate of inflation has decreased due to severe governmental restrictions, such as wage and price controls and a limitation of bank credits and monetary circulation.

The balance of trade, which has been positive since 1964 has been dependent on the copper exports. Iron ore is the second leading export. About one third of exports have gone to the United States, and another third have been absorbed by the European Common Market. As for imports, one third come from the United States and the European Common Market provides about a fifth.

Formation of the Joint Mining Company

Negotiations with the Alessandri Government. In the early sixties, Kennecott decided to seek a substantial expansion and made the necessary technical studies. The U.S. corporation asked the Alessandri Government for certain fiscal and other guarantees, as a necessary condition for expansion. In order to make these guarantees effective, special legislation would have had to be enacted. The government regarded this as politically impossible. Kennecott decided to bide its time until such guarantees would be granted.

The need to obtain these guarantees can be illustrated by the fiscal treatment of the large copper companies. In 1960, Chile had suffered from a very serious earthquake. On that occasion the government had decided to raise two temporary, supplementary taxes of eight percent and five percent. These special taxes had been progressively abolished for every taxpayer except Kennecott and Anaconda. In addition, the Chilean Government imposed higher taxes on the copper companies than on other business and also distinguished between the larger and the smaller copper companies. This fiscal system was of course discriminatory, but from a Chilean point of view it was justified on the ground that the large copper companies are Chile's most prosperous enterprises.

However, Kennecott was, at that time, paying in taxes between 81 percent and 87 percent of its gross income. Such a high rate can hardly be described as a strong incentive to engage in major expansion. In Kennecott's view, taxes had to be lowered to a more reasonable rate and, what is more important, guarantees had to be obtained that the new rate would not be changed from one year to another.

The Agreement with the Frei Government. Shortly after Chile's new President, Eduardo Frei, assumed office on November 4, 1964, Kennecott began discussions with a Presidential Commission to explore the possibility of expanding production in line with the new administration's economic program. On the American side, the main negotiators were F.R. Milliken, President of Kennecott, C.D. Michaelson, Vice President of Kennecott, and R.H. Haldeman, Vice President of the Braden Copper Company. On the Chilean side, the main negotiators were R. Saez, who was Head of CORFO (Corporación de Fomento de la Producción), J. Lagarrigue, Executive Vice-President of the Copper Corporation, and E. Simián, who was then Minister of Mines.

On December 3, 1964, the Chilean Government and Kennecott concluded a basic agreement. On December 18, 1964, Kennecott's Board of Directors authorized the management to proceed with the carefully-conceived plan. On December 21, 1964, in a nationwide broadcast to the Chilean people outlining a series of agreements with U.S. copper companies operating in Chile, President Frei announced the agreement reached between Kennecott and the Chilean Government.

The purpose of the agreement was to expand, activate, and improve the mining operations of the El Teniente Mine, in order to increase the installed copper production capacity from approximately 180,000 short tons annually to an estimated 280,000 short tons per year. It was expected that the expansion program would take about five years to complete.

However, important steps had to be taken before construction work could begin. The actual enactment of the relevant Chilean legislation took a certain amount of time,[2] as did the gathering of the considerable funds necessary for expansion, which involved long negotiations with the Export-Import Bank of Washington (Eximbank) and the Agency for International Development (AID). In fact, two years and four months were spent in discussions before the basic agreement made in December 1964 could be implemented.

On September 16, 1966, a stock corporation named Sociedad Minera El Teniente S.A. was created. On April 13, 1967, the Braden Copper Corporation, a foreign corporation organized under the laws of the State of Maine (U.S.A.), and with an agency authorized to operate in Chile, transferred its assets and liabilities to the new Sociedad in exchange for all of the capital stock of the Chilean company. Braden was exempted from all taxes, contributions, or charges for transferring its assets to El Teniente.

That same day, April 13, 1967, important decisions were put into effect. Braden sold a 51 percent interest in El Teniente to an agency of the Chilean Government, the Copper Corporation, in exchange for

2. *Braden-El Teniente Copper Laws 1955–1967:*
May 5, 1955   Law N. 11,828 (Basic Copper Law which does not deal only with Kennecott operations).
March 30, 1960   Decree with Force of Law 258 ("Foreign Investor's Statute")—implementing Law N. 11,828.
March 31, 1960   Decree with Force of Law 268—amends Law N. 11,828.
January, 25, 1966   Law N. 16,425—Titles I and IV modify Law N. 11,828 and DFL 258. Titles II, III and IV (in part) constitute new copper law.
April 21, 1966   Decree with Force of Law 61—Regulations governing the export trade of copper and its byproducts under emergency monopoly situation, provided by Law N. 11,828, Art. 15-A.
April 25, 1966   Law N. 16,464—modifies Law N. 11,828, and DFL 258. Modifies Law N. 16,425, Titles II and III. Articles 233 and 239 represent portions of the Frei Administration proposed Law N. 16,425, which were knocked out in the original passage, but inserted as riders to subsequent legislation in 1966.
June 28, 1966   Decree with Force of Law 91—replaces Article 4 of DFL 61.
August 30, 1966   Decree with Force of Law 114—Regulations for Applications of Article 13-A of Law N. 11,828. Reinvestments of net profits in Chile.

80 million dollars.[3] Formed in 1965, the Copper Corporation was in fact a redesignation of the Copper Department, which had existed for many years. Unlike the Copper Department, the Copper Corporation had received the power to own stock in mixed mining companies. Braden sold a 51 percent interest not only in the existing properties, but also in the planned expanded facilities. The Chilean Government thus became the majority shareholder of El Teniente. The Board of Directors of the new Sociedad was constituted with four government representatives and three Kennecott representatives.

Meanwhile, financial and fiscal arrangements were guaranteed by a decree of the Ministry of Economy, Development and Reconstruction, dated March 20, 1967.[4] The decree guaranteed full stability of tax rates and exchange arrangements for twenty years. This text also described in detail the loans financing the investment.

Whereas Braden in Chile does not have any interests or activities other than El Teniente, Kennecott now has entirely separate exploration activities.

Financing and Foreign Exchange

The Sociedad's equity capital ($160 million) represents the value placed on El Teniente's properties before the expansion for the purpose of the transaction. The loan capital of approximately $230 million is destined for financing the expansion.

Equity Capital. The Sociedad's capital stock amounts to $160 million and is divided into 160 million registered shares, having a par value of one dollar, which have been issued in four series, that is:

Series A : 65,280,000 shares;
Series B : 62,720,000 shares;
Series C : 16,320,000 shares;
Series D : 15,680,000 shares.

Series A and Series B are ordinary shares, whereas Series C and D constitute preferred stock. The Copper Corporation owns Series A and C and Kennecott retained Series B and D.

The transactions of April, 1967, brought about an important

3. As a result of the sale, Kennecott (Braden) realized a gain of $27.6 million because the "book value" of the entire Braden investment had been depreciated over a long period of years.

4. See *International Legal Materials*, VI, pp. 1151–61 (November 1967).

change in Kennecott Copper Corporation's general accounts. Prior to the sale of a 51 percent interest in El Teniente to the Copper Corporation, Braden's sales and earnings were included in the consolidated income account of Kennecott, and its assets, liabilities and equity were included in the consolidated balance sheet. Since the transaction, El Teniente's production and sales have been presented separately. Kennecott's financial interest in El Teniente has been shown on the balance sheet as an investment and the dividends and interest received have been reported accordingly.

Government Participation. In exchange for the 51 percent participation in El Teniente, the Chilean Government has agreed to pay $80 million to Braden. The government has paid only a minor part of its debt in cash. The rest is represented by notes with an interest of 5¾ percent, which are receivable in various amounts until July 1, 1970. Amounts received by Braden on the principal of such notes are to be concurrently loaned to El Teniente on 5¾ percent notes receivable in 30 biannual instalments commencing December 31, 1971. Interest earned on the latter loans will bring about the issuance of additional 5¾ percent notes.

In other words, Kennecott (Braden) has lent $80 million to the government, which has to repay them between 1967 and 1970. The reimbursed funds (plus other funds) are immediately lent again by Kennecott (Braden) to El Teniente, which has to repay them between 1971 and 1986. This system has two advantages for the government: firstly, it permits an amortization in the repayment of the government's debt; second, by avoiding the repatriation to the United States of considerable funds, it helps to preserve Chile's foreign exchange.

Kennecott's management is confident that the government will find the funds necessary for the loan repayment. Normally, the government should receive sufficient funds for that purpose from dividends on its 51 percent interest.

Preferential Shares. Shares in Series C and D have no voting rights and constitute preferred stock. This preference, as regards the Sociedad's profits made available for dividends, consists in preferential payment of 6.5 percent on their par value, in dollars. Should the net profits of one fiscal year not be sufficient to pay all or part of the stipulated 6.5 percent, it would be paid preferentially, without interest, out of the net profits of subsequent fiscal years. The 6.5 percent received in any year is credited to the amount of the dividend that the preferred stock is entitled to receive.

These preferential shares were adopted at the request of the Chilean Government, which may in the future sell them to the public. A few years ago, Braden's management examined the problem of the public issue of shares: at that time, it was found that the local investors expected a much higher return than the one Braden could offer. It is not now possible to forecast when El Teniente's preferred stock will be sold to the public. The sale of stock will depend on the government's initiative, but presumably this will not occur within the next few years. Kennecott's executives consider that the sale of shares to the public will be politically advantageous to El Teniente.

In many developing countries, nonvoting shares are not popular, even if they constitute preferred stock. In El Teniente's case, the decision to give voting rights to the preferred shares will be taken by the government. If voting rights were given to these preferential shares, sales to the public would dilute the voting rights of the main partners. Even if the government's majority were to be diluted, however, it could still use various methods to keep control of the enterprise. Furthermore, in developing countries (as in developed countries) the public generally does not attend the corporation's General Meetings. Consequently, a voting, preferred stock would not endanger the government's control of El Teniente.

Loan Capital. El Teniente was authorized by a decree of the Ministry of Economy, Development and Reconstruction, to make investments in Chile of approximately 230,241,000 dollars.[5] These investments were made possible by credits granted by the Export-Import Bank of Washington, by Braden, and by the Copper Corporation. More specifically, El Teniente has benefited from the following loans:

1. Eximbank Loan	$110,016,000
2. Braden Copper Co. Loan	80,000,000
3. Copper Corporation Loan	23,700,000
4. Braden and Copper Corporation Loan	16,525,000
Total	$230,241,000

The Eximbank loan is employed for purchases and expenses abroad. The other loans are used for purchases, payments, and other expenses in the country. The Braden and Copper Corporation loan can also be used for purchases, payments, or expenses abroad.

5. See *supra,* note 2.

The Chilean Government has guaranteed the Braden loan and the Eximbank loan.

The total amount of the investment will be amortized within a period of 15 years, commencing in 1971.

The Eximbank Loan. The Eximbank loan will be repaid with an annual interest of 6 percent, payable biannually on amounts drawn, and of ½ percent, payable twice yearly on the amount not yet drawn of the credit at the disposal of the Sociedad. El Teniente will amortize the total amount of these credits in 30 successive half-yearly payments, commencing three months after completion of the construction work. The service on the other loans granted to El Teniente shall be subordinated to the prior service of the Eximbank credits which are due and demandable.

Kennecott assisted El Teniente in the conclusion of this loan. Eximbank wished to be fully informed concerning the financial, legal, and engineering aspects of El Teniente. Although long discussions were necessary to determine the conditions of the loan repayment, Eximbank did not require any structural change be made in the enterprise. The main condition demanded by Eximbank was that the mine should be run by Kennecott (Braden); the management contract and the advisory sales contract concluded between El Teniente and Kennecott (Braden and Kennecott Sales) were viewed as essential. In addition to this it is required by United States law that the bank's credit be a "tied loan": as a result, the equipment necessary for expansion was bought in the United States.

Eximbank had no objection to the fact that the government was El Teniente's majority shareholder and could, therefore, interfere in Kennecott's day-to-day management. The decree issued by the Ministry of Economy, Development and Reconstruction has guaranteed El Teniente's specific status. All of Eximbank's rights are also indirectly guaranteed by the decree.

The Braden Copper Company Loan. This credit of $80 million bears an annual interest of 5¾ percent, payable in biannual instalments. El Teniente is committed to amortize the entire amount represented by these credits in 30 equal and successive half-yearly instalments, commencing on December 31, 1971. This loan is insured by the Agency for International Development (AID) under its Special Risk Guaranty Program.

The Copper Corporation Loan. The Chilean agency has extended a credit of $23.7 million to El Teniente. The amount will be delivered in escudos. The loan bears an annual interest of 5¾ percent payable in dollars every six months. The amortization of this loan will be made in 30 equal and successive biannual payments, commencing on December 31, 1971.

Kennecott's management is confident that the Copper Corporation can find these funds. The amounts will be provided progressively, as the successive steps of construction are realized. The whole credit will be spent in Chile.

The Braden and Copper Corporation Loan. Under this credit, the Copper Corporation has granted $3,782,000, and Braden, $12,-743,000. These credits correspond to a figure equivalent to the total interest that the Sociedad will pay to Braden and to the Copper Corporation up to December 31, 1971, pursuant to the terms of the Braden Loan and the Copper Corporation Loan. The same terms laid down for these loans apply to the Braden and Copper Corporation loan as regards interest and amortization. The total of these credits will be equivalent to the total of the amounts actually paid out as interest by the Sociedad.

The purpose of this loan is to amortize the interest on the Braden loan and on the Copper Corporation loan. For instance, Braden has agreed to lend $80 million to El Teniente and to re-loan such sums corresponding to the interest as long as the construction is under way. Consequently, the total credit granted by Braden is equivalent to $93 million.

The interest had to be amortized because the new facilities will not provide revenue until construction is completed. Because Chilean law forbids compound interest, a complementary loan was used. In Chile, this arrangement is a common practice among large industrial undertakings.

Foreign Exchange. El Teniente is guaranteed the right to keep abroad the necessary foreign currency resulting from the export sale of its copper, to carry out its foreign financial obligations, including debt interest and amortization, the payment of dividends to Kennecott, and various other costs outside Chile.

In Chile, the Sociedad is guaranteed the right to sell the proceeds in foreign exchange arising from its exports at the same exchange rate governing other exporters. Accordingly, an exchange rate that is or may prove to be discriminatory, shall not be applied.

Furthermore, the Sociedad has the right to free access to the foreign exchange market as regards the foreign exchange that it brings into the country or invests in accordance with the decree. It may also sell such foreign exchange through the Central Bank of Chile at the most favorable rate or treatment of exchange in force for investments at the time of the sale.

Taxation

The Fiscal Status of El Teniente. The Sociedad has the guarantee that taxation levied on profits or income is a single and invariable tax at a rate of 20 percent on taxable net income.

Furthermore, the Sociedad's stockholders have the guarantee that only a single and invariable tax, fixed at 30 percent, can be levied on dividends or profits distributed to them by the company.

Moreover, the Sociedad has to pay a 2 percent general housing tax on its profits, following payment to the Corporación Viviendas (Corvi) of $10,555,000. These payments finance part of the accelerated housing plan that Corvi carries out in accordance with the agreement made with the Sociedad. The value of the new houses constructed for El Teniente's personnel constitute a contribution towards the 2 percent mentioned above, as also do the cost of repairs, additions, or improvements to the houses. This also applies to any expenses incurred for town planning and works destined for welfare, recreation, and physical culture instituted in the respective housing developments. In the opinion of President Frei, these arrangements satisfy the housing requirements of El Teniente's personnel. Kennecott's executives could not object to this tax, which is imposed on all corporations alike and is, therefore, nondiscriminatory.

Finally, the Sociedad is subject to the usual property taxes and other variety of taxes.

El Teniente's fiscal arrangements are guaranteed for twenty years, beginning in 1967.

Guarantees Against Fiscal Changes. El Teniente benefits from two other important guarantees against fiscal changes. Firstly, the Sociedad and its stockholders are exempted from any new general tax that may be levied on ordinary or excess profits, and its stockholders are totally exempt from taxes on the undistributed profits due to them. Secondly, the Sociedad shall not be burdened with any new discriminatory special taxes or duties, liens or charges, or with any increase in the existing ones.

Nevertheless, various groups have asked for an increase in the taxes levied on copper companies. For instance, the Socialist Party has repeatedly called for much higher taxes, even though this would lead to breaches of the prevailing copper agreements. There have been several concrete proposals for such tax increases. There has also been a proposal for enforced savings, which would be the equivalent of a tax increase. Furthermore, an export tax on copper has been proposed. Such a tax would have direct repercussions on the copper price, which has to remain competitive.

Until now, these various proposals have all been rejected. The government, which is El Teniente's major shareholder, would not benefit from a new tax that would reduce the dividends of the Sociedad. Quite to the contrary, a change in El Teniente's fiscal status could considerably damage the government's good record with respect to its commitments. Consequently, the government informed the Congress that the President would veto any additional tax.

A change in El Teniente's fiscal status could also endanger the support given by international financial institutions to Chilean development. For instance, the government gave its assurance to Eximbank that notwithstanding internal opposition to the copper companies, the decree of the Ministry of Economy, Development and Reconstruction would be carried out. A breach of the copper agreements could, indirectly, have far-reaching consequences for the future of international aid to Chile.

Finally, a Kennecott executive observed that it is "good politics" for the political opposition to advocate new taxes on copper companies. This same executive stated, however, that the government's political opponents would likely adopt a different attitude if they were in power, as they would then hesitate to endanger the smooth running of the enterprise, which is regarded as essential to the country's economic development.

Management

Control. During negotiations with the Chilean Government, Kennecott's executives at first considered the possibility of entering upon a 50-50 joint mining venture but, feeling that such a split could easily bring trouble, they later decided on a minority participation. In their opinion, ultimate control is always with the government. For instance, export permits can be granted or refused at will. High taxes are another means of pressure, which was used, for instance, against

Kennecott and Anaconda under the Alessandri regime. Although there is a limit to what a government can do, it nevertheless has at its disposal a wide range of administrative controls. Furthermore, in Chile (more than in many other developing countries) the economy is greatly influenced by the government. Finally, Kennecott's executives hoped that the Chilean Government would feel more responsible for the success of the enterprise if it were a majority shareholder in El Teniente.

Until recently, the situation of the other major U. S. copper company operating in Chile, Anaconda, was quite different, for in most cases it operated with wholly-owned subsidiaries. The Copper Corporation was Anaconda's partner only for the exploitation of a new mine, Exotica. Even in this venture, the Copper Corporation had only a 25 percent share and the American Company retained a majority of 75 percent. Nevertheless, on June 26, 1969, the Chilean Government instituted, in agreement with Anaconda, the "long-term nationalization" of all Anaconda assets in the country. It was agreed that the government would buy shares corresponding to 51 percent of the company's assets. The government must also buy the remaining 49 percent some time during the period 1973–1981 and thus become gradually the only possessor of the mines.

The Board of Directors. As in most developing countries the number of people who understand business problems is relatively small in Chile. However, the country has an appreciable number of very competent businessmen. Kennecott's executives were impressed by the capability of the Chileans on El Teniente's Board of Directors.

Since the transfer of Series A and C shares to the Copper Corporation, there have been seven board members, i.e. four for the Copper Corporation and three for Braden. The President of the Board is Eduardo Simián, who acquired business experience in the United States and was later Chile's Minister of Mines.

El Teniente's Board of Directors makes decisions on important questions, such as, dividends or the overall financial policy. Until now, the government's representatives on the board have always voted in agreement with their ministers.

Day-to-day Management. Because Braden concluded a management contract with El Teniente, Kennecott's subsidiary is responsible for technical management. Until now, the government has never interfered with El Teniente's day-to-day management. Seven of Braden's employees work on a permanent basis with El Teniente. The

U.S. corporation does not receive any management fee in exchange for its services but only charges for costs. The Sociedad uses four different sets of audits in Chile to determine these costs.

The two main corporate officers dealing with day-to-day management are a U.S citizen and a Chilean citizen. Robert Haldeman, a mining engineer, has worked for Braden since 1941 and became Executive Vice-President in 1957. He is now also Executive Vice-President of El Teniente. Eugenio Silva Barros has acquired business experience with U.S. corporations and is now El Teniente's General Manager. He is responsible for administrative matters but leaves all technical questions to Braden's employees, as provided by the management contract.

The distinction between technical and administrative responsibilities is not clear cut in El Teniente. Nevertheless, the management responsibilities are defined with great care and are clearly divided between the partners. Consequently, day-to-day management has functioned without any major divergence between the partners.

The Sociedad management will handle the construction work until completion. Contracts have been concluded with U.S. and Chilean firms for the design, procurement, and construction supervision of the mine expansion, construction of a new concentrator, expansion of smelter, power and industrial water installations, and construction of a new highway to replace the existing railway. Work is currently ahead of schedule and may be completed a year earlier than planned.

Financial Policy. The Chilean Government and Kennecott have agreed that El Teniente's primary objective is to maximize copper production through expansion and to earn the highest possible net profits. The 1964 agreement also stipulates that these profits are to be distributed almost without limitation. In the distribution of profits, priority is given to the preferential shares of Series C and D.

Before distributing the dividends, the Sociedad is obliged to invest 4 percent of its annual profits. The management is free to decide where these funds are to be invested, though they have necessarily to be placed in non-copper investments. The obvious purpose of this governmental requirement is to diversify the Chilean economy.

A decree of the Ministry of Finance, dated November 14, 1966, states that part of El Teniente's net profits may be ear-marked for the creation of special funds for specifiç purposes. The creation of large reserves is nevertheless unlikely, as the basic principle agreed upon between the partners is that the profits are to be distributed as they are earned. The basic agreement between the Chilean Government and Kennecott stipulates that profits will not be devoted to any further expansion without the mutual consent of El Teniente's shareholders.

In September, 1969, Kennecott acceded to the demand of the Chilean Government for a new formula for distribution of dividends. The government proposed revision of the original agreement on the ground that the high price of copper on the London Metal Exchange had not been anticipated at the time the agreement was negotiated. Consequently, the charter and by-laws of El Teniente have been modified to authorize a distribution of dividends that varies according to the price on the London Metal Exchange. This "overprice formula" gives the government a larger share of the dividends whenever the price per ton exceeds 40 cents. When the price of copper is 40 cents or less, dividends are distributed as originally contemplated. When the price exceeds 40 cents, however, the government's share increases, as indicated in the following examples:

	Overprice Formula	
	Share of Dividends	
Copper Price	*Braden*	*Chilean Government*
40 cents or less	49.0 percent	51.0 percent
50 cents	38.2 percent	61.8 percent
60 cents	31.3 percent	68.7 percent
70 cents	27.5 percent	72.5 percent

Assuming that copper prices remain above 40 cents a pound, the new agreement will reduce Kennecott's before earnings significantly below those expected under the previous formula. Moreover, Kennecott would have sold the property at a higher price if it had anticipated the higher copper prices, because the purchase price was based on anticipated earnings of the mines. The Chilean Government, however, has made no offer to readjust the purchase price.

Even if Kennecott had not gone into the joint venture, it is likely that the high price of copper would have led to a government demand for a larger share of the profits. This would tend to indicate that the joint venture formula is not a panacea to the problem of foreign investment in developing countries. However, it should be emphasized that the new sharing of profits has not affected the relations between the partners, which have remained more than satisfactory.

Labor. Although some 7,000 employees are at present on El Teniente's payroll, only about 20 are foreigners. This extensive use of Chilean personnel at all levels is not a policy resulting from the partnership between Kennecott and the Chilean government. The U.S. corporation applies this policy in every situation, even in wholly-owned subsidiaries, as it is considered both economically and politically advantageous.

At present, most of the employees have moved or are engaged in moving from the mountainside to newly-built homes in Rancagua, in the Central Valley. Eventually, all of the employees will be resettled there. They will own their own homes and commute by a new highway to a new mine shaft that will take them to the mine working level. These changes in the employees' conditions of life are some of the most important parts of the expansion program.

The labor situation has not always been calm. In 1964, there was a five-week illegal strike. In 1966, production stopped during the whole first quarter because of a strike. These strikes were brought about by a desire for higher wages to cover the inflationary cost of living. During the long copper strike in the United States, however, mining operations continued normally in El Teniente. More recently, the labor situation in the company has been relatively calm.

Sales

Kennecott Sales Corporation has concluded an advisory sales contract with El Teniente under which it represents the Sociedad in the sale of its copper and by-products. K. S. C. acts as an agent and advisor, but has no title to the copper. Ultimate control of prices and all sales policies rest with El Teniente's Board of Directors. The Sociedad is only charged for costs, which, like management costs, are determined by four sets of audits in Chile.

The Chilean Government does not take any part of El Teniente's production. The Kennecott Copper Corporation does not normally take this copper for its own consumption either. Nevertheless, during the long strike in the United States, the Chilean production reached a record level: exceptionally, Kennecott claimed a portion of the production for itself after the sales contracts with third parties had been fulfilled. In this respect, Anaconda follows a different policy and uses the Chilean copper in its own U.S. plants.

Usually, El Teniente's entire production is distributed in Europe, where the Sociedad has different kinds of customers. In France El Teniente's copper is sold to the government, which then resells it. The Sociedad sells directly to private customers in Belgium, Germany, England, and Italy. The contracts are concluded for one year, but in actual fact buyers are long-term customers.

As has been mentioned previously, Chile at present does not impose any export tax on copper.

Evaluation and Prospects

Problems. The economic risks of this investment seem limited. On the one hand, the world economy offers good opportunities for an increasing use of copper. Although El Teniente's reserves have not yet been evaluated with great precision, it is known that these reserves are substantial and justify the expansion. Kennecott has long experience in the operation of copper mines and its research laboratories are trying constantly to improve mining methods.

Political risks in Chile, however, seem much more substantial. In a country where the fear of foreign political or economic interference has traditionally been very strong, the U.S. Government and corporations often encounter hostility from some influential Chilean circles. On this topic, a *New York Times* correspondent in Chile wrote:

> There is a specifically anti-American flavor to Chilean socialism as opposed to the tacit philosophy of coexistence held by the Communists.
> The Socialists intend to continue pressing toward nationalization of all foreign interests, especially the huge Anaconda, Kennecott and Braden copper mines, which produce about a seventh of the world's copper. . . .
> The Communists, on the other hand, have not pressed nearly so hard for nationalization.[6]

More generally, the whole Chilean political scene appears uncertain. At present, right-wing and left-wing extremists unite against President Frei and his experiment of "Revolution in Freedom." Frei was elected President in 1964 for a period of six years but cannot be re-elected in 1970. The election of March 1969 considerably weakened the President's party and strengthened the right-wing nationalist opposition. Nevertheless, it is to be hoped that any new government

6. M. W. Browne, "Chilean Marxists' Split Is Deepening," *The New York Times,* April 2, 1968.

will not lightly interfere with the structure of enterprises that are essential to the country's future.[7]

El Teniente and Kennecott. In 1967, the Board of Directors of the Kennecott Copper Corporation met in Chile. This exceptional event demonstrated that Kennecott's executives recognize the great importance of the Chilean operations.

The agreements between the Chilean Government and Kennecott will permit the implementation of an important expansion program involving considerable financial resources. El Teniente's case shows that foreign investors do not deliberately avoid investing in developing countries altogether, as is sometimes contended, but that they become more and more selective in their investment decisions.

The Sociedad's earnings will benefit because of a substantial reduction in applicable Chilean tax rates, the production and sale of an additional 100,000 tons of copper annually, and lower unit operating costs resulting from this expanded output. Although Kennecott is now in a minority position on the Board of Directors, it has retained the venture's day-to-day management. Consequently, the management remains unified. The possibility of a conflict between the government-controlled Board of Directors and Kennecott's managers cannot be excluded but, in this respect, Kennecott has taken a calculated risk. It appears, however, that no such conflict has occurred as yet.

Kennecott will receive more in dividends with a 49 percent participation and a 52 percent tax rate than it used to receive in dividends with a 100 percent ownership and an 87 percent tax rate. The overprice formula,[8] however, reduces Kennecott's earnings from El Teniente.

Finally, in becoming co-owner with the Chilean Government and in giving to this government the satisfaction of being a majority partner, Kennecott will be more closely identified with the aspirations of Chile, which should prove to be a net advantage in an investment association extending over a large number of years. The management hopes that the joint venture approach will change the role of the gov-

---

7. The Allende government, formed in October, 1970, is firmly committed to the full nationalization of all foreign mining interests. This will put an end to the hopes placed on the form of joint venture illustrated by the Kennecott experiment —at least in Chile.

8. See *supra,* p. 94.

ernment from imposing negative restraints to exercising a positive interest.

More important than the specific guarantees obtained by Kennecott or the financial control granted to the Chilean Government is the partners' common will to fully develop the exploitation of this essential natural resource.

El Teniente and Chile. The Chilean Government will also gain substantial revenue as a result of the increased copper production and equity participation in the Sociedad. The government will receive more with dividends, plus taxes at their present rate, than it previously obtained from taxes at an 87 percent rate. Moreover, an increasing percentage of El Teniente's copper will be processed by the government refinery. Furthermore, as 90 percent of El Teniente's copper is exported and sold for hard currency, this will be a real boon for Chile's foreign exchange. Finally, the government seems convinced that the continuing presence of Kennecott is necessary to ensure the efficient management of the enterprise and easy access to foreign sources of capital and research facilities.

Chile's economic development requires new investments. As the Chilean economy is still very dependent on copper sales, expansion should be linked with a diversification of the production. In fact, the accrued financial resources that Chile will draw from the copper ventures generally, and from El Teniente in particular, should allow for the expansion's financing. The birth of a manufacturing industry, which would be partially turned towards export, is especially important in a country where apparently agriculture cannot be greatly developed and diversified.

As both partners have something to contribute to the enterprise and, as they both can greatly benefit from the venture's success, El Teniente will be a valid test of partnership between a government and a foreign corporation. On the other hand, as the 1969 events that led to the "long-term nationalization" of Anaconda assets have shown, El Teniente's future is likely to be closely dependent on the political evolution of the country.

V: REFINED SUGAR AND OTHER FOOD PRODUCTS IN WEST AFRICA

Grands Moulins de Paris

Grands Moulins de Paris. Grands Moulins de Paris (GMP) is a group of companies that is controlled and managed by the Vilgrain family. The main corporations of the group are GMP, the Grands Moulins Vilgrain (GMV), and the Grands Moulins de Bordeaux (GMB). GMP owns 59.60 percent of the capital of GMV and 25.84 percent of the capital of GMB. By the end of 1967, the total assets of the group represented more than 260 million FF.[1] The capital was 42.3 million FF., the long-term debts were approximately 63.5 million FF., and the short-term debts stood around 125 million FF.

GMP holds participations in a number of companies in France and abroad. The total portfolio is worth more than 20 million FF.

Milling in France. In 1967 the consumption of bread decreased in France whereas the population increased. National milling for internal needs decreased by 1.82 percent and amounted to 48.5 million quintals.[2] On the other hand, thanks to a high demand on the international market, national milling for exports reached the record of 8.45 million quintals, which marked an increase of 28.50 percent on 1966.

1967 Results. The GMP Group milled 5,579,000 quintals for the national market and supplied 11.50 percent of national requirements. It also milled 3,658,150 quintals of wheat for export and thus ac-

1. FF = francs français. $1 is about 5 FF.
2. 1 quintal = 100 kg.

counted for 42.30 percent of French flour exports. Altogether, the metropolitan group of GMP milled 9,237,220 quintals, which constituted (exports included) 16.22 percent of French national milling. The group also produced 1,866,727 quintals of cattle fodder.

The group had a consolidated turnover of 688,923,000 FF. After taxation, it showed a gross return of 14,350,000 FF. After provision of depreciation of 11,203,000 FF., there remained a net return of 3,147,000 FF.

Congo (*Brazzaville*)

Profile. Congo (Brazzaville) is a state of western equatorial Africa and covers 342,000 square kilometers. It is surrounded by the Atlantic on the west; the Gabon, the Cameroon, and the Central African Republic on the north; the Congo (Kinshasa) on the east; and the Portuguese enclave of Cabinda on the south.

In 1966 the Congo had 850,000 inhabitants. The capital of the country is Brazzaville, which has 131,000 inhabitants. The main harbor is Pointe-Noire. The population is composed of various races, the most important of which are the Batékés on the high plateaux, the Bakongos and the Balalis, who cultivate the Pool area to the West of Brazzaville, and the Bahembas. As well as being engaged in farming, these tribes also hunt and fish.

The main mineral resources are lead and gold. Since 1960 oil has been extracted near Pointe-Noire, but the annual production remains at approximately 100,000 tons. The main plantations produce palm oil, coffee, bananas, cocoa, tobacco, sugar cane, and peanuts. The most developed agricultural area of the country is the Niari Valley where manioc, peanuts, and cane sugar are cultivated and where cattle are raised. There are also considerable potash deposits about to be exploited.

Recent History. Formerly the country had been under French colonial administration, but it became independent in 1960. The Congo (Brazzaville) was first ruled by a Catholic priest, Abbé Fulbert Youlou. The regime of Youlou encountered economic and social difficulties which were met by increased authoritarianism. As a result of riots that broke out in Brazzaville during a general strike, he was overthrown in August 1963. Jailed, Youlou escaped in 1965 and took refuge in Congo (Kinshasa), and later in Europe. In 1966 he published a book entitled *"J'accuse la Chine."*

The presidential type Constitution of 1961 was replaced by a constitution that gave effective powers to Parliament. This is a notable exception in Africa. At that time the functions of head of state and head of government were separated. After elections made by a limited electorate college, Massamba-Debat became President of the Republic in December 1963. He appointed Pascal Lissouba as Prime Minister.

Beginning in 1964, Youlou's followers and the Christian trade-unionists favored a leftist orientation of the regime. The *Mouvement national de la révolution* (MNR) became the single political party and moderate elements were eliminated from the government, which, consequently, became increasingly socialist and "anti-imperialist." Nevertheless, the economic development of the country was still very much dependent upon foreign investments, and France remained the main financial support of the country.

However, Congo (Brazzaville) then established closer links with the U.S.S.R. and China, and loosened its ties with the member states of the *Union africaine et malgache*. It gave its support to the Congolese rebels, which was a source of great difficulties with the government of the ex-Belgian Congo. In 1965, close relations were established with Cuba, which sent specialists as advisers to the Presidential Guard and to a newly-created militia.

Pascal Lissouba resigned in April 1966. He was replaced by the leader of the MNR, Ambroise Noumazalay. As a consequence of this change, the single party assumed an enhanced role and the regime became even more radical. As a reaction, an attempt was made in June 1966 by some Army elements to overthrow the regime, but this was crushed by the Presidential Guard. In January 1968, however, the President dismissed Noumazalay, which brought about a return to a more moderate policy. In summer 1968, this regime was in turn displaced by a military government that is seeking to establish national unity and improve or reestablish relations with both western and eastern countries.

The Beginnings of Sian

The Peanut Experiment. An important river of the Congo is called Kouilou in its lower part, and Niari in its upper part. The Niari Valley is an extremely fertile area. The French colonial administration aimed at insuring the development of this area. Consequently, a group of French industrialists came in 1949 to study the potentialities of the Niari Valley. Among them were representatives of the GMP Group.

In the Niari Valley, public authorities were carrying out studies and experiments in the field of tropical oils. The Compagnie Générale des Oléagineux Tropicaux (CGOT) was, apparently, a well-equipped company and had the use of a pilot plant and of several laboratories. In particular, it had begun the cultivation of peanuts. The authorities asked the GMP Group to buy land in the valley and to take up the cultivation of peanuts for commercial purposes. In exchange, the French industrial group would receive the help of public authorities and of the CGOT. The GMP agreed to the proposal. The Société Industrielle et Agricole du Niari (Sian) was thereupon established.

This peanut experiment, however, turned out to be a failure, understandable for various reasons. One of them is that the traditional occupation of GMP was milling. Moreover, the local resident sent from France to be Manager did not have at that time sufficient practical experience. Furthermore, although CGOT had at its disposal modern technical means, it also lacked experience.

Sian lost a great deal of money and serious consideration was given to the liquidation of the company. However, the public authorities used strong pressure to keep it open: a closure would have had deplorable political effects and would also have caused unemployment.

Reconversion from Peanut to Sugar. The local manager visited a sugar plantation in the Belgian Congo. He at once laid out a sugar plantation in the Niari Valley and his crop throve. As a result, a complete conversion from peanut to sugar was carried through. Considerable new investments were needed. A French government fund, the Fonds d'Investissement des Territoires d'Outre-Mer (FIDES) took subscriptions from Sian and made loans to the company. Two civil servants of the colonial administration were placed on the Board of Directors of the company. Again the venture turned out to be a failure. The GMP did not have any greater experience in sugar production than it had in the cultivation of peanuts. The substantial sums absorbed proved insufficient to put the venture back onto its feet. The lack of competent personnel also was strongly felt. Once again, Sian was on the verge of ruin.

The Company's Recovery. Fortunately, in 1957 several factors concurred to aid the company's recovery. First of all, an experienced manager, Mr. Urbain, was sent from France to take over the running of the enterprise. In order to assist Mr. Urbain, GMP's executives decided to provide Sian with a more effective and extensive assistance than previously. In particular, they obtained the support of the newly-created Compagnie Financière pour l'Outre-Mer (Cofimer), a private financial institution which benefits from official government support. It takes equity shares in African ventures, acts as an intermediary between potential partners, and has succeeded in becoming a catalyst of private capital.

The positive effects of Mr. Urbain's management were rapidly felt. New sections of sugar cane were tested. Fertilizers were used extensively. Great emphasis was placed on the training of personnel. The year 1958 was one of remarkable success. Productive capacity was subsequently increased from 10,000 tons to 35,000 tons a year.

Although Sian's development was not without problems, it has become a successful enterprise.

The Development of Sian

Geographical Developments. Voluntarily, Sian's executives chose a policy of growth and diversification. GMP's and Cofimer's executives also favored this policy. A powerful incentive in this direction was the fact that in Africa sugar is sold in highly protected markets.

This evolution was not the result of the desire of only the foreign investors. Several African governments showed their interest in the activities of the company and asked to participate. Without any doubt, they were attracted by the prospect of good profits. They offered to take an equity participation and could, therefore, expect to receive from these ventures both high dividends and substantial taxes. However, profit was not their unique motivation; somewhat like a steel factory or an oil refinery, a sugar refinery for a country is also an element of national prestige. Almost everywhere, companies for studying and testing were created. Each case had to be judged on its own merits because climates differ greatly in Africa. On the whole, sugar is a profitable product for Africa, but the further north one goes, the more the cost of production increases.

In the beginning, Sian developed in the neighboring countries of the Congo, which are not among the most developed countries of Africa. Previously, the territories of French Equatorial Africa were

part of a Customs Union. After independence, a free trade association was maintained amongst the new States: Congo (Brazzaville),
Gabon, Cameroon, the Central African Republic, and Chad. Sian
naturally took advantage of this free trade association, which has
now been merged with the larger *Organisation Commune Africaine et
Malgache* (OCAM).[3] Consequently, Sian invested in other countries
situated further north. So far, however, it has not invested outside
former French territories.

Lateral Development. The African governments also asked Sian to
engage in new activities. GMP's management calls this evolution the
"lateral development." As a result, affiliated companies now produce
flour, soap, cattle fodder, and other articles.

Milling is the most important part of this lateral development.
Like sugar refineries, flour mills are also an element of prestige for
African governments. GMP was glad to be able to launch in Africa
the business that constitutes its traditional field of operations in
France. From an economic point of view, however, milling in Africa
does not have as sound a basis as sugar. Even if one takes into account transportation costs, locally produced flour is often more expensive than flour imported from France. In developing countries,
however, the soundness of an investment cannot be appreciated only
from a purely economic point of view. Moreover, it is likely that
products such as flour, soap, or cattle fodder are often more beneficial to an underdeveloped country than a steel factory or an oil refinery.

New Ventures. As a result of its policy of growth and diversification, Sian has initiated a number of ventures in the former French
territories.

In the Congo (Brazzaville) the main development was the creation
of the Société Sucrière du Niari (Sosuniari), which is a second Sian
but more important. Sian is the main shareholder of the new company.
The Congolese Government, which is not a shareholder of Sian, acquired an equity participation in Sosuniari. The initial purpose of the
new venture was to supply the world market with sugar. With the creation of the Grands Moulins du Congo (GMC), Sian also initiated
milling. Cattle fodder and the recuperation of molasses are two other
new activities.

By African standards, Chad is a relatively highly populated country. Part of the population is Islamic and, therefore, a great con-

3. On OCAM, see pp. 112–14.

sumer of sugar. Chad absorbs between one-half and two-thirds of Sian's production. Chad's Government was interested in launching a local sugar industry and so became the partner of Sian in a venture for refining sugar and producing confectionery, the Société Sucrière du Tchad.

In Cameroon, Sian and the government became partners in 1967 in the Société Sucrière du Cameroun. This new venture is an important sugar producer. With the formation of the Société Camerounaise de Minoterie, milling also started in 1967.

In the Ivory Coast, the government, Sian, the Raffineries de Saint-Louis, Cofimer and two other corporations became partners in the Société Sucrière de Côte d'Ivoire. The government wanted to produce sugar for a variety of agricultural and industrial purposes. A German group and an American group were ready to invest. After long negotiations with the government, Sian and the Raffineries de Saint-Louis obtained the bid. The day-to-day management is mostly in the hands of Sian. At present, the venture is still at the studying and testing stage. Some agricultural problems have first to be solved: climate, adaptation of varieties, diseases. No industrial realizations will come about before 1970 or 1971. In addition to Sosuci, Sian has an independent venture of perfume plants in the Ivory Coast.

In the Central African Republic, Sian formed the Société Industrielle Centrafricaine des Produits Alimentaires et Dérivés. This agro-industrial enterprise is situated in Bangui, where it started operating in February 1968 and which includes an oil mill, a flour mill, a soap works, and a plant for the production of cattle fodder.

One should finally mention: in Senegal, a flour mill, the Moulins Sentenac of Dakar; in Upper Volta, a sugar enterprise which started at the end of 1968; in Gabon, a soap works.

Sian negotiated for quite some time in Nigeria, without success, because no suitable local partner could be found. The negotiations ended before the outbreak of the Biafran war. Undoubtedly, Sian feels more comfortable in the former French territories where the language is still French and where the legislation is quite similar to French legislation, at least as far as the basic principles are concerned. The Nigerian case shows that Sian's geographical diversification has some limitations at present. Nevertheless, the situation might change in the future, particularly if the African markets become more integrated and if competition on the Continent becomes more intensive.

Financing

Financial Involvement. From a financial point of view, there is a great difference between mining ventures, which generally involve considerable financial backing, and agricultural industries, which involve substantial, but less considerable financing. Mining ventures frequently require an investment of the order of $100 million, and Lamco in Liberia has a capital investment of almost three times that amount. Sian is certainly an important agro-industrial enterprise, but its capital is only of the order of $10 million. Even if the loan capital is added to this amount, the difference between this and mining outlay remains striking. As a result of this basic difference, ventures such as Sian and its affiliated companies are somewhat less dependent than mining ventures on massive loans or investments from financial institutions. They generally need a larger number of smaller investments. Most of the affiliated companies are financed by Sian itself in conjunction with Cofimer and local partners. Such institutions as the French government-controlled Caisse Centrale de Coopération Economique and private banks also often give loans.

Economic and Financial Profitability. Sian's development in new activities has concentrated primarily upon products related to sugar production. For instance, a by-product of the sugar refining is molasses, which the company uses to produce cattle fodder. The African governments are certainly interested in sugar production and by-products, but they also want other products. Since the profitability of some of these products if questionable, one might wonder why Sian and the governments in question engage in these ventures.

The answer is the distinction between economic and financial profitability. The economic profitability of a product can be appreciated if its cost is compared with the cost of the same product produced elsewhere. From this point of view, Sian and its affiliated ventures are certainly profitable in the production of sugar: Sosuniari has one of the lowest cost ratios in the world, if not the lowest one. On the other hand, the flour production of the Sian Group is not economically profitable. In this connection it should be noted that at present practically every developing country aims at the construction of a flour mill and that, consequently, this trend is certainly not specifically African.

Nevertheless, these enterprises survive because they benefit from strict protection, which will probably outlast the "infant industry" stage. Because of this protection, these ventures are financially profitable and dividends come very quickly. Even when they are only financially profitable to some extent these can be defended by African governments, because of their beneficial indirect effects: notably, that they create employment opportunities and that they constitute a marked improvement when compared with the purely prestige projects that were so much in favor a few years ago.

Sian's Capital and Sosuniari's Capital. Sian is a mixed holding company, incorporated in Kayes, Congo. Its assets include the company's physical properties in Congo and its participations in affiliated companies, both in Congo and in other African countries. The equity capital amounts to 41,125,200 FF. and the reserves to 2,440,598 FF. The capital is divided among the partners in the following way:

Grands Moulins de Paris	40.5 percent
Fonds d'Aide et de Coopération	19.5 percent
Dutch interests	8.0 percent
Cofimer and other French interests	32.0 percent

The Dutch interests consist mainly in a bank, which was among the promoters of Sian. This bank had experience in the sugar business, which was not the case with GMP. When Sian started to show a profit, the bank progressively took a more passive role. Apart from Cofimer, the French interests are individuals linked with the Vilgrain family. GMP's share is slowly increasing.

When the holding was created, the independent state of Congo did not exist. The French colonial administration supported the venture through the intermediary of the public fund FIDES, which was a shareholder of Sian. After independence, FIDES was replaced by the Fonds d'Aide et de Coopération (FAC). In 1966, it was agreed that the FAC would transfer its share to the Congolese Government. The transfer was not carried out because the government was not able to find the necessary funds. In the Group of Sian companies, Sian itself is the only one in which the government has no participation; however, this exception is partly historical. Moreover, a venture such as Sian could not work without a close partnership and co-operation with the government. Finally, the Congolese Government did not insist on obtaining an equity participation; it is apparently more interested in Sian's main subsidiary, Sosuniari.

The capital and reserves of Sosuniari amount to 26 million FF. The capital is divided among the partners in the following way:

Republic of the Congo	25 percent
Sian	38 percent
Dutch interests	12 percent
French interests	25 percent

The French interests are: GMP; the Compagnie Française pour l'Afrique Occidentale; Cofimer; and some banks. GMP and Cofimer participate twice in Sosuniari, once directly and once indirectly through Sian.

GMP and Cofimer Participations. GMP and Cofimer participate twice in all ventures created by Sian. The indirect participation of the French Group, through Sian, is generally important. The governments also ask GMP and Cofimer to participate directly in these affiliated ventures. For prestige reasons they want French business enterprises to be shareholders in the companies. It would be difficult for Sian, which is incorporated in an African country, to do business in other African countries if a French company did not directly participate; and we should bear in mind too the desire of GMP to act as the promoter of these new ventures.

Government Participations. Partly for historical reasons, the Congolese Government has no share in the Sian venture itself; however, this is an exception to the rule. Governments have become partners in all affiliated ventures. According to a GMP executive, it is extremely desirable to do business in Africa by asking the government to participate. By way of payment, the government generally brings land, harbors, concessions, and other assets into the venture.

For this same financial reason, governments always have minority shares in Sian's ventures. They do not even apply for the majority of the shares. This may seem surprising at a time when the new states show their fear of neocolonialism and foreign economic interference. In this respect, the case of Cameroon is interesting. According to a GMP executive, Cameroon is, among all the countries in which Sian has invested, the country that is the most concerned about its economic independence; yet the government only has a 30 percent participation in Sian's affiliated companies. When some shareholders withdrew, the government asked to take over these shares, to which Sian agreed, but the government participation has not been the cause of any other argument.

Loan Capital. Governments do not provide any cash. GMP of Paris is not willing to commit directly substantial funds. Sian's capacity to reinvest its profits in new ventures is not unlimited. Thus, the bulk of financial resources has to be found elsewhere.

More than 50 percent of these investments are financed by long-term loans. There is a great variety of lenders, such as French public funds and banks. In particular, the constant co-operation and help of French public authorities have permitted Sian to have a major part of the investment in all its ventures financed by long-term loans.

Management

An Agricultural Industry. Mining ventures in Africa are generally linked with powerful multinational corporations. The ores are transported to the factories abroad where they are processed into semi-manufactured or manufactured articles or put to industrial use. These mining ventures will very often remain almost without any connection with the local economy.

The situation of an agricultural industry is quite different. Most of the time, the products will be sold mainly on the local markets. An agricultural industry has important stimulating effects for the local economy. Nevertheless, agriculture has its specific uncertainties: a particular seed or fertilizer might succeed under certain climates and soil conditions and then unexpectedly fail under slightly different conditions; meteorological phenomena can make the success or the failure of a harvest.

Although these difficulties should not be underestimated, it has often been admitted in recent years that in Africa greater emphasis should be placed upon agricultural industries that allow the people to maintain their traditional activities and that can be well integrated into the local economy.

System of Exploitation. The managers of an agricultural industry face a difficult dilemma: should the company have its own plantations or should it merely conclude supply contracts with individual farmers, i.e. the *paysannat* system?

Sian chose to have its own plantations. Other corporations have adopted the *paysannat* system but this is contrary to Sian's practice. Sosuniari's costs per unit are perhaps the lowest in the world. According to a GMP executive, the *paysannat* could not produce at a competitive cost. Another advantage of the plantation system is seen in the fact that it gives to the workers the certainty of fixed income.

On the other hand, the *paysannat* system presents several difficulties. For the good management of a sugar refinery the uncertainties that are inherent to agriculture must be kept to a minimum. A strict vigilance against diseases must be observed. A company has to start its refining operations on a certain day and terminate them within a specified time. Machines have to be used carefully. In brief, precise planning is very important for the success of the venture. In the experience of GMP, such precision cannot be observed within a *paysannat* system.

Of course, the plantation system has one inconvenience: it is easily attacked as "capitalism." Here again, Sian's experiment is interesting. Generally speaking, the governments pay their share of the equity capital by contributing the land to be cultivated. It would thus be easy for them to insist on the use of the *paysannat* system. In fact, they have not objected to the use of the plantation system. In particular, the Government of the Congo (Brazzaville), which is socialist, has never questioned the plantation system adopted by Sian.

GMP has technical assistance agreements with Sian and all affiliated companies, Sosuniari excepted. In return for this technical assistance, GMP receives royalties and never has any difficulty in having them transferred.

Government and Management. The executives of GMP and Sian would not accept any joint venture with only a minority participation, unless it were a very small share: 5 percent for instance. At present, that is, they would not agree to a 40 percent investment in which the government would have 60 percent. Management control seems to them essential to the satisfactory running of the business.

The governments generally do not interfere with the running of the business, and they do not take any part in the day-to-day management. In 1966, a GMP executive reflected that, in the long run, governments would wish to participate in the management of these ventures. In 1969, the same executive was no longer so sure about this. Between 1966 and 1969 absolutely no evolution was perceptible. Even in the socialistically-inclined Congo there was no change. To be sure, the government wished to negotiate the sale of sugar to the U.S.S.R., but the transaction was never made. If there is any evolution, it is likely to be an extremely slow process.

The great risk of African participations is derived from the political changes that periodically affect African governments. If the faction in power changes, the representatives on the Board of Directors also change. In order to avoid any repercussion on the management of the ventures, Sian's executives have developed an interesting and somewhat unusual system: one seat on the Board of Directors is given to the government, but to that seat 4 or 5 persons are designated; if one of them suddenly falls out of favor with the government, the others still retain their representative function.

At any rate, the GMP executive could not remember any instance where a government representative contested a decision; these representatives only control results and profits. As to day-to-day management, there would be no objection in GMP against the nomination of a national as assistant manager, but again the effects of a change of government would be feared.

Financial Policy. There has never been any conflict as to profit policy. The main reason for this harmony is probably due to the fact that, on the whole, the Sian Group is a successful business. GMP's Board of Directors was not willing to invest regularly considerable funds, but it very much aimed at Sian's expansion. Thus, profit policy is a policy of reinvestment and each year new ventures are created. As long as the business is successful, it is also possible to distribute fair dividends. GMP never had any difficulty in transferring its dividends to France.

Africanization of Personnel. The Sian Group does not resist the "Africanization" of personnel in any way.[4] The company applies a gradual system of replacement. Africans replace European employees in the lower positions first of all and later then in the upper ones. Africans come to the headquarters of GMP in Paris for training. The main obstacles in the way of training Africans are again the political changes that bring about changes in the factory personnel.

Congo (Brazzaville) is especially insistent on the "Congolization" of personnel. In 1968, a decree stated that administrative jobs in companies would be filled by Congolese. The decree dealt generally with secondary jobs. Sian was not affected, as the management had anticipated this governmental move. In Senegal, some corporations experienced difficulties as to labor contracts, but GMP remained unaffected.

Labor Situation. In 1966, the unions in the Congo decided to strike. As a result, Sian's factories stopped production. According to

4. Sian: 2,000 employees (150 Europeans); Sosuniari: 3,000 employees (50 Europeans); Sosucam: 750 employees (10 Europeans).

a GMP executive, this came as a surprise. The government's reaction was severe: army and police were sent to factory sites. Since then, the labor situation has been calm.

Sales

The world sugar market is extremely unstable and has been characterized by a succession of shortage and overproduction crises. Regular attempts have been made to organize the market by international agreements. In 1902 the Brussels Conference concerned itself with remedies against overproduction. The First World War brought about a severe sugar shortage. In 1937, the London Conference had again to deal with overproduction problems. There was also a further shortage during the Second World War.

As a result of these international conferences, markets became strictly protected by tariffs and quotas and internal prices were supported by subsidies. European countries are especially protectionist: the cost of beet sugar is higher than the cost of cane sugar and production can, therefore, only flourish thanks to strict protection. Undoubtedly, these measures are favorable to agriculture and industry but, at the same time, they are detrimental to the consumer.

In the late sixties, the situation deteriorated because of a new overproduction crisis. The market was being torn apart by dumping. The developing countries that are sugar producers suffered especially from this crisis, which diminished one of their main sources of income. In the fall of 1968 more than 70 countries participated in the second United Nations Sugar Conference in Geneva. On October 24, they concluded an international agreement for price stabilization and price fixing. This agreement regulates the quotas of exporting countries and re-exporting countries. The participating countries also made arrangements to improve the returns of the sugar-exporting developing countries. The period of validity of the agreement is five years. It came into force on January 1, 1969. The countries of the European Common Market did not recognize it.

Organisation Commune Africaine et Malgache. The purpose of the Organisation Commune Africaine et Malgache (OCAM) is to establish closer ties between the French-speaking African and Madagascan States. One of its most concrete achievements was the organization of the sugar market. OCAM was created in February 1965 in

Nouakchott (Mauritania) and replaced l'Union africaine et malgache (UAM). It has 14 member states: Cameroon, Congo (Brazzaville), Congo (Kinshasa), Ivory Coast, Dahomey, Gabon, Upper Volta, Madagascar, Niger, Central African Republic, Ruanda, Senegal, Chad, and Togo. The Charter of OCAM was signed in Tananarive (Madagascar) by the respective heads of state of the member countries in June 1966. Its main organ is the Conference of Heads of State which meets alternatively in the capitals of member states and which is assisted by a permanent Secretariat in Yaoundé (Cameroon). In January 1968, the Heads of State met in Niamey (Niger) and were able to improve economic cooperation between their countries; special attention was devoted to the organization of the sugar market.

Sian's Sales. Sian never reaches the consumer directly, for it sells to large, well-established commercial companies. These French companies have been well adapted to the post-colonial period. Their local operations are now often managed by nationals. For Sian, the use of these intermediaries obviates any credit problem. Any direct contact with the peasants is maintained by the commercial companies; thus Sian's managers do not have to worry about the collection of debts.

Originally, Sian was designed to supply the Congo and neighboring countries, especially Chad. When its production increased, it looked around for new markets. The creation of OCAM provided it with good outlets. OCAM has two groups of sugar producers: first, the Sian Group; second, the sugar group of Madagascar, i.e. the Sucreries de Saint-Louis, a French company. The organization of the sugar market was discussed by the member states in 1966, and again in 1968. As a result of the sugar agreements, both groups benefit by protection within OCAM. The member states buy from the two groups at a preferential price. Not only are the OCAM markets protected against third parties, but they are also divided between the two companies. A substantial proportion of Sian's production is thus exported to OCAM's markets. Moreover, it refines the proportion of Sosuniari's production that is destined for these markets.

Sosuniari's Sales. Although Sian was originally designed to supply the Congo and neighboring countries, the initial purpose of Sosuniari was to produce for the world market. The economic performance of the company seems to justify this ambitious goal. Its capacity is at present 60,000 tons per year and will later be 100,000 tons. It can produce more than all of Sian's ventures put together. Its cost per unit of production is probably the lowest in the world.

Whatever the economic performance of Sosuniari, however, its financial success demanded as a precondition the basic soundness of the world market. This market was sound at the time of the company's formation but the situation has since changed markedly.

Because of the overproduction crisis, most markets have become highly protected. Only surpluses are now sold on the world market. In order to sell these surpluses the traders proceed to frantic dumping. In particular, the European Economic Community provides very large subsidies in order to protect its production of beet sugar. A few years ago, the price offered on nonprotected markets was 12 cents a pound. Because of the dumping, sugar is now sold in these markets for 1.40 cents, which is half the cost price of Sosuniari. If the Congolese company could sell at 4 cents a pound, it would be a very prosperous enterprise.

The solution for Sosuniari was to find protected markets. To a certain extent the company was forced to withdraw to Africa. Part of the production is now sold in OCAM markets. Moreover, for the past few years a series of agreements have been negotiated with several countries, especially with Algeria and the U.S.S.R. An agreement might also be concluded with the U.S.A.

Temporarily at least, Sosuniari has sufferred from inadequate sales and a shortage of working capital. The managers of the company are studying the means to insure more stable sales.

Increase in Local Consumption. Surprisingly enough for a company that was to supply world markets, it is possible that the long-term solution to Sosuniari's problems might be found locally. The executives of the Sian Group have noted an interesting phenomenon: after introduction of the locally produced product, consumption increases beyond that previously imported, even when the price established in the now protected market is higher than the earlier import price. Presumably the existence and qualities of a local product are discussed among themselves by the local inhabitants. Perhaps also the African standard of living is improving, even if the trend is slow. But the fact remains that the phenomenon has been observed in each country where local production replaced importation; moreover, it has been observed not only in connection with sugar, but also with flour. Today this phenomenon is the great hope for Sosuniari: if sales on the world market do not improve, improvement in African sales might compensate in the long run.

Governmental Relations

Government Reactions to Sian's Proposals. According to a GMP executive, the African governments are enthusiastic when Sian people come to them with investment proposals. These governments are eager to have factories built and they show a special interest in products destined for local consumption.

They are also in great need of financial resources and they know that Sian's ventures are generally successful. Although the managers of any such venture are likely to apply a relatively conservative pay-out policy, the governments can reasonably expect substantial dividends. Moreover, the government is not only a shareholder in these ventures, it is also a tax collector. In Congo (Brazzaville), the corporate tax is 30 percent and the withholding tax 14 percent. In other countries where Sian is established, the corporate tax varies between 28 percent and 35 percent, and the withholding tax varies between 14 percent and 18 percent.

Advantages of Partnership with Governments. As a condition *sine qua non* of the investment, Sian's negotiators ask for the conclusion of a *convention d'établissement,* which is a kind of basic agreement between the foreign corporation and the government. This document will embody the respective rights and obligations of the partners. Sian for instance, receives a tariff or quota protection, sometimes even a monopoly. The foreign corporation also receives the guarantee that it will be given enough foreign exchange for the importation of machinery and equipment and for the free transfer of interests and royalties; but this point generally does not cause difficulties since these countries are still in the French franc zone.

To a large extent, the success of an African venture depends upon a constant and close cooperation with the respective government. According to a GMP executive, Sian's ventures receive more assistance from local administrations now than they used to receive from colonial administrations before independence. In Africa, foreign investment is occasionally considered to be a form of neo-colonialism, but Sian's managers have never encountered any such accusation. This is all the more surprising in Congo (Brazzaville) in that it has sometimes been subject to Russian and sometimes to Chinese influence.

The country is periodically affected by nationalistic waves. One would have expected these socialist influences and internal resentments to constitute a perpetual sword of Damocles over Sian. In fact, the group always received the support of the Congolese Government and was never in this kind of danger. Sian seems to be respected for several reasons: economic success of the group; good relations between the group and the government; presence of the government as a shareholder in Sosuniari; and employment opportunities offered by the group.

The Risks of Partnership with Governments. For obvious reasons, both GMP and Sian fear political changes; they would like to stay outside internal politics. Each change of regime is likely to bring accusations that the group was too closely associated with the preceding regime.

Nevertheless, the ideological importance of the changes, which usually only involve small numbers of rival power groups, should not be exaggerated. Ideology plays a smaller role than is often assumed in American or European newspapers. Sometimes personal or tribal rivalries are involved, and most of the country usually lives outside these disputes. Therefore, it is generally advisable for foreign investors to remain as far as possible independent of any particular faction.

Evaluation and Prospects

Problems. At present, the managers of the Sian Group face three problems that should not be underestimated: a political problem; a market problem; and an expansion problem.

The political problem consists in the need to avoid being identified with any tribe or political party in any African country. There is little that Sian's executives can do to solve this problem. Sian's ventures and African governments are partners and the managers daily require governmental cooperation. They can only refrain from engaging in any activity not connected with their business. The real solution to this problem would be greater political stability in Africa.

The instability of the world sugar market and sugar prices is another difficult problem. As a result, sugar enterprises that are important producers, like Sosuniari, often suffer from shortages of working capital. Several solutions are available, but none of them are likely to bring about rapid results. Market organization and price stabilization may be assured by international agreement, like the Geneva Agreement of the fall of 1968; however, these agreements have their limits and not all producing countries adhere to them; they involve a complex system of bargaining that can only produce results slowly. A second solution may be regional integration, and OCAM is a step in this direction; independence is so recent for most African States, however, that they are not likely to delegate substantial powers to a regional organization easily and rapidly; it remains true that, in the long run, the formation of a political and economic African organization may open attractive new markets for Sian's products. Finally, the increase in local consumption, which has been observed each time locally produced goods replace imports, might provide a solid basis for the development of the group's sales; it is not certain, however, that this increase will be sufficient to absorb the high production level of Sosuniari; and African standards of living are only slowly improving.

Sian's management should be able to deal more easily with the expansion problem. African governments have asked for, and generally obtained, a diversification in the company's activities. Although these new ventures are not always economically profitable, they are profitable financially.[5] The group has been growing very fast and each year new factories are created. The group's executives have to decide if this expansion should continue indiscriminately or if a stricter selectivity should be adopted. The pressure of competition makes it a necessity for the Sian Group to expand; but this is not inconsistent with a more circumspect investment policy.

Positive Aspects. In developing countries especially, the viability of enterprises has to be appreciated in a long-term perspective. Much to its credit, GMP was not discouraged by the venture's initial setbacks. Since GMP took over the direct management of the Sian Group, the business has become very successful. The support of the French authorities, the resources and the advice of French and other foreign financial institutions, and the experience of French commercial companies have greatly contributed to this success. The Sian case is a striking example of the continuing strength and variety of the ties that bind France and its former African territories.

The Sian case also demonstrates that some current preconceived ideas concerning "capitalist" enterprises and ways of exploitation should in future be subjected to close examination. It might be

5. For this distinction, see pp. 106–07.

thought that several features of the Sian Group would cause resentment on the part of newly-independent states: substantial support from one foreign country; foreign financial and managerial control of all enterprises; and use of the plantation system. In reality, not only do the African governments not resent the presence of Sian, but they consciously seek it. French support is viewed as a necessity and is even welcome. The governments have never asked for a majority participation. Their role in the management of Sian's enterprises has so far been very limited. These ventures, therefore, have a unified foreign management, although the necessity for a progressive africanization of personnel is not denied. The plantation system has never been questioned. Relations between Sian and the government have been especially good in the socialist Congo. Nevertheless, the Sian Group has of course no absolute guarantee that the favorable situation of today will continue tomorrow.

The present harmony results from the fact that Sian contributes substantially toward the development of the recipient countries. Dividends and taxes constitute an appreciable source of income for the governments. As an agricultural industry, Sian allows the exploitation of fertile lands that might otherwise remain idle. Since the products are destined in general for local consumption, the Sian Group has close ties with the local economy. Finally, it provides good employment opportunities.

In brief, Sian faces serious problems, but its prospects may be a source of optimism.

VI: POWDERED MILK IN CENTRAL AMERICA

Nestlé

THE GROUP

The Growth of the Group. The origin of Nestlé goes back to 1866 when both Henry Nestlé in Vevey, and the Anglo-Swiss Condensed Milk Co. in Cham, started their respective enterprises. In 1905, after 39 years of rapid growth, the two enterprises merged. This is how the Nestlé Group was formed. In 1929, the group bought the company Peter, Cailler, Kohler, Chocolats Suisses S.A. In 1947, Nestlé entered into an industrial and commercial collaboration with S.A. Alimentana, Kempttal, the affiliated companies of which manufacture the "Maggi" products. In the same year, the corporate name of the group became Nestlé Alimentana S.A. In 1950, the group acquired a controlling interest in Lamont Corliss and Co., one of the most important American chocolate enterprises. In 1960, Nestlé bought Crosse and Blackwell (Holdings) Ltd., London, a well-known British enterprise of food products. In 1961, Nestlé took an important equity participation in the Italian Company, Locatelli S.p.A., Milano, which produces cheese, sausages, and canned tomatoes in its factories of central and northern Italy.

In 1962, the group took an important step towards diversification: in collaboration with the Swedish group, Marabou-Freia, it formed a Swiss holding company, Findus International S.A. This holding company controls the Findus Companies, which produce and distribute frozen foods in several European markets; at that time, Nestlé took an 80 percent participation in the capital of Findus International

S.A. In 1963, the group acquired an important minority participation in the American company, Libby, McNeil and Libby, which produces canned food. In 1967, an agreement was concluded between The Nestlé Company Ltd. (U.K.) on one side and two British companies, the Union International Company Ltd. and J. Lyons and Co., Ltd., on the other; they agreed to cooperate in the frozen food trade in the United Kingdom. Moreover, Nestlé acquired an equity participation in an ice cream enterprise that belongs to these two British companies. In 1969, Nestlé bought the remaining 20 percent participation in the capital of Findus International S.A. and thus became its sole shareholder.

Activities. Nestlé manufactures and sells four main categories of products.

	1959 = 100	*1959*	*1968*
I	*Milk, dietetic specialities, butter, cheese:* —sterilized milk, condensed milk, milk products; —dietetic milk foods for children, such as "Eledon" and "Pelargon"; —cereals for children, with or without milk, such as "Nestum" and "Cerelac."	100	145
II	*Soups, bouillons, condiments, precooked dishes, ice cream, frozen foods:* —soups, bouillons, aromas, condiments, sauces; "Maggi" products; —frozen foods: "Findus" products (fish, poultry, vegetables, fruit).	100	669
III	*Chocolates, cocoa, and confectionery:* —chocolates: "Nestlé," "Peter," "Cailler," "Kohler."	100	184
IV	*Instant beverages:* —soluble powder beverages: "Nescafé," "Nescoré," "Nestea," "Nesquick," "Quick;" —fortifying beverages: "Nescao," "Milo" (which was the official beverage in the Olympic Games of Mexico).	100	234

Profile in Figures

	1959	*1968*
Sales to third parties (in million of FS) *	3,672	8,478
Capital, reserves and accumulated profits (in million of FS)	801	1,437
Participations in, and loans to, subsidiaries and affiliated companies (in millions of FS)	806	2,209
Distributed profits (in millions of FS)	56	121
Self-financing of the two holding companies (Nestlé and Unilac) (in millions of FS)	51	150
Capital expenditures (land, buildings, machinery, equipment, etc.) (in millions of FS)	155	353
Administrative units	63	78
Sales offices and depots	338	536
Factory personnel	39,200	54,935
Administrative and sales personnel	21,572	35,140
Total personnel	60,772	90,075
Factories	139	208

* FS = Swiss Franc—A U.S. dollar is about 4.30 FS.

Remarks:

Nestlé is active in more than 70 countries and has one or several factories in most of them. They are mainly located in nine countries: Great Britain and Ireland (19); France (28); U.S.A. (15); Italy (12); Spain (11); West Germany (10); Brazil (10); Holland (11); South Africa (9). Although Nestlé is a Swiss company, it has only four factories in Switzerland itself.

In 1968, the Annual Report of Nestlé included, for the first time in the group's history, a consolidated balance sheet and a consolidated profit and loss account.

Organization. Nestlé has applied a policy of decentralization, which is shown by the degree of independence of its subsidiaries and affiliated companies. Since 1936, these companies have been controlled by two holding companies: by Nestlé and Anglo-Swiss Condensed Milk Co.; [1] and by Cham and Vevey and Unilac Inc., Panama. When this structural transformation took place, for each Nestlé share the shareholders received a cash bonus and one ordinary share of the Unilac holding: the Nestlé share and the Unilac share constituting an indivisible stock and bearing the same number.[2] This transaction was made possible by drawing on the reserves. Meanwhile, the subsidiaries and affiliated companies were allotted between the two holdings.

Unilac was given control of the group's interests in the Western Hemisphere, the Sterling Area and the Pacific Area, and Nestlé was placed in charge of the subsidiaries and affiliated companies of Continental Europe. In 1950, a Bahamian company, Nestlé's Holdings Ltd., was set up to hold the participations in the Sterling Area. In 1964, Nestlé Alimentana bought the participations that Unilac had in the United States. Unilac and the Canadian subsidiary have the right to buy the shares of Nestlé's Holdings Ltd. until 1970.

In 1959, the capital of Nestlé Alimentana and the capital of Unilac were both tripled. In order to preserve and even reinforce the Swiss character of the enterprise, Nestlé Alimentana issued linked registered shares; its capital has since been composed of 652,000 bearer shares and of 1,304,000 linked registered shares (each share with a par value of FS 100.). Bearer shares and registered shares are quoted separately on stock exchanges.

The main administrative center of the group is in Vevey, Switzerland. During the Second World War, a second center was established in Stamford, Connecticut, U.S.A.

Policies. Nestlé is one of the largest multinational corporations. With the exception of the 1959 capital increase, the group has internally financed its expansion and consolidation. In particular, these huge financial resources have permitted the purchase of Crosse & Blackwell and of Findus, as well as their integration into the Nestlé organization. By tradition, the group follows a policy of strict internal financing, which has been a decisive element in its growth. An important part of the operating companies' profits is thus left to them for direct investment. Similarly, a large part of the two holdings'

1. After 1947: Nestlé Alimentana S.A.
2. *Actions jumelées,* or twin shares.

(Nestlé Alimentana and Unilac) net profits is not distributed but used by the group. Whereas the annual capital expenditure already stood at 155 million FS in 1959, it amounted to 352 million FS in 1968.

The uninterrupted growth of the group is mainly due to excellent management, to the security of its financial basis, and to the constant improvement of the products by its research and control laboratories. Particular emphasis is placed on the training of the executives and on their constant *recyclage*. Nestlé has created the *Institut pour l'Etude des Méthodes de Direction de l'Entreprise* (Imede) in Lausanne; [3] executives from numerous European countries and a great many corporations take part in a difficult training program, which is inspired by the methods followed in the Harvard Business School. A characteristic feature of the institute is that the "students" must have some experience of management behind them. Such an institution is unique in Europe.[4]

On the occasion of its Centenary, Nestlé created a foundation to which it granted a capital of 20 million FS. This foundation was created for the study of worldwide alimentary problems and especially of the means of improving the supply in the most impoverished areas of the world.

Because it operates in so many countries, Nestlé has to accept political and economic risks in some of them: nationalization, excessive taxation, foreign exchange difficulties, devaluation, etc. Moreover, there is sharp competition in the food industry. The prospects of the group are excellent, however, because demand is constantly increasing for both traditional and new products. This tendency, which can be felt in developing countries as well as in developed countries, is reinforced by the rapid increase of the world population.

JOINT VENTURES IN DEVELOPING COUNTRIES

Nestlé in Developing Countries. For a long time most American corporations were satisfied with the outlets provided by their national market and did not feel the need of going abroad. Nestlé's policy has been different. The Swiss group preceded most large American corporations by engaging in important investments abroad. This expansion outside national frontiers was necessary because the Swiss market is very limited.

3. The Institute is under the patronage of the University of Lausanne.

4. The conception and methods of the INSEAD in Fontainebleau, France, are quite different.

As a result of its widely spread international interests, the group takes a calculated risk in some countries, especially in those that are underdeveloped. Sometimes, the risk materializes: in 1960, the Government of Cuba nationalized the three Nestlé-controlled enterprises.[5] Nevertheless, in most of the developing countries there is no hostility toward foreign enterprise. Nestlé's investments in developing countries constitute about 15 percent of the group's total investments. A large part of these investments in developing countries is to be found in Latin America, where there are companies manufacturing and selling Nestlé products in most countries.

Nestlé operations are often well integrated in the national economy, because its activities involve transactions with a great many people. In many countries, raw materials are supplied by a multitude of small local producers, whereas in others the group has to face a few important suppliers. This factual situation can have important consequences for the development of the local company's operations. A further link between the group and the national economy is the fact that food products are destined for the consumer market as a whole.

A few decades ago, foreign corporations were rarely incorporated in the country of investment but merely established branches or agencies. Nestlé was a pioneer in the use of subsidiaries, i.e. of locally incorporated companies. With very few exceptions, Nestlé has always established local subsidiaries.

Wholly-owned Subsidiaries vs. Joint Ventures. Although Nestlé has mostly operated through wholly-owned subsidiaries, it has nevertheless entered into many joint ventures. In the experience of Nestlé, it is rather difficult to find suitable local partners. Frequently, local private investors do not have substantial financial means. When they do, they often prefer to invest these funds in real estate or other short-term investments yielding a high rate of return or to transfer them abroad. In fact, there sometimes is no other partner available but the government. Although Nestlé has never gone into any joint venture with the government itself, in a few cases it has become the partner of a governmental corporation.

Nestlé agrees to joint ventures when the local law or governmental policy requires a local participation, or for some other commercial or

5. Compañia Nacional de Alimentos S.A., Latas Modernas S.A., and Conservas Selectas S.A. On March 2, 1967, the Governments of Cuba and Switzerland concluded an agreement on compensation.

financial reasons. The group's experience has shown that governments of developing countries want, above all, local manufacture, regardless of whether on a joint venture basis or not. At times, special local circumstances also make it necessary for Nestlé to look for a local partner: for instance, the market is too small for two factories or local resources are insufficient to supply them; such a situation leads Nestlé to strive to cooperate with the existing local producer.

Nestlé believes that joint ventures might bring about political or psychological advantages in certain cases. However, the accusations of neo-colonialism might subsist even if local interests participate in a venture. One of the ways to gain acceptance by the national community lies in the contribution to the development of the country by the economic success of the enterprise and by the employment of nationals at all levels, with only a few Swiss left in key posts. Although Nestlé applies this policy almost everywhere, it is sometimes difficult to find nationals who are able to exercise important functions. In many cases, however, only one Swiss occupies a senior managerial post. Moreover, the mobility of the senior personnel brings about a progressive internationalization: for instance, a Spaniard might be the manager of a Latin American venture.

Nestlé's usual policy is to take depreciation as rapidly as possible. This might not necessarily be the case under a joint venture, because of a possible disagreement with the local partner on that matter.

Control in Joint Ventures. When Nestlé goes into a joint venture for commercial and financial reasons, it usually tries to acquire the majority of the shares and to control the enterprise. The requirements of coordination between the multinational operations of the group are a powerful incentive to seek a majority participation. Moreover, it is difficult in developing countries to find local partners who wish or can take a majority of the shares.

This does not mean, however, that Nestlé is *a priori* opposed to a minority participation. Nestlé is in a minority position in various joint ventures, either because the law requires it, or for other particular local reasons. The Philippines is an example of a country whose laws require a majority participation for local investors.

When Nestlé does not have the voting control of a joint venture, it nevertheless tries to have as large a participation as possible. Moreover, the group asks for as large a degree of management control as possible; for instance, through a management contract. In cases where Nestlé has management control, although it is only a minority shareholder, it continually keeps the majority interest informed of the operation of the enterprise.

Finally, Nestlé has also entered into some 50 percent joint ventures. This kind of venture requires especially careful drafting of the agreement in order to avoid conflicts and to make clear who is responsible for the management.

Changes in the Partners' Relationship. It is Nestlé's experience that joint ventures are not rigid structures. For example, in case of expansion individuals and governmental corporations might have difficulty to provide their share of the capital increase. As a result, and in order to continue the company's development, Nestlé might have to provide for the necessary additional funds and consequently increase its participation. Nestlé prefers not to finance an expansion by providing debt capital.

As a rule, the basic agreement includes the right of first refusal in the case of a partner's withdrawal. Nestlé has seldom withdrawn from any venture. Not only is the company convinced that in developing countries the withdrawal from an enterprise would create bitterness and that the group's reputation would consequently suffer; it further believes that even if, temporarily, a business seems to be in a bad condition, this would not justify a withdrawal. The problem is viewed in an entirely different manner in developed countries where a withdrawal has neither the same meaning, nor the same impact. But this does not mean that Nestlé will easily withdraw from companies operating in developed countries.

Generally, Nestlé takes a pragmatic rather than a doctrinal approach towards the problem of joint ventures in developing countries. The group is in a position to adapt its policy to prevailing circumstances.

Prolacsa

THE CENTRAL AMERICAN COMMON MARKET

The Customs Union. Both the Central American Common Market (CACM) and the Latin American Free Trade Association (LAFTA) are the fruit of the efforts made in favor of regional integration by the Economic Commission for Latin America (ECLA).

Created in 1960, the CACM includes Costa Rica (since 1962), El Salvador, Guatemala, Honduras, and Nicaragua: its total population consists of about 12 million inhabitants. The progress of this important experiment in regional integration was seriously threatened by a short but bitter war between Honduras and El Salvador in 1968, which also disturbed the trade pattern. As this book goes to press, CACM is making serious efforts to salvage the Common Market.

The CACM today is a free trade area on its way to becoming a full customs union. Its members have abolished tariffs on nearly all their trade with one another. The exceptions mainly concern a few agricultural products. The Agreement on Tariff Equalization (1959) stipulates that a common tariff be established within five years on goods imported from outside the region. A common external tariff now exists for practically all items, but the few exceptions relate to important products.

A regional customs union can provide larger markets and increased competition while maintaining sufficient tariff protection against the low-cost manufactures of the industrial countries: these conditions create new opportunities and incentives for its members to industrialize.

Progress in regional integration has been much more rapid in Central America than in South America. All five countries are at a relatively early stage of industrialization. No one Central American country is so much larger or more advanced industrially as to arouse fears in the other countries of political or economic domination. Nor has integration been hampered, as it is in much of South America, by the vested interests of high-cost industries that have developed behind high tariffs. Moreover, price levels and exchange rates have generally been more stable in Central America than in Latin America generally.

Monetary cooperation is carried on through the Central American Clearing House and the Central American Monetary Council. Both the future expansion of intraregional trade and the probable price fluctuations for the member countries' agricultural commodities on the world markets will increase the need for a cooperative approach to monetary policy. Unless the growth of money supplies and credit is coordinated, unmanageably large payment surpluses and deficits within the Common Market might bring about the reimposition of import restrictions.

Trade Evolution. Over the period 1960–1966, intra-area commerce expanded several times as rapidly as members' total trade. Over the period 1960–1967, intra-zonal imports have increased almost five times. The growth of intraregional trade has been accompanied by a significant change in its composition. Exchanges of manufactures and semi-manufactures among the five republics have risen at an annual rate of more than 60 percent since 1960. Industrial products now correspond to about two thirds of intraregional trade.

Central America's traditional export structure has not yet been materially affected by the Common Market. A few agricultural commodities (primarily cotton, coffee, sugar, and bananas) still amount to about two thirds of total exports.

Foreign Investment. The regional market has been a major force in attracting international funds and technological expertise. Foreign private investors are participating not only in large-scale industrial ventures which can take advantage of the regional market but also in smaller ventures, many of which have been acquired from local owners. So far, local private investment has continued to flow mostly into small to moderate-sized operations of a traditional nature.

Although each country should have its share of the Common Market's opportunities, economic criteria must also be applied in the location of new industries. A balance between the political and the economic criteria has to be found.

The Role of Financial Institutions. For CACM to succeed, all five members must feel that they share in its benefits. Created in 1960, the Central American Bank for Economic Integration (CABEI) is a development bank that finances long-term industrial and infra-structure projects of regional importance. In doing so, it can affect the location of new industries in order to maintain an equitable balance among the member countries, as well as to generally promote industrial development. Most of its loans have been to the private sector, but the bank also plays an important role in the public sector through its administrative control of the Central American Fund for Economic Integration, which finances transportation, communications, and energy projects.

The Inter-American Development Bank (IDB) also plays an important role in the implementation of regional integration. IDB especially encourages multinational investment projects and contributes to the intermediate-term financing of purchase and sale of equipment goods between the Latin American countries.

NICARAGUA

Profile. The Republic of Nicaragua is surrounded by the Honduras in the north, Costa Rica in the south, the Pacific Ocean in the west, and the Caribbean Sea in the east. Nicaragua has a total area of 148,000 square kilometers (53,000 square miles). Whereas volcanic high plateaux, mountains, and forests occupy the interior of the country, the eastern and western coasts are mostly cultivated.

In 1966, Nicaragua had 1,715,000 inhabitants and Managua, its capital, 274,000. The country's official language is Spanish.

Between 1961 and 1966, the annual average growth rate of the gross national product per capita was 5 percent in Nicaragua, as compared with 3.3 percent in Central America and 1.5 percent in Latin America as a whole.

Recent History. Formerly a Spanish colony, Nicaragua attained independence in 1821. The country suffered U.S. military occupation from 1912 to 1933 (with an interruption in 1925–1926). In 1933, a nationalist uprising provoked the withdrawal of the U.S. troops. After the death of Sandino, the leader of the uprising, in 1934, Anastasio Somoza opened a new era (1937–1956). The regime was supported by the U.S.A., which had a strong economic and financial predominance in the country. Somoza repressed internal political opposition as well as the workers' discontent. After his assassination in September 1956, his son, Luis Somoza, succeeded him in February 1957. In June of that year, rebels unsuccessfully called for his resignation. The election of René Schick as President of the Republic in 1963 did not bring about any fundamental change in the country's policy: Schick, a member of the Liberal Party, was a faithful pupil of the "Somoza Clan." He continued, however, the relative liberalization of the regime that had been begun by Luis Somoza.

The death of Schick, in August 1966, created a serious crisis: Conservatives and Christian Democrats united to oppose the elder son of Somoza, Anastasio, nicknamed "Tachito." During the election campaign in January 1967, riots broke out in Managua. The elections of February were a new victory for the "Somoza Clan." Tachito has since devoted his efforts to modernizing the country's economy.

The Economy. The government places considerable emphasis on modernizing and diversifying agriculture and therefore extends credits to the development of new land, through cultivation, irrigation, and the promotion of fertilizers. Nicaragua's economy is still to a large extent dependent on the production of cotton and coffee. Other important agricultural products are bananas, sugar cane, sesame, rice, and cocoa. The country's forests offer important quantities of mahogany. The main exports are cotton (almost half of the total

value of exports), coffee, and meat. Shrimp and banana exports are
in the process of developing.

Nicaragua also has substantial mineral resources such as gold
(which is an important export product), silver, and copper.

With the assistance of foreign capital the industrial sector has
steadily expanded in recent years. Construction activity of all kinds
has been particularly remarkable. Road construction and residential,
commercial, and industrial building have all proceeded apace. Manufacturing production, which until now has largely been concentrated
on consumer goods, is now turning to certain intermediate and capital goods as well. Exports of industrial products are developing.

Most of the trade is carried out with the U.S.A. Imports that are
necessary to feed the growing industrialization and increasing consumer demands tend to rise slightly more rapidly than exports. The
resultant deficit has been more than offset, however, by an increasing
inflow of foreign capital, especially to the private sector.

Of the five members, Nicaragua's share of the Common Market's
trade is the smallest, with exports to the region accounting for a
small part of the country's total exports. Meanwhile, Nicaragua's imports from other Common Market countries have substantially increased since 1960.

The currency used in Nicaragua is the cordoba. At present, one
U.S. dollar is equal to seven cordobas.

NEGOTIATIONS WITH NESTLÉ

The Negotiations. In 1958, Nestlé's products were being sold in
Nicaragua through an independent agent. That year, the government
contacted Nestlé with regard to the construction and operation of a
powdered milk factory. Nestlé sent an agronomist who prepared a
comprehensive report.

Nicaragua is an ideal country for stock-breeding. As the production of milk exceeds national demand, surpluses are exported. Powdered milk is sold in limited quantities only, because Nicaragua is a
country that essentially consumes fresh milk.

In view of these facts, Nestlé's experts realized that the Nicaraguan market did not have the necessary conditions for a sound operation of a powdered milk factory. Although the prospect of regional
integration was an interesting possibility, in 1958 the CACM was
still only at the negotiating stage. As Nicaragua could not favorably
compete with other traditional milk-exporting countries like Holland,

Nestlé executives thus concluded that investment risks greatly exceeded other positive aspects. Although the negotiations virtually came to a standstill, Nestlé and the government did not completely lose contact.

The government again approached Nestlé in 1961. The following year, and several times since, Nestlé sent agronomists to Nicaragua. By that time, CACM had been formed. As the inhabitants of the other four countries are fairly important consumers of powdered milk, Nestlé informed the government that a powdered milk factory could be built under certain conditions.

The main idea of the Nestlé negotiators was that the factory should be planned on a scale sufficient to supply the demands of the Common Market. Everything was to be done in order to give the enterprise a Central American character, with Nestlé taking a relatively limited equity share. The financing of the enterprise was to be provided by the shareholders of the five countries. This conception also meant that the signing of an intergovernmental protocol limiting imports of milk products was necessary as it would guarantee the distribution of the products throughout the Common Market.

Protocol of San José. In July 1962, representatives of the five countries signed the Protocol of San José (capital of Costa Rica).[6] The main guarantee given by the five governments was that milk imports from countries not pertaining to the Common Market would be restricted.[7]

The protocol applies the principles of economic integration. Locally-produced milk products would freely circulate between the countries of the Common Market, i.e. without being taxed as imports. As far as milk products from countries not pertaining to the Common Market are concerned, the five members would increase or decrease in varying degree their import duties so that a common external tariff could be adopted; even Costa Rica, which has a powdered milk factory cooperative would have to decrease its duties. To reinforce this protection, import quotas to be determined according to the Central American production would be introduced into the five countries. Finally, even when Central American factories will have a production equal to the needs of the Common Market, there will still be the possibility of importing 15 percent of the requirements in

6. This protocol is an addition to the Agreement on Tariff Equalization (1959): see *supra* p. 127.

7. For the time being, the protocol deals only with powdered milk.

order to maintain a certain degree of competition from external suppliers.

FINANCING

Multinational Financing. The financial structure of the venture was first discussed seriously in the second half of 1962. Nestlé experts undertook economic and feasibility studies. According to calculations made, the enterprise would need a capital of around $2 million, not including the working capital. The enterprise was to be named Compañía Centroamericana de Productos Lácteos S.A. (Prolacsa).

The Nicaraguan partner in the venture was to be the Instituto de Fomento Nacional (Infonac), an institution financially dependent on the government. Nestlé and Infonac would each take a 15 percent equity share.

As Nestlé and Infonac were to provide only part of the financing, they first requested the Central American Bank for Economic Integration (CABEI), to grant a long-term loan to the venture, to take a participation in the equity capital, and to place part of the capital among Central American investors. This would have given the future company a truly Central American character and an excellent assurance against economic and political risks. After prolonged negotiations, however, no agreement was reached.

Nestlé and Infonac then approached the Inter-American Development Bank (IDB), who confirmed Nestlé's idea that Central American investors should have an important participation.

Nestlé had proposed the division of Prolacsa's capital into five series of shares:

Series A	15 percent Nestlé
Series B	15 percent Infonac
Series C	20 percent Central American investors
Series D	20 percent Central American investors
Series E	30 percent Nestlé and Central American investors

Although Nestlé did not ask for the majority control, it nevertheless wished to exercise a certain managerial control. It was therefore agreed that the group would take 51 percent of the Series E shares. In accordance with this financial arrangement the Board of Directors would have five members; two seats for Nestlé, one seat for Infonac and two seats for the other shareholders.

After prolonged negotiations, an agreement appeared to have been reached in 1966 when, suddenly, Infonac claimed a larger financial participation for Nicaragua. This request was based on the fact that the factory would be established in that country and that it was only normal that local investors were given a larger participation. It was finally agreed that the Nicaraguan investors would have an additional 20 percent share of the capital, but Nestlé insisted that the venture should include investors from all other countries of the Central American Common Market. A compromise was reached: these investors would provide a share of 34 percent and although they would control only one series of shares, they would hold two seats in the board. To this effect, the Stock-breeders' Association of Nicaragua, which would control one series of shares, agreed to elect an investor of another Central American country as the director representing that series. This financial structure was accepted by all parties concerned and has not since been subject to any change. The capital (10 million cordobas) of 100,000 shares is divided in five series, as follows:

Series A	15 percent Nestlé
Series B	15 percent Infonac (Nicaragua)
Series C	20 percent Stock-breeders' Association of Nicaragua (11 percent) and Central American investors (9 percent)
Series D	20 percent Central American investors
Series E	30 percent Nestlé (16 percent), Nicaraguan financial institution (9 percent), Central American investors (5 percent).

Prolacsa was incorporated on December 15, 1966. In the Spring of 1967, the promoters of Prolacsa started looking for private investors in the other countries of the Common Market. Nestlé insisted on dividing the share devoted to Central American investors equally among the four countries: about 8.5 percent for each country. The shares were to be placed among the financial circles of the four countries. Most of the shares have since been subscribed and only a small part remains to be placed. The first general meeting of shareholders was convened in 1968.

No right of first refusal has been provided for the case of withdrawal of a partner, because with five series of shares and a relatively large number of shareholders, such a device would be too complicated. Nevertheless, the shareholders have an option in cases of capital increase; both the percentage devoted to each series and the percentage allocated to each shareholder in his series would be respected.

IDB Long-term Loan. In 1967, IDB granted to Infonac a loan of $1 million, to be repaid over a period of ten years. Repayment will start three years after the conclusion of the loan agreement. The loan has been granted to Infonac in dollars, then Infonac has lent these funds to Prolacsa in cordobas. This means that Prolacsa will reimburse the amount in the same currency. As a result, Prolacsa does not incur any devaluation risk.

IDB granted the loan on the condition that these funds would be used only for imports of machinery and equipment. A certain number of rules were imposed by IDB and/or Infonac. For example, machines worth over $50,000 were to be chosen on a public tender basis.

MANAGEMENT

The Factory's Construction. Although third parties execute specific construction jobs, Nestlé supervises and assumes responsibility for the entire construction under a contract with Prolacsa.

The factory has been built in Matagalpa, in the interior of the country. Production started in the second half of 1969. At the beginning, the factory will have a capacity of 3 to 4 million pounds of powdered milk a year. The final goal is to reach a capacity equal to total consumption in the Common Market, which, at present, is of some 9 to 10 million pounds. An expansion of the factory will be necessary to reach such a capacity. Two brands of powdered milk will be produced: "Nido" (28 percent fats) and "Lirio Blanco" (26 percent fats).

The Board of Directors. As each series of shares is entitled to select one director, the board has five members. An annual rotation system is applied for the election of the board's chairman. Nestlé has two seats (Series A and E), while Infonac has one seat (Series B). Although the Stock-Breeders' Association has the voting majority of Series C, it was agreed, as mentioned previously, that this series would elect a non-Nicaraguan director, i.e., a personality from one of the other four countries; at present, the seat is held by a Honduras financial institution.

All decisions have to be approved by a majority of four votes out of five. This system gives Nestlé a *de facto* right of veto. Since Prolacsa is a multinational company, however, it would have been difficult for any single shareholder to expect to control the board. Even though its minority position in the board might constitute a certain risk, Nestlé does not anticipate any serious problem. It counts on the cooperation of all shareholders and their respective board representatives to solve any problem.

Day-to-day Management. As the quality of the product was to be insured by the foreign partner, Infonac never objected to Nestlé controlling the day-to-day management of Prolacsa. As will be seen below, the distribution problem has already been solved. Prolacsa has to deal with manufacturing problems; accordingly, the company mainly needs good technicians.

All main corporate officers are designated by Nestlé:

General Manager;

two Assistant Managers;

   an Administrative Assistant Manager (Chief Accountant);

   a Technical Assistant Manager (Production Manager);

a Laboratory Chief;

a Head Mechanic.

The present organization of the day-to-day management may be subject to change.

Financial Policy. A statutory provision stipulates that the company will observe the legal requirements concerning the compulsory reserve. Any formation of additional reserves has to be accepted by a majority of shareholders in each series. As a result, each important shareholder has a right of veto in this matter. No decision on financial policy can be taken without a true consensus of all main partners. Nestlé thought that since Prolacsa would have numerous passive shareholders, these would normally prefer to cash any available profits. Therefore, the creation of voluntary reserves would be a matter for the stockholders to decide upon.

TRADEMARKS AND TECHNICAL ASSISTANCE

Nestlé's Policy. As early as the time of the first negotiations, Infonac asked Nestlé to assume the day-to-day management and to license its trademarks to Prolacsa. The question of the trademarks for Prolacsa products was the object of much thought by Nestlé. When the Protocol of San José was signed, it was known that the imports of Nestlé products in the CACM countries would be restricted, but that the other importers would also be affected by the intergovernmental agreement. These competitors could, therefore, attempt to manufacture locally; this possibility was viewed as an argument for Nestlé to license its well-known name and trademarks to Prolacsa; but as a condition, Nestlé asked to be entrusted with the day-to-day management of the venture.

Since Prolacsa uses the Nestlé trademarks and processes, technicians go to Matagalpa to apply Nestlé methods. All tasks related to technical assistance will also be executed by Nestlé.

Technical Assistance. For Nestlé, technical assistance has a broad meaning. An essential aspect of this assistance is the quality control of the products. Wherever in the world Nestlé's products are manufactured the group controls their quality through its regional and central laboratories. In the case of Prolacsa, Nestlé also gives an extended technical assistance to the stock-breeders: improvement of grazings, of milking methods, etc. This, as well as other aspects of Nestlé's contribution, should have lasting benefits for the country.

In exchange for this broad technical assistance (trademarks, patents, quality control, education of the farmers), Prolacsca pays to Nestlé a remuneration equal to $0.02 per pound of milk powder produced. In view of the difficulties that usually affect production at its start, Nestlé asked for a minimum payment whatever the actual volume of production would be. This point was the object of considerable bargaining between Nestlé and Infonac. A compromise was finally reached, whereby Nestlé would cash such minimum remuneration only when profits would exceed a certain percentage of the share capital. The payments are to be made in U.S. dollars, which protects Nestlé against any risk of devaluation.

SALES

Distribution System. It was unnecessary for Prolacsa to create a sales organization from scratch, because a distribution system of Nestlé's products existed in Guatemala, El Salvador, Costa Rica, Honduras, and Nicaragua. The local company in Guatemala supervises and coordinates the distribution and sale of Nestlé products in Central America. This managerial integration was effected in 1961 as a consequence of the creation of the Central American Common Market.

Prolacsa has signed distribution agreements with the companies selling Nestlé's products in each of the Central American countries. These organizations act as selling agents for Prolacsa and, therefore, receive a commission. No objection was made by Prolacsa's shareholders to the appointment of Nestlé as the marketing agent, because the goods were to be sold under the Nestlé trademarks.

Competition in the Common Market. Since local production of milk powder in the region is very small, the protectionist provisions of the Protocol of San José will practically come into force only when Prolacsa starts production. Imports will be restricted (but not eliminated) by a tariff and quota protection. How the competitors of Nestlé and Prolacsa will react in this changing situation cannot be foreseen. Some of them may try to start manufacturing within the Common Market.

At present, the main competitors are Dutch cooperatives which export from Holland, and a local cooperative in Costa Rica.

GOVERNMENT RELATIONS

Infrastructure Work. The factory is in the city of Matagalpa, which is linked by road to Managua and the coast. As most of Prolacsa's suppliers are individual stock-breeders, it was essential to build a system of roads between the factory and the farms. The Government of Nicaragua committed itself to establish a road network that would facilitate the collection of milk from the stock-breeders. Such a network will cost about 14 million dollars. Nestlé cooperated to a large extent in the preparation of the program.

Besides, while Nestlé was ready to give any necessary technical assistance to the stock-breeders, it was understood that the government would deal with the financial aspects involved: the purchase of cows, improvement of grazings and milking methods, etc. This modernization program will cost about $5 million.

Consequently, the total cost of the infrastructure construction amounts to around $19 million. Infonac asked IDB for a special loan of about $13 million. IDB has already agreed to grant a credit of $9.6 million. In addition, local financing will provide approximately $6 million.

Taxation. Prolacsa has a special fiscal status. The company is exempt from excise duties on imports of machinery, fuel, and tin. For a period of five years, the company is totally exempt from the corporate tax on profits; during the five following years, only half the normal tax will be applied. Nevertheless, these exemptions do not apply to royalties and other fees, which, although generally assimilated to profits, are fully taxed from the beginning. Prolacsa does not have to pay the tax on capital. The company did not ask for any special guarantee against a change in its fiscal status.

Foreign Exchange. Normally, the foreign exchange situation in Nicaragua should not present serious difficulties. The transfer of capital and profits abroad as well as interests and royalties is not restricted. In recent years, Nicaragua has not suffered any devaluation and the risk for the future is remote. However, both Prolacsa and Nestlé, as mentioned before, have taken precautions to prevent the detrimental effects of a possible devaluation.

EVALUATION AND PROSPECTS

Evaluation. At the origin of this multinational joint venture lies Nestlé's confidence in Nicaragua as a country suitable for the production of powdered milk, and in the Central American Common Market as a good outlet for the consumption of this product. The enterprise should, consequently, have as much as possible a regional character with sales being based on exports to the other Central American countries.

The negotiations between Nestlé, the Government of Nicaragua, Infonac, CABEI, and IDB were long and difficult. Between the first official approach and the start of production, twelve years elapsed. This extended negotiation was partly caused by the fact that the parties involved in the discussions had different outlooks. In the beginning, moreover, nobody could foresee the emergence of the Common Market.

As the Common Market turned out to be a success, Nestlé showed a growing interest in the establishment of the enterprise. Moreover, the regional character of Prolacsa was viewed as a good guarantee against economic and political risks.

Prolacsa will bring important and ever lasting advantages to Nicaragua and the CACM. This agricultural industry will be integrated in the Nicaraguan economy, especially through its relations with the supplying stock-breeders. The government's assistance with regard to the infrastructure work has, naturally, closely associated it with the venture. This truly regional enterprise will supply all countries with a basic consumer product and should bring profts to each country's shareholders. The multinational character of the company rests on policy as well as financial considerations. To the best of our knowledge, Nestlé has been the first international corporation to seek the creation, in a developing country, of a regional enterprise with shareholders coming from all the region's countries.

Prospects. The short-term prospects of Prolacsa are good because the Common Market provides excellent outlets for powdered milk and because these five countries are, at present, politically stable.

In a longer perspective, Prolacsa's expansion would be a delicate problem. The manufacture of other products for the Common Market may have a different economic basis. Nestlé's position is that a diversification in the manufacture of its products has not necessarily to be linked with Nicaragua and Prolacsa.

The future of Prolacsa is also dependent on the evolution of economic integration. Although the CACM has made a good start, a great deal remains to be done. The willingness of the Common Market Members to cooperate with each other and to adopt regional rather than strictly national policies, will determine the speed with which the Market's longer-term goals can be attained.

Although the CACM is progressing, it has always been understood that the final goal would be the economic integration of all Latin America. On April 14, 1967, the Chiefs of State and representatives of 20 American nations met at Punta del Este (Uruguay), to approve a "Plan of Action" committing the Latin American Governments to establish a Latin American Common Market (LACM), which is to be "substantially in operation" by 1985. Serious difficulties lie ahead: for instance, there is a widespread belief that a Latin American Common Market will not be viable as long as the Latin American countries pursue widely divergent monetary policies.

Even though Prolacsa must evaluate all the consequences of such a development, the concrete problems of Latin American economic integration will not arise for several years to come.

VII: BREWING BEER IN HONG KONG

Carling Brewery (Hong Kong) Limited is one of two local producers of beer in the Colony of Hong Kong. It was formed in 1965 as a 50-50 joint venture of a large Canadian brewing company and a consortium of Hong Kong business men. It represents the first business conducted by the Canadian partner in the Far East, even though its beer sells in about sixty countries of the world. It is the first venture into brewing for the local partners, whose other business interests consist of large scale construction and importing operations.

Origin of the Enterprise

Before the formation of the joint venture, only one of the approximately forty brands of beer consumed in Hong Kong was manufactured within the colony. Through their close ties with the local market, the Hong Kong partners of the company realized the potential for another local producer, and began searching for a partner who could supply the requisite brewing know-how. In 1962, four North American brewing corporations were approached, among them Schlitz, Anhauser-Busch, and the Canadian company that became the eventual partner. From the meetings and negotiations that ensued, the Hong Kong promoters chose the Canadian company to enter into the joint venture as an equal partner.

For the Canadian company, entry into the venture signalled basic changes in the manner of conducting its foreign operations. It had not attempted before to tap the Far Eastern market on a large scale because of unfamiliarity with the local production and marketing conditions. The licensing agreement it entered into with the joint venture represented the first occasion on which it had licensed its brand names to a company in which it did not have majority control. These changes were made for two principal reasons. Firstly, a feasibility study prepared by the company showed the possibility of a fair return on capital investment. Secondly, the Hong Kong partners were individuals whom the Canadian partner considered to be compatible for the sharing of ownership and control, and who could provide the local knowledge of markets, language, institutions, and personnel that was essential. It was the company's conclusion that "there can be no doubt that in the consumer products field, Chinese partners are an essential in this market. . . . It would be difficult to find better partners."

Accordingly, on April 12, 1965, the Hong Kong and the Canadian partners entered into the joint venture agreement for the formation and operation of a brewing company in the Colony of Hong Kong. The agreement stressed the extent to which the Chinese partners were essential, and the different, but complementary roles both partners in the venture were to play.

ORIGINAL CAPITAL STRUCTURE AND
TECHNICAL ARRANGEMENTS

A limited liability company, incorporated as of September 28, 1964 under the laws of Hong Kong, was chosen as the vehicle for the joint venture. Consulting by telephone and letter, Hong Kong and Canadian counsel required about six months to work out the terms of the Memorandum and Articles of Association. The company was incorporated under the name of "Associated Breweries Limited" with dummy incorporators and nominal share capital. "Associated" became party to the agreement spelling out the terms of the joint venture. At the request of the Hong Kong partners, its name was changed as of June 30, 1965 to the present one of Carling Brewery (Hong Kong) Limited. In the local language, "Carling", roughly translated, means "good health". It was also felt that considerable good will could be gained from the international reputation of the new name.

The total capitalization of the joint venture, and the amount contributed by each partner have not been made public to date. But, in accordance with the joint venture agreement, the authorized share capital was set at 1,060,000 common voting shares with a par value fixed in terms of Hong Kong dollars. The partners subscribed for 530,000 or half of the shares each, and paid up one half of the par value, the balance remaining on call. The Hong Kong partners had advanced the purchase price of the land for the plant to the company, and this debt was repaid through the issue to them of shares paid up as to 50 percent. An additional sum of money was raised by way of loan from The Hong Kong and Shanghai Banking Corporation, and secured by a fixed-charge debenture on the land, plant, and equipment. Further capital was raised by a call of 20 percent of the par value of the shares outstanding, as authorized by a directors' meeting of December 1, 1965.

The capital raised by the above methods was sufficient to finance the construction and equipping of a moderate sized brewery of a net capacity of 40,000 Canadian barrels per year. The plant also contains its own bottling facilities.

The joint venture agreement was executed as of April 12, 1965. It consists of three parts. The main text of the agreement, to which the Canadian and Hong Kong partners and Associated were parties, set out the basic provisions of the joint venture, such as capitalization, termination, and control. Schedule A, executed by the Canadian partner and Associated, specifies the responsibilities of the Canadian partner for the provision of technical, engineering, and advisory services to the joint venture. Schedule B, executed by Associated, the Canadian partner, and The Carling Breweries Limited, the latter being an Ontario company and subsidiary of the Canadian partner, is a licensing agreement for the use by the joint venture of the Carlings brand names in return for royalties. Together, the agreement and its two schedules comprise the joint venture arrangements and the responsibilities of the partners.

Under Schedule A, the Canadian partner assumed the obligations of supplying all of the know-how for construction of brewing facilities having a net annual capacity of 40,000 Canadian barrels (1,-000,000 Imperial gallons) with a peak monthly ouput of at least 100,000 gallons. It was responsible for selecting and placing orders for all of the machinery and equipment necessary; planning the machinery layout in the plant; and giving specifications for the piping, refrigeration, electricity, waste disposal, and dimensions of the buildings. At its own cost, the Canadian partner supplied a project engineer to assist with the construction for a period of six months. After six months, the engineer became a salaried employee of Associated. It also was charged with selecting and training a head brewer, who was to become an employee of Associated, and with providing whatever other technical supervision that might be required. In return for the know-how as above stipulated, the Canadian partner received an agreed-upon lump sum payment.

Schedule A set out the responsibilities of Associated as well. Associated had to choose a suitable site for the plant, and to engage local architects and engineers to design the buildings, and facilities for waste disposal, electricity, and refrigeration according to the specifications provided by the Canadian partner. Such architects let the construction contracts and oversaw the execution of the whole project.

In Schedule B to the joint venture agreement, The Carling Breweries Limited authorized the use by Associated of its following brand names: Carling's "Black Label" Beer, Carling's Pilsener Lager Beer, Carling's "Red Cap" Ale, Carling's Extra Stout, and "Cinci" Lager Beer. In return, Carling receives continuing royalties related to the volume of sales. Associated covenanted not to sell the beer outside of the Colony of Hong Kong, and to refuse to sell to anyone who might in turn do so.

To protect its brand names, Carling had them registered in Hong Kong and retained the right of inspection and quality control. Associated agreed that wherever necessary, it would obtain covenants of nondisclosure of manufacturing processes and trade secrets from its employees. As further protection, upon termination of the right of Associated to utilize the "Carling" name, it would become obligated to make available for purchase by Carling all inventories and equipment bearing that brand name, and to destroy such items that Carling declined to purchase.

By Schedule B, Associated obtained the right to use the Carling brand names for a period of ten years from the end of the first calendar month of production by Associated. Accordingly, the license agreement, and thereby the entire joint venture agreement terminates as of November 30, 1977, at which time it becomes subject to renegotiation. If before that date, Associated should breach any of the terms of the agreement, and the breach should not be remedied following 60 days' notice, or if Associated should become insolvent, then the Canadian partner has a right to terminate the joint venture.

As stated above, the actual identity of the Hong Kong partners was of paramount concern to the Canadian partner. The Hong Kong partners are three relatives who have combined their interests into a holding company, and this holding company is the actual partner to the joint venture. But to protect against a change in ownership of the holding company, and thereby an actual change in the individual local partners, the agreement stipulates that at any time the three individuals cease to control 51 percent of the shares of the holding company, then the Canadian partner acquires the option of terminating the joint venture.

Upon termination, by lapse of time or otherwise, provision has been made for a buy-sell procedure. The company's auditors will prepare a valuation of the company assets. Then the Canadian partner will have 90 days in which to purchase all the shares of the joint venture held by the Hong Kong partners at one half of the valuation established. If it chooses not to exercise this option, then the reciprocal right of purchase within a further 90 days accrues to the Hong Kong partners. If neither side should exercise its option within the 180 days, then the "rights and obligations shall be determined according to law" and the terms of the joint venture agreement. This would entail a winding-up and distribution of assets to the shareholders. In the event that one partner or the other exercises its option to purchase, then the selling partner agreed to execute a covenant not to compete within the Colony of Hong Kong for a period of seven years from the date of transfer of the shares.

MANAGEMENT AND PERSONNEL

Both parties contributed equally to capital, and are equal owners. This equality was maintained also with respect to management and control. The Board of Directors has six members. The Memorandum and Articles of Association of the company provide that each of the two partners shall have the right to appoint three of the directors. Alternates may be appointed, and ownership of qualifying shares is not required. The chairman is specifically precluded by the memorandum from exercising a casting vote in case of deadlock.

As stated, it was the obligation of the Canadian partner to provide a head brewer who would be an employee of the company at an agreed salary. At the December 1, 1965 meeting of the directors, the head brewer, a former employee of the Canadian partner, was appointed General Manager and Head Brewer of the joint venture. Two of the Hong Kong partners were appointed Joint Managing Directors. All offices are held at the pleasure of the board. Although the General Manager is the chief executive officer of the company, and is responsible for the day-to-day operations, his expertise is restricted mainly to the technical aspects of production. The local partners serving as officers deal chiefly with marketing problems, and because of language, handle most of the employee relations.

Since coming into operation, the plant has employed about 30 persons, including management. This relatively small work force has been made possible through the modern equipment and plant. None of the employees are represented by a union. In dealing with the employees, the language barrier proved difficult at first. The local partners were able to deal with routine matters, but a translator was required to explain technology to the workers. Now that the workers have become familiar with plant operations, and the General Manager has acquired some knowledge of Chinese, language presents fewer difficulties. When need arises, the Chinese foreman still acts as a translator. By 1967, after one year of operations, the General Manager is the only Canadian working in the plant or serving in a supervisory capacity. All the remaining employees are local Chinese. The General Manager is the only one of the three directors appointed by the Canadian partner who resides in Hong Kong. The other two commute from Canada for the requisite meetings.

The Brewing Industry in Hong Kong

The city of Hong Kong is 90 miles to the southeast of the Chinese province of Canton. The Colony of Hong Kong is an area of 398 square miles, consisting of the island of Hong Kong, Kowloon, and the New Territories. The New Territories include land on the mainland and 235 small islands.

The standard of living is among the highest in the Far East, with an average income of about US$400 per year per person. Of the five million inhabitants, however, about 5.6 percent are classified as "very rich", relegating a large percentage of the population to an annual income considerably below the average. Population is increasing by about 6 percent annually, and the economy is expanding by about 10 percent.

Adult consumption of beer is estimated at about three gallons per year, indicating a market for about eight million Imperial gallons for 1967. Most of this beer is sold in 23-ounce bottles. This market is shared by some forty different brands of beer, only one of which, before 1966, was brewed locally.

San Miguel beer, produced in Hong Kong by Hong Kong Breweries Limited, supplied 60 percent of the market, or about five million gallons in 1966. It is owned 75 percent by San Miguel Breweries Limited of the Philippines, and 25 percent locally within Hong Kong. Of its directors, one is Chinese and three are British, all resident in Hong Kong. The remaining five directors are nonresidents. In addition to paying a substantial management fee of about 10 percent of its profits each year to its parent company, all its profits are distributed each year as dividends. Its marketing policy has been to sell through local distributors only, and not to go direct to the market.

About forty brands of imported beer account for the remaining 40 percent of the Hong Kong market. Of the imported beers, one brand, "Tsingtao" beer from mainland China, accounts for approximately 40 percent of imports. Carslberg beer comprises about 18 percent of the imports; three Japanese brands, "Sapporo," "Asahi," and "Kirin" combine for 12 percent, and Malaysian Breweries sells about 8 percent. More than thirty other brands compete for the other 22 percent of import sales.

"Tsingtao" beer enjoys its dominant position among the imports because of its pricing policy. It is the cheapest in Hong Kong, selling for even less than San Miguel. Its market position would be even stronger were it able to increase production, but with its limited supplies, its present dealers have to be placed on quotas. Were it able to supply sufficient quantity to meet the demand at the existing prices, competitors would be forced to drop their prices to compete.

Operations of Carling Brewery (Hong Kong) Limited

Plant construction was begun in October, 1965, and completed in August, 1966. The contracting firm was owned by the Hong Kong partners of the joint venture, and all laborers were engaged locally. The brewing equipment was imported from Canada, the United Kingdom, and Germany, and the bottling machinery from the United States. The first beer was produced in November, 1966.

The company hired a local firm of marketing and publicity agents, Ling-McCann Erickson Limited, to assist with promotion. Although Carling Brewery (Hong Kong) Limited is free to use any of the "Carling" brand names it wishes, it has directed the bulk of advertising towards sales of the "Black Label" brand in 23-ounce bottles. Its promoters expected the joint venture to capture about 10 percent of the total market during its first full year of production, giving it sales in that year of approximately 800,000 gallons. As had been anticipated, the Carling beer faced vigorous competition from the time its was first sold. San Miguel cut prices immediately, and the company was forced to follow suit. Figures for the first full year of operations are not available, but the Canadian partner indicated its satisfaction with the progress made.

Previous to the establishment of the Hong Kong brewery, "Black Label" beer had been sold in over sixty countries of the world. Most of these markets had been serviced from the United Kingdom, and from the Natick, Massachusetts and Tacoma, Washington plants of Carling. But the high cost of transportation had been an inhibiting factor to increased international sales, with one exception. The United States government pursues a policy of patronizing American suppliers for its worldwide needs. Under this policy, Carling brands have enjoyed a good market in the Far East, Europe, and other offshore military bases. As of 1967, no arrangements had been made for supply to the Far East markets from Hong Kong by the joint venture. For this to be done, the "Hong Kong only" market provided for in the joint venture agreement would have to be renegotiated. The problem also exists of whether the United States government would continue to extend its preferential purchasing to a brewery located in Hong Kong with 50 percent of its ownership in local hands. An additional problem could be the need to produce a different brew for the Far Eastern markets, now serviced by Carling from the United States.

Negotiations commenced in 1967 between the Canadian partner and Carling Brewery (Hong Kong) Limited for supply of the Malaysian market from Hong Kong. Whether the markets of the joint venture will be extended beyond the Colony of Hong Kong will depend on how much such exports might cut into the world markets presently supplied by the wholly-owned producing affiliates of the Canadian partner. The issue is whether the Canadian partner can increase its total profits by supplying through the joint venture and taking half its profits, as opposed to keeping all the profits from shipping to those same markets direct from England and North America with the added transportation costs. Since the storage and transportation costs of beer constitute a substantial portion of its selling price, and since price is the main determinant of beer's saleability in oriental markets, it is foreseeable that agreement will be reached for the joint venture to undertake supply of markets in the Far East outside of the Colony of Hong Kong.

Should export markets or increased sales within Hong Kong necessitate expansion of brewing capacity beyond its present one million gallons per year, it is expected that the bulk of the cost would be financed through retained earnings. Through its own position and that of the local partners, the company would have little difficulty raising additional sums from banks and other financial institutions. Provision was made for expansion in the joint venture agreement, and subscriptions for shares from the public can be entertained on terms acceptable to the two partners. Accordingly, financing expansion does not present an obstacle to it being undertaken as viewed presently.

The laws of Hong Kong encourage a healthy competition in the brewing industry. The colony does impose import duties on tobacco, soft drinks, oil products, and alcoholic beverages. The duty imposed on imported beer, combined with the excise taxes, amounts to about HK$1.90 per Imperial gallon. But this is not sufficiently high to afford local producers much protection, as their taxes amount to HK$1.60 per gallon. This differential works out to about only six Canadian cents per gallon. The importation of capital equipment for brewery construction is not taxed at all.

On the export side, beer can be freely exported from Hong Kong. Although there is a corporate tax of about 12.5 percent, no withholding taxes are imposed on dividends or other funds paid out of Hong Kong, nor are there any exchange controls that have inhibited payments to the Canadian partner. The government requires licensing of all breweries, but this is more an administrative formality than a device for preclusion of competition or raising of revenues. British Common Law forms the basis of the legal system of the colony.

Evaluation

The joint venture agreement provides that "all disputes arising out of" the agreement and its schedules are to be referred to binding arbitration. The Hong Kong Arbitration Ordinance of 1963 governs the arbitration proceedings in all material respects, and the law of Hong Kong has been made the law applicable. To date, recourse to arbitration has not proven necessary, nor is such recourse anticipated.

With respect to management of the joint venture, difficulties could ensue from the 3-3 split of directors and the absence of a casting

vote by the chairman. Again, problems in this area are not anticipated. The General Manager and Head Brewer, who is also one of
the Canadian partner's three appointees to the Board of Directors,
provides the technical and brewing know-how essential to the operations. For their part, the Hong Kong partners possess the knowledge
concerning local financing, marketing, language, and the government,
all of which are conditions precedent to successful operations. They
obtained the brewing license, acquired the land, established credit
through their banking connections, hired the contractors, and hired
the employees. It was their knowledge of market conditions in Hong
Kong that gave rise to the formation of the venture. Despite the diverse contributions that each partner can make, there is complete
consultation on all questions of management and operations. For example, in developing a brew that would be acceptable to the local
market, the head brewer relied on the judgment of the Hong Kong
partners.

At this stage of the company's existence, it could not function
without the cooperation of both partners. As the employees become
more skilled in the art of brewing, and as the Canadian partner
learns more about local conditions, the present state of interdepen-
dency will weaken, and either of the partners would be able to "go it
alone" were it not for the covenant not to compete. Disputes could
arise, especially if profits do not accrue as quickly as anticipated. Financial results for the first full year's operations are not compiled,
but indications are that the partners are content. The local partners
could become disgruntled if the opportunity for exporting is not
made available to the joint venture. But again, such disputes are not
anticipated in view of the highly satisfactory relationship to date between the partners.

From a financial point of view, newcomers to the market are subject to strong competition, especially from San Miguel and Tsingtao.

The possibility of Hong Kong being overrun from the mainland
was another factor considered before the Canadian partner made its
investment. As long as Hong Kong continues to supply mainland
China with such a large percentage of its foreign exchange, a takeover is considered unlikely.

In conclusion, the Canadian partner admits that the joint venture
is the only method by which it would have entered the Hong Kong
market. Whatever problems might arise through this method of conducting business will be solved, it feels, out of the good will of the

partners towards each other. Good will and mutual respect between partners is fundamental to a joint venture, especially where ownership and control are shared equally. After one year of operations, and more than five years of cooperation, the Canadian partner is quite satisfied with its first joint venture of this nature, and would advocate its use again where compatible local partners can be found.

Venture between Multinational Corporation,
Local Corporation, and Local Investors

VIII: ENGINEERING AND CHEMICAL GOODS IN INDIA

Formation

Volkart Brothers. Volkart is a Swiss company that has a long tradition in trading. They went to India in 1851 and thereafter developed an extensive distribution network throughout the country. After World War II and the independence of India in 1947, the Indian Government took steps to induce a more rapid rate of economic development than had occurred in the past. This tendency had also its influence on the activity of the importing and engineering divisions of Volkart. Because of government policy it appeared necessary not only to expand the whole distribution organization but also to start local manufacturing requiring substantial additional capital and additional technical personnel that in the past had been recruited in and sent out from Europe. It also became necessary to offer Indian nationals more scope and to employ a greater number of Indian personnel in the executive posts as well. Volkart felt that such an expansion and change in the structure of the company could only be achieved by bringing in Indian capital as well as Indian managerial talents.

As early as 1950, Volkart started discussing plans for "Indianization" with the Indian Government. In 1953, Tata Sons and Volkart agreed to a mutual approach and started negotiations for the formation of a joint venture.

Tata Sons Ltd. Tata is India's largest industrial enterprise. It accounts for something like 10 percent of the total Indian investment in organized industry. Its share in the value of industrial production is about 6 percent. It manufactures a great variety of products: steel; steel tubes; locomotives; commercial vehicles; chemicals; soda ash;

cosmetics; perfumes; textiles; consumer products; etc. According to an Indian economist who has studied the formation and methods of business empires in the country, Tata has a reputation for "clean and honest" practices. It shows a constant willingness to consider the important national purposes and aims.

Voltas Ltd. The negotiations between Volkart and Tata were successful. In 1954 Voltas was founded, absorbing Volkart's engineering and marketing departments. Both partners were attracted by the resources and the reputation of the other. Apart from the common objective of expansion there was not very much of a preconceived plan at the outset, but the partners were bound by a feeling of mutual trust. The Swiss company feels that the choice of local partner in a foreign venture is very important, even more so than the degree to which this partner is to participate in the equity capital.

Volkart of India. The Swiss company continued its own separate activities as before, especially dealing in cotton, coffee, coconut fibres, and other produce. In 1961, Volkart of India merged its cotton business with the Indian concern Patel Cotton Company Limited, and the coffee business was merged in 1966 with the Indian Company Consolidated Coffee Limited. In 1968, the remaining business of produce export and shipping agencies, so far carried on under the name of "Volkart (India) Ltd.," was also merged with Patel-Volkart. The merged company Patel-Volkart Limited is very close to a 50-50 joint venture. The main purpose of the partners was to combine financial and managerial resources.

It can be seen, therefore, that in addition to its participation and role in Voltas, Volkart Brothers maintains substantial separate activities in India.

Financing

The financial problems of Voltas are especially delicate. First, distribution costs can be very high. Moreover, trading involves a good deal of administrative work, which considerably increases the costs. Furthermore, the company very often takes over from its principals the burden of financing involved in marketing operations that begin right after a product is manufactured. Finally, the development of Voltas' own manufacturing operations involved in recent years the investment of considerable funds.

Equity Capital. The composition of the equity capital has changed substantially since 1954:

1954—Volkart: 45 percent, Tata: 55 percent.
1965—Volkart: 12 percent, Tata: 18 percent, Life Insurance Corporation and Unit Trust of India: 22 percent, Public: 48 percent.
1968—Volkart: 10 percent, Tata: 18 percent, Life Insurance Corporation and Unit Trust of India: 25 percent, Public: 47 percent.

Voltas has an authorized capital of Rs. (rupees) 50 million (approximately $6.6 million).[1] In 1968 it had an issued, subscribed, and paid up capital of Rs. 43.3 million (approximately $5.7 million). As of August 31, 1968, reserves and surplus stood at Rs. 34.0 million (approximately $4.5 million). Over 9,200 shareholders were registered.

Decrease of Volkart's Participation. During the 1950's and 1960's Vokart has followed a definite financial policy in connection with Voltas: if funds were available in India for reinvestment, the Swiss company had no objection to their being thus used; but if new capital was needed, no general prediction could be made about the extent of its participation. As Volkart was interested in decreasing its equity participation, it sold a proportion of its shares and failed to subscribe to some new capital increases.

This decrease was not the result of any political pressure, but rather of an internal decision on the part of Volkart. Volkart's attitude in India was essentially part of an overall company policy, which was based on an evaluation of the situation in Asia generally, and in India more specifically: Volkart decided not to invest and not to expand operations in Asian countries. According to the company, at that time such a policy was reasonable, because no one could foresee how these countries would develop. Large sums would have been required in order to pursue competitive operations in the East. Volkart's activities in the Western Hemisphere were, moreover, flourishing precisely at that time.

This did not mean that Volkart was willing to give up the Indian market. The Swiss company showed a sustained interest in the activities of Volkart of India. At present it takes an active interest in the new concern Patel-Volkart, the activities of which are more closely related to other activities of Volkart. Volkart still has a 10 percent

1. One US dollar = 7½ rupees.

participation in Voltas, receives dividends from it, and also receives commissions for its buying agent function in Europe.

Broadening of Ownership. Together with Volkart's, Tata's participation has also decreased, although it always remained larger than the share of the Swiss company. Voltas' management aimed to comply with government policy, which favors a broad ownership of industrial securities. The government is very concerned with the development of a broad and active capital market. Consequently the Life Insurance Corporation (now the only life insurance organization in India), the Unit Trust of India (a financial institution set up in 1964), and the general public at present hold about 70 percent of Voltas' shares. In 1965 the general public held almost an absolute majority of the shares. In relative terms the share held by the public has since slightly declined and that held by the financial institutions has slightly increased. The Indian capital market was rather depressed in the years 1966–1968 and financial institutions had to take a more active role in the market.

Loan Capital. Because of these depressed capital market conditions, it has not been easy in recent years to find large amounts of local money in India. Voltas issued debentures, but relied also very much on reinvestment of earnings.

Through the years Voltas obtained several foreign loans from Swiss, U.S., and Indian banks. In recent years foreign exchange loans were granted to the company by the Industrial Credit and Investment Corporation of India Ltd., Continental Bank International, U.S.A., and the Commonwealth Development Finance Company Ltd., U.K. The outstanding aggregate balance on these loan accounts stood at Rs. 13.24 million (or $1.77 million) as on August 31, 1968:

ICICI	Rs.	5.75	million
CBI	Rs.	4.56	million
CDFC	Rs.	2.93	million
Total	Rs.	13.24	million

Management

Directors and Managers. Both on the Board of Directors and in day-to-day management the number of Swiss employed by Voltas has gradually decreased. From the start, Volkart expected Tata to contribute executive personnel. A substantial number of Indians, however, were trained in Volkart prior to the formation of Voltas, and many of them are still employed by Voltas today. This is true especially for the managerial posts that are immediately below the key positions.

There are no longer any Swiss employed in Voltas. B. Reinhart, one of the brothers heading Volkart of Switzerland, is on the Board of Voltas, but rarely attends board meetings. Nevertheless, Mr. Reinhart takes a personal interest in Voltas and is fully informed on the policy and progress of the company.

Voltas has a succession problem: several executive officers have left because they had reached retirement age; others will leave in the next few years for the same reason. New candidates will have to be found for senior executive posts. Promotion has generally been from within the firm. As Tata's influence is now predominant, it is reasonable to assume that most of these jobs will be filled by employees from Tata companies.

Voltas' personnel does not really go to Volkart of Switzerland for training as such, but managers and employees of the sales and engineering divisions do go to visit principals and manufacturers of the products distributed by Voltas. They do so not only to improve their technical knowledge, but also to gain some experience of European countries, people, ways of thinking, etc. Volkart often acts as an intermediary between the visitors and the manufacturers.

Development of an Independent Management. The participation of the Life Insurance Corporation (LIC), a governmental agency, in the management of Voltas, would seem a convenient way for the government to influence policy. In fact LIC does not try to influence the management. As a rule, LIC is a mere passive investor: it does not even attend the annual general meetings and does not appoint directors. When it wishes to intervene, it does so privately. The company is very satisfied with LIC's presence as shareholder, because Voltas' prestige is thereby handsomely reinforced.

The role of the general public in management is even more limited.

Because of this the management system, goals, and methods had to be established by the two main partners, Volkart and Tata. As has already been shown, they followed no preconceived plan. Their common aim was the growth of the enterprise. They were aware that certain specific sectors were extremely promising: for instance, Volkart of India was a pioneer in air conditioning, and the partners decided to exploit fully the potentials of this new field. By and large, however, the management policy had still to be elaborated. In this respect both partners agree today that the respective participations held in the capital and the alterations in the percentages of participation were not unimportant, but did not have a decisive influence on management.

In the beginning, Volkart insisted on the importance of installing a professional management, which would think essentially in terms of Voltas. For some years there was a juxtaposition of Tata and Volkart employees: it was their task to create an effective team and in time they did succeed in establishing the professional and independent management Volkart had envisaged. A Voltas executive said that even today, Voltas has a significant degree of autonomy, and that the managers enjoy a substantial delegation of powers. The Tata representatives on the board do not put pressure on the other members by forcing them to implement Tata's views.

Even in the beginning, however, the power and influence of Tata were always present in the background. A Tata officer explained that Volkart had agreed that the Indian concern would decide on the main policy issues. In addition, the gradual replacement of Swiss by Indians, and of Volkart employees by those from Tata, played a decisive role. R.F.S. Talyarkhan is not only Chairman of the Board and Chief Executive of Voltas, but also a director of Tata Industries. Tata first waited to see how the venture would develop. When its success was apparent, the large Indian concern displayed an increasingly active interest in it.

Now Voltas has grown almost independent of Volkart. It has developed, under the umbrella of Tata, at a very rapid rate. This is understandable, because Tata is an influential enterprise, and because, for the reasons already mentioned, Volkart decided not to invest substantial amounts of money in the company. A Volkart officer said that the increased influence of Tata could have been forecast as early as 1954; in his view, the results should be favorable, because Voltas will benefit fully from Tata's great managerial, financial, and technical resources. But he noted also that the company might be in danger of losing its original identity.

Financial Policy. The partners stipulated in the basic agreement that the company has to follow a policy of expansion and growth, and therefore also of reinvestment of earnings. In the several capital increases, the new shares were stock dividends.

Activities and Sales

Organization. Voltas has its head office in Bombay, and branches in Calcutta, Delhi, Madras, Bangalore, and Lucknow. In addition there are regional offices, sales and service depots, and dealers all over the country. During the year 1967–1968, 81 percent of the goods sold by the company were manufactured in India, and 19 percent were imported. While the percentage of the goods imported is decreasing, the absolute level of such imports is increasing.

Voltas has two sectors of activity: distribution and manufacturing. The distribution sector has nine engineering divisions and two marketing divisions. Voltas is still primarily a distribution and service organization, but the manufacturing activities are growing rapidly.

As sales increase, the foreign corporations using the services of trading organizations are often concerned to have their own system of distribution. Also there is a general tendency in the business world today to eliminate the "middle man." In a country as large as India, however, it is extremely difficult to dispense with the services of a distributor, at any rate during the initial period. Besides, when companies create their own system of distribution, newcomers often in turn use for some time the services of a trading organization. Some small manufacturers never succeed in dispensing with an intermediary, particularly if they are interested in selling on a country-wide basis. It remains true, however, that this trend against intermediaries is likely to increase in the future. Distributors will have to prove that they are still useful. It will no longer be sufficient to give special care to after sales service, as Voltas traditionally has done. Existing distribution methods will have to be improved and new distribution methods will have to be found.

In India, which has a mixed economy, a trading organization has to take into account the fact that the government is an important potential buyer. Nevertheless, transactions with the government can be long and complex. Moreover, in 1967 and 1968 the government delayed the implementation of some public projects, and the direct impact of these decisions on Voltas' activities will be shown below. The company is convinced that government business should not be neglected. It would be dangerous, however, to rely too much on this market, and a diversification of outlets should be sought.

Engineering. Traditionally, Voltas emphasized engineering, and it still represents approximately two thirds of the company's total sales. However, the relative importance of this sector has declined as the distribution costs of some products were too high for them to remain a good business proposition. Because of this Voltas is seeking to concentrate on the more profitable items. Profitability, however, should be assessed in a long-term perspective: there are some lines in heavy engineering, like electrical products, where the results may be profitable only after a few years of marketing have passed.

Voltas also engaged in construction projects, or "turn-key contracts." This part of the company's activities, however, suffered from several drawbacks. It is difficult to find the right type of men to conduct these activities. There is also a legal problem: in turn-key contracts the interest of Voltas is to buy in the cheapest market. It is questionable whether the company is infringing its agreement with a manufacturer for whom it is distributor if it buys elsewhere.

The creation of the project engineering division was intended to give a new impetus to this type of activity. The division tackles a variety of construction projects, such as aerial ropeways, electrostatic precipitators, chemical plants, industrial furnaces, and food processing plants.

Marketing. At the moment marketing activities represent approximately a third of Voltas' sales. Recently the emphasis has shifted from engineering to distribution of consumer products, and the proportion is increasing. This sector has a chemicals division and a pharmaceuticals and consumer products division. The products distributed by these divisions are: fine, heavy, and industrial chemicals; bulk vitamins; processed foods; and pharmaceuticals. These products are made in India and abroad. The pharmaceutical sector is promising because, although costs can be high, there is a large volume of sales and the profits are substantial.

Since the Indian Government has shifted its efforts from heavy industry to agriculture, fertilizers have become a very promising field. Consequently Voltas decided to enter the field of imported fertilizers and has associated with one of the world's largest manufacturers of fertilizers in the U.S.A. More generally, the management feels that the new government emphasis on agriculture as well as the increase in farmers' income call for a complete reorientation of the company's marketing strategy.

Manufacturing. As early as 1954 Volkart operated a small unit for manufacturing air conditioners, and this activity was taken over by Voltas. Manufacturing operations have increased considerably since. During the year 1967–1968 they accounted for Rs. 73.5 million (almost $10 million).

The manufacturing works are located in a 120-acre site at Thana, near Bombay. The products manufactured in the factory are: air-conditioning and refrigeration equipment, room air conditioners, water coolers, electrical overhead travelling cranes, hoists, fork-lift trucks, core drilling equipment, and diamond drill bits. On the same site Voltas has engaged in a joint venture with Scottish Machine Tool (Overseas) Ltd. for the manufacture of machine tools, and in another joint venture with Merlin and Gerin of France, for the manufacture of switchgear and allied electrical equipment.

As has already been mentioned, India is a mixed economy and the government is an important potential buyer. In 1967, however, Voltas' manufacturing operations suffered directly from the delaying of certain governmental projects. Substantial quantities of mining drills, for example, were not collected according to contract and now remain idle on the premises, though attempts are being made to convert them for other purposes.

Voltas is directing its efforts, therefore, to fields that are not only profitable but also have a diversity of buyers. In this respect, air conditioning, where Volkart was a pioneer, is one of the most attractive fields, but Voltas cannot rely only on the items that it has been manufacturing hitherto. Perhaps the two most promising markets in India today are agriculture and electronics (in the broad sense of the term). The possibility of entering the field of electronics is at present the object of study.

As to the attractions of agriculture, the management had already made up its mind. An agro-industrial products division was created. The hard core of this division's operations is the sale and servicing of the tractors and implements made by the International Tractor Company of India Limited, a joint venture supported by International Harvester Company (U.S.A.), Mahindra and Mahindra (an Indian concern), and Voltas, which acts as sole distributor for the products made by the joint venture. This is certainly a field that will benefit from strong governmental encouragement. This is also a field where the demand is constantly increasing and where there is a great diversity of buyers. Nevertheless, Voltas might have to adopt new distribution methods: the purchase of a tractor, for example, is often too expensive for one farmer to contemplate alone; it is therefore desirable for farmers to have the possibility of leasing tractors or other agricultural equipment, rather than buying them.

Government Relations

Foreign Exchange and Devaluation. The economic situation of the country and the devaluation of 1966 undoubtedly affected directly Voltas' operations. The tone of the Annual Report for the year 1965–1966 leaves no room for doubt in this respect:

> The country suffered a major devaluation of the currency for the second time in its post-independence period. . . . The economic situation of India makes it virtually impossible for Voltas to plan and forecast its sales for even short periods ahead. . . . The Company had the usual, and in some cases inordinate, delays in respect of raw materials and sub-contracted items. . . .
>
> The impact of devaluation on the Company's working—apart from what has been mentioned in the Directors' Report—will be felt in our manufacturing costs, which have risen on account of higher depreciation and interest charges, and also because of enhanced rupee prices for imported and locally-bought raw materials and components. . . .

Voltas also suffered from the shortage of foreign exchange. The company is privileged in comparison with other corporations, however, in that its main foreign exchange needs relate to manufacturing activities, which still constitute only a minor proportion of its total concerns; but this proportion is expected to increase sharply in the future.

Taxation. At the beginning of its establishment in the country, Volkart of India was a general partnership. As the tax imposed on this kind of business organization is on a progressive basis, the fiscal burden on Volkart was very heavy. It was therefore decided to change the nature of the business organization and to adopt the corporate form. This change alleviated Volkart's fiscal burden, because a company in India is subject to a corporate tax on profits which is not progressive, but proportionate.

Voltas has been organized as a company since its inception. It pays a corporate tax amounting to between 53 and 60 percent of its profits.

Export Sales. Because of Indian foreign exchange requirements there is a strong government drive to encourage exports. Since Tata has always been very anxious to comply with national objectives, Voltas makes every attempt to assist this drive. In particular, a new division—International Operations—was set up in 1968.

Ideally the company would like to export the products it manufactures and also the products of principals who are represented by it: but whatever is manufactured or distributed by Voltas is under license. As the licensors have their own multinational network, they wish to ensure that the products exported by Voltas do not compete with their own products manufactured or distributed in other countries. Consequently, the agreements concluded between Voltas and the licensors were originally very restrictive on the company's exports. Generally speaking, the licensors have now come to realize that the Indian Government is quite strict in this matter. Therefore, they have become more flexible, provided they are given some kind of compensation. Voltas is gradually developing its export trade, but only in a quite selective manner since some foreign collaborators are more difficult to deal with than others. All this involves extensive bargaining and discussion.

There is yet another way in which exports can be developed: Voltas, as has been mentioned previously, undertakes turn-key projects abroad and also exports engineering skills. The Indian Government favors this manner of joint venturing abroad, as it does not involve the outflow on a permanent basis of large amounts of money. On the contrary, construction fees, wages and salaries, and royalties could in the long run contribute significantly to the Indian balance of payments. This aspect of Voltas' activities is still limited, but it does seem to have a promising future, especially in developing countries. At present Voltas is devoting its efforts to Asian countries, especially those in Eastern and Western Asia. The company's management is also examining various proposals for joint ventures in certain countries.

Finally, the bilateral trade agreements between India and some Eastern European markets could provide useful outlets for products distributed or manufactured by Voltas.

The Government and Voltas. Even when there was a truly joint management between Tata and Volkart, the Swiss company was in a minority position. It is questionable whether the fact that foreign interests were in such a minority position assisted the company in obtaining the necessary governmental permits. A Voltas officer said that in general terms, the extent of foreign participation does not make any difference in this respect; the government relies, he added, more on the reputation of the company and its contribution to the country's economic development. A Vokart officer said that the government has now become more flexible about the extent of foreign participation; basically it favors a widely-distributed ownership of shares, and this is the case with Voltas.

A high-level government official confirmed these views, saying that Voltas is considered a first-class company. He saw proof of this in the fact that Voltas is one of the few companies on which, on the stock exchange, investors can speculate in advance: this is called "forward trading". Also, the government regards Voltas very much as an Indian company and as a Tata company. Since it is an Indian company, it may engage in any activity, except in the public sector. At a time when the general emphasis in India is on manufacturing, it may develop its distribution activities if it so wishes.

The case of Voltas shows that the degree of participation held by the foreign partner is not necessarily considered by the government to be of paramount importance. Other elements, such as a broad distribution of ownership, the reputation of the company, the contribution to the country in economic terms, are also viewed as essential. The government endeavors to make a total assessment of a company and bases its judgement on this appraisal.

Voltas in New Joint Ventures

Voltas, itself a joint venture, has also sponsored other joint ventures. The company acted in several occasions as a promoter and an intermediary between a foreign and a local collaborator. Its main role lies at the very start, in bringing partners together.

Voltas contributes its name and its knowledge of India. As it knows the country, the market, and a large number of products, it is in an adequate position to make project reports and marketing analyses. It can also help to obtain the necessary governmental approvals and permits. Usually it takes only a small equity participation in these concerns, because it is interested not so much in dividends as in acquiring distribution rights.

The Lakshmi-Rieter venture is a typical example. Rieter Machine Works Limited is a Swiss company, for which Voltas was distributor. Complications arose over importation, so that it became necessary to manufacture the machinery in India. Voltas succeeded in finding a local partner for Rieter. After long negotiations a new company was formed: Lakshmi Machine Works Limited, which manufactures the complete range of "Lakshmi-Rieter" cotton-spinning machinery. Voltas and Rieter each hold an equity participation, but the Indian Lakshmi concern has the majority. The new company has benefited from Voltas' reputation and experience, while Voltas has acquired the distribution rights for the machinery.

This aspect of Voltas' activities is worth attention, because it is rather rare in a developing country for a joint venture to become the promoter of other joint ventures. Though not all are thriving, these collaborations have on the whole been satisfactory. It is difficult to foresee what significance this experiment may have in the future. The government grants only a few licenses for each industrial field, and in some fields there are no more licenses available, so that Voltas sees some limits to the experiment.

Prospects

Voltas is India's largest and most versatile distributor. Financial results show that while the sales have been increasing rapidly, the margin of profits has declined in recent years. To a certain extent, the general state of the economy, devaluation, and the increases in costs are responsible for this decrease in the profit margin. It is obvious, however, that the company has experienced a kind of "inflationary growth," that it is now at a turning point, and that it has to face several important and difficult alternatives.

Trading vs. Manufacturing. Traditionally trading has been a very important industry in India. In recent years, however, the utility of intermediaries has been questioned. Also, the government has directed its efforts to the encouragement of manufacturing industry. Therefore, the question is whether Voltas should remain primarily a trading organization or stake its future on manufacturing.

With some nuances, Volkart, Tata, and Voltas officers seem to agree that the emphasis on trading should be maintained. A Volkart officer was convinced that Voltas should remain a trading company as before: trade is the traditional business of Voltas, the field they really know. Manufacturing, he said, should mainly support distribution. Voltas should achieve a kind of vertical integration: the firm could engage in the manufacture of products related to other products that were already manufactured or distributed by the company. A Tata officer agreed with him that Voltas should remain primarily a trading organization. In his view, although the manufacturing divisions should grow, it should not be at the cost of the distribution divisions.

Diversification vs. Selectivity. Voltas is active in many fields and deals with a considerable variety of products. The decline in the general profit margin now compels the company, however, to question the wisdom of thus continuing to diversify. Some feel that, on the contrary, a strict policy of selectivity should be adopted, and that the company should eliminate more of the less profitable lines.

The answers to this question were not really inconsistent, but the emphasis varied from one person to another. A Tata officer maintained that diversification, both regarding distribution and manufacture, were necessary; he recognized, however, that there should also be a degree of selectivity. In the Annual Report of 1966–1967 the main advantage of diversification was clearly underlined: the profits in one field compensate for the losses in another field, and the same is true with regard to products. A Voltas officer, on the other hand, stressed the importance of selectivity: the company, he said, ought to concentrate only on the more profitable items and should drop other lines: this has already occurred in some cases, and the employees and workers were being retrained for other activities. A Volkart officer stated that selectivity and expansion should both be encouraged, but that diversification was not at the moment of prime importance. A new product, he added, should always be chosen to be complementary to its existing line of products and with due regard for its success and acceptance on the local Indian market of tomorrow. He concluded that if these conditions were fulfilled, most of the problems would be solved, because Voltas has the capacity to sell almost anything. On the whole therefore, although the need for some selectivity is recognized, the continuance of a substantial diversification seems likely, because Tata, which operates the enterprise, has the expansionist views of a very large concern.

Related to this problem is the question of business organization. It is questionable whether the present structure, with all divisions combined in one organization, is still adequate to the efficient management of such diversified operations. It is also debatable whether, within this framework, each division is really able to develop sufficient autonomy and is not in fact hampered in its operations by the top-heavy organizational structure. Perhaps subsidiary companies should be created, which would then be responsible to a holding company; but this would raise difficult tax problems.

Use of an Automatic Data Processing System. As trade is to a large extent an administrative affair, Voltas has a correspondingly large number of administrative personnel. Consequently, salaries represent an important and ever-growing proportion of operating costs. It seems that Voltas has reached the limits of what can be achieved in distribution (especially of chemicals and pharmaceuticals) by mere clerical work. The introduction of an electronic data processing system is now indispensable.

Such a system will not only increase the efficiency and diminish the costs of the distribution system. It will also be an invaluable tool in the hands of Voltas' management, with regard to studies, forecasts, planning, projecting, problems of factory production, etc. More generally, the system will allow for more modern, precise, and efficient methods of management.

Nevertheless, use of computers to automate the company's administrative work meets with great resistance on the part of the employees and of the unions. Moreover, the government is concerned about India's serious labor problems and is aiming to have as many people employed as possible. No cut in Voltas' labor force will be made without consultation with the government. Perhaps the solution may lie in retraining those who were employed in distribution for other activities. Voltas' management is making every attempt to find an answer to this grave social problem, because it refuses to revoke its basic decision to adopt automation. For the time being, Voltas is using the Tata computer, but it is conceivable that in the future it might acquire its own machine.

Evaluation. Voltas is not a wholly-owned subsidiary of Tata, but the Indian concern has, over the years, substantially increased its influence over the company. The management has, for example, become a Tata management to a large extent. This change in the balance of influence of the joint venture was not so much the result of basic differences in business philosophy as of developments in economic policy. While Volkart decided to observe a relatively cautious attitude in relation to Asian countries, Tata was induced by the profit opportunities to take an increasingly active part in the thriving concern. While in some cases of joint ventures the foreign partner gradually takes over the concern and eliminates the local partner, Voltas illustrates the opposite development. Although the evolution will not be a rapid one, we shall probably witness more and more cases in the future where the local partner gradually increases his influence or even takes over.

It has been recognized that Voltas will derive great advantages from being a Tata concern. Tata has its own traditions and is a strong and dynamic firm, esteemed in India and abroad for its honesty and integrity. It is perhaps regrettable, however, that Voltas seems bound to lose its original independence. It might possibly suffer from becoming only one component of a centralized organization; yet this is only a hypothetical risk, whereas the advantages of combining with Tata are certain.

Although the role of Volkart in Voltas has decreased, it has not become unimportant. Volkart has contributed to Voltas its traditions, methods, and managers. The influence of this contribution will be felt for a long time. Moreover, the Swiss company still holds a minority participation in the capital and acts as a buying agent for Voltas.

The problems faced by Voltas are not inconsiderable. While some of these difficulties are dependent on the general state of the Indian economy, others are growth problems. Finally, the most serious problem of all might be the succession in management: as has been mentioned earlier, several highly-placed managers and directors are reaching retirement age. Voltas is at a turning point. It seems, therefore, essential and urgent to find first-class executives who will be able to conduct the company successfully through the years ahead.

Ventures between Multinational Corporation,
Local Companies and Investors,
and a Labor Union

IX: FACTORY MACHINERY
IN WORLD MARKETS

General Outline of Fives Lille-Cail

THE ¨COMPANY

Background. The company of Fives Lille-Cail (FLC) was the result of the merger in 1959 of the Fives Lille Company, already 100
years old, and the Cail Company, which dates from the beginning
of the 19th century. It developed further by taking over the Apple-
vage Company in 1963, and the firm of Maison-Bréquet in 1966. In
1968, FLC split up into a holding company, the Compagnie industrielle et financière Fives Lille-Cail, with a capital of 66 million francs,
and an FLC working company, with a capital of 70 million francs.[1]

In February 1970, FLC entered into a merger with La Société
Française des Constructions Babcock & Wilcox, a subsidiary of the
British firm of the same name. Under this arrangement two shares of
Babcock & Wilcox will be exchanged for five new shares of FLC.
The new company is named Compagnie Industrielle et Financière
Babcock-Fives. The merger was negotiated with the active support of
the Banque de Paris & des Pays-Bas, which is a shareholder both in
FLC and in Babcock & Wilcox. The new group, which comprises ten
factories and about 11,000 employees, will be the largest French en-
terprise in the field of heavy engineering equipment, with annual
sales of about 1.5 billion of French francs.

Main Activities. FLC produces the heavy equipment required for
most industries. It specializes in the designing and equipping of

1. The franc has a par value of $0.18004.

whole factories: sugar factories, cement factories, ironworks, complete handling plants for the iron and steel industry, and power plants. Among other things it supplies equipment for hoisting, and for the treatment of ores, compressors, and boilers.

Sales. FLC employs 5,000 people and has five factories—three in northern France around Lille, one in the Paris region, and one at Givors, near Lyon. Sales vary between 300 and 600 million francs ($60 = 120 million). After 20 to 25 million francs have been set aside for amortization, the net profit varies between 5 and 8 million francs.

Foreign Operations. The percentage of exports in FLC's sales is one of the highest in France: an average of 50 percent. Although operations have been established mainly in the developing countries, which receive about three-quarters of the exports, they have also been set up with the Common Market countries and Eastern Europe. Factories have been installed in Mexico, Brazil, Ecuador, Venezuela, Thailand, India, Pakistan, Morocco, Algeria, Tunisia, Congo, Cameroon, Egypt, Israel, Iran, Iraq, U.S.S.R., and Rumania.

POLICY TOWARD JOINT VENTURES

Incentives. FLC is not a financial group seeking, above all, to extract revenue from its joint undertakings; neither is it a company that gives priority to developing its products outside France. It is first and foremost a producer and exporter of equipment and it is interested only in production of goods. Its present policy is to develop sales. Its joint enterprises are the result of a sales promotion policy and not of a move toward establishment of foreign operations. FLC is therefore often led to establish joint enterprises with its clients, either at the client's request or in order to obtain a contract to sell equipment.

Methods. FLC has three types of foreign joint venture:

(a) Ventures to provide technical and commercial services, i.e., companies that examine and sell installations. These companies benefit from the technical expertise of FLC. In theory FLC has control of these companies, provided the local regulations allow it. The variety of arrangements that are used may be illustrated by several ventures that act as FLC's agent in foreign countries. FLC do Brazil is a wholly-owned subsidiary staffed by Brazilians. FLC Iberia is a 50-50 joint venture with Spanish interests. And Sedic, which represents FLC in Belgium, is 60 percent owned by Belgian financial institutions and 40 percent by FLC; the firm is staffed by Belgians.

(b) Ventures with a client as a condition of sale. A client wishing to order a complete factory requests or imposes as a condition the participation of FLC as the supplier of the machinery and engineering skills. By this association the client obtains additional financial resources and technical guarantees, and FLC plays an active part in seeing that factory functions satisfactorily. FLC provides considerable technical assistance, and often helps the local company to draw up its budgets. As a general rule, FLC's participation amounts to about 5 percent to 25 percent. Portland de Mallorca, in Spain, and Azucarera Tropical Americana S.A., in Ecuador, come into this category of joint venture.

(c) Ventures to establish local engineering and manufacturing companies that, in view of government policies in some semi-industrialized countries, is a condition of continued export to these countries. In fact these countries wish to develop their industries starting with the least complex materials and therefore restrict the importing of these materials. It is therefore in the interest of FLC to have its equipment produced on the spot, using its own know-how, in order to keep open or encourage a market that has already indicated its potential. FLC hopes to maintain its sales either by a number of signed contracts, e.g., the case of Fives Lille Industrial do Nordeste S.A. (FLIN), or by possible future contracts, e.g., the venture with Krishna Corporation Private Ltd., which failed.

FLC's participation may reach or even exceed 50 percent of the capital and it plays a decisive part in controlling operations. The Koch Company in the Saar may also be placed in this category. It is an association with local interests for the manufacture of goods complementary to those of FLC. In this association, each partner controls 50 percent of the shares.

The main joint ventures in the developing countries are: a sugar factory in Madagascar (set up during the 1950's); four cement factories in Turkey (1954–1956); a cement factory in Niger (1962); a cement factory in Majorca (Portland de Mallorca—1962); a cement factory in Spain (1965); a sugar factory in Ecuador (Aztra—1966). These joint enterprises are of the "client-investment" type. FLIN (1967) and the KFC project (1964), on the other hand, are of the type of company that manufactures locally.

The four joint ventures selected, KFC, Portland de Mallorca, Aztra, and FLIN, are the most representative. Aztra and Portland de Mallorca have involved large-scale investments. The abandoned venture with Krishna Corporation Private, Ltd. and FLIN reflect a deliberate policy of establishment in a market that otherwise would have remained closed.

Krishna Corporation Private Ltd. and Fives Lille-Cail Private Limited

THE ECONOMIC-POLITICAL CONTEXT

The Policy of the Government of India. Since 1956, the Government of India has vigorously encouraged local industry to take out manufacturing licenses while at the same time imposing strict limits on the currency available to them for imports. In practice, the only European firms that have been authorized to keep up their imports are those that have granted manufacturing licenses to local firms. These imports have been diminishing gradually, as the Indians have found it possible to manufacture the aforesaid equipment themselves. In August 1957 this was the situation facing the Cail Company—which later merged with Fives Lille to form FLC—and consequently they signed a licensing agreement with Krishna Corporation Private Ltd. (KCP), which at that time was the fourth most important industrial group in India, with its headquarters in Madras. When the merger took place, Cail's contracts were assumed by the new company, and later agreements were signed to make these contracts complete and binding on all parties. Because of these agreements, FLC was able to import its equipment into India, to the tune of approximately 300,000 metric tons per annum.

The third five-year plan in India, beginning in 1961, aimed at developing plants producing machinery for heavy industry. The Indian Government placed orders for the new plants with Indian suppliers, who held licenses for building such plants. The authorized imports were greatly cut down and only available to foreign companies with a stake in Indian companies.

American policy toward aid to developing countries. In 1961 changes in United States foreign aid policy reflected concern for problems with its balance of payments. American aid allocated to developing countries was, in general, tied to purchases from the United States or from other developing countries. India was considered a developing country, and was therefore able to offer material produced in India to other developing countries receiving American aid.

THE NEGOTIATIONS

Both Indian policy, which was very restrictive toward imports and very favorable to foreign investment, and American policy on aid to developing countries combined to make the prospect of forming a joint venture in India particularly interesting for FLC. And so, with this project in mind, contacts were made in India in 1961 with KCP in Madras, with which the FLC had had links for many years.

This Indian company, whose only means of offering complete factories, especially cement factories, was through an association with FLC, studied this offer, which was particularly advantageous to it. An initial project aimed at forming a joint venture associating KCP with FLC and with a French paper manufacturing group, in order to manufacture and sell material for cement and paper making factories, turbines, and boilers. The capital, 10 million rupees, was to be subscribed as follows: 25.5 percent by KCP, 25.5 percent for the two French groups, and the remaining 49 percent to be placed with the Indian public.

This first project had to be abandoned after the withdrawal of the paper manufacturing group. It was replaced by a more limited project for association between KCP and FLC. The company thus to be formed was to take the licenses granted by FLC to KCP and to sell in India the imported material for cement manufacturing. The capital of this engineering company, shared equally between FLC and KCP, was to be very limited.

The Indian Government vetoed this project, stressing (a) that engineering companies do not have the right to sell material but only to carry out engineering work, as their profits—and therefore the transfer of money abroad—should not be disproportionate to the total invested capital from foreign sources; and (b) that the licenses ceded to an Indian company by a foreign company participating at a 50 percent share in an Indian company should not be subject to royalties.

In these circumstances the two partners returned to the formula of a manufacturing and construction company with a capital of 4 million rupees, of which KCP and FLC would each hold 50 percent. The additional capital required to make the planned investments was to be raised through a loan from the Madras Industrial Finance Corporation. On this understanding a protocol agreement was signed in 1963.

EVALUATION

In fact, this project was never carried out. FLC attributes the failure to reach agreement to the slowness of the Indian administrative procedure and the hesitation of the Indian partner, who seemed to continue to consider the possibility of a solution that would not involve the proposed association.

It is obviously impossible to make any judgment on a joint venture that never took place. However, the reasons for which FLC was led to consider its formation should be stressed—it was the most effective way in which this company could strengthen its position on the Indian market. Subsequent developments confirmed this view, since, apart from the continuation of licensing agreements, the contracts concluded after 1965 have up to now only concerned the supplying of material and not of complete installations.

The desire to maintain a position in a closing market is behind the creation of the FLIN, the joint venture in Brazil, in which the FLC participates.

Fives Lille Industrial do Nordeste S.A. (FLIN)

THE ECONOMIC-POLITICAL CONTEXT

The Policy of the Brazilian Government. In Brazil there are two trends concerning foreign capital. The liberal point of view is that, as internal savings are weak, foreign contributions constitute the major source of investment. The "socialist-nationalist" point of view is that foreign investments are the main instrument for foreign exploitation of the country.

The policy of the Brazilian Government toward foreign investments demonstrates uncertainty. The Superintendência da Modea e do Credito (Sumoc), in its instructions of January 1955, renewed in January 1965, wished to facilitate short-term entry of foreign equipment companies. The foreign capital law 4.14(1) of September 1965 limited to 10 percent per annum the delivery of dividends by foreign companies; this law has now been neglected. But these fluctuations are not favorable to the placing of foreign investments.

Neither are the statutes concerning subsidiaries of foreign companies very favorable to the foreign investor. Into this category falls any company of which at least 50 percent of the shares giving right of vote belong, directly or indirectly, to a foreign enterprise. As regards the fiscal authorities, the transfer of funds from the branch to the parent company is not authorized. Tax on the dividends deducted at source is 25 percent if the dividends are to go to foreign persons, 15 percent if they go to persons whose residence or company headquarters is in Brazil. A tax of 30 percent is also levied on incomes sent abroad. Finally, national companies are granted easy loan conditions by the specialized agencies, which the branches of foreign companies do not enjoy.

The Northeast of Brazil. The northeast of Brazil is a particularly underdeveloped region. On account of this the government has agreed to special conditions for companies that consent to establish there, and has formed a special body responsible for encouraging economic development in the region—the Superintendência do Desenvolvimento do Nordeste (Sudene). If this body approves the establishment of an industrial project, the beneficiary enjoys considerable exemptions from taxes and customs duty.

THE NEGOTIATIONS

In April 1967, the Banque de Paris et des Pays-Bas, on the initiative of FLC, signed a financial agreement with the Brazilian Institute for Sugar and Alcohol Production, for the exporting from France of 60 million francs worth of equipment. The Sudene insisted on the installation of a workshop for the construction of machinery and the maintenance and manufacture of material for the sugar industry.

Within the terms of this agreement, FLC undertook to build the workshop, and as the main beneficiaries of the agreement were in the state of Alagoas, the Factory Workers Union in this state proposed that the workshop should be built there.

The new joint venture was formed by FLC putting up the whole of the capital increase of the Industria Metalurgica Alagoana, which changed its name to become Fives Lille Industrial do Nordeste (FLIN). The initial capital of the company is to be divided as follows:

Factory Workers Union, Alagoas	98,000 cruzeiros (49%)
FLC	102,000 cruzeiros (51%)

The new resources are to be used first to buy an area of land of 50 hectares upon which to build the workshop for which FLC will supply equipment and technical assistance.

The question arose as to which company would make the investment, the parent company or its Brazilian branch, Fives Lille do Brazil. On the understanding that changes might later be made to the structure of the Brazilian group, it was the branch company that, in spite of the original stakes, held the participation in the FLIN.

It must be noted that the elaboration of the project gave rise at times to violent opposition from competitors, who did not take kindly to the installation of FLC in Brazil. Once these difficulties had been overcome and the French authorities had given their permission, FLC paid over, in September, 1967, the 102,000 cruzeiros agreed on, and sent an engineer to Maceio, capital of Alagoas, to study the industrial project.

The Sudene approved the FLIN project and the agreement was signed in November 1967.

FINANCING AND MANAGEMENT

Financing. The final distribution of capital was to be as follows: (a) shares including right of vote: $1 million (FLC has 51%, and the Factory Workers Union 49%); (b) shares without right of vote: $1 million (Sudene fund); (c) loans at 8 percent from the Nordeste Bank: $2 million. In fact, the Bank's participation in the form of loans was replaced by the contribution from the Sudene of an equivalent sum in shares without right of vote. Apart from this slight change, the initial scheme (75% put up by Sudene without control of the management, the remaining 25% being divided between FLC and the Factory Workers Union) has been preserved.

Out of an authorized capital of 20,000,000 cruzeiros, 12,000,000 were subscribed and the distribution in August was as follows:

FLC	1,530,000
Factory Workers Union	1,470,000
Sudene	9,000,000

These figures were reached after five increases in capital in which FLC participated as set out above, through the local branch, Fives Lille do Brazil. It must be noted that for fiscal reasons the Brazilian partners would like to see the FLIN become listed on the stock exchange. Although FLC was reticent over the addition of new shareholders, it would not reject this development if the shares sold to the public belonged to the Brazilian group.

Management. At the General Assembly of Shareholders, FLC holds 51 percent of the votes and the Factory Workers Union 49 percent. On the Board of Directors FLC appoints the Vice-Chairman, the Sales Manager, and the Technical Manager. The Factory Workers Union appoints the Chairman and the Head Supervisor. Each year the Assembly elects a Fiscal Board of three members.

As FLC controls 51 percent of the capital, it was necessary to provide some form of protection for the Brazilian partners. At the

General Assembly, the most important decisions—modification of capital, by-laws, and loans involving mortgage guarantees—are made with a two-thirds majority. Decisions of the Board of Directors other than those concerning the usual running of the company are made with a majority of four out of five directors.

ACHIEVEMENTS

It is too early to develop this aspect. It is, however, possible to give a brief idea of the results of the joint venture during the two years of its existence.

Technical Assistance. This is industrial assistance rather than financial. Financial aid is, however, by no means negligible and is conducted through the Brazilian branch of FLC. Industrial assistance has consisted mainly in a study course for a Brazilian engineer in France and a visit to Ecuador by the representatives of the factory workers in Alagoas, who examined the Aztra sugar factory, another of FLC's joint ventures. Finally, FLC plans to send out to Maceio two French engineers and three foremen.

Management of the Company. On this point the agreement has not been entirely respected. Out of the three members of the Board of Directors that FLC is authorized to elect, FLC has only appointed two: the Vice-Chairman (a Director of Fives Lille do Brasil) and the Technical Director (a Frenchman who has worked twelve years in the FLC at Denain).

Results of Operations. At the end of November 1969 the technical offices were completed, the factory covered, and a third of the machines delivered. The factory will not be entirely completed until the end of 1970. But the canvassing for clients has already begun and is going well. Firm offers of 1 million new cruzeiros have already been made and orders worth 13 million new cruzeiros from 42 clients are being considered. When the factory is running at full capacity, it should have annual sales of approximately 12 million new cruzeiros.

From the orders received the beginnings of a new development can be seen—FLIN is ready to produce not only boilerworks material for the sugar industry, as was intended at the outset, but also other material, in particular light framework for factories.

EVALUATION

It is impossible to give a complete judgment on a joint venture set up so recently, but it can be noted that the partners seem satisfied with their association, which is functioning without major setbacks.

In general, relations between the company and the government, or rather its local representative, the Sudene, are highly satisfactory.

The joint venture also seems to correspond to the hopes of the partners. For the government, the installation of a workshop for the manufacture of machinery in this particularly underdeveloped region is a very positive step, as it is for the Factory Workers Union in Alagoas. For FLC, FLIN is the best way to obtain new orders in Brazil and to renew a policy of active presence in this country—a policy that had lain dormant for over twenty years.

Portland de Mallorca S.A.

THE ECONOMIC-POLITICAL CONTEXT

The Policy of the Spanish Government toward Foreign Investment. With regard to foreign investment, the Spanish Government is in an ambiguous position. Nevertheless, since the law of July 27, 1959, a certain number of principles have been laid down. The repatriation of profits is theoretically free, although reinvestment in Spain is strongly encouraged. Direct investments require the authorization of the Spanish Government, and in any case, if a joint venture is formed, 50 percent of the capital must remain in Spanish hands, unless the authorities have given express and exceptional permission.

The Cement Market in the Balearic Islands. Portland de Mallorca S.A. was set up in order to construct a cement factory near the town of Palma de Mallorca in the Balearics. There was in fact no doubt of there being a market for cement on the island of Mallorca, given the spread of tourism to the island, the planned development of the airport, and the need to build a dam. According to official statistics, cement consumption was as follows:

Year	Tons	Year	Tons
1954	28,500	1960	52,000
1957	40,600	1961	60,000
1959	48,500	1962	70,000

These figures do not take into account purchases on the parallel market, and are in fact 20 percent less than the actual consumption. Consumption has risen steeply in more recent years, exceeding 150,000 tons in 1965, and it is likely to exceed 350,000 tons in 1969.

There was no local cement factory to supply this market and it was necessary to import cement produced on the east coast of Spain. This in itself was not sufficient, and an Italian company imported cement from Tarenta where there was excess production. Mallorca is in fact on the route from Tarenta to the Catalan coast. The setting up of a cement factory in Mallorca therefore seemed an attractive proposition.

THE NEGOTIATIONS

After rejection of the initial project to construct a cement factory three kilometres from Palma, Portland de Mallorca decided to construct a cement factory at Lloseta on a piece of land in its possession, near the chalk and slate quarries. The company obtained the necessary authorizations and on June 7, 1962, the agreement of the General Assembly of Shareholders.

On June 13, 1962, FLC signed a contract with Portland whereby FLC would provide a factory worth 6 million francs of which it was to subcontract a little over half to Spanish industry. This order was bound by the signing of two special and separate contracts. On the one hand FLC agreed to undertake the engineering of the whole project and carry out work until the factory could be used, in return for a renumeration of 10 million pesetas payable in installments of 5 percent on the annual profit of the company. Moreover, FLC had to subscribe an increase in capital of 10 million pesetas. FLC obtained the necessary permission from the French authorities, in return for certain obligations.

FINANCING AND MANAGEMENT

Financing. At the General Assembly of Shareholders of Portland de Mallorca on June 7, 1962, it was decided to increase the capital from 29 million to 40 million pesetas in order to allow FLC to participate. Ten million pesetas were subscribed by FLC, and 1 million by the local Spanish group (mainly Mallorcan).

The capital of 40 million pesetas soon proved to be insufficient. It rose to 70 million at the end of 1964. The new distribution of shares was as follows: 15 million pesetas for an industrial group in Madrid; 10 million pesetas for the original Mallorcan group; 25 million pesetas for the new Mallorcan shareholders; 20 million pesetas for FLC and its Spanish associates (mainly the technical director of Portland appointed by FLC and its Spanish subsidiary, Fives Lille-Cail Española, which was later to become Fives Lille-Cail Iberica).

The beginning of 1966 showed a further increase in capital of 50 percent, which brought the total of 105 million pesetas to cover operations and for accounting purposes. FLC and the associate Spanish group held between them a total of 27 million pesetas (of which 15 million belong directly to FLC). The increase in capital decided in June, 1968 (from 105 to 157½ pesetas) was approved by FLC, which did not participate directly, but the associate Spanish group held 3½ million pesetas in new shares. FLC, directly or through its Spanish associates, therefore controlled about 20 percent of the capital stock at the end of 1968.

Management. At the General Assembly, before changes in 1969, FLC held a number of votes proportional to that of its shares. At the meeting of the Board of Directors, it held three seats, in spite of the variations in its capital participation. Two of these seats were held by the Chairman-Managing Director and the Sales Manager, the third by the representative of the associate Spanish group.

According to the law of July 17, 1951 on the legal system governing corporations, each shareholder or group of shareholders controlling more than 10 percent of the capital has standing to request that an extraordinary session of the General Assembly be held and, by taking legal action, to oppose the decisions taken by the General Assembly.

DEVELOPMENT OF THE JOINT VENTURE

Technical Assistance. The technical assistance given by FLC to the Portland de Mallorca is very considerable. According to the initial agreement, FLC undertook to supply the necessary personnel for the organization and direction of the production and commercial departments. Separate agreements were signed. Moreover, during the construction of the factory, FLC not only secured the installation and initial functioning of equipment, but also looked for the site, examined the land available, supervised the civil engineering work, and controlled the operations of the factory.

As has been mentioned previously, in return for its technical assistance, FLC was to receive 5 percent of the net annual profit of Portland de Mallorca until the total sum received should reach 10 million pesetas. As the operation of the factory has not yet shown a profit, this clause of the contract has not yet come into play.

Activities and Development after 1968. From 1966 onward the factory functioned at its full capacity and production was 100,000 tons per year. It soon became obvious that the possibilities of the

Mallorcan market were such that cement production was on the increase. At the start, FLC and its Spanish partners seemed in agreement on this point.

Contacts were therefore made with English and Swiss cement-producing groups likely to be interested, and a project for increased production was realized when the U.S. company, American Cement Corporation, agreed to become an associate, on condition that its participation in Portland de Mallorca was at least 50 percent. When the decision to expand on this basis was taken by the Board of Directors in March 1968, the representative of FLC noted the general economic factors (difficulties likely to occur in Spain connected with the probable diminishing of its tourist trade, the incidence of devaluation, and less sure earning capacity) for not signing the agreement with the U.S. company. The agreement was nevertheless signed and came into force at the beginning of 1969. American Cement took twelve of the twenty-four seats on the Board of Directors. FLC's participation was reduced to about 10 percent of the shares and to two seats on the board.

Portland de Mallorca had set off to a good start. After a fairly serious crisis (in 1967 and 1968) due to the slump in tourism in Spain, the business progressed very satisfactorily. The technical assistance supplied by the French company was by no means a negligible factor in this success. Relations between the French and Spanish partners were good, although complicated by the division into several groups on the Spanish side.

After 1969. It is too early as yet to know how relations between the three groups within the company will evolve. However, it seems obvious that the almost total control exercised by the American group leaves little initiative to the two other groups—this is not really a "multinational joint venture" since the management is not in fact shared. FLC has nevertheless preserved its representation on the Board of Directors, which was enlarged considerably. In this way it considers that it will ensure that the financial management of the business will allow the appreciation and profitability of its own participation, as well as the payment for its technical assistance.

Azucarera Tropical Americana S.A. (*Aztra*)

THE ECONOMIC-POLITICAL CONTEXT

The Policy of the Government of Ecuador. Ecuador enjoys an economic (especially monetary) stability that is rare in Latin America.

This stability is one of the factors favoring foreign investment, which the government is trying to encourage. The laws of 1962 and 1964 governing industrial development are a considerable encouragement to investment in industry, without any discrimination as to the origin of the capital.

These laws protect the food industries in particular (including the sugar industry) and aim to stimulate investment in the least-developed parts of the country.

Role of Government in Aztra. Aztra produces sugar. For several reasons it was understood at the outset that the company would receive assistance from the public authorities. The factory is situated 80 km. to the southeast of Guayaquil in the heart of one of the poorer provinces, Azuay y Ganar. Moreover, the military junta that was in power until 1966 attempted—mainly for political reasons—to break the sugar monopoly. In fact, sugar was produced in Ecuador only by two or three factories whose capital was highly concentrated.

There had been no sugar refining in Ecuador previously. Therefore the prospect of a fairly important home market, especially for refined sugar, combined with the U.S. system of sugar quotas made the installation of a new sugar refinery a serious project, especially as a by no means negligible contribution was to be expected from the government.

THE NEGOTIATIONS

In 1964 Aztra was formed to grow sugar cane, to produce and sell sugar and its by-products, and to encourage auxiliary industries. The capital was theoretically 60 million sucres. The capital actually put up was 20 million sucres, divided into 20,000 shares of 1,000 sucres each, held by the promoters of the company and the owners of the land used for growing sugar.

The construction of the sugar factory was laid open to international offers. The only offers to remain in the running for final adjudication were those by an American company, a German company, and FLC.

The Government of Ecuador agreed to guarantee the contracts undertaken by Aztra on several conditions:

(1) an increase in capital from 20 to 100 million sucres, in which government participation could theoretically be 20 million sucres;

(2) the setting up in the government's favor of a mortgage on the total capital of Aztra;

(3) a contract guaranteeing the placing on the foreign market of

the sugar produced during the period covered by the financial engagements.

As the American and German competitors had both offered to put up 18 million sucres ($1 million), FLC agreed to accept the same obligations and carried off the deal after obtaining the agreement of the Compagnie Française d'Assurances pour le Commerce Extérieur (Coface). By the contract signed on October 16, 1964, FLC undertook to deliver a complete sugar factory able to turn out 7,000 tons per day, and a refinery attached to it, with a capacity of 150 tons per day, for a total sum of $13,998,000. The contract came into force after an agreement on March 17, 1966, between FLC and Aztra, laying down among other things FLC's participation in the capital of Aztra. A contract had previously been signed between Aztra and the French export-import group, Louis-Dreyfus, for the placing of part of the production abroad.

FINANCING AND MANAGEMENT

Equity Capital. On March 18, 1966, FLC paid half of its share of the increase in Aztra's capital, i.e., 9,400,000 sucres (about $500,-000). The rest was paid slightly later than the fixed date of payment (March 1967), in the summer of 1967. As no clause was included to cover the resale of the shares subscribed, it was originally understood that FLC would transfer some of its shares to its local agents, but in fact this transaction did not take place.

The new government of Ecuador, which came into power after the coup d'état of 1966, was less interested in the business than the previous government and, contrary to the intention of the latter, did not share in the increase in capital. The total sum of the capital subscribed was therefore only 60 million sucres: a third by the promoters, a third by FLC, and a third by new subscribers, especially landowners.

A first increase in capital, 20 million sucres, took place in 1968. FLC cancelled debt owed to it by Aztra in exchange for shares worth 200,000 sucres, and, in total, increased its participation to 24 million sucres. Following the decision of the General Assembly in March 1969, to increase the capital by 20 million sucres, FLC stated that it would not subscribe to any additional shares. But in order to remain in control of 25 percent of the capital, it did in fact participate to the extent of 1,200,000 sucres. Its share was therefore 25.2 million sucres in a total capital of 100 million.

Loans. No outside loan was provided for at the outset. In fact,

Aztra received a loan of 10 million sucres granted by the Corporacion Financiera Nacional on reasonably advantageous conditions. The loan was for buying additional agricultural land. Aztra also received considerable credits in 1969 (30 million sucres) and will do so in 1970 (40 million sucres).

Management. At the Board of Directors of the joint venture, FLC holds two of six seats, those of the second vice-chairman and of the director-in-chief. Two heads of departments in the French company hold these positions.

At the General Assembly, FLC had 25.2 percent of the votes. It was in order to keep this percentage that FLC finally agreed to participate (to a limited extent) in the capital increase decided on in March 1969. Legislation in Ecuador stipulates that a group holding over 25 percent of the shares may in certain circumstances oppose majority decisions.

ACHIEVEMENTS

Delivery and Technical Assistance. The factory was delivered in normal circumstances. The first structural parts were sent out in September 1966. Construction began in December 1966, and was completed in October 1967. In late 1967—early 1968, the sugar factory and refinery carried out a set of tests over a period of one and a half months, corresponding to the amount of sugar cane available. For these tests Puerto Rican experts were called in. But in the spirit of the 1966 agreement, and at the request of Aztra, FLC supplied the experts to carry out subsequent sets of tests as part of its technical assistance.

FLC's technical assistance also touched on the financial sphere (on account of the presence of its two representatives on the board) and the agricultural sphere, especially on account of the intervention of a French specialized body, the Technical Center for Research on Sugar Cane.

Governmental Assistance. The Government of Ecuador gave Aztra several advantages. In doing this, it followed two objectives— the development of an under-developed area and the splitting up of the sugar monopoly.

For these reasons, the government had intended taking part in the capital increase decided in 1964, but the government established by the *coup d'état* of 1966 did not carry out that intention. However, it did extend to Aztra the benefit of the industrial development law of

August 8, 1962, which granted exemption from all taxes on exported material, on transfer of capital, and on increase of capital. Moreover, as the company was classified in a privileged category, it enjoyed the following advantages:

(a) 100 percent exemption from taxes on sales and from local and government taxes during the first five years, from the date of actual production;

(b) 75 percent exemption from income tax during the same period;

(c) 100 percent exemption from customs duty and import stamps on the material necessary for the functioning of the factory;

(d) when required, accelerated depreciation.

Results of Operations. During 1969, 250,000 tons of sugar cane were handled. In 1970 the capacity will reach 500,000, which corresponds to an increase of sugar production 25,000 to 50,000 tons. At the same time, sales will rise from 2.5 million sucres in 1969 to 5 million in 1970. The number of people employed during the whole year ranges from 160 to 200, but this figure rises above 3,000 during the period following the harvest in which cane is converted into sugar.

Operations produced a deficit in 1967 and 1968, but should break even in 1969 and subsequently produce a large profit. The possibilities concerning placement of production are very encouraging—a third of the production is to be placed in the home market (especially refined sugar of which Aztra is the only producer in Ecuador) at the price of 100 to 120 sucres per ton; a third is to be sold at the same price on the American market; and the remaining third will be absorbed into the world market at an approximate price of 40 sucres per ton. The total production is to rise in 1971 to 100,000 tons of sugar (a million tons of sugar cane handled)—about half the total production of Ecuador.

EVALUATION

Aztra is typical of the kind of joint venture requested by the client. FLC only participated in it at the outset because its participation was one of the conditions of a large order. But FLC, although not a sugar-producing company, does maintain an interest in the running of the business. The French company is directly concerned in the smooth running of the joint venture, which constitutes the only guarantee of payment for the sugar factory.

The relations between the partners, although difficult at first, have

become very satisfactory; confidence was shown on both sides. It is
in FLC's interest to associate actively with its partners in Ecuador,
who have acknowledged that they have common interests.

As for the Government of Ecuador, it seems satisfied, if one is to
judge by the advantageous conditions of rediscount offered by the
Central Bank, obtained for the credit allocated to the 1970 operations.

X: FERTILIZERS IN INDIA

Formation of Coromandel

Indian Agriculture. According to the 1961 census, the population of India was 439 million and statisticians put the rate of population growth at about 2.1 percent. Today the growth rate is on the order of 2.5 percent and a projection made by the Planning Commission is that by 1971 the population is likely to be on the order of 560 million. The task of feeding this population is tremendous. This is one of the reasons why the Indian Government has placed an increasingly greater emphasis on agriculture.

Up till now, the government relied very much on imports of agricultural products. Self-reliance is the goal, however, as was pointed out by the Planning Commission:

A major objective of the Fourth Plan is to move towards self-reliance as speedily as possible. A process of development sustained by continuous foreign aid cannot be healthy. The attempt should, therefore, be to reduce foreign aid inclusive of food aid—and net of interest and loan repayment—to about half the present level by the last year of the Fourth Plan. This will entail concerted effort both in reducing imports and increasing exports.[1]

Because the needs are so important, the goals fixed by the Planning Commission in agriculture are ambitious:

In the agricultural sector, the main endeavour has to be two-fold: first, to provide the conditions necessary for a sustained increase of about 5 percent per annum, over the next decade, in agricultural production; and secondly, to enable as large a section of the rural population as possible

1. *Approach to the Fourth Five Year Plan,* Planning Commission, Government of India, p. 2 (1968). The Fourth Plan runs from 1969–1974.

—including the small cultivator—to participate in development and share its benefits.[2]

As a consequence of this agricultural drive, the government encouraged in every way the installation of fertilizer plants. Nevertheless, some Indian and foreign entrepreneurs did not wait for the fourth plan to engage in this field. In 1959 two American companies and one Indian concern started negotiations for the creation of a major fertilizer plant on the east coast of India.

The Promoters of Coromandel. The three promoters of the venture are the Chevron Chemical Company, of San Francisco (Chevron), International Minerals and Chemical Corporation of Skokie (IMC), and E. I. D. Parry Limited, of Madras (Parry's).

Chevron is a wholly-owned subsidiary of the Standard Oil Company of California. It ranks among the world's leading producers and marketers of industrial petrochemicals and agricultural chemicals. With a production of 1,250,000 annual tons of ammonia and 600,-000 tons of complex fertilizers, it is one of the world's largest food plant manufacturers. The company's participation in agriculture encompasses insecticides, fungicides, and weed killers.

IMC is the world's largest independent producer of fertilizers, with an annual output exceeding 10 million tons. It manufactures and markets all three major plant nutrients—nitrogen, phosphate, and potash. In addition to huge mines in Florida and New Mexico, (U.S.A.), and Saskatchewan (Canada), IMC operates 50 mixed fertilizer plants in the U.S. and has several other fertilizer ventures outside North America; it is partner, for instance, in a phosphate mine in Senegal. It is also a member of an international consortium that will develop agriculture and industry in the Dominican Republic.

Parry's, with its subsidiaries, is India's largest private fertilizer producer and seller. It benefits from 60 years' experience with Indian agriculture. Its main activities are in sugar, chemicals, ceramics, fertilizers, distilleries, carbonic acid gas, confectionery, and engineering.

The Joint Venture. The government of India has a definite policy in favor of joint ventures, and would not allow a fertilizer project to be wholly-owned by foreign interests. This is why Parry's, which has a rich experience in distribution, was invited to join the venture. Because the Indian economy was passing through a difficult phase and the project implied considerable financial, technical, and managerial

2. *Id.,* at p. 9.

resources, IMC and Chevron decided to join forces in order to share the financial risk and the financial burden. They did not cooperate to combine distinct technical expertise: technically, either company could have done it alone.

The negotiations started in 1959. The promoters obtained the necessary government clearance in 1963. In April 1964, Coromandel Fertilizers Limited was incorporated. Production started in December 1967. This $80 million project is the country's first major private-sector fertilizer company.[3] The plant is in Visakhapatnam and the corporate headquarters are in Secunderabad. Both cities are in the State of Andhra Pradesh.

Before the plant came into operation, eight years had been spent in negotiating, planning, and construction.

The Plant. Several companies were hired by the promoters for the construction of the plant. Both Chevron and IMC are accustomed to being very demanding towards their contractors. Although U.S. companies or their subsidiaries were the primary contractors, many Indian firms were employed as subcontractors.

The plant is located on a 500 acre site adjacent to the Caltex refinery and 2½ miles from the Visakhapatnam harbor, on India's east coast. The site has been leased from the Visakhapatnam Port Trust for 50 years with options to renew. This location offers a good harbor for importing raw materials, a local source of naphtha, and significantly, access to one of the nation's finest crop-growing regions. At the port, Coromandel operates its own bulk cargo raw materials unloading berth.

The operation is utilizing indigenous materials in manufacture, such as jute bags. The Caltex refinery furnishes the plant with naphtha. Indigenously produced sulphuric acid catalyst is also used. Phosphate rock and sulphur are the raw materials that have to be imported.

All these raw materials are converted into ammonia, sulphuric acid, and phosphoric acid, which in turn are made into the end products, complex fertilizer and urea. Within the plant are the five main process units: ammonia, urea, sulphuric acid, phosphoric acid, and

3. This amount includes the value of the physical plant, considerable investment in working capital, interest during construction, and losses incurred during the formation period. The amount is comprised of expenditures made before devaluation at Rs. 4.76 = 1 dollar and those made after devaluation at Rs 7.5 = 1 dollar.

complex fertilizers. Supporting facilities—storage, utilities, bagging, shipping, raw materials, unloading, maintenance, and administration —are also within the plant. This self-contained complex requires only outside sources of basic raw materials, fresh water, and electrical power.

The Coromandel plant has a rated capacity of 80,000 tons of nitrogen and 73,000 tons of phosphate per year in the form of complex fertilizers and urea. The principal product is a high analysis complex fertilizer, (28-28-0 formula, the most concentrated high nitrogen-phosphate sold in India), at an annual rate of 260,000 tons. As demand develops, the plant will be capable of manufacturing other varieties of fertilizers. Approximately 16,500 tons per year of finished urea also are being manufactured for the market.

Financing and Foreign Exchange

Original Financing and New Financing. After the promoters had received governmental clearance in 1963, they worked on the financial arrangements, which were finished early in 1964. The three promoters realized that, although previous offers of shares to the public in projects in which U.S. companies were involved had been oversubscribed, in 1962 border confrontation with China had drastically upset the capital market in India. Investors were extremely cautious. Therefore, it was arranged to have Coromandel's issue underwritten by several Indian financial institutions. As was anticipated, the underwriters were required to take up most of the public issue. In addition, Coromandel obtained long-term loans from the Export-Import Bank of Washington, D.C. (in dollars), and from the U.S. Agency for International Development (in rupees). At this point, the total financing of the project amounted, in pre-devaluation rupees, to Rs. 30 crores.[4]

Subsequently, higher duties were levied on imported equipment; labor and material were affected by inflationary tendencies; and the rupee was devalued on June 6, 1966. Consequently, additional funds for Coromandel became necessary. New equity was sought with existing shareholders. As for the debt capital, long-term loans in rupees were obtained from the Industrial Development Bank of India and again from the Agency for International Development. Rs. 12 crores (in pre-devaluation rupees) thus completed the financing of the

4. Rs. = rupees. One crore = Rs. 10 million.

venture. In terms of 1967 rupees (post-devaluation), project costs were about Rs. 48.4 crores, which represent approximately $64.5 million.

Because of the magnitude of the investment and the general state of the Indian economy, Coromandel had to overcome serious financial problems. During this critical period the venture benefited from the understanding and support of regional and central governmental authorities. During the first five years of its operations, Coromandel will receive substantial help from its tax holiday.[5]

Equity Capital. The equity capital was supplied in the following amounts of rupees and dollars:

Currency	Original financing	New financing
	(in crores of rupees)	
U.S. Dollars	4.0	0.5
Rupees	4.5	0.6

The partners hold shares in the capital in the following proportions:

Chevron	25 percent
IMC	22 percent
Parry's	7½ percent
Financial institutions and individual investors	45½ percent

As can be observed, the majority of the capital is Indian. In this respect, Coromandel has complied with government policy, which favors a broad Indian ownership of the shares. In terms of control, however, it should be noted that the two American companies together hold nearly 50 percent of the share capital. Coromandel has about a thousand individual shareholders, who have a very limited share. The shares are listed on the major stock exchanges in India and trading activity is expected to increase now that the plant is in operation. Besides, several Indian financial institutions have a substantial share. Among them one might mention: Andhra Pradesh Industrial Development Corporation Limited, Hyderabad; Industrial Credit and Investment Corporation of India Ltd., Bombay; Industrial Finance Corporation of India, New Delhi; Punjab National Bank

5. This means a tax exemption on profits up to 6 percent. Coromandel not entirely exempt from taxes.

Ltd., New Delhi; and Life Insurance Corporation of India, Bombay.
Long-term Loans. The ratio of equity capital to loan capital is
approximately one to four. The loans are as follows:

Source and currency	Original financing	New financing
	(in crores of rupees)	
Eximbank (U.S. dollars)	12.9	—
AID (Rupees)	8.4	3.9
IDBI (Rupees)	—	7.0

Foreign Exchange Requirements. Foreign exchange for purchase
of imports of machinery and equipment is presently limited to replacement items, but Coromandel has heavy foreign exchange requirements for the purchase of phosphate rock and sulphur, and for
the service of its dollar loan from Eximbank. According to a corporate officer in New Delhi, Coromandel has been given sufficient foreign exchange and no problem is anticipated in this respect in the
foreseeable future.

Apparently, the fact that the foreign interests are in a minority position has no bearing at all on the question of foreign exchange permits or other governmental permits. The management of Coromandel
does not depend on Parry for this purpose but deals directly with the
government. The position and influence of L. Bharat Ram, Chairman, is very rarely used either. The government deals directly with
the management of Coromandel. Generally speaking, the relations
between Coromandel and the government have been quite cordial
and satisfactory.

Foreign Exchange Savings. The product made by Coromandel was
previously imported. According to estimates, the production of the
venture replaces imports that amounted to $33 million in foreign ex-
change a year, but the net foreign exchange saving is about $24 mil-
lion. The company is not committed to save a determined amount of
foreign exchange yearly.

Management

Board of Directors. The Indian shareholders, who have a majority
of the capital, are no more passive than the shareholders of any large
U.S. or European corporation. Actually, the Industrial Development
Bank of India, the Industrial Finance Corporation of India, and the

Andhra Pradesh Industrial Development Corporation in particular, are very active through their representatives on the Board of Directors. Chevron and IMC together hold 47 percent of the stock; foreign corporations in other joint ventures often exercise control with smaller shares. The importance of financial participation is not the only factor to be taken into consideration; the power and strength of the partners have also to be considered and both Chevron and IMC are able to exert considerable influence. The partners try, however, to reach agreement by discussion rather than by the exercise of voting power.

Chevron and IMC do not have a majority on the Board of Directors, but they hold half of the seats. The board is comprised of twelve members: the chairman, who is neutral; three each from Chevron and IMC; one from Parry; two from government organizations; one from the Industrial Finance Corporation of India, in which the government has 50 percent of the capital; and one neutral outsider.

L. Bharat Ram, Chairman of Coromandel, is an important Indian industrialist, who manages a great variety of businesses. Although he is Chairman of Coromandel, he is not involved in its day-to-day management. While he communicates directly with the Coromandel management, he does not normally deal directly with the three founding shareholders. As the promoters are three dynamic and important groups, it was thought appropriate to elect as chairman a man who would not be connected with any of the promoters.

Day-to-day Management. The contributions of the partners are quite specific. In addition to the equity capital, Chevron and IMC have jointly contributed know-how in the form of secret formulas, secret processes, and engineering and manufacturing data for the construction and operation of the plant. They are parties to a technical assistance agreement with Coromandel. They were given shares in exchange for know-how, but do not receive any royalties. Parry's contributes both its well-established sales organization and its experience of marketing in India.

Although the partners' contributions are specific, their responsibilitites in day-to-day management have not been laid down in writing. The only function unique to Chevron is its right (not an obligation) to appoint the managing director of Coromandel. IMC has a similar right (likewise no obligation) to appoint the deputy managing director. Also to be mentioned is the plant manager, who is a man from Chevron. The managing director, deputy managing director, and plant manager are the only personnel classified as senior management. In subordinate positions, Chevron and IMC both have employees in various operating positions. Although many important positions are still held by foreigners, the number of foreigners is being reduced as rapidly as conditions allow. The secretary and two special directors are now Indian nationals, as are a number of middle management positions.

The U.S. companies are not directly involved in the day-to-day management of the project. This function is performed by the managers the U.S. companies have loaned to Coromandel. These managers play a very important role in technical and administrative matters. They also have more than a say in commercial matters. Chevron and IMC as such deal with general policy decisions through their representation on the Board of Directors and through their share ownership at the general meetings. Parry's has an essential role in the everyday operations since it is located in India and is an integral part of the Coromandel picture through its position as principal sales agent and marketing advisor.

Dividend Policy. Since the project costs were considerable and since production started only at the end of 1967, the problem of dividend policy had not then arisen. No prior policy has been established as to the disposition of profits. A majority of the stock is held by the three founding partners, but the stock is listed on the major stock exchanges of India. When the management wishes to establish dividend policy it has to take this fact into account. On the other hand, Coromandel benefits from a development rebate in the form of extra depreciation, 80 percent of which cannot be distributed as dividends for eight years. In addition, the loan agreements with Eximbank, AID, and the Industrial Development Bank of India require that certain conditions be met before dividends can be paid and the agreements also limit the dividends until the loans have been repaid.

Labor. The enterprise has begun to provide training and gainful employment for some 700 Indians. During the construction phase, an additional 7,000 Indians were hired.

Since the manufacture of chemical fertilizer is not a labor-intensive industry, a high premium must be placed on individuals with specialized skills. Rather than formal training abroad, the emphasis has been placed on training through operational experience. As the necessary abilities are developed, more of the management and operations will be carried out by Indian personnel, and a commensurate reduction in the number of U.S. technicians will take place. By far the largest number of Coromandel employees is from Visakhapatnam and Andhra Pradesh. Only where positions could not be filled satisfactorily by qualified local or regional personnel have others been hired.

Labor relations in Coromandel have generally been harmonious. There has been only a work stoppage of two weeks in early 1967, during the construction of the plant. The troubles were not only a question of wages; there were also some additional points of contention. No labor problems have arisen since the start of plant operation, in spite of the unrest to be found in several parts of the country.

Sales

Education of the Farmers. Well before breaking ground for the plant, it was decided that the cultivators of Andhra Pradesh must be introduced ahead of time to the product that Coromandel intended to manufacture. Emphasis in India, previously, has been on straight nitrogen fertilizers such as ammonium sulphate and urea. In addition to known nitrogen needs, Coromandel foresaw that phosphate deficiencies would soon restrict crop yields in the key areas of intensive cultivation.

The U.S. promoters' agronomic and chemical research developed a nitrogen-phosphate fertilizer (the 20-20-0 analysis) specifically to meet these needs. From 1962 to 1967, market development was carried out in the form of a "seeding program." It served to introduce "Gromor" (the registered trade name for Coromandel fertilizers) in Andhra Pradesh, while developing the marketing and distribution system necessary to support what would be the country's largest fertilizer plant. Over 200,000 tons of imported 20-20-0 were sold under the program.

Farmers learned of the product's advantages by many means. The sales agency organization of Parry's established over 1,500 distributors and offered extensive agronomic advice. Several promotional techniques were used, the most successful of which was demonstration plots. More than 1,000 were planted.

Marketing and Distribution System. The system now operating is the natural extension of that developed during the seeding program. Coromandel and Parry's cooperate closely in this task. Coromandel maintains a marketing and promotion staff in Secunderabad, including its Farmers' Advice Bureau, which was established to counsel farmers on matters related to crop raising. Parry's field sales force of over 80 trained agriculturalists and several agronomic advisers operate from nine regional sales offices in Andhra Pradesh. Both organisations work through the more than 1,500 private dealers and cooperative societies.

At initial production in Visakhapatnam, a 28-28-0 product was offered rather than the 20-20-0 sold during the seeding program. This 40 percent increase in plant food content offers the farmer and sales distributors a reduction in storage space, transport costs, and handling.

The government has an option to buy 30 percent of the production. In the State of Andhra Pradesh, there are some remote areas that would not be attractive from a purely commercial point of view. Nevertheless, the desire of the government to have this option is not merely to serve these remote areas and it is Coromandel's desire as well to distribute fertilizers in all areas, remote or otherwise. The real motive of the government in asking for an option to buy 30 percent of the production was to use this as a lever by which prices could be kept within reasonable bounds during a period of scarcity. This purpose could be achieved by selling the fertilizers at special prices. The government would probably prefer, however, not to use the option and furnish these remote areas with imported products.

The demand of Andhra Pradesh could absorb the entire production, but Coromandel also sells its products in the neighboring states. Sales are for the most part to private distributors or cooperatives; very little is sold directly to farmers. The company will not be committed to any exports as long as internal demand is in excess of production.

Parry's is the selling agent, but this does not mean that the management of Coromandel has nothing to do with marketing. Parry's deals with direct sales to farmers, dealers, and cooperatives, while the management of Coromandel deals with advertising promotion, provides advice on agronomic innovation, and works in cooperation with various foundations to improve Indian agriculture. A senior Parry's officer said that hitherto the U.S. companies have not interfered with the Indian concern's distribution methods. A Coromandel officer observed that although the management does not interfere with Parry's distribution methods, it nevertheless tries to influence them when necessary. A Chevron officer pointed out that Coromandel management has the final word on marketing and distribution policy, since these decisions directly influence the venture's total performance. Although the respective responsibilities in marketing and distribution methods are well defined, in fact, the partners have to cooperate very closely in order to avoid friction and to operate efficiently.

Relations between the Partners and with the Government

The Problem of Imported Products. As has been mentioned previously, under the seeding program Coromandel imported 200,000 tons of fertilizers, which were intended for the education of the farmers. The program met with a serious setback in June 1965, however, when the state government put the authority for distribution in the hands of the Director of Agriculture of Andhra Pradesh. The government explained this change by the fact that there was a shortage of fertilizers in the state. Because of this fact, Coromandel was required to sell only to those to whom the government were ready to give a permit and a system of rationing and control of the stocks was aimed at.

The U.S. companies were not pleased with this decision. They maintained that it was understood that Coromandel would have the right to distribute freely and that the freedom to market was essential to the success of the venture. Consequently, Coromandel's association with the seeding program was withdrawn in the second half of July 1965.

In the following months, the government revised its attitude on that subject. At the end of April 1966, Coromandel was informed by the central government of the release of 100,000 tons of ammonium phosphate to be imported for the period 1966–1967 for distribution by Coromandel. At this point, IMC asked the Government of India to guarantee Coromandel's right to distribute freely in the future. The government declined to grant such a guarantee. In spite of this, Coromandel's right to distribution has since been respected and relations with the government have been quite cordial.

Relations between Parry's and Coromandel. H. V. R. Iengar, who is Chairman of Parry's, was previously in governmental service. After he retired, he became chairman of several joint ventures between Indian and foreign interests. According to a senior government official, he is very much respected both in India and abroad.

H. V. R. Iengar became the first Chairman of Coromandel. He was personally interested in the project as Chairman of Parry's and as a patriotic Indian. No conflict arose on the technical side but difficulties did ensue over the problem of imported products, which has just been related. Mr. Iengar was of the opinion that during a period of scarcity of fertilizers, the state government had some responsibility for ensuring that there was no black marketing and that the distribution was fair. He disagreed, however, with the particular method adopted by the state government and tried to negotiate with it for a modification of its proposal. The U.S. partners felt that the government should not interfere with the right to free distribution, which was regarded as essential to the satisfactory operation of the enterprise.

Although this was a serious problem, it would actually be difficult to select one item with enough import to be labelled the principal divergence. There was, rather, a difference in philosophies in general and, as a result, the three promoters decided it would be best if a neutral person were chairman. Accordingly, H. V. R. Iengar resigned as chairman and L. Bharat Ram was elected as his successor on March 13, 1967. It was agreed that the new chairman would use his influence to help Coromandel whenever necessary, but that he would not directly participate in the day-to-day management.

According to all parties concerned (including H. V. R. Iengar), this resignation was felt to be beneficial. This is because his resignation crystallized the points at issue and led to a review of attitudes and policies that had caused the resignation. It is a tribute to the three companies that they did not permit the situation to affect their relationship.

Relations between IMC and Chevron. One of the interviewees mentioned that the joint management of the American corporations has not been without problems. The major cause for any problems has been communications. It has been very difficult and expensive to keep directors and corporate officers in India, San Francisco, Chicago, New York, and London informed and up-to-date.

Chevron and IMC are both large companies. Chevron has a slightly greater share of Coromandel's capital and appoints the managing director, but otherwise they are practically equals in Coromandel. Actually, the U.S. companies have not had to be concerned about one or the other becoming too powerful. The basic structure of the project limits this possibility. Also the fact that Chevron and

IMC are large companies contributes to the harmonious relationship. The representatives of the two meet as equals, neither feeling subordinate to the other. This might not be the case if one of the two companies were much larger than the other.

It remains true, however, that the managing director and the deputy managing director hold loyalties to different corporations and to different men. One of the officers who held the position of managing director declared that he would give his loyalty first and foremost to Coromandel. The principle seems sound, but it is probably not always easy to put it into practice. For this reason a great deal will depend on the men sent from the U.S. and on their capacity of getting along together.

The Deputy Managing Director recognized that it is difficult to have two powerful groups working together. However, he added, there is no trouble at present because the individuals sent from the U.S. work well together and because the management of Coromandel enjoys a great deal of autonomy. In his view, a clear distinction has to be made between the construction period, during which differences of opinion as to technical processes might easily arise, and the operational period, when things are easier. On the whole, the cooperation between the two American companies is now considered to be highly satisfactory.

Evaluation and Prospects

In the course of our enquiries on joint ventures, it has appeared clear that true joint management works only under certain conditions: managerial responsibilities have to be clearly defined and the managers have to be able to get along with one another. If Coromandel experienced some difficulties at the start, it was probably because these conditions were not really met. Considerable effort has been made, however, to improve cooperation between the partners.

Parry's brings to the venture a very useful assistance as selling agent and fulfills an important role as Indian advisors to the Coromandel management and as Indian friends of Chevron and IMC.

The cooperation between IMC and Chevron will be dependent on the ability of senior executives to work together and in maintaining the equilibrium, not only in Secunderabad, but also in New York and San Francisco. At the present time the cooperation between the American companies is effective and advantageous to both. Coromandel seems destined to enjoy an excellent commercial and economic future: the prospect of increasing returns might provide an additional cohesive factor. The investments in the venture are so high that there is every incentive for the partners to make a continual effort to work together.

It is likely that relations between Coromandel and the government will continue to be satisfactory. Sometimes foreign corporations experience initial difficulties in India, precisely because they are newcomers. With time, they learn the ways of the country and this is often reflected especially in their relations with the government. The Indian Government is determined to contribute to the success of any enterprise in such a vital field as fertilizers.

For India, Coromandel is a major step toward its goal of fertilizer self-sufficiency by the early 1970's. Substantial foreign exchange savings should be realized. It is expected that the fertilizer output of the enterprise will ultimately produce enough extra food in Andhra Pradesh to feed 8 to 10 million people: this will represent a considerable contribution toward lessening the critical food shortage. It is also likely that the education of the farmers will have lasting beneficial effects. Furthermore, Coromandel is a significant addition to the economic expansion of the port of Visakhapatnam, as well as to the industrialization of Andhra Pradesh. Finally, the venture will in the future employ an increasing number of Indians in skilled or even managerial jobs.

It was an advantage for Coromandel to start operations precisely at the time when the Indian Government decided to make a vigorous effort in agriculture in general and in fertilizers in particular.

*Venture between Multinational Corporation
and Government Investment Bank*

XI: STEEL PIPE MANUFACTURE IN TURKEY

Mannesmann

Activities. Mannesmann A.G., of Germany, mines coal and iron
ore, smelts coke and pig iron, produces steel, and rolls steel into
plates, sections, and strips. The main activity of the enterprise is the
steel processing industry. Mannesmann makes seamless and welded
pipes and tubes of all sizes, of all wall thicknesses, and from all types
of steel; supplies pipes and tubes and lays pipelines for transporting
oil, gas, and water; delivers pipe scaffolding tubular and plate constructions, containers, apparatus and sprinkler irrigation systems;
builds couplings and transmissions, engines, and other machines,
transportation facilities as well as turn-key tube rolling mills, and
tube welding plants. For the last several years the production program also included plastic pipes and tubes made from low-pressure
polyethylene and polyvinil chloride.

Mannesmann has branches and sales offices in all parts of the
world in addition to factories bearing its name in Brazil, Canada,
Turkey, and U.S.A.

Joint Ventures in Developing Countries. Mannesmann has important joint ventures in Brazil and Turkey, established respectively in
1952 and 1954. The Turkish venture is the object of this case study
and will therefore be described below. In Brazil, Mannesmann has
several joint venture affiliates, but the principal one is the Companhia Siderúrgica Mannesmann, which produces iron, steel, steel pipe,
and rolled products, and in turn has various subsidiaries and affiliates
in iron ore mining, construction, and sales. About 72 percent of this
enterprise is held directly and indirectly by Mannesmann, and the

balance is owned by local official and private interests. Good progress was made towards settlement of the "notes affair," in which the company became involved when promissory notes were illegally issued by misuse of its name; an agreement was reached with the Brazilian Government in the spring of 1966; Companhia Siderúrgica Mannesmann has since granted compensation in the manner agreed upon with the government to all bona fide bearers of notes issued in misuse of its name who are prepared to compromise. Various court proceedings are still pending. Mannesmann also holds a two-thirds interest in an affiliate in Argentina.

In addition to these equity joint ventures, in recent years Mannesmann has concluded an increasing number of engineering and turn-key contracts in developing countries, especially in Asia, the Middle East, and Africa. Contracts have related to a great variety of items, such as pipelines, welding plants, irrigation systems, pumps, and dolphins.

The Control Problem. When Mannesmann invests in an equity joint venture, it has a strong preference for a majority participation. The company may accept minority participations in Germany, but there is no exception to the general policy in any developing country. If the government of a developing country insists on a majority of the shares being held by local interests, Mannesmann considers that in such a case it is better not to invest. The main asset of the German concern is its technical expertise. Mannesmann thinks that it can put its technique to work only if it has a decisive say in management. Either the company gets more than 50 percent in an equity joint venture or it implements turn-key projects or construction jobs with technical assistance. In the experience of Mannesmann, a company that does not have a majority control of a venture is too easily subject to the constant interference of the other partner or party involved.

Sümerbank

The Bank. Sümerbank is a Turkish state economic enterprise. It was established in Turkey in 1933 by a special law (Statute No. 2252). Pursuant to this law, the bank engages in industrial banking transactions of various kinds. The law states the purposes of the bank as follows:

1. To operate the factories turned over to it by the State Industrial Office (Devlet Sanayi Ofisi), and to administer the participation shares of the State in private industrial establishments, in accordance with the provisions of the Code of Commerce.

2. To study projects for, and the management problems of all industrial institutions which would be created with state capital, except the factories to be founded under powers given by special laws.

3. To participate in or to help within the limits of its own capital, industries, the establishment or management of which would be economically useful for the country.

4. To train specialists for industry and seek measures for the development of national industry.

Sources of Finance and Degree of Autonomy. Sümerbank has only public funds and does not draw money from the capital market or from private financial institutions. It naturally gets dividends from those industrial firms of which it is a shareholder. Some of these firms make profits, others make losses.

Sümerbank is a state-owned industry holding company, and the degree of its autonomy is therefore rather limited. If the bank officials want to invest in any company, the government must approve. To a large extent Sümerbank is controlled by the Minister of Industries. If the holder of this post is replaced, it is not unreasonable to suppose that the President of Sümerbank will also be replaced.

Formation

Establishment of the Joint Venture. In 1954, Sümerbank approached Mannesmann concerning its interest in building a plant for the manufacture of steel pipe in Turkey. The proposal by Sümerbank, which plays an important role in the industrial development of Turkey, was accepted by Mannesmann, and a joint venture was established under the name of *Mannesmann-Sümerbank Boru Endüstrisi T.A.S.* (Mannesmann-Sümerbank Steel Pipe Manufacturing Corporation), in accordance with the Law for the Encouragement of Foreign Capital (Statute 6224, enacted on January 1, 1954).

The aim of the corporation is to manufacture the steel pipe needed in the country and thus save a considerable amount of foreign exchange.

Factory's Machinery. The factory was built by Turkish workers with materials imported from Germany. The plans of the factory were entirely German. Most of the machinery has been provided by Mannesmann. Some machines were bought from French firms. The German company did not insist on being the only source of supply for machinery and equipment. The partners looked for the cheapest source of supply. However, Mannesmann was by far the most important supplier, and this was the way in which it paid its share of the capital.

If new machinery were required, a specific authorization of the government for the expansion would be needed. The government then would ask for an international bid to be made, in order to secure the cheapest source of supply. This is the general policy of the Turkish Government. However, an outsider might wonder whether this is not mainly theory and whether Mannesmann would not, in fact, stand good chances of getting the bid.

Factory's Site. The factory was established outside the town of Izmit, which is situated on the Sea of Marmara and is about 100 kilometers from Istanbul. It is connected by a state highway system and a railroad to Istanbul and Ankara.

Mannesman-Sümerbank has at its disposal a total of 739,000 square meters of land, of which it acquired 632,600 square meters (Köseköy-site near Izmit) in 1964. About 63,000 square meters are actually used for mill works purposes. The following are the main reasons for the establishment of the factory at this site:

1. The land originally acquired belonged to Sümerbank and could thus be bought by the company at favorable terms.

2. There is access to a plentiful water supply, which is an essential element in the manufacture of steel pipe.

3. The site has transportation facilities (sea, railway, and highway connections).

4. It is close to adequate labor supplies.

Factory's Production. At the start, the one-shift capacity of pipe production of the factory was 15,000 tons. In the late fifties, the factory produced at a rate of about 25,000 tons per annum by working extra shifts. The capacity depends on the mixture of sizes, but at present, capacity approximates 100,000 tons per year.

At the beginning, the size of welded tubes ranged from ½ to 2½ inches. The range has since been progressively extended up to 40 inches. The number of sizes has thus increased considerably.

Financing

Equity Capital. The Mannesmann-Sümerbank Steel Pipe Manufacturing Corporation is established as a stockholding company in accordance with the provisions of the Turkish Code of Commerce.

In the beginning, the capital of the corporation was 5,600,000 TL, of which 3,200,000 TL were subscribed by Mannesmann.[1] The German company brought this amount to Turkey in the form of machinery and equipment. The capital was later increased to TR 35 million (a little less than $4 million), of which TL 20 million were contributed by Mannesmann, and TL 15 million by the Sümerbank. Again, Mannesmann paid its share of the increase with machinery and equipment.

Thus, 57 percent of the capital belongs to Mannesmann and 43 percent to Sümerbank. Actually, the capital subscribed by Mannesmann was provided by four different German firms, but they all belong to the Mannesmann Group. The capital subscribed by Sümerbank was provided mainly by the bank itself, but also partly by Karabük Iron and Steel Works and by Izmit Paper Mill.

Any new capital increase for expansion would have to be agreed to by the Turkish Government, because the importation of new machinery would involve a foreign exchange problem.

In case of a capital increase or of the withdrawal of one of the partners, no right of first refusal has been provided for in the statutes, but the government might object to any change.

No arbitration clause is contained in the basic agreement. Matters that are not regulated by the statutes are regulated according to the Turkish laws.

Loan Capital. It is almost impossible for Mannesmann-Sümerbank to get long-term loans from abroad. The joint venture was able to get a long-term loan from the European Investment Bank, but this was an indirect transaction through the intermediary of a Turkish Development Bank, named Sinai Kalkinma Bank. The company does not solicit directly foreign or international financial institutions, because the risk of devaluation in Turkey is substantial and no foreign bank would take the risk. Nor could the joint venture go to the Eurodollar

1. TL = Turkish Lira. Until August 1970, one dollar = 9 TL. After the devaluation of August 1970, one dollar = 15 TL.

market, because the Turkish Government would not accept it. More-over, Mannesmann has not made loans to the company, although it is true that until now there has been no urgent need for such loans. In view of this situation, any credit furnished by Sümerbank is ap-preciated. In addition to its capital contributions, Sümerbank has granted substantial credits to the joint venture.

Expenses. The costs of the venture can be classified as follows:

Raw materials and equipment costs	70 percent
Wages	10 percent
General expenses	20 percent

These proportions have not changed materially since the late fift-ies. The raw materials constitute a major proportion of the venture's costs.

Management

Board of Directors. Mannesmann-Sümerbank has a Board of Directors consisting of five members, elected by the general meeting of shareholders. Three of the members are representatives of the Mannesmann Group and two of the Sümerbank. Two of the persons representing Mannesmann are Germans. The third is a Turk, who has represented Mannesmann in Turkey for 25 years. He knows Mannesmann and Turkey well and acts as a coordinator between the German company, Sümerbank, and the Government. The President is one of the German members.

The board normally meets three times a year, either in Turkey or in Germany. Its functions are similar to those of an *Aufsichtsrat* in Germany.[2] Members of the board have nothing to do with day-to-day executive questions.

Operating Management. Mannesmann-Sümerbank has a true joint operating management. It has a Turkish managing director appointed by the board, who is in charge of commercial affairs, and also a Ger-man managing director cooperating with him, who is responsible for the technical matters. Although they are called managing directors, they are not members of the board. They form a kind of executive

2. Under German company law, the *Aufsichtsrat* is entrusted with general policy supervision, and the *Vorstand* with the day-to-day management of the company. In practice, the distribution of functions between the two organs varies considerably according to the by-laws of the company.

committee that is similar to the *Vorstand* of German company law. There is no subordination of one managing director to the other. They try to handle any problems between them. Any matters of importance have necessarily to be referred to the board: for instance, increased expenses. The same is true when any divergence arises between the managing directors.

Can a True Joint Operating Management Work? According to a Mannesmann executive, the answer to this question depends to a significant extent on the behavior of the partners. Until now, no serious difficulties have occurred in the case of Mannesmann-Sümerbank. As a matter of fact, the management works smoothly, which also is a consequence of the separating of technical and commercial duties.

Although the managing directors are of different nationalities, they get along together well. Mannesmann has a majority participation in the venture, but does not exploit it. The German partner does not "put its fist on the table," but constantly tries to work out arrangements with its partners. The majority position is a means of control that Mannesmann prefers to keep in reserve.

According to this Mannesmann executive, the management of the joint venture is as autonomous as any management of any company. Any matters of importance have to be referred to the board, but for buying, selling, etc., the managing directors are free to do as they choose. Of course, it all depends on what is considered a matter of importance. If the Board of Directors interprets its function in an extensive way, the autonomy of the operating management might in fact be rather limited. However, it seems that a substantial delegation of powers has been granted to the managing directors.

Technical Responsibilities. There is no technical assistance agreement between the Mannesmann Group and Mannesmann-Sümerbank, and the German concern does not receive any royalties. However, it is the policy of Mannesmann to communicate technological developments to the Turkish company and to see that it is always up to date. In the Turkish venture, Mannesmann is satisfied with the dividends it receives. This is the policy of the German company in every country: it does not get royalties from companies in which it has a majority participation.

In the late fifties, five Germans were employed in Mannesmann-Sümerbank: the technical managing director and four foremen. At present, only two Germans are still employed in Turkey. Firstly, there is the technical managing director, who has a decisive say in every technical question, but who closely cooperates with the Turkish managing director. Secondly, there is a technician in the plant, who is fully informed on all points pertaining to the manufacture of tubes. The same system of employment is applied to both: they work under a three years' contract. At the expiry of this period, the contract may or may not be renewed.

Commercial and Administrative Responsibilities. Up to 1966, the commercial managing director always came from Sümerbank. In 1966, there was a promotion from within: the company appointed a Turk who had been working in the venture for many years. The heads of the different service divisions work under the Turkish managing director. The company considers that administrative work must be done by Turkish nationals.

Financial Policy. In comparison with a nominal capital of TL 35 million, the legal reserves amount to about TL 11 million and free reserves amount to about TL 24 million. The total of the reserves is thus equal to the capital.

Although Mannesmann-Sümerbank distributes a fair amount of profits, the reserves are quite high. According to a Mannesmann executive, reserves have been increased to a larger degree than usual in an American-Turkish venture. Sümerbank agreed to this policy. The government also looks favorably on this conservative dividend pay-out policy. Capital and reserves are sufficient to meet the company's requirements.

Labor. In 1959, Mannesmann-Sümerbank had 46 administrative employees, and 328 workers. In 1968, there were 84 administrative employees and 508 workers employed in the company.

Most of the workers are members of a union. There was a partial strike in November and December 1965. Rates of pay are the subject of constant negotiations between the company and the union.

The Raw Materials Problem

The manufacture of steel tubes requires certain raw materials, mainly skelps. They are raw materials in the sense that they are an input of the steel tubes factory. However, they previously were the output of a steel factory; they had gone through a process, and in that sense they are already products.

The Foreign Exchange Problem of Imports. In the first few years of the factory's production, the raw materials were not available in

Turkey. Accordingly, they had to be imported from Mannesmann. Turkey suffers a chronic shortage of foreign exchange; this difficulty severely limited the volume of production.

At that time, the price of the raw materials was not a problem. Sümerbank never maintained that the prices of the materials supplied by Mannesmann were too high. The materials were imported from the German concern under the condition that no cheaper source was available.

The Price Problem of Local Manufacture. The Turkish Government has gradually required local purchase of most factory inputs in an attempt to alleviate the foreign exchange problem. Some raw materials can still be imported, but neither skelps nor tubes can be imported. Mannesmann-Sümerbank has practically become independent from imports of raw materials. At present, materials come partly from Karabük Iron and Steel Works, which is a small shareholder of Mannesmann-Sümerbank. Most of the skelp, however, is supplied by the Eregli Steel Works. Both American interests and the Turkish Government have an equity interest in Eregli.

Thus, the foreign exchange problem has disappeared, but it has been replaced by another serious problem. At present, the price of skelps made locally is about 70 percent higher than the international price. This, of course, has a direct and substantial impact on the price of the steel tubes made by Mannesmann-Sümerbank.

Neither Mannesmann nor the joint venture can do anything to reduce the costs of raw materials. This is a problem for any company in Turkey. Great factories are built, and large amounts of money are needed to service the debt financing. Industrial prices in Turkey are higher than international prices and Turkish products therefore cannot meet international competition. The internal market is protected and exports are not competitive. Turkey is an associated member of the European Common Market, but there is no immediate prospect of full membership.

Sales

Sales in Turkey. The Turkish Managing Director is responsible for all commercial matters. However, Mannesmann can give its advice in the Board of Directors and the Mannesmann representatives do this frequently.

Most of the tubes are distributed by selling agencies, which are financially independent from Mannesmann-Sümerbank. They are associated with the joint venture by contracts. No commission is paid. The agencies buy at net prices; they pay in advance 30 percent of the value of the goods they purchase, and 70 percent after the goods are sold; transportation costs and a certain percentage of profit added to the price offered by the company make up the final selling price. The agencies sell only to the private sector.

Some governmental authorities—the Water Supply Commission, for instance—buy directly from the joint venture. Large state-owned companies do the same. The state receives no favorable treatment as to prices, but it enjoys fiscal advantages.

The Turkish Army does not take any part of the production, except for nonmilitary purposes, such as gas and water connections.

Quite frequently, the most important reason for the refusal of a foreign corporation to enter upon a joint venture abroad is the problem of coordination between this joint venture and its other operations around the world. Mannesmann does not have this problem in the case of the Turkish joint venture. Mannesmann-Sümerbank has relatively few transactions outside of Turkey. The joint venture, in effect, manufactures in Turkey for the Turkish market.

Exports. Mannesmann-Sümerbank has recently exported some hundreds of tons of steel pipes. These exports are directed mainly to neighboring countries, especially Lebanon. Efforts are being made at present to increase exports; however, this drive might not be very successful, because exports depend partly on the price of skelps from Turkish sources, and on taxes.

Mannesmann of Germany has substantial exports: tubes, sheets, plates, and machinery that cannot be manufactured in a developing country. Large factories cannot be established anywhere. Potentially, Mannesmann and Mannesmann-Sümerbank could compete in certain countries and with certain products. In fact, this is not likely to happen until the steel tubes made in Turkey become more competitive internationally.

Domestic Competition. Because imports of steel tubes in Turkey have been completely banned, there is no external competition. In recent years, however, other companies have started production of tubes in Turkey and domestic competition is now growing stronger. A Turkish company manufactures steel tubes; other companies make plastic tubes; and still others make cement tubes. Sümerbank is not financially involved with any of the joint venture's competitors.

Mannesmann-Sümerbank is not pleased with this competition, but considers it as a normal development. From the beginning, the partners knew they would not always be alone in the field. Demand is strong and prospects are considered to be good for the next few years.

Government Relations

It is common for a government of a developing country to assume an essential role in all sectors of the economy. As has already been mentioned, the Turkish Government is especially active and keeps a close look on the activities of enterprises. Perhaps the best example, in this respect, is the case of a company which wants to proceed to an expansion: contrary to what the Indian Government does, the Turkish Government will not, as a condition of the expansion, ask for a greater local participation in the equity capital of the company or for a public issue of shares; but it will control very closely all the economic aspects of the expansion.

In the case of Mannesmann-Sümerbank, governmental relations are the joint responsibility of the Board of Directors and of the operating management. The management of the joint venture calls on the authorities and also on governmental officers, but the Turkish members of the board also have contacts with the ministries.

Both the Turkish and the German managing directors are of the opinion that the Turkish Government is constantly willing to help the company in its operations. This reflects the nature of the Turkish participant in the company, and the importance of pipe manufacturing in Turkey.

Day-to-day relations with the government have always been good. Mannesmann-Sümerbank has not had such problems as restrictions on the transfer of profits out of the country—problems which are often the source of endless headaches for foreign corporations doing business in developing countries. However, there is a well-developed bureaucracy in Turkey, and it takes time to deal with it. Moreover, although the attitude of top government officers is extremely positive, the reaction of some departments is sometimes less positive.

More generally, there is one point that irritates foreign investors increasingly. As has already been mentioned, any capital increase requires the consent of the Turkish Government. Recently, it has been the policy of the Turkish Government to agree only to a capital increase by forcing the companies to take on export commitments. The government maintains that, in general, any profit transfers abroad must be covered by exchanges through exports. Since the Turkish industry cannot yet compete with world market prices, export sales do not cover the costs, which means that exports cause losses.

Results and Evaluation

Expansions. The expansions undertaken in recent years by Mannesmann-Sümerbank constitute a significant sign of the enterprise's health.

In 1963–1964, a second welding line was installed for tubes from one and one-half to six and five-eighths inches. The company proceeded to a capital increase. The machinery was invested by Mannesmann, while Sümerbank paid its share in cash.

In 1966, a spiral tube welding plant was added for tubes from eight to forty inches. There was no capital increase. The plant was financed by Mannesmann-Sümerbank out of profits. Also the European Investment Bank granted a seven-year credit of $430,000 to the company, but, as has been mentioned, this was made indirectly through a Turkish development bank, Sinai Kalkinma Bank. The interest paid by Mannesmann-Sümerbank to the bank is 8 percent, plus 1 percent commission.

Any further expansion would involve other sizes or other types of tubes. The government would probably not agree to something other than tubular products. As has been mentioned, the consent of the government is necessary for any expansion.

Evaluation. Since it started operations, Mannesmann-Sümerbank has always made a profit. The main problems that the company has to face are dependent on the Turkish economy: raw materials are too expensive; the economic system is too closed; the government is cautious when an enterprise seeks to expand; and domestic competition is growing. Mannesmann-Sümerbank has been able to develop and has been a successful venture, but the problems cited indicate some limits for the time being. There is very little that the company can do in response to these problems.

Relations between the partners have been satisfactory. They realized a truly joint operating management, because the individuals were able to get along together and because the respective managerial responsibilities were clearly defined. Problems have been worked out between the partners by discussion and compromise, and not by majority rule.

Generally speaking, relations between the government and the company have also been satisfactory. By import substitution the venture has contributed to the saving of a substantial amount of foreign exchange.

The problems to be faced should not be underestimated, but on the whole, prospects for the next years are considered to be good.

XII: COMPUTERS IN WORLD MARKETS

The Company

The Growth of the Company. In 1914, Thomas J. Watson, Sr. left his post of Commercial Manager of the National Cash Register Company. He then became Manager of the Computing-Tabulating-Recording Company, which was in fact a loose group of three small corporations.

In 1924, this group became the International Business Machines Corporation, commonly known as IBM. At that time, the company sold mainly punched cards and tabulating machinery. Like many American corporations, IBM had modest beginnings but gradually grew into a venture of considerable size.

During the Great Depression, IBM decided to run the risk of undertaking an expansion program. In 1935, the U.S. Congress passed the Social Security Act: after a public tender IBM was chosen to supply one of the largest accounting operations the world had ever seen.

From then on, the company has grown rapidly. Until the end of the Second World War the bulk of its sales were made on the U.S. market. Although it has developed a wide range of products, it has concentrated primarily on the manufacture and sale of computers.

International Operations. IBM began operations overseas through branches, agencies, and subsidiaries in the early part of the twentieth century. A foreign department was set up in 1928. At that time, international transactions were predominantly sales and licensing arrangements, and the company had only a few manufacturing operations outside the U.S.A. Realizing the growth potential abroad, the company formed the IBM World Trade Corporation (a wholly-owned subsidiary) in 1949 to deal with foreign sales. At present, foreign sales are increasing faster than domestic sales.

Partly due to the formation of the Common Market, a special effort was launched in Europe, where IBM gradually established several manufacturing plants: Germany (3); France (3); Netherlands (1); Italy (1); United Kingdom (2); Sweden (1). The company has also built a factory in Japan and another in Canada.

IBM's manufacturing effort has not been restricted to developed countries only. On the contrary, IBM has manufacturing facilities in five developing countries: Argentina, Brazil, Colombia, Mexico, and India. Moreover, the company has sales branches and agencies in many countries. As far as communist countries are concerned, IBM sells in the Eastern European countries of Bulgaria, Czechoslovakia, East Germany, Hungary, Poland, and Rumania. In addition, the company does business in Yugoslavia, to which the U.S. Government does not apply the trade restrictions that affect the other Eastern European countries. On the other hand, IBM does no business in Albania, Cuba, North Korea, North Vietnam, Communist China, or the U.S.S.R.

It can be seen, therefore, that in some form or another, IBM is at present active in a great many countries.

Organization. The development of domestic and foreign branches and subsidiaries has involved considerable investments. IBM's capital needs have been further increased by the fact that it has supplied the market with a broad range of products and services. Consequently, the company has had to issue stock to the U.S. public and to solicit aid from financial institutions.

In the early fifties it appeared that IBM was too monolithic and that the rapidity of decision-making was impeded by the burden of a top-heavy administrative structure. In 1956, a major decentralization project was initiated. Today, IBM consists of eleven divisions and three wholly-owned subsidiaries, all of which are entrusted with a substantial degree of autonomy. As there has always been a close link between all IBM activities, however, these divisions and subsidiaries operate in close cooperation with one another. Supervision over the divisions is exercised by the Corporate Office, composed of the Chairman of the Board of Directors (Thomas J. Watson, Jr.), the President of the Corporation, and a Senior Vice President. The Corporate Office is assisted by two top management committees and five staff and line executives. These committees and executives deliberate and act upon such matters as establishing broad objectives, plans, and policies; establishing management structure and practices to accomplish objectives; approving plans and programs of divisions and subsidiaries; and appraising performance throughout IBM.

The Nature of the Industry

A Common Approach. The use of computers throughout the world has considerably increased over recent years. The large computers have been given extensive publicity. But besides the rare "super-computers," which are used by the large research centers, a great number of smaller machines have been in operation in banking, commercial, and industrial enterprises. Although each computer company has usually presented a main product line, the market has been supplied with an extremely wide range of models.

The computer industry is undeniably unique. Computer systems, in the extreme sophistication and complexity of technology, are unlike anything else, with the exception perhaps of satellites and communication systems. Although many different companies seek to enter this promising field, with time they all arrive at a common approach to the special organizational problems that this industry poses. This is true even for large companies that manufacture and sell many different products. At first, the computer department may be influenced in its methods by the other departments but, sooner or later, it transforms itself into an autonomous division that obeys the specific requirements of the computer industry.

This similarity of pattern is reinforced by the rapidity of technological change, which requires great adaptability from the manufacturing companies.[1] The successive changes in the activities of the IBM Poughkeepsie, N.Y., factory are a good example of this flexibility: during the Second World War it manufactured armaments; after the war it concentrated on producing electro-mechanic materials; and in recent years it has devoted itself to producing calculating machines. These technological changes have of course spectacular effects on the efficiency of the machines produced. The increasing

1. An indirect, but important consequence of this rapid evolution has been the formation of an active secondhand computer market in the United States. Dozens of business organizations are specialized in the purchase, resale, and leasing of such machines.

number of calculations of which a computer is capable in a second is a good example of this progress: 1944, 3 calculations per second; 1952, 16,000 calculations per second; 1961, 225,000 calculations per second; 1968, 1,000,000 calculations per second.

The future character of the industry is clearly indicated by the accelerating trend towards using computers as the basis for "on-line," "real-time" information systems. The term "on-line" refers to the accessibility of the computer, and the term "real-time" refers to the speed with which the computer can respond.

"On-line" terminals, connected to the computer, are devices through which a person communicates directly with a computer, either to give it information or to ask for and receive the results of computation or a file search. Terminals may take many forms. Some are similar to typewriters, accepting information and queries through a keyboard and responding by typing out the answer. Others, called graphic displays, look like television sets, on the screen of which appear words, diagrams, and drawings. And still others, as simple as a touch-tone telephone, respond with spoken words generated by the computer.

"Real-time" means that the persons using these terminals exchange information, questions, and data processing results with the computer immediately. Modern data processing equipment operates so rapidly and can store and manipulate such large amounts of information that it can solve problems and find information for many users at what appears to be the same time. When a computer is used in this manner by more than one person, the process (which will be described in greater detail below) is known as "time-sharing."

These dramatic changes in the use of computers obviously provide industry, government, and science with remarkable instruments for the execution of their tasks.

Specialization of Manufacturing Units. The company's policy is not conducive to a proliferation of manufacturing facilities. The factories cooperate in the realization of a carefully integrated production. Not even one manufacturing unit produces all the constituents of an IBM 360, and this is true even in the U.S.A. According to a highly-developed specialization process, each unit has the task of producing a certain component module, and no more.

IBM production is highly integrated, but not entirely so. It is more economical to purchase certain components from outsiders. IBM makes substantial use of supplying companies, with which it is very demanding as regards components' specifications. For instance, IBM buys from outside sources a small transformer. These outside purchases, however, represent only a small part of the entire manufacturing process.

Coordination between Manufacturing Units. All these various elements contributed by different manufacturing units have to be properly assembled. In the assembled and operating computer an information pulse must travel at a specified and constant speed. Consequently, the design and the implementation of production methods require extreme precision.

Thus, the production of a general product line has to be carefully coordinated. Basic directives come from the parent company in New York, but the national managers have substantial autonomy in the implementation of the basic objectives. If these objectives are not realized, the parent corporation may send to the respective country an officer whose task is to find a solution to the problem in collaboration with the national manager. Although IBM avoids unnecessary interference in the operations of a foreign subsidiary, it does offer guidance and assistance in such areas as finance, engineering and manufacturing coordination, patents and copyrights, and uniform corporate design.

Special difficulties in coordination arise when a computer company merges with another company. For example, in Great Britain, International Computers Limited (ICL) merged with English Electric (EE) and Elliott-Automation (E-A). In the long run, this merger should improve the competitive position of ICL, but on a short-term basis, it has created some coordination difficulties; no sooner had ICL developed its own integrated family of computers than it had to accommodate a whole new, and completely different range manufactured by EE and E-A.

Market Requirements. Each computer company seeks to create a family of complementary machines having a broad general compatibility; the customer has to be able to adapt the "architecture" to his ever-changing needs. With the 360 general product line, introduced in 1964, IBM made a special effort to provide the customer with the constant possibility of easily increasing his family of machines. This "family growth" no longer requires the expensive outlay for a new programming at each purchase. This effort was continued with the introduction of the System/370 in 1970. The merger of computer companies in Great Britain similarly aimed at the formation of a better and wider family of compatible machines.

Although the specific operational needs of each customer may differ considerably in detail, the general market requires substantially the same basic computer system. A computer company has to ensure that the same work can be executed similarly for a bank in Wall Street and a bank in Vienna. In this respect, a computer is different from a consumer product like soap or food: the consumer product industries have often to differentiate their products according to the various needs of each market. On the other hand, a computer system may generally be applied unchanged in any country. Actually, some requirements may differ from one country to another: e.g. the alphabet is not the same all over the world. These adaptations, however, do not change the basic structure of a computer system.

In particular, there is no fundamental difference between the market of a developed country and that of a developing country in this respect. A customer in a developing country may welcome a reduction in the size or price of a machine, but special adaptations or conditions may be required equally well in a developed country. Of course, so far the customers from developing countries have not been very numerous. Nevertheless, many computer companies have undertaken an educational effort in these countries. The fundamentals of the data processing science are taught in specialized institutes and sales agencies have been established nearly all over the world.

Leasing. The material elements of a computer system are referred to as *hardware,* while *software* denotes the nonmaterial elements, such as know-how, services, and programming. In addition to sales of computers, IBM leases hardware and software on a large scale. The customer operates the system, but maintenance is provided by IBM. One advantage of the lease for the customer is that when the machine becomes obsolete he can replace it in part or as a whole without making a large investment.

IBM not only sells and leases directly to customers but also sells computer systems to computer-leasing companies. These companies, which have not been in existence for long, buy the machines from IBM and then lease them at a price lower than that charged by IBM. Leasing companies are able to do this because they depreciate their equipment over a period upwards of ten years, whereas IBM depreciates equipment over five years. As a product line is usually replaced by a new one after only a few years, the leasing companies take a serious risk and may suddenly have to replace part of their stocks. If this were to happen, the price of leasing would be raised for a while, only falling after a time under the pressure of competition.

Time-sharing. The central (or treatment) unit of a computer works more quickly than the entry-exist units. Consequently, the central unit has some "leisure." In order to make use of these "leisure" periods, research scientists had the idea of connecting the central unit up with several entry/exit units corresponding to different programs. Under this scheme, each program is allowed an equal share of treatment by the central unit. These motions occur so rapidly that an apparent simultaneity between the treatment of all programs is achieved. A new activity was developed out of this principle in the computer industry: the process of "time-sharing," which became a commercial force in the market place in 1965. Experts anticipate that in 15 years or so the time-sharing work will represent 75–80 percent of total computer activity.

IBM's time-sharing activities are dealt with by the Service Bureau Corporation (SBC), a wholly-owned and independently operated subsidiary of the company. IBM provides customers with a broad range of terminal-oriented computing choices. SBC's customers range from small businesses whose basic data processing needs are handled on a regular basis to some of the nation's largest companies for whom SBC can provide expert assistance in dealing with sophisticated data processing tasks.

IBM is not the only computer company, however, that is at present making a determined effort to take advantage of this promising new field. General Electric and Control Data Corporation (CDC), among others, have extensive time-sharing operations. CDC, for example, which is a profitable competitor of IBM's in the United States, has invested $50 million for the establishment of a data processing national network based on six of its "super-computers," 6000 Series, which are installed in New York, Boston, Washington, Houston, Minneapolis, and Los Angeles. This system permits CDC to offer its services to thousands of clients simultaneously.

The Company's Policy towards Joint Ventures

Doing Business Abroad. IBM's recent history does not include a single case of equity joint venture with a business partner. On the other hand, IBM shares are listed on principal stock exchanges in Europe and, therefore, are available to any member of the public that may wish to invest. But until now, the company has not issued shares to the public in any developing country.

This fact may seem surprising, since the computer industry is generally considered to be a very "sensitive" industry by numerous governments. Government statements and newspaper articles in many countries point out that the predominance of foreign computer companies represents an economic interference that is detrimental to national interest. Because governments tend to be important customers of the industry, they are especially conscious of this problem. One might have expected these governments to force the foreign computer companies to associate with local partners, or at least to issue shares to the public.

Actually, governments as a rule have neither compelled nor even exercised strong pressure on IBM to accept local participation. In France, for instance, the computer industry is largely dominated by foreign interests and IBM maintains a wholly-owned subsidiary, even though the government tends to be suspicious of any foreign (especially American) domination in the advanced technological sectors of the economy. When the joint venture between Bull and General Electric experienced some internal difficulties, the government agreed on an increased foreign participation. The example of Japan is even more significant; although as a rule foreign companies cannot make investments in the country except on a joint venture basis, IBM is one of the few that have managed to establish a wholly-owned subsidiary. The Indian Government also has a definite policy in favor of joint ventures, but IBM has a branch operation in India, which includes some manufacturing. If the Indian operations of the company were expanded to any extent, however, it is highly probable that the government would then insist on a public issue of shares.

The reasons for the governments' lenience in the case of the computer industry can only be speculated upon. There often are, of course, differences or nuances between government statements and government practice with regard to all kinds of problems. Governments probably tend to consider the presence of a computer industry as necessary for the national economy, even if a local industry does not yet exist. Consequently, they tolerate the predominance of foreign corporations for the time being, while at the same time offering powerful incentives to the development of a national, locally-bound industry.

Whereas IBM has not been compelled to enter upon any joint venture, the question remains to be discussed as to why the company has neither voluntarily sought an association with an industrial partner in any country, nor proceeded to a public issue of shares in any developing country.

Reasons for the Company's Policy. Many chemical companies avoid combining with others on a joint venture basis because they fear that the local partner might gain the technical know-how from them and start manufacturing independently. This fear usually does not exist to the same extent in the computer industry. Certainly, the desire to protect its technical secrets is not the main reason why IBM has hitherto refused to form any equity joint venture with a local partner. IBM follows an open patent licensing policy. If a company has a large technical lead over its competitors, this will tend to protect it from being too severely damaged as a result of theft of any specific know-how.

IBM is not opposed to joint ventures as such, but wholly-owned subsidiaries have proved to be an efficient vehicle through which to carry out the company's objectives. An IBM executive observed that at the present time he could not imagine a single case where a joint venture would improve the efficiency of the existing system of operation. Moreover, whereas a consumer product industry may seek a local partner, so as to be better able to manufacture a special product for a given market, the computer industry does not face such an incentive. Finally, joint ventures between other companies in the computer industries of France and Italy did not have encouraging results: in France one of the partners gradually assumed control, and in Italy the joint venture was abandoned after a relatively short existence.

Nevertheless, it should be emphasized that the control of the parent company over all its subsidiaries does not exclude in any way a large delegation of management responsibilities to foreign executives. In line with principles of decentralization, IBM has delegated major operational responsibility to the country level. The country manager, within the framework of centrally coordinated policy, has full responsibility for personnel programs, marketing, and customer service. Responsibilities for product development and manufacturing are centrally assigned to various specialized development laboratories and plants throughout numerous countries. Under this system each development laboratory is highly specialized in a particular technology and each plant manufactures a specific range of products for the local market and for export. This creates an interdependence among foreign and domestic plants which rely on each other for parts and components. By rationalizing its multinational production to a great degree, and by following a policy of manufacturing on a product by plant basis, IBM not only cuts high production costs, but also constantly improves the quality of the entire production.

The Extensive Employment of Nationals. Although IBM refrains from associating itself with local partners, this does not mean that the company is indifferent to the problem of acquiring a local identity. For psychological and economic reasons, IBM extensively employs nationals at all levels. In the early stages of any foreign venture several experienced IBM officers are needed in order to overcome the numerous initial difficulties. Later, these expatriates are gradually replaced by nationals. Contrary to the practice of many American corporations, IBM makes even the senior executive positions available to nationals; in Japan the whole organization is run by nationals, from the lowest ranks to the very highest. There is also a consistent policy to "internationalize" senior personnel and the manager of a company may be a national from a third country. After the initial period of operation, the parent company may from time to time send abroad officers to fulfill a function of control.

IBM has successfully implemented this policy in the majority of countries in which it has established branches or subsidiaries. The policy has also been carried out in developing countries, and has been viewed as a compromise between the need for closer direction over foreign companies and the need to acquire a local identity. In each country the company has applied its particular principles of personnel training, such as the *recyclage,* or continuing education, of the employees.

In order to gain general acceptance and recognition abroad, IBM has also consistently abstained from becoming involved in local politics or indulging in certain dubious local practices. Meanwhile, it has made contributions in such areas as social service, local educational programs, community development, health, and language programs.

Evaluation and Prospects

Antitrust Problems. On January 17, 1969, the Antitrust Division of the United States Department of Justice filed a civil antitrust complaint against IBM, charging it with monopolization of the data processing industry. The Department claimed that, both with regard to sales and manufacturing policies, IBM had resorted to questionable methods that have prevented its rivals from gaining an adequate share of the U.S.'s fastest growing industry and that its size should be curtailed. The Department also pointed out that in the year 1967, IBM received about 74 percent of the growth revenue from the U.S. sales of general-purpose computers.

IBM's competitors, which have exerted strong pressure on the Department of Justice in recent years, had two particular goals in mind.[2] First, their attacks were not aimed so much at the computer market itself, where IBM has a firm lead, but rather at the latest innovations in the data processing industry, such as time-sharing; secondly, the leasing companies were demanding that IBM separate the hardware from the software costs, in order to permit the development of a data processing industry independent from manufacture.

IBM has been at issue with the Department of Justice before (for instance in 1952) and emerged more or less intact. Early in 1969 it made two attempts to ward off the "antitrusters": it surrendered its whole recently-developed time-sharing service to its Service Bureau Corporation (a subsidiary which is operated autonomously), and promised a new pricing policy. At the end of June 1969, IBM decided that henceforth its clients in the United States would pay separately the hardware price and substantial portions of the software price. These changes may stand the company in good stead as it struggles through the case, which may well drag on for years.

In the course of the case the company will no doubt argue that the very strength and proliferation of the industry—80 systems manufac-

---

2. The pressure of IBM's competitors has not been only indirect. Three civil antitrust suits have been filed against IBM by competitors charging violation of the antitrust laws. Control Data Corporation filed a complaint on December 11, 1968, charging monopolization in the industry, alleging damages in an unspecified amount and asking for injunctive relief. On January 3, 1969, a complaint was filed by the Data Processing Financial and General Corporation, a computer leasing company. It accused IBM of various violations of antitrust laws, alleged discriminatory policies against leasing companies, and asked for treble damages totaling more than one billion. On April 22, 1969, another complaint was filed by Applied Data Research Inc., a computer software supplier. It charged IBM with the violation of the antitrust laws, asked for immediate separate pricing of all computer software and services and sought treble damages of $900 million. On August 20, 1970, Applied Data announced an out-of-court settlement that called for a reimbursement of $1.4 million for costs related to the claim and for further study of an arrangement that called for the supply by Applied Data of a computer program to IBM, for a period of three years at $600,000. In each case, IBM has denied that it has violated the antitrust laws in any respect.

turers, 4,000 companies dealing in related equipment, support, and services, annual sales of $6.7 billion—refute the charges against it. It will further observe that technological advances have come at a very rapid rate, and from all corners of the industry, not just from IBM. It will also point out that in Great Britain—though nowhere else—it has been overtaken by another manufacturer with regard to market shares. According to one estimate, International Computers Limited (ICL) has 45 percent of the U.K. market against 30 percent for IBM. ICL's comparative achievement is partly due to the extensive research work on computers carried out in Britain after the war, and partly to the success of its so-called "1900" Series.

The Company's Future. Because IBM has been firmly established in foreign markets for some time, it is unlikely that the company will be affected in the short term by U.S. governmental restrictions on investments abroad. These restrictions, however, will have an impact on IBM's activities in the long run, because the company is growing so rapidly.[3] Consequently, IBM will have to find additional funds on foreign financial markets, e.g. on the Eurodollar market, if it is to continue to thrive.

On the whole IBM seems to face a bright future. Towards the end of the twentieth century there is every reason to suppose that more powerful as well as smaller and cheaper computers will be produced. There is practically no sector of industrial, governmental, or scientific life in which their influence will not be felt. In this greatly expanded market, however, IBM will increasingly face tough competition. In the United States, its competitors will in particular devote their efforts towards capturing a substantial share of the market of the new computer activities, such as time-sharing. Abroad, especially in Europe and in Japan, governments will strongly encourage the creation of national computer industries, which are generally recognized to be necessary to a country's economic independence and development. Nevertheless, a multinational effort may appear to be the only way to form a strong computer group capable of competing efficiently with U.S. companies. Because of the nature of the computer industry, transnational mergers would seem to have a relatively greater chance of success than transnational joint ventures. Although

3. It should be noted, however, that the Nixon Administration which took charge in January 1969, seems inclined to reduce the extent of these limitations. It has already taken a few steps in this direction.

the realization of transnational mergers is at present meeting with legal, economic, and political obstacles, such hindrances should gradually be overcome.

Meanwhile, IBM has taken a strong, and perhaps decisive lead on the U.S. and international markets, and the company will continue to abide by the principles that have contributed towards its success. At present, IBM has no intention of entering into any joint venture with a business partner, not because it is against joint ventures as a matter of principle, but because this form of association does not seem fully compatible with the nature of the industry. Nevertheless, it should be emphasized that the management would not in the least be opposed to a joint venture if in any specific case this would be the best course in reaching an objective. IBM's executives have considered a number of joint ventures in the past and will continue to do so in the future. Meanwhile, the management feels that the company is contributing to the economic development of foreign countries by other means: it introduces to these countries the highly advanced technique of a modern and essential industry and provides nationals with employment opportunities at all levels.

Those among the developing countries that have already progressed towards industrialization, or which have great industrial potential, are becoming attractive markets for computer companies. Some of them, which are indeed seeking earnestly to attract the computer industry, may allow IBM to operate with a wholly-owned subsidiary. Other countries, however, which have a definite policy in favor of local participation in foreign enterprises, might insist at least on a public issue of shares. This would present IBM with a delicate problem, especially if its competitors are only too ready to make this kind of concession.

*Venture between Multinational Corporation
and Local Investors*

XIII: BUSINESS FORMS AND OFFICE MACHINES IN CENTRAL AMERICA

Origin of Moore Business Forms de Centro America S.A.

Moore Business Forms de Centro America, S.A. is a joint venture in El Salvador, owned 49 percent by Moore Corporation, Limited (Moore Corp.), a Canadian company, and 51 percent by Salvadorians. It produces business forms and markets the forms and related business machines throughout Central America. Its formation resulted from a combination of three principal factors, namely: the formation of the Central American Common Market (CACM); the nationalization by Castro of Moore Business Forms de Cuba, S.A.; and the acceptance by a Salvadorian of a program to expand his printing business in conjunction with Moore Corp.

The CACM is the culmination of a number of treaties entered into, for the most part, by Guatemala, El Salvador, Honduras, Nicaragua, and Costa Rica, for the dissolution of tariff and trade barriers *inter se* and the establishment of a common external tariff. The first of these treaties was signed on June 10, 1958. Subsequent treaties and agreements have been directed towards the further integration of the economies of these countries, and their evolution towards a single integrated economy, although it will be some time before these latter objectives are fully achieved.

With the tariff reductions provided for among the CACM countries, markets for a local producer are vastly expanded, making profitable operations that would not have been undertaken on a country by country basis.

Not a great deal of progress has yet been made in the formation of the Latin American Free Trade Area (LAFTA), but should this trading group become viable, most of South America would be included in a form of common market. This being the case, it is expected that LAFTA and CACM would form a working relationship that would extend mutually the trading opportunities of one group within the other. But even without the potential advantages of LAFTA, the increased market provided by the CACM arrangements encouraged Moore Corp. to set up production facilities in one of the member countries.

Prior to 1962, Moore Corp. had owned 70 percent of the shares of Moore Business Forms de Cuba, S.A., a company that employed about 100 persons. The remaining shares were owned by Cubans. Under Castro, the minority shareholders, a number of whom were employees of the company, were forced to leave Cuba. Their shares became forfeit to the Cuban government, which in turn became the minority shareholder. Although it owned only 30 percent of the shares, the government dictated conduct and management of the company, leaving Moore Corp. with no real alternative but to sell its majority interest to the Cuban government. The amount of compensation was agreed to, but since 1962 the method of payment has been under negotiation. It is anticipated that payment will be eventually made in kind, i.e., sugar.

The *de facto* expropriation by Cuba left Moore Corp. without production facilities in the Central American region, at a time when markets were increasing and the CACM was making good progress towards lowering its internal trade barriers. In addition, a number of the personnel from the Cuban operation were seeking to re-establish themselves elsewhere in Latin America. Because of these factors, Moore Corp. sought out a new base for operations in Central America, and met with Alex Dutriz, a Salvadorian businessman with interests in newspapers and printing. Dutriz was interested in expanding his printing operations, and agreed to form a joint venture with Moore Corp.

FORMATION OF THE ENTERPRISE

Pursuant to the agreement reached between Dutriz and Moore Corp., Dutriz had incorporated, as of February 6, 1962, under Salvadorian law, Formas Centroamericanas, S.A. to engage in the production and sale of business forms and related accessories and equipment. Arrangements were made for Armando Criado, the former General Manager of Moore Business Forms de Cuba, S.A., to relocate in San Salvador, and to become General Manager of Formas. Dutriz held a majority of the Formas shares, and minority positions were taken out by Criado, by the manager of Dutriz's already existing general printing company, and by two other Salvadorians.

By agreement dated December 20, 1961, these original shareholders of Formas granted an option to Moore Corp. to acquire up to 49 percent of the ownership of the company, or its successor. Then Formas entered into a technical assistance agreement, dated January 12, 1962, with Moore Business Forms, Inc. (Moore Inc.), an American subsidiary of Moore Corp. In return for royalty payments, Moore Inc. agreed to supply know-how to Formas for the manufacture of business forms, and to permit use of the Moore patents and trade names. This agreement had a termination date of December 31, 1966.

At a shareholder meeting on September 28, 1964, it was resolved to increase the capitalization of Formas as a necessary step in expanding the productive capacities of the company, and to make way for the participation by Moore Corp. It was also resolved to change the company's name from Formas Centroamericanas, S.A. to Moore Business Forms de Centro America, S.A. The increase in capitalization became effective at the same time the articles of incorporation of the new company were issued. On February 19, 1965, Moore Corp. exercised its option to acquire a 49 percent ownership, and achieved this position by subscribing for the newly authorized shares.

ORIGINAL CAPITAL STRUCTURE
AND TECHNICAL ARRANGEMENTS

The authorized capital of Formas was 30,000 colones ($12,000), divided into 300 shares with nominative value of 100 colones each. All these shares had been issued to five residents of El Salvador. When Formas became Moore Business Forms de Centro America, S.A., the authorized capital was increased to 200,000 colones ($80,000) consisting of 2,000 shares with nominative value of 100 colones each.

All shares of the joint venture are issued and fully paid-up. Moore Corp. owns 979, and Mr. John Macdonald Kirkpatrick, Chairman of the Board of the joint venture and Manager of the International Division of Moore Business Forms, Inc., owns 1 share for a total of 980 shares or 49 percent of the capital stock of Moore Business Forms de Centro America, S.A. Of the remaining shares, 51 percent are owned by Dutriz, Criado, and three other Salvadorian residents. Of these shareholders, Dutriz is the largest, holding about 33 percent of all the shares.

El Salvador, unlike some other developing countries, does not place limitations on the degree of foreign ownership of Salvadorian companies. But under the terms of its Industrial Development Law, tax and other concessions are made available to companies that are majority-owned by nationals. Accordingly, in order to qualify the joint venture for these benefits, Moore Corp. restricted its ownership to 49 percent.

When the new company was formed, Moore Corp. took its shares under the option agreement from the newly-issued shares of the joint venture, up to 979, and the remaining authorized but unissued shares were distributed to the five original shareholders of Formas on a basis whereby they maintained the same proportionate equity position as amongst themselves.

As mentioned, Formas had entered into a technical assistance agreement with Moore Inc. Upon formation of the joint venture in 1965, Moore Inc. entered into a royalty and technical assistance agreement under virtually the same terms as the previous agreement with Formas, for the use of know-how, trade names, and brand names of Moore Inc. by Moore Business Forms de Centro America, S.A. throughout the Central American market region. Moore Inc. receives a royalty that is calculated on the production levels of the joint venture. In order to provide for the transfer of know-how, it was not necessary for Moore Inc. to send many personnel from the United States to El Salvador, because Armando Criado and others from the defunct Cuban operation were familiar with the operations and could supply the required expertise.

The initial capital requirements of the company were fully met by the subscriptions for shares, and no debt financing was required. The low cost of commencing operations resulted because Formas, and its successor, used the existing printing plant of Dutriz, and needed only to convert some of the presses and purchase others. The physical plant was in existence, and the joint venture rented this from Dutriz.

MANAGEMENT AND PERSONNEL

The Board of Directors of Moore Business Forms de Centro America, S.A. has five members, namely: John Macdonald Kirkpatrick, Chairman of the Board, Alex Dutriz, Armando Criado y de Varona, Alfredo Ortiz Mancia, and Joaquin Koloffon Carrasco. The latter four directors are all residents of El Salvador, and J. M. Kirkpatrick is resident in Canada. All directors serve in that capacity without compensation. Since Moore Corp. owns only 49 percent of the shares, and there is no provision for cumulative voting, it could theoretically be frozen out of placing representatives on the board. However, that eventuality is not anticipated since Moore Corp. can exercise the required control of operations through its ownership of Moore Inc. which licenses the patents, trade names, etc., to the joint venture.

Mr. Dutriz is President of the company, and Mr. Criado is Secretary and General Manager. Since arriving in El Salvador, Criado has taken out local citizenship, and it is contemplated that other former members of the Cuban company will do likewise. In addition to Mr. Criado, the Assistant General Manager, Sales Manager, and two of the plant supervisors were formerly with the Cuban operation. As General Manager, Criado is the chief executive officer in charge of day-to-day conduct of operations. As of December, 1967, the joint venture had about 150 full time employees. None of the employees are unionized, because local labor laws offer a certain degree of employee protection, and also because labor organization and collective bargaining have not yet become accepted practices in Central America.

The productivity per laborer in El Salvador, even with comparable capital equipment, is below that of the average North American worker. To overcome this gap, modern equipment was introduced into the plant, and training for the present employees has been provided by former members of the Cuban company. In addition, under a technical service agreement with Moore Corp., provision is made for the supply of qualified personnel to instruct in the latest techniques of production. To date, several persons have come from North America to provide this instruction and training for short periods of time.

Laws of El Salvador

El Salvador is the most highly industrialized, though not the largest, of the CACM countries. It is one of the few countries in Latin America that has managed to stabilize its currency. Like a number of other developing countries, it has embarked on a policy of encouraging foreign investment, and grants additional incentives where there is local participation.

Under the Law of Industrial Development, passed January 18, 1961, certain advantages are made available to foreign investors who establish industries in El Salvador that are "new" and "necessary as a producer of goods to meet primary needs." A further qualification is that 51 percent of the capital must be owned by Salvadorians, or sold to Salvadorians within 4 years from the incorporation of the company. A "Salvadorian" is considered to be any citizen of that country, even though he might be a permanent resident of a foreign country. The principal industries covered are manufacturing and food processing, but others can qualify where there is substantial investment in capital goods, and a sizeable number of workers are provided with permanent employment.

Upon meeting the above criteria, an industry can receive from El Salvador the following benefits:

(1) exemption for 10 years from import duties and charges on machinery, equipment, construction materials, and raw materials not available locally;

(2) exemption for 5 years from all organisation, production, sales, capital, and income taxes;

(3) reduction by 50 percent for an additional 5 years of the taxes mentioned above.

In addition to the above advantages offered by El Salvador to a qualifying industry, the incentives of the five CACM countries are also available to any industry established within one of the member countries. National treatment is accorded to goods produced in any one of the countries, meaning that there are no import or export restrictions or taxes on such goods flowing between member countries.

To protect the colone from devaluation, and to discourage the withdrawal of foreign investment, El Salvador has imposed certain exchange controls. An amount equal to only 10 percent of the total money invested by a foreigner can be withdrawn in any one year, whether the money to be withdrawn is income or capital. In addition, the law of June 1, 1961, requires that all foreign exchange must be purchased through the Exchange Control Department of the Central Reserve Bank of El Salvador, and prior written approval is required for all remittances abroad of foreign exchange.

Under the technical assistance and royalty agreements between Moore Inc. and Moore Business Forms de Centro America, S.A., all payments are remitted to Moore Inc. in U.S. currency and deposited in a U.S. account of that company. To date, Moore Inc. has experienced no problems in receiving its payments. Profits have not been remitted to Moore Corp. as dividends. All profits have been retained to meet future expansion requirements, and excess funds are placed in colone bank deposits and savings certificates in San Salvador.

Conduct of Operations

The CACM population is estimated at about 12 million. Moore Corp. estimates that total sales for Central America will reach about $2 million annually, but this figure would be greatly increased if the company could gain access to the South American markets. This would happen if LAFTA and the CACM were to establish a working relationship with each other, but for the present, the company's market is confined to Central America. It has one main competitor in the field of business forms, a Guatemalan firm with a minority interest held by Mexicans.

Moore Business Forms de Centro America, S.A. manufactures continuous forms, "Speedisets" and register forms. Most of the papers used are imported from Canada and the United States. A small portion comes from Guatemala and some of the tissue paper is Scandinavian. All of the paper is purchased competitively in world markets. The company also manufactures its own carbon paper. On its paper imports, there is an exemption from import duties under the laws of El Salvador, since the company qualifies for the industrial incentives, and the paper required for production of the business forms is not available locally.

None of the handling or dispensing machines used in conjunction with the forms is manufactured locally. They are imported from the wholly-owned manufacturing subsidiaries of Moore Corp. in the United States, Kidder Press Company, Inc. of New Hampshire, and Stacy Machine Company, Inc. of Massachusetts. Because these machines are not used in the manufacture of products locally, they do not qualify for exemption of import duties. Moore Corp. has rejected any thought of producing such machines in Central America because the large production runs of the American plants generate economies of scale that more than offset the applicable tariffs.

All sales of both the business forms and imported machines are made directly to customers by salesmen who are employees of the company, except for sales to Panama, where an agency arrangement exists. The company plans, however, to open its own direct sales outlet in Panama, and supply it from El Salvador even though Panama is not part of the CACM.

To protect its competitive position, the company has not made available its profit or production or sales figures since it began operations in 1965.

PLANS FOR EXPANSION

The company's present premises in San Salvador are rented from Alex Dutriz, who uses part of them for his general printing operations. Dutriz wants to expand his own operations into the part now used by the joint venture, and the joint venture also wants to expand its own production capabilities by 50 percent. Accordingly, the company is undertaking to build a new plant in San Salvador.

Under the existing technical services arrangements, Moore Inc. drew the plans for the new plant in collaboration with a local contractor. Including land and structure, but excluding machinery, the total cost of the new plant will be about $300,000. All of the machinery will be leased from Moore Inc. Financing will be provided through retained earnings, supplemented by a loan from the Instituto Salvadoreno de Fomento Industrial (Insafi). Insafi is a government-owned development agency, organized to assist in the financing of new and necessary industries in El Salvador. To obtain this assistance, the following steps are necessary.

1. The architectural plans, with detailed cost estimates, must be submitted to Insafi for approval.

2. Insafi must approve the plans and determine that the industry is new and necessary.

3. The developer must finance himself at least 20 percent of the cost of the land and buildings, and at least 40 percent of the cost of the machinery.

4. At least 85 percent of the personnel to be employed by the company must be Salvadorian citizens.

Moore Business Forms de Centro America, S.A. has already met these conditions and expects to secure Insafi financing for the balance of its costs. The loan will be long term, at commercial rates, secured by a mortgage on the land, premises, and equipment.

PROBLEMS OF DOING BUSINESS

Although the five CACM countries, El Salvador, Costa Rica, Honduras, Guatemala, and Nicaragua, have made considerable progress towards establishing a common market, they have not succeeded completely, and they have not progressed very far in integrating their economies.

For example, the joint venture must still make allowance for the divergent national laws when it imports business form machines from the United States. Import duties are payable to El Salvador, but further import duties are payable to Guatemala when they are shipped for sale to that country. To avoid this double taxation, the company has established wholly-owned subsidiaries in both Guatemala and in Costa Rica to import directly from the United States the machines it sells in those respective countries.

A further problem arises from having to deal in five different currencies. Accounts receivable in the cetsalas of Guatemala must be converted to the colones of El Salvador for bookkeeping purposes, and different price lists are required for each country. In addition, uncertainty is caused by the different exchange rates as they fluctuate from day to day.

Evaluation of the Joint Venture

Moore Corporation, Limited had total world sales for 1966 of $278,733,871 and earned almost 10 percent net profit after taxes. Through its wholly-owned subsidiaries it conducts business in Canada, the United States, Puerto Rico, and Mexico. Since 1964, Moore Corp. has entered into three joint ventures, acquiring a 20 percent interest in Lamson Industries Limited of England, a 45 percent interest in Toppan Moore Business Forms Co. Ltd. of Japan, and a 49 percent interest in Moore Business Forms de Centro America, S.A.

The latter is the first experience of Moore Corp. as a partner in a joint venture in a developing country. It chose to conduct its operations in El Salvador as a minority partner of a joint venture because that country offers tax holidays to new and necessary industries that are owned at least 51 percent by local nationals. Moore Corp. also feels that local ownership offers other advantages to the foreign investor in a developing country through creating better relations between the foreign investor and the local government, the employees, and the customers. As an example, Mr. Kirkpatrick cites that while Insafi loans are available even to companies that are wholly foreign-owned, he feels that the excellent and speedy cooperation that body gave for the construction of the new plant, was to some degree a reflection of the good will arising from local ownership. He feels also that because Salvadorians own a majority of the company and because the government is actively encouraging such joint ventures, nationalization is a very remote possibility.

The largest single criticism against joint ventures is that joint ownership means joint control, thereby precluding business decisions that the foreign investor considers to be in its own best interest. Moore Business Forms de Centro America, S.A. has not experienced this problem, because no business decision has yet arisen where the foreign and local owners have been at odds. Second, Moore Corp. enjoys an ultimate power of control over the operations through the licensing agreement. Third, individuals and not the government, are the local partners. Individual shareholders, regardless of their nationalities, are more likely to agree on policies to maximize returns, and national policies are not as likely to be considered, thereby eliminating certain possible disagreements. On the other hand, since the government is not a shareholder, the full weight of governmental authority could not be as readily mobilized to support programs that would benefit the company.

In the typical joint venture, the foreign partner usually contributes know-how and capital, and the local partner provides knowledge of local markets, institutions, and conditions. In this instance, the local partners had a limited role to play. They had to provide 51 percent equity ownership, and Alex Dutriz provided employment for personnel displaced from the Cuban operation and premises for the company to begin production. Knowledge of local conditions was less important because Moore Corp. had available the top personnel from its Cuban company, who were already familiar with the problems of doing business in Latin America.

When tax holidays for the joint venture expire in 1975, the principal reason for Moore Corp. not owning all of the capital of the joint venture will no longer be tenable. By that time, however, the government could introduce further incentives for local ownership, such as other tax holidays, decreased withholding taxes on dividends paid to foreigners, and differential exchange controls. Apart from such specific measures, Moore Corp. feels that it has much to gain from continuing local ownership by way of better relations with customers, employees, and the government. It has, therefore, no plans to buy out the local shareholders once the Industrial Development Law benefits expire. Nor does Moore Corp. intend to alter any of the other terms of the joint venture arrangement, as it is very satisfied with the results of its first joint venture in a developing country.

Venture between a Multinational Corporation and Local Company

XIV: DRUGS IN INDIA

General Policy of Merck & Co., Inc.

THE COMPANY

Merck & Co., Inc. is the result of the merger in 1953 of Merck & Co. and Sharp & Dohme Incorporated. It is engaged primarily in the production and marketing of compounds for human and animal health. With implementation in the U.S. of the Medicare and Medicaid programs, the relatively small proportion of drug purchases previously paid for by the government is increasing.

On January 31, 1968, Calgon Corporation merged with Merck and became a wholly-owned Merck subsidiary. Calgon's rapid growth in recent years demonstrates the potential of water treatment products and services for the home, industry, and municipalities. The merger places Merck in promising new fields such as water pollution treatment.

In 1967 the company's net sales were $528,162,000, from which international sales accounted for $176,682,000. The net income came very near $90 million. As a rule, approximately three-fourths of the earnings come from developed countries. The company had 51,800 stockholders and 18,300 employees.

As the 1967 results show, the international share of Merck's operations is substantial. In the same year, international operations accounted for approximately half of the company's sales gain. The contributions of Merck's international operations to the U.S. balance of payments, amounting in 1967 alone to approximately $75,000,000, have over the years greatly outweighed the company's investments outside the United States.

Merck products are comparatively small and light and transportation costs are relatively small. Therefore, exporting from the U.S. is economically attractive. However, because of other considerations, including tariff and quota regulations, the company has established manufacturing operations in twenty-two countries abroad. The company has also a number of licensing arrangements in the United States and other countries.

In the great majority of cases Merck has wholly-owned subsidiaries, including those in Canada, Europe, Latin America, Australia, South Africa, Lebanon, and the Philippines.

POLICY TOWARD JOINT VENTURES

According to Merck's management, the company was indeed compelled to establish joint ventures in Asian countries because of law or government policy. Merck has joint ventures in Japan (50%-50%), Thailand (60%-40%), New Zealand (75%-25%), Pakistan (75%-25%), and India (60%-40%). The company has no case of minority participation and has only one case of equal participation.

Most foreign corporations emphasize that they do not have any definite policy toward joint ventures and that they deal with each case on its merits. Merck on the contrary has developed a definite policy toward business ventures. The company wants to exercise three controls: (1) control of management; (2) control of production; (3) control over the distribution system. Consequently, Merck looks for the largest possible majority. The reason for this strong preference, in addition to normal management considerations, is a specific desire to protect patents and know-how.

In only one case does Merck not have voting control: the 50 percent to 50 percent Japanese joint venture. Since the products sold by this company are entirely the result of the Merck's U.S. research program and because of Merck's broad marketing expertise, the Japanese partners generally have accepted the American management's position in questions of policy. This equal joint venture, an important exception to Merck's policy, was motivated by the great attraction of the Japanese market and by the very strict attitude of the Japanese Government toward foreign participation. Merck prefers majority positions in foreign ventures, although it is willing to consider each situation on its own merits.

All this does not mean that Merck is indifferent to the problem of acquiring a local identity in the country of investment. The company strongly prefers to employ nationals of the country in which the for-

eign venture is located. A training program in all aspects of management insures the formation of a cadre of trained nationals and allows
the promotion of nationals of these countries to replace foreign nationals over a period of time.

Merck's preference for a majority does not mean that only a
perfunctory interest will be lent to the local partner. The local participation may be financially substantial. Also, Merck has been willing
to give the local partners responsibility for the distribution system. In
these instances, the local partner, with the advice of Merck, has set
up a separate sales company. Whatever the solution chosen in any
specific case, however, Merck always shows a keen interest in distribution methods and commercial results.

Merck's policy toward joint ventures is guided by a number of factors. Among them is the desire to protect patents and know-how. In
the future, Merck might face a situation where the advantage of
being or remaining in an attractive market will outweigh the disadvantages of being or becoming a minority partner. Similarly, Merck,
although traditionally reluctant to undertake ventures with governments, might have to form a joint venture with a government or a
governmental corporation, if a market seems very attractive and
there is no private partner available.

Merck Sharp & Dohme of India Ltd.

FORMATION

The Negotiations. Merck has been involved in the Indian market
for a long time. It marketed finished goods through two local distribution firms. The initiative for the formation of the manufacturing
joint venture came from Merck in response to the interest of the Indian Government—expressed in connection with its second Five-
Year Plan—in the local manufacture of drugs to provide employment, to build up native skills, and to save foreign exchange. In an
address delivered on January 6, 1958, Dr. A. N. Rao, Chief Industrial Adviser to the Ministry of Heavy Industries, indicated that
the manufacture of basic drugs and pharmaceuticals chemicals would
be a part of Indian development plans.

The market for these products became a contest between Russian
and American competitors. In order to get the bid, the Russians offered very attractive financial conditions, i.e. long-term loans at low

interest rate. Merck made a proposal that was twofold: the company would give technical assistance to a governmental corporation for a streptomycin plant, in exchange for a low fee; it would also form a 60 percent to 40 percent joint venture with private Indian interests for the manufacture mainly of vitamins and steroid hormones.

The Indian Government showed immediate interest in the Merck proposal. However, as to the second part of the deal they made a counter-proposal: they wanted a 50 percent to 50 percent joint venture with a governmental corporation. Merck's management rejected this offer, which, in its view, seemed to contain potential conflicts of interest.

The negotiations relative to the streptomycin plant came to a conclusion in April 1958. Merck gave know-how and technical assistance to an Indian governmental corporation and received a moderate fee. In October 1958, after considerable discussion and bargaining, the Indian Government gave its approval to a 60 percent to 40 percent joint venture between Merck and Indian private interests. Tata Sons, Ltd. had agreed to become the local partner in the new venture, Merck Sharp & Dohme of India Ltd.

One might wonder why the government finally renounced its proposal and accepted the Merck proposal. On this, a top government official said that other private 60 percent to 40 percent joint ventures had been accepted previously and the government wanted to avoid discrimination. Moreover, and according to this official, a primary goal of the government is not so much to ensure control by nationals as to create a broad capital market and to stimulate Indian entrepreneurs. In the Merck case, the substantial shareholding of the Tata group appeared to the government a satisfactory way of associating Indian capital with the benefits of the enterprise. This one example would tend to indicate that the attitude of the Indian Government toward foreign control is in fact more flexible than is sometimes imagined abroad.

Formation of the Venture. A temporary plant was put into operation in 1959, but the formal opening of the new facilities at Bhandup, near Bombay, did not take place until March 1, 1964. The manufacturing facilities were installed for a full pharmaceutical line, including an antibiotic subdividing unit, a general organic unit, and a basic Vitamin B_{12} manufacture unit. Initially the chemical production line consisted mainly of steroids, diuretics, and some sulpha drugs. The production has since been expanded and diversified.

FINANCING

Equity Capital. Merck Sharp & Dohme of India Ltd. (MSDI) has an authorized capital of 42 million rupees, which is approximately the equivalent of $5.6 million (pre-devaluation).[1] The capital is divided into 4,200,000 shares of 10 rupees each. The paid-up capital amounts to 18 million rupees, which is approximately the equivalent of $2.4 million ($3,750,000 pre-devaluation when the investment was made.) Both partners paid in the amount corresponding to their share in the capital. The Tata interests, which had made a substantial investment in the venture, expected to receive reasonable profits out of it. MSDI management has kept this in mind in proposing the annual dividend of the company.

Loan Capital. No long-term loan was concluded. The company, which has received normal services from the banks, has dealt primarily with the Punjab Bank.

The equity capital and the loan capital invested in MSDI are substantial. However, if compared with the sums involved in mining investments, they are small. Consequently, a company such as MSDI is less dependent than mining companies on the assistance of foreign or international financing institutions. MDSI was not influenced by third parties in determining the structure and the main features of the venture.

MANAGEMENT

Board of Directors. In 1968 the composition of the board did not reflect exactly the composition of the equity capital. The board has nine members: six Merck representatives and three Tata representatives. Of the current directors, three have British citizenship, one is American, and five are Indian nationals. The board surveys and approves the general policies and operations of the joint venture. It also serves as a channel of communication between the partners. It usually meets from six to eight times a year. The Tata representatives participate very actively in the board proceedings.

Day-to-Day Management. For practical purposes, the enterprise has been managed in the same way as a wholly foreign-owned subsidiary. There has been no interference of Tata in the operation of the enterprise.

1. The Indian devaluation of 1966 established the rupee at 7.5 = $1.00. The old rate had been Rs. 4.76 = $1.00.

Of the higher officers responsible for operating management, the managing director is an Indian national, the sales manager is Australian, the chief of production is British-American. An Indian who joined the company as an accountant is now secretary.

In the future, senior top management of MSDI will be even more predominantly Indian. The country has now excellent financial specialists, a reflection of the country's tradition. This is less true for manufacturing and technical personnel. Senior Indian personnel come fairly regularly to the United States for training and discussion.

Financial Policy. From the beginning, Merck & Co., Inc. has accepted a policy of long-range growth for India, and accordingly wants to apply profits liberally to reinvestment. Although the financially powerful Tata group expects to receive reasonable profits, it also has a full understanding of long-range growth requirements. Incidentally, Tata's management observes that too often foreign collaborators in India want to distribute high dividends because the rupee is a weak currency. In 1967, total reserves were in excess of 5 million rupees (approximately $660,000). This policy of long-range growth and reinvestment has allowed the company to carry out several expansions.

Labor. The company's total staff exceeds 600 employees. With three exceptions it is Indian. The management of MSDI chooses the personnel; Tata does not interfere in the selection. Employees all come from the general labor market. At the end of 1967 they organized a union. Labor relations have been harmonious.

The social benefits provided by the company include medical services, accident insurance, retirement benefits, and a subsidized canteen.

TECHNICAL ASPECTS

Majority Participation and Licensing. In 1958, in a letter addressed to Mr. Rao, a Merck executive—Mr. Ekaireb—wrote:

Many of our present patent license agreements from others provide that the license goes to Merck and Co., Inc. and its subsidiaries, or that Merck may license its subsidiaries. A subsidiary is defined in such terms as to require Merck ownership. We would expect to follow that pattern in the future and would hesitate to suggest a change because of the questions it would raise in the licensors' minds as well as the difficulties it would create where we are licensors.

Speaking of the trademarks, patents, and know-how that Merck would provide to the joint venture, Mr. Ekaireb added:

We would want to reserve the right to terminate the use of any or all of these in the event of any change in the ownership or control of the joint company not resulting from action considered by us voluntary on our part.

In fact, Merck wanted mainly to insure that its patents and know-how would be adequately protected. This, in effect, was accomplished through the majority ownership.

For years, the transfer of foreign technology into Indian hands has been a primary concern of the Indian Government. One might then wonder why the government, in the case of MSDI, permitted technology to remain in foreign hands. On this, a government official said that in this case technology could remain in foreign hands, because MSDI is a well-established business. Although some official statements on this problem of transfer of technology might seem rigid, the case of MSDI shows that the government is willing to examine each case on its merits and tries to take all factors into account.

Royalties. As to technical assistance, patents, know-how, and trademarks, the rights and obligations of the partners were laid down in a formal agreement. However, no royalties were provided for. Why did Merck not ask for royalties?

A Merck officer simply stated that "in this case we considered we would be satisfied with dividends," but another officer wondered if the parent company should not have asked for royalties. In April 1963, all prices of pharmaceuticals were frozen. Some vitamin prices decreased. When the cost decreases, the government expects the manufacturing companies to reduce its prices. If royalties had been granted to the American company, they could have been added to the cost.

SALES

Indian Market. Sales increased from 32.1 million rupees in 1966 to 38.5 million rupees in 1967, and to 43 million rupees in 1968. MSDI does not import finished goods from the parent company; it imports only raw materials and intermediate goods. The major part of MSDI products are sold in finished form. As to competition, all major world producers are present on the market—the Russians have a streptomycin plant.

The Relation with Voltas. Voltas [2] is the distributing firm for MSDI products. The shareholders of Voltas are: Volkart Brothers (a

2. See the Voltas case, *supra* pp. 151–66.

Swiss company), Tata, the Life Insurance Corporation, the Unit Trust of India, and the general public. The role of Tata is predominant in the company. Voltas is engaged in manufacture, but is traditionally a marketing firm.

MSDI and Voltas are in continuous discussions on distribution methods. MSDI considers Voltas as a very efficient organization. Consequently, it leaves the trading firm largely free to conduct the distribution of its products.

Exports. Often a foreign corporation is concerned that the products manufactured by the joint venture will compete with the products it manufactures in or exports to other countries, although, in a sense, patent licensing agreements tend to lessen this concern. In developing countries the problem is often even more remote because the products manufactured by the joint venture are seldom internationally competitive.

In the case of MSDI, the joint venture has exported in a moderate degree. The exports have primarily gone to various countries in Africa and Southeast Asia. Until now there has been no conflict between the company and the government policies for encouraging exports, largely because MSDI has been one of few pharmaceutical companies able to satisfy the Indian Government's policy. There is no formal restriction on exports by MSDI to any part of the world. Actual export policy is coordinated with exports from other Merck subsidiaries in various countries.

GOVERNMENT RELATIONS

The management has to deal with several governmental ministries, for instance: health; petrochemicals and chemicals; and industry. The company feels these relationships have been satisfactory.

Internal Prices. As has been noted, all prices for pharmaceuticals were frozen in 1963. For new products the company must submit cost information and negotiate prices. The Ministry of Petrochemicals and Chemicals deals with these questions. On June 6, 1966, the government put into force a devaluation of 36.5 percent. This increased the cost of imported materials and consequently reduced the profits; the devaluation had a strong impact on MSDI. In spite of these difficulties the company managed to maintain a margin of profit.

Foreign Exchange Requirements. The company has still to import raw materials and intermediate goods. Although the situation seemed to improve in 1968, India had experienced several years of foreign exchange difficulties. The impact of these difficulties on the company was felt mainly in 1965. It was difficult to obtain the necessary exchange permits, but this never affected the production. At times, however, there was only a small margin of safety.

Foreign Exchange Savings. The second Five-Year Plan provided the opportunity for the formation of MSDI. One of the primary goals of the plan was the saving of foreign exchange through replacement of imports. Merck's management said that the savings realized for India by MSDI have been substantial. Tata, a strong supporter of the implementation of national goals by private enterprises, also recognized this. Finally, a government official said that the contribution in this respect of MSDI to the country is satisfactory. There is thus a general agreement on this point.

Taxation. Since the Chinese invasion taxes have been increased in order to support the Indian military effort. The corporate tax is 60 percent. Because MSDI benefits from some general fiscal incentives, the actual rate of the tax levied on the company is generally slightly less. On the other hand, MSDI does not benefit from any special tax exemption. In the opinion of the management of MSDI, the fiscal burden in India is very heavy.

EVALUATION

At the origin, Merck was successful in getting allocated to private enterprise an activity that might easily have been taken over entirely by public enterprise. In the shaping of the venture the U.S. company asked for a majority participation in order to have a unified management and to protect patents, trademarks, and know-how. It is true that most of the time management has to be unified in order to be efficient. The desire to protect patents and know-how is also understandable. It might be questioned whether a majority participation was really necessary in order to implement these goals. However, in this case, the answer to the question is perhaps not of the utmost importance because, from all indications, both the government and Tata have agreed completely to the proposals of the American company.

Tata as a passive investor does not interfere with the management of the venture. As an investor, the Indian concern, of course, hopes for fair dividends from the venture, although it fully recognizes the need for long-range growth and reinvestment. Tata's role is greater than it might seem at first, because Voltas is the distributing firm for

MSDI products and Tata has the control of Voltas. Tata has been satisfied until now with its cooperation with MSDI. However, difficulties might arise if some day, as sales expand, MSDI were tempted to create a distribution system of its own. Friction might arise also if Tata decided some day to engage in the manufacture of pharmaceuticals. According to Tata, however, this will not happen in the near future. Merck clearly recognizes that the prestige of Tata—one of India's oldest, largest, and most experienced enterprises—has been very helpful in the development of the joint venture, and the relationship between the partners has been entirely harmonious.

The Indian Government looks on MSDI favorably because of its good record. Moreover, it notes that the company has complied with objectives of the plan and has carried out a fair amount of Indianization of the staff. Because of these positive elements it does not object to the foreign control of the venture and accepts that the technology remain in foreign hands. Nevertheless, a government official said that if MSDI were to undertake a substantial expansion, the government would then ask the management to make a public issue of shares, which would increase Indian financial participation. In any event, the MSDI case shows that the government can be quite pragmatic and flexible and tries to take a global view of business ventures.

In brief, points of friction and difficulties are not to be excluded in the future, but so far the venture seems to have been on the whole satisfactory for both the partners and the government.

Venture between Multinational Corporation and the Government

XV: ELECTRONIC PRODUCTS IN INDONESIA

N.V. Philips Gloeilampenfabrieken

ACTIVITIES

N.V. Philips' Gloeilampenfabrieken (Philips) is a much diversified Dutch company. The main product divisions are:

1. Lighting
2. Domestic appliances
3. Radio, television, and record-playing equipment
4. Electronic components and materials
5. Electro-acoustics
6. Telecommunications and defence systems
7. Industrial equipment
8. X-ray and medical equipment
9. Pharmaceutical-chemical products
10. Allied industries and glass
11. Computers

In the field of records, Philips has engaged in a 50—50 joint venture with the German company Siemens: Philips' Phonographic Industries/Deutsche Grammophon Gesellschaft. The venture has been successful and broadened its interests to include the entertainment industry, music publishing, and artist management. Along with the large market for records, the scope for marketing musicassettes has considerably increased. Sales of this product have gone up accordingly.

Computers. The European market for computers is no longer left to American corporations. In 1968 the first series of general-purpose computers, the P 1000 family, comprising three types, was supplied to users within the Philips organization. Beginning in 1969 deliveries were made to third parties in the European market. This series will be provided with an extensive package of software, peripheral equipment, and documentation. The marketing and service organization built up has the necessary systems analysts on its staff, as well as hardware and software specialists. Placed with national Philips organizations, they will handle the rapidly growing market for computers in selected areas.

Air-traffic Control. The work done and techniques utilized by Philips in various technologically-advanced and complementary fields have allowed it to participate in the important effort to control the rapidly increasing world air traffic. The first of the new type of computer-controlled automatic switching centers for telegraph and data traffic was supplied to KLM at Amsterdam. This center will form part of the Société Internationale de Télécommunications Aéronautiques (SITA), the backbone of which is constituted by highspeed data circuits between Amsterdam, Frankfurt, Paris, and London. The exchanges for Paris and London too will be supplied by Philips. At Schiphol Airport, near Amsterdam, the "Airlord" system supplied to KLM is now in operation, permitting very fast handling of passenger data. The electronic "Airlord" system for the automatic handling of passenger data include the check-in units in the departure hall and equipment for feeding the principal flight data to the computer. The radar equipment was also provided by Philips.

World Distribution of Sales and Assets. More than 90 percent of sales realized by many large U.S. corporations are on the domestic market. For Philips, the proportion is approximately inverse; about 90 percent of its sales are made abroad. This shows why name and reputation around the world are so important for the Dutch company.

Sales are distributed in the following way:

Europe	73 percent
Western Hemisphere	16 percent
Rest of the world	11 percent

The Western Hemisphere comprises the Americas and Oceania. The rest of the world is Asia and Africa mainly. The share of the "rest of the world" is even smaller when we consider the distribution of assets:

In millions of guilders [1]		
	1967	1966
Netherlands	3,616	3,647
Other European countries	5,394	5,169
Western Hemisphere	1,506	1,436
Other countries	574	528

JOINT VENTURES IN DEVELOPING COUNTRIES: GENERAL POLICY

Exports and Manufacture. Because of various economic factors, Philips has often expanded its foreign sales organizations to include manufacturing activities. In the beginning, Philips only exported. Sales organizations involve not only much time and many people but also considerable capital investments—generally more than those required in factories. Long-term commercial considerations make it necessary to stay in a country. Philips' reputation is involved: a withdrawal would have a detrimental effect on relations with the government. Long-term investment makes further development necessary. When there is an existing sales organization and when sales are sufficient, the local company is mature enough to start manufacturing operations, mostly beginning with the assembly of components.

Philips has factories in 26 developing countries. In most of these countries, the operations are relatively small. Several problems have been encountered, but two in particular have been objects of concern. Firstly, the activities of a concern like Philips can reduce the foreign exchange requirements but practically never eliminate them. The reason is that many components can be made at a reasonable price only if really large outputs can be produced, and the markets of the developing countries are not wide enough to allow the production of such large outputs. Consequently, imports of components and raw materials remain necessary together with imports of know-how. These foreign exchange requirements create problems in those developing countries that lack foreign exchange. Other concerns such as those that process local raw materials for the market of industrialized countries do not have this foreign exchange problem because they often earn more foreign exchange than they use. Secondly, operations of an electronic industry for a limited market employ relatively small

1. The guilder is equal to about $0.26.

numbers of workers, although considerable employment is generated in distribution channels.

As many developing countries are especially concerned with foreign exchange shortage and widespread unemployment, any electronic company is indirectly affected by the fact that its contribution in either respect is unavoidably inferior, in relative terms, to that of other industries.

Formation of Joint Ventures. Once Philips has decided to manufacture in a developing country, it may do so alone, or it may form a venture jointly with a local partner. At any moment joint venture agreements are being negotiated in one or more developing countries. Sometimes Philips is obliged to enter into a joint venture with a local partner because government policy requires the participation of local interests. In the Philips' experience, "compelled" joint ventures are more often the result of government policy than the result of a law. Moreover, it has sometimes been obliged to take the government itself as the local partner. On the other hand, Philips has little experience with local development banks as partners in joint ventures.

In the Philips' experience, the nature of the product has an influence on the decision to form or not to form a joint venture. For instance, Philips has few joint ventures in its traditional fields (such as light bulbs). The governments of developing countries usually are not interested in these traditional fields, either because they are not regarded as a priority objective of economic development, or because they are not expected to be very profitable.

At the other extreme, joint ventures are undesired by foreign investors in the manufacture of very sophisticated products. A joint venture uses more managerial energy than a wholly-owned operation. To run a business for a very sophisticated product requires good management capacity. It is easier for two managerial teams to cooperate in a simple assembly operation. Moreover, in the manufacture of electronic microscopes, for instance, the partner would be a partner only on paper: there are few firms in the world competent in this field, even in developed countries.

Once the decision to create a joint venture has been made, Philips looks for the establishment of a basic agreement, which is a preliminary contract embodying the principles and policies that the partners intend to apply. The agreement is made in writing and its content varies from one case to another.

Management Problems. One of the most difficult problems facing the partners is the alternative between a unified management or a truly joint operating management. Philips' executives unhesitatingly agree that it is better to have a unified management; where this is not possible, there should be a clear division of responsibilities. An example cited below will show the inconveniences of a situation where the respective responsibilities were not clearly defined. As a rule however, the management of Philips' joint ventures is unified.

Another problem that is often the source of conflict between partners in joint ventures is the profit policy: to what extent should profits be distributed and to what extent should they be reinvested? The attitude of Philips towards this problem is that a venture has first to make profits and provide long-term employment. As to the dividend pay-out policy, Philips does not believe in the "quick dollar" and applies a rather conservative policy. Reinvestment of earnings and growth are viewed as essential, but of course shareholders everywhere expect a fair dividend. There is one thing about which Philips is very definite: to sell out is absolutely contrary to the philosophy of the company; it does not pay to withdraw when a venture suffers a temporary setback.

Finally, the possibility of competition between the products made by the joint venture and the products made or sold by the foreign corporation in other countries can cause bitter conflicts between the partners. Philips regards this problem as somewhat theoretical, because in many cases it is difficult to export from a developing country; however, the Indian joint venture has been able to export to neighboring countries. In the long run, Philips sees a solution to this delicate problem in an international specialization among the company's ventures around the world.

Philips Joint Ventures. After describing the general attitude of Philips towards joint ventures in developing countries, it seems appropriate to illustrate this attitude by a few cases.

In India, Philips established a public limited company and floated shares on the Indian capital market, which is much more developed than the capital market of most developing countries. It is an important joint venture and has about 5,000 employees. The company produces lighting articles, radio receiving equipment, electronic measuring and testing equipment, and most of the component parts of these articles. Philips-India is a case where, due to the size of the market and government pressure, an intensive import-substitution effort has been made.

In the Philippines, Philips was forced to industrialize locally and to form a joint venture with local interests. The government then granted protection to the new venture. Everything should have functioned properly. Unfortunately, the venture failed because of smuggling from Hong-Kong and Taiwan. Smuggling of complete radio sets was possible because the customs are not in control of the coast line of the hundreds of islands comprising the Philippines. In the future, with integrated circuits applied in radio receivers, the essential parts for, say, 200 sets can be transported in a matchbox. This makes customs control of electronic components virtually impossible and as a consequence the markets of many developing countries for such goods may in fact become open markets.

A final example: the government of a certain country stipulated that Philips should train local technicians selected by the government. It also wanted Philips to provide a technical manager. The technicians were not then selected by the government on the basis of their ability. When Philips pointed this out, the government refused to reconsider its candidates. Philips then sent a technical manager. When anything was wrong the government declared that it was the technical manager who was at fault. When the technical manager made any requests, he was rebuffed on the grounds that he was in an advisory position. According to a Philips executive, this case shows clearly that a joint venture will not work when the respective responsibilities and powers of the partners are not clearly defined and divided. Moreover, a manager's power must correspond to his responsibilities.

THE CONTROL PROBLEM AND THE SUCCESS
OF A JOINT VENTURE

Degree of Participation. In its joint ventures abroad Philips has various degrees of participation. If a venture is going to be very profitable, Philips naturally prefers to have as large a majority as possible. Nevertheless, Philips has often a minority participation, at least at the beginning of a venture.

In cases of minority participation, Philips prefers to leave the management in the hands of the local partner. As Philips is very anxious to preserve its reputation, it wants to avoid the possibility of a conflict between a locally-controlled board of directors and a foreign executive committee. Therefore, the Dutch company does not seek the conclusion of a management contract. All this does not mean, however, that Philips is content to be a passive investor. It insists on the right and effective opportunity to exercise adequate measures of control over the operation of the enterprise, especially in planning and accounting. Also it asks for a right of veto for certain important decisions.

When Philips is in a minority position it still quite often grants the right to sell the product under its trademark. Even in mere technical agreements it sometimes grants this right. However, Philips is concerned to protect its name and its reputation: the partners therefore agree that the right to the trademark can be withdrawn if the product does not meet specified quality standards.

It may occur that Philips starts with a 50 percent participation. It has no objection on principle to 50 percent to 50 percent joint ventures. In such cases persuasion and mutual trust are even more vital than in other joint ventures.

Philips often starts with a minority or equal participation, but this does not mean that it will always remain in such position. Quite frequently Philips proceeds from a minority to a majority position even if this step had not been provided for from the start: for instance, where the company proceeds to a capital increase for expansion, and the local partner cannot provide its share of the increase.

When its reputation was at stake, Philips has been known to buy out the share of the partner. The reputation of the company is viewed as something very important vis-a-vis the public, the government, and other interests in the country.

The Success of a Joint Venture. To Philips there is much more to a joint venture than formal points such as the degree of participation and control. According to a company executive, voting power is a means of last resort. Even in such a sophisticated field as electronics, the formal matter of control is not viewed as so important. Nor is control viewed as essential to insure profitable operation. If things are going badly in one venture, the group would lose money, but would not suffer very profoundly. Considering its reluctance to withdraw from its ventures, it would find a compensating profit for its risks in other ventures.

Many foreign corporations are concerned about the coordination between their worldwide operations. Majority control of joint ventures appears to them essential in order to ensure a satisfactory coordination. Philips considers a large degree of autonomy of managements abroad as essential; the formal instrument of voting control, which the parent company enjoys over an affiliated company, should only be exercised in exceptional cases. Even the wholly-owned subsidiaries outside the Netherlands have a considerable autonomy.

Philips sees several elements that are more likely to ensure the success of a joint venture than the degree of participation. For instance, the flow of know-how from the foreign corporation to the joint venture is viewed as essential. Moreover, all persons interviewed in the Philips organization insisted on the extreme importance of the choice of the local partner. There should be no prejudice in this choice; some foreign corporations would under no circumstance enter a joint venture with government, but Philips takes no dogmatic stand on this matter, as will be shown below by the Indonesian case. In the experience of the Dutch company, it is rather rare to find local partners in developing countries who have business experience. Joint ventures have strong personal aspects; it is therefore essential to provide for preemption rights that can be used in cases of capital increase or when a partner wishes to withdraw. Finally, if the local partner is good, it would only be detrimental to abuse a position of power. Philips prefers to convince. It aims at studying the planning, the results, and the accounting and afterwards giving its opinion. The real force is rather in the knowledge that the executives and the employees of an enterprise have between them. Philips feels that it does have the arguments and the knowledge necessary to convince its partners.

Indonesia

HISTORY AND ECONOMY

Profile. Indonesia has a total land area of about 2 million square kilometers or 735,000 square miles. It is an archipelago nation of over 2,500 islands. The five major islands are Kalimantan, Sumatra, Sulawesi, Java, and West Irian. The capital is Djakarta.

The country has 112 million people who constitute the world's fifth most populous nation; 72 percent live in agricultural areas. There is overpopulation in Java, which has three fifths of Indonesia's total population. Immigration to Sumatra and even more to Kalimantan is not only an economic necessity, it could also be a factor of national unity.

The natural resources of the country are substantial. The main cultivations are rice, maize, and millet. The main plantations are rubber, sugar, tea, coffee, copra, pepper. Among the mineral resources one should first cite oil: the fields of Palembang, in Sumatra, were the foundation of Shell's fortune. Indonesia also has coal, iron, tin, bauxite, manganese, nickel, and gold.

It is difficult to make an accurate evaluation of the country's natural resources. Mr. Hamengkubuwono IX, Sultan of Jogjakarta and Indonesian Minister of State for Economy, Finance and Industry, has rightly observed:

The popular world view is that Indonesia is a treasure-house of natural resources. In all frankness, nobody knows exactly the wealth there is in and on the ground and in the seas around Indonesia. Only 5 percent of the country is on the geological maps, 40 percent on the geographic, and under 1 percent on the oceanographic maps.[2]

Recent History. Until the end of the Second World War, Indonesia was under Dutch colonial power, but in 1945 Dr. Sukarno declared the independence of the country. In 1946 the Republic of Indonesia was formed and was recognized by the Netherlands. However, guerilla warfare between Indonesia and Dutch soldiers poisoned relations between the two countries. In the 1949 Hague Conference, the Netherlands transferred their sovereignty to the United States of Indonesia, but a union continued between the two countries. In the same year separatist movements in some islands struggled against the central government, which asserted that they were fomented by foreign capitalists. In 1950 Indonesia became a member of the United Nations and adopted a unitary constitution. In 1954 the union between the Netherlands and Indonesia was dissolved.

In 1956 and in the following years the New Guinea (or West Irian) problem led to further deterioration of the relations between the two countries. All the Dutch had to leave the country. In 1957 an attempt against Dr. Sukarno's life was also attributed to foreigners and a new nationalistic wave broke out. All Dutch organizations and corporations were taken under custody. In 1959 Dr. Sukarno transformed Indonesia into a presidential type of democracy, and in 1960 he dissolved Parliament and created an Assembly of the People. In 1962 the Netherlands and Indonesia reached an agreement on the transfer of West Irian. In 1963 this area, which was previously under Dutch control, was transferred to Indonesian administration, after a brief period of direct administration by the United Nations.

2. "Indonesia plans a brighter future", in *Progress*, p. 166, N. 2, (1968).

In 1965 a Communist-backed attempt to seize control of the government was blocked by the Army. The Indonesian Communist Party was subsequently eliminated as an open, organized political force. In 1966 a new cabinet was formed with a five-man Presidium headed by Army Chief, General Suharto.

Foreign Aid. The new government inherited a total debt to foreign countries of no less than $2.4 billion. With the assistance of the International Monetary Fund, the government is implementing an economic stabilization program. The United States is providing support to this program through participation in Indonesian debt rescheduling and economic assistance conferences, Food for Peace commodity sale agreements, and several programs financed through the Agency for International Development.

The United States and several other major Indonesian creditors met in Paris in December 1966 to reschedule payments due on the large Indonesian debt. The resulting agreement provided for a consolidation of all payments on arrears and also those debts falling due between July 1966 and December 1967. Payments on the consolidated amount will only start to be made as from 1971 onwards. This agreement released some of Indonesia's foreign exchange for development use.

A meeting was held in Amsterdam in February 1967. The conference of creditors examined the requirements for foreign assistance during the year 1967 to support the economic stabilization program. New economic assistance was granted to meet Indonesia's essential import requirements. In the autumn of 1968, the creditor countries again met in Amsterdam. The creditors decided to meet regularly and follow closely the development of the situation. Indonesia affirmed its determination to accord all creditors, those from communist countries as well as those from Western countries, nondiscriminatory treatment.

Indonesia has renewed its active membership in the United Nations, the International Bank for Reconstruction and Development. and the International Monetary Fund, and has joined the Asian Development Bank. In order to bolster American private investments, an Investment Guaranty Agreement was concluded between Indonesia and the United States at the beginning of 1967.

Return to Equilibrium. Early in 1966 the People's Provisional Assembly, known in the abbreviated form as Madjelis, adopted a decision giving the highest priority to improvement of the economy. It ordered the use of market forces instead of administrative and political pressures. It insisted on a democratic economy to call forth the initiative and creative capacities of every citizen. The Madjelis decision ordered decontrol—and debureaucratization—to give the economy maximum freedom. For the Indonesian people, who had been living for many years under a regime that tried to include every sector of life under its direct control, the Madjelis decision constituted a strikingly radical change.

This new economic philosophy was applied to the implementation of the government's goals: combat inflation, improve production, and bring the balance of payments into eventual equilibrium. The government took the decision to abandon nonproductive prestige projects; more than 400 projects were thus abandoned. Greater emphasis was placed on the production of food and export commodities. A differential interest rate ensures the use of bank credits for these priority objectives.

The government decided to rehabilitate existing enterprises rather than launch new projects. It also took the decision on a matter of principle to return to their owners foreign properties that had been taken over.

The government also decided to compel state corporations to operate under conditions similar to those governing private enterprise; as part of the overall stabilization program, subsidies for state enterprises are being phased out, noneconomic prices and rates for many products and services corrected, and preferential, unrealistic credit terms eliminated. The objective was to force state enterprises to compete in the market under the same conditions as govern operations of private firms. Prices for gasoline, diesel oil, kerosene, natural gas, postal services, electricity, metered water, telecommunications, ocean shipping, and bus and rail fares are among those that were significantly increased.

THE FOREIGN INVESTMENT LAW

The performances of the takeover teams (i.e. the official teams that were imposed by the Sukarno regime and that took custody and management of the enterprises) were very often disappointing. The government led by General Suharto realized that a "take-off" of the economy would necessitate a great improvement in the investment climate. It agreed to the principle of compensation to foreign corporations, but the financial problems of the country will render such a compensation difficult. In fact, the government has been trying mainly to make arrangements with these corporations so that their properties could be given back and operated by them again. The government has aimed at getting rid of the problems of running these enterprises.

In September 1966, Indonesia and the Netherlands concluded an agreement for compensation of the nationalized Dutch assets. Philips has as yet not received any cash compensation pursuant to the compensation agreement concluded by the Dutch Government. According to this agreement, private persons and small companies tend to be favored in respect of the date of judgment so that the relatively small amount that Philips may receive as compensation will be minimized by the fact that this payment takes place towards the end of the century.

On December 12, 1966, a Presidium Instruction authorized the return to their owners of non-Dutch foreign enterprises taken over during the "Malaysian confrontation." On December 24, 1966, the Foreign Investment Law was adopted. On January 10, 1967, an explanatory and complementary Presidium Instruction was issued.

Direct Foreign Investment. The Foreign Investment Law permits direct foreign investment in all fields except defense industries. In fields vital to the public welfare, however, such as transportation, telecommunications, and electricity, the law specifies that foreign capital may not exercise "full control." This provision opens up the possibility of some form of joint ventures in such industries.

The government may also designate certain fields closed to foreign capital, establish priorities in accordance with its development plans, and cite conditions to be met on a case-by-case basis. Without being specific, the law calls for Indonesian participation in foreign enterprises after an appropriate period of time.

In brief, since the law allows for a good deal of flexibility, much will be left to the initiative and decision of the government, which is resolved to encourage the formation of joint ventures.

Priorities. The essential and constant concern of the government is the external financial position of Indonesia. Consequently, the priorities for investment will be assigned in the following way: foreign exchange earners; foreign exchange savers; quick-yielding projects and investments providing large-scale employment opportunities, introducing new technology or working methods, and providing modern equipment to increase productivity or lower costs. For the foreign corporations that are foreign exchange earners and foreign exchange savers, the return to full control is not excluded.

Procedure. After an investment proposal has been approved by the appropriate governmental department or ministry and by the Technical Team for Foreign Capital Investment that is to assist in processing the application, the proposal is forwarded by the minister to the Chairman of the Presidium, who is also Chairman of the Advisory Body for Foreign Investment.

If approved by the Advisory Body, the draft of the contract has to be approved in writing by the Presidium Chairman. The contract has then to be signed by the appropriate minister, duly delegated for the purpose on behalf of the Indonesian Government. The Department of Basic and Light Industry and Power must be approached by most manufacturing industries.

In principle, an operation permit cannot be granted for more than 30 years. It seems, however, that in fact extensions beyond this limit will be possible.

Fiscal Incentives. The Foreign Investment Law provides for a large range of fiscal exemptions and abatements.

It offers a tax holiday on corporate income and dividend payments for a maximum of five years. Most companies can obtain a four or five years' holiday except in mining where the present policy is to limit the tax holiday provision. At the end of the tax holiday a foreign enterprise is able to negotiate with the Department of Finance for reduction of corporate income tax if it can prove that the viability of the enterprise requires an extra period of tax relief. It may also be allowed to offset losses during the period of exemption against profits subject to taxation in the abatement period. Foreign enterprises might receive further abatements by accelerated depreciation of fixed capital assets.

The law offers exemption of import duties on equipment, machinery, and tools needed for the project. The Minister of Finance has also decided to give extra duty-free privileges for the importation of raw materials in the first two years of operation.

Loan capital does not enjoy benefits in the form of tax exemption or other advantages. The approach taken is that the equity capital places the least strain on the balance-of-payments position of Indonesia and is therefore entitled to the greatest encouragement.

Guarantees. The government is willing to allay the fears of foreign corporations as to possibilities of new nationalizations or takings under control, as is shown in Article 21 of the Foreign Investment Law:

The Government will not carry out a comprehensive nationization/revocation of ownership rights of the foreign capital enterprises nor take steps to lessen the right to control and/or manage the enterprises concerned, except if it is declared by Law that the interests of the State require such a step.

The terminology of the article implies that an Act of Parliament would be required. If such a measure were taken, the foreign corporations would receive a fair compensation.

The government has also tried to minimize the restrictions on the transfer of funds. Profit transfer is guaranteed by law and the government imposes no restriction as to the amount. Repatriation of capital is not allowed while the enterprise is still enjoying a tax holiday. Loan capital must have a grace period as long as the tax holiday, since the transfer of the debt service is viewed as repatriation of original capital; but both principal and interest repayments are recognized as costs that may be granted the right of transfer in the original foreign exchange in which the funds were introduced in Indonesia. Foreign currency expenditures necessary for personnel working in Indonesia are also allowed.

FOREIGN EXCHANGE SYSTEM

Indonesia has gradually moved from a multiple foreign exchange rate toward a single fluctuating exchange rate for most import transactions. Moreover, it has increasingly relied on free market forces to determine import priorities. Indonesia has for a long time linked imports with exports through the bonus export (BE) system, the content of which has varied with time.

The Previous BE System. Formerly Indonesia had at least two foreign exchange rates. There was first a rate for the BE certificates that originated from loan credits: this is the foreign currency given by aid countries to the Central Bank. The second rate applied to the BE certificates that originated from Indonesian exports.

The Present BE System. The Suharto regime endeavored to simplify and strengthen the foreign exchange system of Indonesia. The first thing to do, of course, was to encourage exports. In order to increase the badly needed foreign exchange reserves, the government simplified administration procedures for exports and set up incentives to exporting companies and provincial governments by allocating them larger shares of their foreign exchange earnings.

At present, Indonesian exports are classified in two categories of products. Distribution of the sales proceeds varies according to the category of products. For some products, the exporter gets 90 percent in BE and 10 percent goes to the government. For other products 85 percent goes to the exporter and 15 percent goes to the government. However, here also, the tendency is toward treating all products in the same way.

The important fact in the changes initiated by the new regime is that Indonesia now has a single market for bonus export certificates. In other words, all certificates have become fungible. Some of the aid giving countries have been opposed to the idea of giving aid through the BE system, but now the origin of the foreign currency is no longer important. Whether they originate from Indonesian exports or from foreign aid, certificates can be exchanged indifferently. It is up to the bank to use either aid or its earned foreign currency.

All the bonus certificates must change hands at the official rate. Transactions take place on an official market, three days a week. The rate for import duty calculations has been gradually increased. The availability of BE for importers has been improved by permitting all banks to participate in financing imports through BE credits. Also, transfers abroad of profits and capital (capital only after the end of the tax concession period) will be on the basis of the BE rate.

As a result of these changes, Indonesia is gradually moving from the system of multiple exchange rates toward a general dependence upon the BE system. This evolution could ultimately produce a single fluctuating exchange rate for most import transactions and greater reliance on free market forces to determine import priorities. The present government believes that a single foreign exchange rate determined by the forces of supply and demand is the best system for a healthy and growing economy. For this reason systematic steps are being taken to reach that goal.

The Struggle Against Inflation. These policies toward a single fluctuating exchange rate constitute an important progress. Their effect on the state of the economy would be minimal, however, if inflationary tendencies cannot be slackened. Although government measures in this direction have been quite successful in recent years, a vigorous and sustained effort will still be needed for many years to come.

The previous government bears a share of the responsibility for the instability of the economy. Nevertheless, one should not forget either that Indonesia has 112 million people or that this population needs huge quantities of rice. The state of the economy depends partly upon factors that are beyond human control. The success or failure of harvests determines the amount of rice imports and this in turn is reflected on the foreign exchange market. Countries like Indonesia depend very much on fertilizers and good seeds but also very much on the hazards of nature.

The government is determined to fight earnestly against inflation. Because of this, it drastically cut nonessential public spending, limited bank credit, reduced the rate of increase in the money supply, and improved tax collection. The government has first to contain inflation within reasonable limits, and then only will it be able to successfully maintain a single fluctuating exchange rate and, more generally, a freer economy.

P. T. Philips Ralin Electronics Ltd.

HISTORY OF PHILIPS INVESTMENT

Before the Taking. Philips was in Indonesia before the Second World War. In 1942, the Japanese took the country. In 1946, Philips returned. At that time Philips was both manufacturing and selling in Indonesia.

There the Dutch concern manufactured light bulbs from imported parts; radio sets; and transmitter equipments. The selling activities were carried out by a joint venture between Philips and Borneo-Sumatra-Maatschappij (Borsumij), a very large, Dutch trading organization.

As has already been mentioned, relations between the Netherlands and Indonesia gradually deteriorated. In 1957, the Philips property was taken under custody. According to the government this measure was not a nationalization. In any case, there was for a short time a complete break between Philips and Indonesia.

After the Taking. From then onward the organization taken under custody was operated independently of Philips by its Indonesian directors. The new directors came from the rank and file of administration. Many among them had limited knowledge or experience in the electrical industry. Practically none from Philips remained except for a few Indonesian engineers. The level and the quality of production decreased sharply.

During this period, unofficial contacts were maintained between Philips and the organization under custody. The Dutch concern forwent its claims and sent parts to the Indonesian organization. During the last years of Sukarno's regime, better and closer contacts were established between Philips and the Indonesian venture.

THE JOINT VENTURE BETWEEN
PHILIPS AND THE GOVERNMENT

Origin. At the time of the political changes, the Indonesian company was in a poor state. The new government proved to be more receptive to foreign investment. It acknowledged its weaknesses and sought to cure them. It realized that outside help would be necessary for recovery. It indicated its desire to cooperate with Westerners. One of the steps it took was to ask Philips to resume activity.

Philips agreed very swiftly to do so. When serious difficulties arise on a given market and foreigners are forced to leave, the philosophy of the Dutch concern is to return as quickly as possible as otherwise some competitor will do so. This applies particularly to as wide and attractive a market as Indonesia. Furthermore, the assistance granted by the country's foreign creditors constituted for Philips a strong impetus to return, because it considered that Indonesia could not realize its recovery alone. Once the decision on a matter of principle was taken, Philips decided to proceed as quickly as possible; it was judged advantageous to return just as soon as the government initiated its policy of encouragement to foreign investment and before the various screening bodies had had to deal with too many investment proposals.

P. T. Philips Ralin Electronics (Ltd.). Philips activities in Indonesia being a small part of the concern's total, the policy followed in that country cannot be considered as representative of the concern's general policy.

Philips and the government conducted their negotiations in 1967. The basic agreement was signed on November 30, 1967. The legal structure was completed on March 18, 1968. A joint venture between Philips and the government itself (and not a governmental corporation) started its operations. The company, P. T. Philips Ralin Electronics Ltd., received the maximum of fiscal incentives provided by the Foreign Investment Law. Should a dispute arise between the partners, the procedure of the World Bank Convention on the Settlement of Investment Disputes, which Indonesia has signed, would be applied.

In terms of production, the venture is set up more or less along the same lines as before, at least initially. The company will produce radios, television sets, and light bulbs. The difference from the past will be in the establishment of an industrially integrated plant making components for bulbs and also electronic components locally. This should greatly ease the foreign exchange problems of the venture.

A New Structure. Although the production, for the moment, will be quite similar to what was done before, the organizational structure of the venture is entirely new. Philips did not want to enter as a shareholder in the previously existing organization. A new legal entity was therefore formed. In the basic agreement the partners agreed upon the general policy of the venture, but this is only expressed in general terms. Only time and experience will provide the structural details of the organization of the venture.

FINANCING

Without any doubt, significant financial means had and have to be found. The financial question is certainly not the last of the problems that the management of the company will have to tackle. It should be remembered, however, that when Philips came back it found an established organization—badly run it is true, but it was at least there. It was not as if it was forced to start completely from scratch.

Equity Capital. In the joint venture, Philips has a 60 percent share and the government a 40 percent share. The capital is 17½ million guilders; 10½ million were subscribed by Philips and 7 million by the government. The latter paid its share with the fixed assets that had previously belonged to the former. Philips paid its share by bringing in machinery and equipment; it is likely that it will later have to bring in new machinery.

Loan Capital. Philips Ralin Electronics Ltd. did not seek long-term loans from foreign or international financial institutions. Nor was Philips of the Netherlands prepared to grant to the joint venture a long-term loan, but this may have to be done at a later stage. Because local finance is to a certain extent available, the operating funds of the venture have been found locally.

Problems. Foreign exchange is a difficult problem, because the joint venture uses a considerable amount for the import of essential parts and for the payment of know-how. To be a large foreign exchange user is difficult in a country where the foreign exchange situation is so serious.

Another financial problem is likely to arise. When the integrated industrial plant really comes into operation, the present financial structure will no longer be adequate. But this problem is unlikely to arise in the immediate future.

MANAGEMENT AND SALES

Organization. The proportions held by the partners in the executive bodies do not correspond to the proportions held in the capital. Philips and the government have an equal participation both in the Board of Directors and in the Executive Board. Two Indonesian directors of the former organization were appointed executive directors of the new venture. Philips also has two directors on the Executive Board. During the first 8 years the Chairman of the Executive Board is appointed by Philips, but he does not have a casting vote. The executive directors decide who fulfills which function. The general manager of the venture is appointed by Philips.

Nevertheless, in order to appreciate how management works in fact, one should not consider the formal managerial organization alone. In the present circumstances, since Indonesia needs Philips, there is more weight on the side of the Dutch concern. On the other hand, Western corporations have for a long time aroused the hostility of the population, because they have been suspected of intervening in Indonesian political affairs. Foreign corporations have therefore to move cautiously in Indonesia.

It appears then that the real balance of power in the joint venture should not be appreciated mainly in terms of seats held in the executive bodies. This is why the problem of a possible deadlock between the partners should not be looked at in an abstract way. On the face of it, in case of deadlock in the Executive Board the partners would take it to the Board of Directors; in case of a new deadlock a general meeting of shareholders would be called where Philips would have the majority. In fact, however, if a conflict were taken to the general meeting, it would mean the end of the joint venture. The real solution for any conflict that might arise between the government and Philips will have to be found by conciliation and compromise.

Management and Government. A related problem is the extent to which the government will participate in day-to-day management. Philips does not expect the government to interfere in the day-to-day management to any extent, because the government knows it lacks scientific management skills. This does not mean that Philips would like the government to adopt the role of a passive partner. In a country like Indonesia a corporation cannot prosper without a government that has a cooperative spirit towards it. This is especially true for Philips Ralin Electronics Ltd., which is one of the largest economic units in the country. The company is of course influenced both by the attitude of government directors and by the decisions of the various ministries. The government itself has to prove that its ideas are better than those of its predecessor. It feels a strong personal interest in the success of the new policy of partnership with Western powers and corporations. In brief, Philips expects cooperation from the government, but no interference.

A problem that is often a source of conflict between a foreign corporation and a government is where and from whom to buy the necessary equipment. Philips encountered this problem in another large developing country. Until now the problem has not arisen in Indonesia. The management of the company has been free to buy where and from whom it chose. This of course does not mean that it may not arise in the future. If it does so Philips intends to use a technological argument: as the existing machinery of the venture came from Philips or from other European firms, it would not be easy to fit into the existing system new machinery of different origin.

Financial Policy. This problem of profit allocation has not been much discussed between the partners. It will be left to the discretion of the Board of Directors. The board will of course take into account some relevant legal provisions of the Foreign Investment Law. For instance, reinvestment of earnings will be tax free. In fact, because growth is the goal, the conservative Philips dividend policy will be applied. It is not Philips' intention to take out profits at an early moment. As soon as it is really available, however, a dividend will be declared.

Technical Assistance. As has already been mentioned, relations between Philips and the organization under control improved at the end of Sukarno's regime. A technical assistance agreement was even concluded at that time. The Indonesians expected that no royalties would be paid for the technical assistance. The Dutch concern did not agree on that, because all Philips affiliated companies—even wholly-owned subsidiaries—pay royalties to the parent company. Philips does not conceal the price it requires from subsidiaries or affiliated companies in exchange for licensing and technical assistance. In this respect the government received the assurance that there would be no discrimination against the Indonesian venture.

Transfers of royalties are guaranteed by the law.

Sales. Many problems relative to the distribution and marketing system have not yet been solved. For instance, it has not been decided whether the existing sales organization will be used or whether a new one will be created or whether two organizations should be used. The management concentrated initially on the solution of production problems and only later turned to the problems of distribution.

The manufacturing activities of Philips in Indonesia may indirectly assist the Dutch concern in the sale of imported products. Indonesia imposes few quotas on imports, but heavy import and sales taxes make the development of these imports difficult. Because of the manufacturing venture, however, Philips will be better placed than other concerns for the sale of imported products, at least in the long run.

The possibility of competition between the products made by the joint venture and Philips products made or sold in other countries has not yet been discussed. Philips did not demand any restriction on exports of products made by the Indonesian enterprise. However, this problem will have to be discussed at a later stage.

THE LABOR PROBLEM

Principles. The principles governing employment problems have been laid down in the Foreign Investment Law in a reasonable and coherent way. The investment proposals that provide for large-scale employment opportunities are regarded as high-priority projects by the screening authorities. The government recognizes the full authority of the foreign investor to select technicians and experts for positions that Indonesian manpower is not yet capable of filling. The law requires foreign firms to train Indonesians for technical and managerial positions.

As to Philips Ralin Electronics Ltd., the basic agreement also lays down some clear and sound principles. The agreement divides the existing personnel into three categories:

1. Personnel to be kept without any change.
2. Personnel to be trained.
3. Personnel to be dismissed.

Apparently the principles of the law and the categories of the agreement would permit a most efficient operation of the venture with a minimum labor force.

Facts. When Philips came back to Indonesia, it had to acknowledge a rather harsh reality: the venture employed 1,200 people, 600 of whom were redundant. The problem is complicated even further by the fact that some incompetent people have retained their jobs while others who could do better are unemployed.

In principle, the solution seems simple: 600 people have to be classified under the third category and should therefore be dismissed. But it would not be feasible for them to become civil servants, because all governmental organizations in Indonesia are overstaffed. The military is trying to solve its problem of excess personnel by engaging in productive undertakings. It cannot now afford to demobilize in great numbers because of widespread unemployment, which also limits the ability of government civilian officers to cut staff. The social consequences of dismissing too many bureaucrats present the government with a major dilemma. Outside the government there is still very little employment for these people. The Indonesian Government cannot risk an increase of the labor unrest.

In addition to the problem between Philips Ralin Electronics Ltd. and the government, there is also a problem between the joint venture and the union, because Indonesian unions easily take a view contrary to the government attitude. Finally, a Western enterprise has to find an answer to the accusation that the result of its coming is a decrease in the rate of employment.

Solutions. This very difficult problem cannot be solved in an abstract way, in a way which can be prescribed in a contract. It will take more time than has been anticipated. At present, the management contemplates two possible solutions. First, when the new activities of the venture begin, some of the surplus personnel might be trained for these new tasks. Second, it might be possible to conclude agreements with other Indonesian industries that would also absorb some of the surplus personnel, but this solution will become effective only by the time the Indonesian economy experiences its real take-off.

PROSPECTS

Prospects for Philips Ralin Electronics Ltd. The first thing to do is to put existing facilities back to 100 percent production. This will be an immediate and definite advantage for Indonesia because before Philips' return, the output was certainly not 100 percent of the productive capacity. Only after this goal has been attained will new facilities and new products gradually be introduced.

As in the past the factory will produce light bulbs, but now the glass shells will also be made by the venture, which will thus save foreign exchange. The joint venture also hopes to begin production of a completely new product: tube glass for fluorescent lights. Semi-manufactured articles and components for television sets and radios were shipped in the last months of 1968 and the first months of 1969.

Philips takes a very long-term view in Indonesia. The Dutch concern is therefore determined to move cautiously and gradually. It will take time to really implement the basic agreement. It is difficult to evaluate this venture because there is not much experience. The main difficulties that the venture has to face are the foreign exchange problem and the labor situation. Certainly, their solution depends to a large extent on the energy and competence of the management, but it also depends on the general state of the Indonesian economy. If these problems can be met successfully, then the future of the venture will be promising because Indonesia is a huge potential market for the products made by the company.

Prospects for Indonesia. The problems that Indonesia has to face will be extremely difficult to overcome: rapid inflation, huge external debt, obsolescence of too many manufacturing facilities, massive open and hidden unemployment, and lack of efficiency in administration. This heritage of the past would be a heavy burden in a small and centralized country; but how can it be dealt with in a country of 112 million people and 2,500 islands? Fortunately, Indonesia has received massive help from its creditors who have thus shown their confidence in the future of the country. Also foreign corporations have shown a vivid interest for the opportunities offered to them. In this respect the departure of the great majority of the two million Chinese who previously lived in Indonesia is regrettable: although some of them were engaged in political activities, it is likely that the majority of them were merely conducting their business activities. The Chinese are extremely good and reliable traders and their absence is felt very much in Indonesia.

If the economic problems of Indonesia seem very serious, the political and social problems of the country seem formidable. There is little that foreigners can do to help in this area; the only thing they can do is to refrain strictly from any interference. The extreme variety of traditions, social structures, and ways of living, and the plurality of religions create a dangerous state of division in Indonesia.

Strong centrifugal forces affect the society and the unity of the nation remains to be achieved.

The harm done by the policies followed under the previous regime has been underlined by Mr. Hamengkubuwono:

In attempting to understand the present political climate in Indonesia, one should appreciate what the society has undergone in the recent past. There has been a glorification of the individual, erosion of the respect of law and human rights, arbitrariness of the powerful, a breaking down of social morals in a prolonged hyperinflation, and an ignored economy. All these took root and therefore the task of recreating a healthy and normal pattern of society calls for a long and painful process of adjustment and perseverance.[3]

Because of this, it is difficult to make a forecast as to the future of Indonesia. What is striking, however, is the absence of prejudices and the great frankness that characterizes official or more private governmental statements. The determination of the government to face the problems and to make the necessary sacrifices for their solution, the vast natural resources of the country, and the foreign aid granted by developed countries will combine to do a great deal for the recovery of Indonesia.

Philips in Indonesia. It is a rare phenomenon that nationalized property is restored to their former owners and it is also rare that these foreign corporations agree to return. In this and in other respects, the case of Indonesia is quite particular.

In fact, the partnership between Philips and the government is not so surprising. The Dutch group is dependent very much on external markets and, therefore, applies abroad a flexible policy; it could not afford to remain indifferent to such a huge potential market with which it was already so familiar. The government resolved to prove that its ideas are better than those of its predecessor and its approach to Philips, which has a good reputation for the quality of its products and which has important financial, technical, and managerial resources, was an obvious step. In these circumstances, the familiarity of the Dutch with Indonesia and its people, is a great advantage, now that the vestiges of colonial domination have disappeared.

3. *Op. cit.*, p. 163.

Venture between Multinational Consortium and Government Corporation

XVI: TEXTILES IN GHANA

The Unilever Group

BACKGROUND

Origin. The Unilever Group was formed in 1929 by merging a Dutch company, Margarine Union, and a British company, Lever Brothers Limited. The main reason for the merger was competition for oils and fats. The basic similarity between the two businesses was that each was engaged in large-scale marketing and household necessities. Their community of interests was that, for expansion, both businesses depended on the rising standards of living throughout the world. Twin headquarters were established in London (Unilever Limited) and Rotterdam (Unilever N.V.).

Organization. In four decades, Unilever has become a worldwide concern that employs 304,000 persons. In 1967, capital and reserves were as follows:

	N.V.	Limited	Total
	In thousands of guilders *		
Ordinary shares	640,165	544,044	1,184,209
Reinvested earnings and other reserves	2,240,883	2,494,175	4,735,058

* The guilder, unit of currency in the Netherlands, equals approximately $0.26.

The English company's shareholders are to be found mainly in the United Kingdom, and the bulk of the Dutch company's shareholders live on the Continent. Since most of the shares of the Dutch company are bearer shares, it is difficult to estimate the total number of the group's shareholders, but Unilever Limited has about 75,000. Practically all the capital of Unilever Limited and Unilever N.V. is owned by members of the investing public. In turn, either one or the other of these parent companies own all the shares of most of the subsidiaries and a majority, or a large part of them in the rest. This means that the parent Boards of Directors are able to exercise a fair degree of control over the total resources of the group.

The English company and the Dutch company each have a Board of Directors, but these boards are identical. These companies are further linked by a number of agreements, the most important of which provides for the payment of equivalent ordinary dividends. The whole organization is dual in appearance but unitary in fact. A special committee of three persons deals with the day-to-day management of the group at the highest level.

The parent companies are responsible for the strategy of the Unilever Group: what major new activities to undertake; how to develop existing resources; and what new resources to plan for. The tactics for each individual enterprise, however, are determined by the company in question. As a result, Unilever products are not usually associated by the public with Unilever but with the subsidiary companies that make or sell them.

Activities. The group does business in nearly every country in the world, excepting China, the U.S.S.R., and the Eastern European countries. Unilever products are mainly consumer products. Because of this Unilever's markets will expand only if standards of living rise throughout the world.

The common factors of the group's activities are skill in the techniques of mass marketing, dependence—which was formerly stronger than now—on oils and fats as raw materials, and, as an historical consequence of the last, a heavy investment in West Africa.

The main activities of Unilever can be classified as follows:

1. Consumer goods for the mass market: margarine and other edible fats and oils; fresh, quick-frozen, canned, and other processed foods, including ice-cream; detergents; toilet preparations.
2. Animal feeding stuffs.
3. Printing, packaging, plastics, chemicals, and other industrial interests (plus services, including transport).
4. Tropical enterprises: merchandise (mainly handled by the

United Africa Company Group); plantations producing palm oil, palm kernels, rubber, and other tropical products: produce (mainly tropical produce handled by the United Africa Company Group, including timber products).

Sales, Profits, and Capital Employed. The distribution by geographical areas of sales to third parties, profits, and capital employed, shows that the bulk of Unilever's operations is carried out in Europe.

Sales, Profits, and Capital Employed

Total in Millions of Guilders		*Distribution in Percentage*			
SALES TO THIRD PARTIES		*Europe*	*The Americas*	*Africa*	*Rest of the world*
1967	19,714	64	15	13	8
1958	13,395	57	16	20	7
PROFITS					
1967	779	70	14	10	6
1958	503	69	12	13	6
CAPITAL EMPLOYED					
1967	8,666	66	14	13	7
1958	5,537	55	13	25	7

All Unilever interests in Africa are included in the table showing amounts and percentages: the United Africa Company Group, industrial interests and plantations. Between 1958 and 1967, largely as the result of a planned withdrawal from produce trading in parts of West Africa, African sales have decreased both in absolute and relative terms. Although profits in Africa have slightly decreased in relative terms, they increased in absolute amounts. Capital employed in Africa decreased both in relative terms and absolute amounts.

JOINT VENTURES IN DEVELOPING COUNTRIES

As a result of the Unilever Group's history and organization, the activities in developing countries are divided between the two parent firms. For instance, United Africa Company Limited, which is the parent of the African ventures, is a wholly-owned subsidiary of Unilever Limited. Whereas each subsidiary or department has autonomy in dealing with particular situations, attitudes common to the whole group and discussed at board level have been developed. These policy guidelines apply to each area in which Unilever operates and are formulated to allow for flexibility and exceptions.

Wholly-owned Subsidiaries and Joint Ventures. Without any doubt, Unilever prefers wholly-owned or majority-owned subsidiaries, because experience has shown that control by Unilever is more likely to lead to success. Joint ventures are formed for a variety of reasons. Sometimes, Unilever goes into joint ventures because partnership with foreign partners is government policy. Sometimes the group seeks a local partner because the association would bring a definite advantage to the venture: for instance, the local partner can sometimes facilitate negotiations with trade unions.

The group's experience shows that joint ventures with a multiplicity of partners are sometimes difficult to handle. The need to share the financial burden with industrial or financial partners is not often felt. It is recognized, however, that in cases of an exceptional risk or initial unprofitability, the presence of a foreign or international financial institution might be helpful.

The Partners. In the experience of Unilever, many problems can arise with private partners. Dividend policy can be, and has been, the source of serious difficulties between the local and the foreign partners. Unilever's policy tends towards growth and reinvestment of earnings. The local partner is apt to look for quick profits and take a narrow-minded viewpoint of the situation. In case of serious conflict, the only practicable solution may be for one partner to buy the other partner's stock. Such difficulties should not overshadow the fact that some joint ventures with private interests are successful.

In general, Unilever's experience is that private interests can be expected to take a more professional view of the enterprise than state or para-state corporations. Moreover, in case of disagreement, a partnership with other corporations can be dissolved and new partners can be sought; whereas the unwinding of a business partnership with a government would have many complications.

Control and Management. Where joint ventures abroad are concerned, Unilever has a marked preference for majority participations. Control might give the local partner a greater sense of responsibility, but even when Unilever is in a minority position, it seeks management control, which it can obtain by concluding a management contract with the local partner. There are examples of the group moving from a minority position to a majority position, and vice versa. The group has also some cases of 50-50 joint ventures. Sometimes it is possible to provide for a deadlock-breaking procedure in such cases.

Unilever usually seeks to utilize three instruments of management in respect of most of its subsidiaries or affiliated companies:

—the submission of an annual plan to headquarters, with an indication of expected performance, profits, and remittances;

—the scrutiny at headquarters of capital expenditures;

—the approval by the board of the nomination of the senior management of the subsidiaries or affiliated companies.

Joint ventures do not in themselves constitute a problem as far as the coordination of Unilever's worldwide operations are concerned, but they do require additional administrative work and special attention. There are obvious advantages in having management stem from one source. When there is a joint day-to-day management, attempts are made to define clearly the respective obligations of the partners. Although there exists an interrelationship between the financial, marketing, and technical responsibilities, Unilever and its partners have not normally experienced serious difficulties in defining their respective obligations.

A difficult problem for a worldwide corporation is the possibility of competition between the products made available for export by the joint venture and the products of the parent concern, wherever they are manufactured. As a rule, Unilever's production in a developing country is destined, for economic reasons, to supply the requirements of that country, and the problem of competition from other elements in the concern is not intractable.

The United Africa Company Group

HISTORY

Early History. The United Africa Company, Limited (UAC), parent company of the United Africa Company Group—the largest group of companies in Unilever Ltd.—was formed in 1929 by merging two great rival trading organizations, the Niger Company and the African and Eastern Trade Corporation. The resulting company is a wholly-owned subsidiary of Unilever Limited.

UAC's early years were difficult—an echo of the world economic crisis. However, by the late 1930s, it began to benefit from reorganization and an increasing improvement in commodity prices, which are the key to African prosperity. In the 1940s Africa entered a boom period and UAC became one of the largest general merchant enterprises in the world.

Changing Environment. First the war, then the emergence of many new sovereign African states, changed the whole political, social, and economic background of the countries in which UAC trades and have, inevitably, brought great changes in the operations of the group.

The postwar system of international produce marketing removed the need for UAC's widespread network of produce buying stations. Moreover, in merchandising of products for the local African market, competition became more severe. Government inducements were given to local industry to develop. Many hitherto small traders became importers themselves. Businesses were set up by both nationals and competitors from overseas. UAC has since adapted itself to these new conditions by withdrawing from most of the produce trade, and by streamlining its merchandise organization. In doing so, it has reduced its dependence on trade goods—the traditional lines that did not change much from year to year—and has turned to selling specialized merchandise to a more demanding clientele. Meanwhile, G. B. Ollivant Limited, a sister company of UAC, continues in the general merchandise field.

Before 1956, UAC had limited experience in industry. It had only exploited some investment opportunities: the plantation industry, the timber industry, and the breweries. Like many trading organizations around the world, circumstances obliged UAC to turn more and more to the manufacturing field. This trend is essentially a matter of redeployment of capital and skills in an area with which UAC is familiar and in which it has considerable experience.

POLICY CHANGES

U.A.C. Industrial Program. In the mid-fifties, UAC realized that many African countries would become independent and that the markets would expand and local manufacture would develop. In 1956, the Board of Directors asked a specialist to examine and report on industrial opportunities in Africa, and eventually, with board approval, to develop those which appeared favorable.

UAC aimed towards the manufacture of products that could be sold in sufficient quantities and with which it had sufficient experience. The UAC Group traded in virtually every product that was known on the African market. Accordingly, there was practically no product that could not be taken into consideration *a priori,* provided the demand for it was large enough to justify investigation. UAC, closely familiar with many products, but lacking the technical knowledge for' manufacturing them, looked for manufacturers who would be prepared to become technical partners. The company tended to form, as far as possible, joint ventures with private investors.

It was foreseen that manufacturing would gradually displace a part of the company's distributing function, since some of the factories would develop their own marketing organizations. UAC's manufacturing activities have developed considerably over the past twelve years. In 1968, the UAC Group operated or had substantial interests in about 70 industrial enterprises in tropical Africa. Most of the 40,000 employees work in English-speaking African countries. Efforts have successfully been made to implement a progressive Africanization of managerial jobs, both technical and commercial.

Joint Manufacturing Ventures. UAC has formed joint ventures with English, American, and Dutch firms that are outside the Unilever Group. The company has sometimes joined with an industrial partner who is within the Unilever Group. By and large, African governments have not so far exercised great pressure on UAC to induce it to accept local partners.

Some joint ventures have three partners: UAC, an industrial firm, and the government. Among these tripartite joint ventures, the largest is the West African Portland Cement Company Limited, which produces 500,000 tons of cement a year in Western Nigeria.

The capital of £8 million is owned by three shareholders: Associated Portland Cement Manufacturers (51 percent), Western Nigeria Development Corporation (39 percent), and U.A.C. (10 percent).

Associated Portland Cement Manufacturers, a British company, contributes its know-how, closely controls the joint venture, and nominates the senior executives, while receiving a fee for its services. UAC supplies the commercial management of the venture and receives a fee in exchange for its service; half a dozen members of the company are permanently in Nigeria as employees of the firm. Although Western Nigeria Development Corporation has no direct responsibility, it asks to be regularly informed and consulted; it receives a fee for the services it provides in government relations.

In cooperation with the Dutch firm Heineken, UAC has established breweries in Nigeria, Ghana, and Sierra Leone. Development banks are also partners in some of these enterprises, but they only have a passive role. Finally, the main distributors (in Nigeria) and merchant companies (in the three countries) are also shareholders. These breweries are successful businesses.

Either alone or in collaboration with partners, UAC has ventured into many other fields, as will be shown below.

Operating Areas. In 1968, UAC did business in more than 30 countries. Its operating areas are: (a) Commonwealth West Africa: Nigeria, Ghana, Sierra Leone, and Gambia; (b) all the French-speaking African countries (other than Guinea, from which it has withdrawn); (c) Congo (Kinshasa); (d) North Africa and the Middle East; (e) East Africa: Uganda, Kenya, Tanzania.

Activities. Although UAC undertakes a great variety of activities, a certain selectivity is observed. Instead of entering a number of entirely new fields, UAC looks for progressive vertical integration. This pattern of investment was underlined by Sir Arthur Smith, Chairman of UAC:

Great emphasis is being placed on vertical specialized development rather than horizontal expansion over a wide field; this is partly in order to try to perfect a more limited number of special skills, but it is also to enable the Company to act in accordance with African governments' known wishes.[1]

Despite the fact that some selectivity is observed, the group's activities are very diversified: they include breweries; timber; departmental stores (Kingsway Stores); motor sales; truck assembly; technical sales; engineering equipment and wholesale electrical businesses; pharmaceuticals and allied merchandise; toilet preparations; foods; textiles; specialized building materials; and general merchandise. The UAC Group also includes a wholly-owned cargo liner company, Palm Line Limited, operating between the United Kingdom/Northern Continental countries and West Africa.

RELATIONS WITH THE GOVERNMENT

Economic Basis for Industry. Without adequate protection against imports, the possibilities of making profits by manufacture in Africa would be almost nonexistent. In almost all cases, costs of production

1. "Catching the Wind of Change: The Redeployment of the United Africa Company," in *Progress* I, p. 196 (1965).

are generallly higher than in developed countries. This is true even of labor costs, after taking into account efficiency and the need for expensive training and supervision. In the experience of UAC, local manufacture has shown an actual saving of foreign exchange by import substitution in only a few cases, for example, truck assembly, cement (local limestone), cigarettes (local tobacco), and beer (local water and bottles).

Necessity for Protection. In most cases, the ventures have to rely on tariff or quota protection to be viable. African governments justify the protection by the "infant industry" argument: the only purpose of protection is to avoid being overcome by experienced competitors in the initial stage of operation. According to some economic experts, the infant industry argument cannot always be applied effectively. During the period of protection, competitors become more efficient; the infant industry remains at a disadvantage and, inevitably, cannot expand. Continued protection is therefore necessary, though not necessarily at the initial level.

Even when the economic basis for industries is questionable, governments sometimes encourage them because local industry provides for employment opportunities. In other words, the indirect and social advantages of local industry are viewed as a fair compensation for their questionable economic results.

Although a government is often obliged to maintain the protection of local industries over a long period, it sometimes tries to decrease its level after the initial period of production. This discourages some investors who have accepted the risk of losses during the initial period on the assumption that they can recoup them under continued protection for some years. In order to protect the consumer, a government sometimes establishes price controls: this does not always work because production costs are high and a minimum profit margin has to be left to the industrialist.

THE GOVERNMENT AS A PARTNER

Use of Public Money. It is sometimes contended that government should not use public money to compete with private interests. Government in any case draws tax revenue from the incomes generated by private investment, even though, for purposes of encouragement, some enterprises are granted tax relief for an initial period of years. Therefore, some business circles feel that governments should not use public monies for risk-taking investment when private risk capital is available for the purpose.

Sir Arthur Smith, Chairman of the UAC Group, has written:

In some enterprises, local African governments are also shareholders—a mixed blessing this, as although it serves to integrate them more closely into the business and thereby lend it their active support, there is a growing feeling among economists that they may be better advised to invest their money in infrastructural activities such as in roads, water supplies or power, instead of in fields where by tradition private enterprise is more often found and where it is ready to contribute the whole of the risk capital needed.[2]

Management of the Joint Ventures. In many countries—both developed and developing—the sharing of management or control at board level with a government can be shown to have disadvantages. If civil servants are on the board, each question may be referred to the ministries: as a result, the whole operation may be slowed down. The problem of decision-making may be even further complicated if government representatives on the board disagree with their ministers.

In a private joint venture, businessmen can get together and quickly decide what has to be done for the best solution of any specific difficulty. One of these difficulties is the buying of goods: when it has been decided to expand, the partners have to agree on the source and the price of the machinery and equipment to be purchased. In a private joint venture, this problem can be settled quite quickly. On the other hand, if a government is a partner in the venture, it may insist on an international tender, which can take a long time. Moreover, if a government has the majority of the seats on the board, it can reject the recommendations prepared by the commercial and technical management; this may not only cause further delay, but may result in other than the best solution from a purely commercial point of view.

Although these difficulties are serious, a foreign corporation often has no choice but to accept partnership with a government. In spite of these problems, where UAC has for one reason or another, entered into joint ventures with governmental corporations or development banks, it endeavors to cooperate to the full with its government partner, and can point to several enterprises of this kind that are conducted comparatively smoothly and with considerable success.

2. *Id.*

RELATIONS WITH THE TECHNICAL PARTNER

Management Responsibilities. Generally, firms procure technical and commercial advice on a contract service basis. UAC however, does not believe in hiring consultants. The company rarely concludes licensing agreements. It prefers to obtain technical expertise by going into partnership with an appropriate industrial company. If the industrial partner does not have a substantial equity share, there is some risk that he will not take enough active interest in the venture. For a similar reason, the industrial partner seeks and in most cases obtains the management of production.

UAC has often had difficulty in persuading manufacturers to become partners. There are some manufacturers who do not like to share their technique with another corporation; there are others who, knowing little about Africa, are afraid of the uncertainties inherent in these markets. Often a manufacturer may undertake a joint investment simply because a competitor would otherwise take his place.

Shareholders as Customers of Venture. Conflicts sometimes arise when a shareholder also is a customer of the venture. UAC and two other companies formed a joint venture for the manufacture of three products. Each shareholder wanted to purchase a different product. The difficulties arose when the general manager of the joint venture quoted, for each product, prices that he regarded as competitive. The two other shareholders felt that the prices were too high. They had hoped that by joining the combined venture they would obtain favorable prices for these products. The ultimate solution was the withdrawal of one of the partners from an unsatisfactory partnership.

This case is an interesting example of conflict produced by the divergent interests of a shareholder as shareholder and a shareholder as customer. It shows that the goals of a joint venture have to be defined very carefully during the negotiations between the potential partners. If the only purpose of an enterprise is to serve the shareholders with certain goods or services, then the joint venture does not need to be autonomous and make a profit. If the enterprise is to pursue its own business goals, then the general manager should be delegated substantial powers.

CONTROL PROBLEM

Pattern of Investment. UAC owns all kinds of participations in the 70 industrial enterprises in which it participates: its degree of ownership ranges between 10 percent and 100 percent. In all but a few ventures, however, UAC has some management control. In the main, it is not content to enter a venture as a mere investor.

UAC's participations in the investment banks of Nigeria and Ghana are passive. In two other ventures, UAC did not become interested in management and is a shareholder only. On the whole, these exceptions to the pattern of investment are few and insignificant.

The main asset of the company is its access to manpower and financial resources in Africa. On the contrary, manpower is a problem for the technical partner who is not often able to send many people abroad for a long period of time. UAC has a reservoir of qualified management personnel at its disposal for work overseas.

Reasons for Control. The efficient management of an enterprise in Africa necessitates a good knowledge of the products and of local markets. In those cases where UAC has this knowledge, it tends to assume the leading role in the joint ventures. UAC's role as a partner often includes that of general manager, as well as that of commercial manager. UAC frequently supplies the senior executive of the joint venture.

A majority participation and/or managerial control by private enterprise is also viewed as essential when the government is a partner. This presents a real advantage to the joint venture; when the company and a government have agreed on a basic decision, this decision can be more expeditiously implemented afterwards. The private enterprise also wishes to be reassured that purely commercial criteria determine management decisions. A majority participation by private enterprise facilitates private management or control and also classifies the company as a subsidiary, which, therefore, can be consolidated in the balance sheet of the parent corporation.

Ghana Textile Printing Company Limited

GHANA

Profile. Previously known as the Gold Coast, Ghana is a member of the British Commonwealth. The country is surrounded by the Ivory Coast in the west; the upper Volta in the north; Togo in the east; the Gulf of Guinea and the Atlantic Ocean in the south. It has an area of 91,843 square miles.

Ghana in 1967 had a population of 8,143,000 inhabitants, of

which 388,400 lived in Accra, the capital. Another major city, Kumasi, had 188,600 inhabitants.

The country is in the tropical belt; the greater part of its territory being mostly savanna.

Recent History. Founded in 1871, the British colony became independent in 1957 and a republic in 1960.

In the early sixties, internal opposition developed against the Nkrumah regime. The country was in serious economic difficulties, which were due to extravagant prestige projects as well as to a decrease in the sales and price of cacao.

In foreign affairs Ghana had, under Nkrumah, established closer ties with Guinea, Mali, the U.S.S.R., and Eastern European countries, while its relations with the U.S.A. slowly deteriorated. Nkrumah acted as a champion of Pan-Africanism, especially at the 1963 Conference of Addis Ababa. In the mid-sixties, relations with the French-speaking countries began to deteriorate. As a result, these countries did not participate in the 1965 Conference of the Organization for African Unity in Accra.

On February 24, 1964, while Nkrumah was on a trip to China, the Army took control of the country without great difficulty. It set up a "National Liberation Council" under the presidency of Lieutenant General J. A. Ankrah. Russian and Chinese technicians and advisors left the country. The political and economic relations with neighboring countries have since returned to normal. When Nkrumah found refuge in Guinea, the situation between the two countries became very tense. In April 1967, an attempted *coup d'état* by a group of Army officers had no success. In April 1969, Lieutenant General Ankrah resigned and was replaced by another Army officer, Brigadier Afrifa.

The Economy. During the past decade, the production of manganese and diamonds has decreased while that of bauxite has only slightly increased. The economy is still very much dependent upon cocoa, the price of which is unstable on the world market. Ghana's production of cocoa, which totals a third of world production, still constitutes a major part of total exports, which are far lower in value than total imports. Massive aid from Western states, especially the U.S.A., replaced Russian and Chinese assistance in 1966. The government undertook a liberalization of the economy and took steps to encourage private foreign investment.

The Volta River Project. The large dam and electrical works of

Akosombo, on the Volta River, favor the industrialization of the country. These provide energy for the factories of the recently created port of Tema (near Accra), which is already an important industrial center.

Before the Volta River Project and its production of cheap electrical power could become a reality, it was essential to find a potential customer for a large part of the electricity to be generated. The Volta Aluminium Company's smelter at Tema fills this need and allows the production of an essential metal that could transform the Ghanaian economy. The smelter's consumption of electric power will rise to 300,000 kilowatts in 1973. By that time, the company will be paying $7 million per annum to the Volta River Authorities.

The Volta Aluminium Company is a private Ghanaian company, which is financed by two of the world's major aluminum producers: Kaiser Aluminum & Chemical Corporation, which has a 90 percent participation, and Reynolds Metal Limited, whose participation is of 10 percent. The total investment in the smelter will be some £46 million. The company expects to produce 145,000 tons of ingots by 1973.

"PACKAGE DEAL" WITH THE GOVERNMENT

Basic Agreement with the Government. In 1960, the Government of Ghana, Alexander Drew and Sons (an English textile company), and Dodwell (an English merchant company) concluded an agreement for the establishment of a textile venture in Ghana. Drew and Dodwell were to act as advisors. Drew appointed a technical manager, who was required to cooperate with a governmental corporation. The foreign interests had no equity participation in the enterprise, which was entirely owned by the government. In 1963, the machinery was still being installed.

Meanwhile a soap factory was being built by Lever Brothers Ghana Limited (LBG), a wholly-owned subsidiary of Unilever. At the time of the factory's inauguration, in the fall of 1963, Nkrumah and the Deputy Chairman of UAC discussed the soap and textile ventures, which are both situated at Tema. In July 1964, a "package deal" was proposed: the government would acquire 49 percent of the equity in the soap company, and a foreign consortium, in which UAC had the leading part, would acquire 49 percent of the equity in the textile company. Unilever retained the management and control of LBG, and the consortium became responsible for the management of the textile venture.

Implementation of the Agreement. UAC took over the management of the textile enterprise on the date of the agreement. It immediately put the weight of its organization to work. One of the first steps it took was to appoint an accountant for bookkeeping. By the end of 1964, it had appointed a managing director and the electrical installation was also in working order. Meanwhile, the government arranged for the termination of the Drew and Dodwell contracts. In January and February 1966, the partners proceeded to the actual exchange of shares. A new company was set up to acquire the textile venture's assets: the Ghana Textile Printing Company Limited (GTP). Production started in March 1966.

FINANCING

The Consortium. UAC is a member of an informal consortium: the Anglo-Dutch Textile Investigation Group, or Adatig. A British company, the Calico Printers' Association, and a Dutch company, Texoprint, are the other members of the consortium. Outside of the consortium, Calico and Texoprint are keen competitors. Adatig provides the commercial and technical management for companies manufacturing printed cotton textiles in Congo (Kinshasa), Nigeria, and Ghana. In particular, the consortium is the foreign partner in GTP.

Equity Capital. The capital GTP is 750,000 Ghanaian pounds[3] It is divided among the shareholders as follows: Ghana Industrial Holding Corporation: 51 percent; the consortium: 49 percent (UAC: 33 percent; Calico: 8 percent; Texoprint: 8 percent).

The consortium paid for its shares in hard currency. The government acquired 51 percent of the capital in exchange for part of the existing fixed assets. This participation was first held by the State Enterprises Secretariat. In 1968, the Ghana Industrial Holding Corporation acquired these shares. The new shareholder is a little more autonomous than the Secretariat; it has, for example, independent accounts.

Loan Capital. Both the government and the consortium contributed loans to GTP, in proportion to their respective shareholdings. These loans were subscribed in Ghanaian currency.

MANAGEMENT

The Textile Industry. Some Far Eastern countries are now large producers of cotton cloth for which they use their own supplies of

3. At par with the British pound before the 1967 devaluation. The capital of LBG is 500,000 Ghanaian pounds.

raw cotton. Others have developed highly efficient industries on the
basis of imported cotton. In most cases, a large domestic market
forms the basis of the industry.

According to some American experts and British businessmen,
printed cotton piece goods can be exported to Africa more cheaply
from Far Eastern countries than the cost of foreign raw materials
and services needed for local manufacture.

If a government gives a local textile industry a tariff or quota protection, this provides for wide employment opportunities, but the
government will at once be forced to sacrifice the revenue it derived
previously from imported goods.

Thus the government faces a basic question and a serious problem.
The question is how soon it will be possible to reduce the tariff or
other form of support so as to induce a fall in prices to the ultimate
benefit of the consumer. The government also faces a dilemma: it
can never be certain that the local industry will ever develop far
enough to be capable of competing on equal terms with the efficient
production of countries in the Far East.

The Board of Directors. The board has five members: three nominated by the government and two by the consortium. The government
representatives on the board have been replaced from time to time,
but not with great frequency.

Up till now, it has probably been somewhat more difficult for the
consortium to manage the textile venture, in which it has only a minority participation than for Unilever to manage the soap venture, in
which it has financial control. This difference is not necessarily due
to the control factor: it is inherent in the nature of the two operations.

Commercial and technical assistance is provided on a service contract basis. As the foreign exchange situation in Ghana is difficult,
there has lately been some delay in transferring its fees to their des-
tination abroad.

Day-to-day Management. The consortium appoints the managing
director. Up till now, it has always been a person from UAC. The
managing director is the senior executive of the company but, in fact,
decisions are made as a result of consultation and mutual consent.
The managing director has to cooperate closely with the technical
manager. The executives of GTP and of the member firms of Adatig
are in frequent contact by telephone, and there are frequent meetings
at management level.

Financial Policy. The policy of UAC—as of most private enterprises—is to aim at growth and to reinvest a substantial part of its profits. This policy is reinforced in Ghana by the fact that the transfer of profits abroad is very difficult. The government favors a policy of growth and reinvestment because in cases of expansion, new employment opportunities are created.

Labor. At present GTP employs 350 persons, 16 of whom are expatriates. To deal with its personnel, the company has access to the advice of UAC's Industrial Relations Advisor. It is recognized in Ghana that the salaries and working conditions of the company's employees are good. Only literate applicants are accepted. No women are employed in the company, not even as telephone operators. On the whole, labor relations have not presented great difficulties for the company, but the importance of long and intensive training has become quite clear.

The company's employees are all members of unions.

SALES

Company's Production The Ghanaian market, like the other African markets, is traditionally-minded with regard to fashion. It is common to see women wearing identical dresses at a party; nor are they disturbed by this fact, as American or European women would be.

GTP produces printed cotton in twelve-yard lengths, forty-eight inches wide. Although part of the cotton cloth for printing is still imported, a substantial part is now made locally. The articles are, technically, roller machine prints, but in the market are called "African Fancy Prints" and "Imitation Waxblocks", according to the kind of design used. The company is at present carrying out an expansion project that will introduce a genuine, hand waxblock operation: this process cannot be imitated. The process is very costly, the resulting article will be of high quality, and its price will be higher than that of ordinary machine prints.

Distribution System. The production, which is protected against foreign competition by tariffs and import licenses, is consumed entirely by the local market. GTP sells its goods to wholesale distributors, which sell the articles to smaller traders and to private customers. Sophisticated stores in the European style and Lebanese traders, who often have their own shops, also buy the company's articles.

GOVERNMENT RELATIONS

The Expansion Problem. Expansion plans involved the acquisition abroad of a large amount of machinery. Consequently, GTP management had to seek foreign sources of financing. By the end of 1968, a loan for a substantial sum had been negotiated with a financial institution in London. The terms of this loan were agreed to in detail by the Government of Ghana.

Foreign Exchange. In principle, the remittance of service fees to Adatig benefits from a priority on the government list of payments to foreign creditors. Because of the foreign exchange situation however, this priority has lately had no effect.

Few firms are at present prepared to ship goods to Ghana, unless they obtain a credit guarantee as to remittances. In practice, therefore, a substantial part of the country's import program must be supported financially by credit insurance in the exporting countries. The government requires a six-month credit term before the date of payment, but it may be even longer before the cash payment actually occurs. The imported goods are often sold on the market long before payment becomes due.

Taxation. GTP has a special fiscal status. It benefits from a five-year tax exemption that covers the corporate tax and import duties. The normal corporate tax is 50 percent of the profits. The government is gradually reducing the withholding tax that is applied to the remittance of dividends.

Arbitration. Adatig would normally include an arbitration clause in any service agreement. The service agreement concluded between GTP and UAC does not contain such a clause.

EVALUATION AND PROSPECTS

The Ghana Textile Printing Company case constituted a departure from UAC's general practice. It was probably unique, depending as it did, on the existence of a wholly-owned Unilever soap factory and a nearly completed government textile factory, which gave rise to the "package deal" as a manifestation of partnership between government and private enterprise. Relations between Adatig and the government reflect the fact that joint venturing with the government sometimes involves more time and discussion than would be the case in a purely private venture. On the whole, however, all difficulties have been dealt with in businesslike fashion.

The financial success of GTP has greatly contributed to establishing harmony between the partners. While the consortium is entitled to fees and dividends, the government is entitled to taxes (after a few years) and dividends. The prospects of the company are similarly good, as long as present conditions continue.

The Ghana Textile Printing Company case demonstrates that it can be to the advantage of a foreign corporation to be flexible when it makes an investment in a developing country.

XVII: REINVESTMENT OF COMPENSATION FROM NATIONALIZATION IN BRAZIL

Since the sale of its telephone utilities in March, 1966 and up to the end of 1967, Brazilian Light and Power Company Limited (Brazilian) [1] has become the minority partner in seven joint ventures in Brazil. These joint ventures are the result of a fundamental change in the relationship between the company and the successive governments of Brazil. This change represents a pattern that could be followed by other developing countries whose public utilities are foreign owned.

Brazilian Light and Power Company Limited

Brazilian was formed in 1912 as a Canadian company to act as a holding and management company for utility subsidiaries that had commenced operations in Brazil as early as 1899. It is now Canada's biggest foreign investment, and represents the largest aggregation of private international capital in Central and South America. At cost, the company's assets total more than $1.1 billion, and present shareholder equity is estimated at over $500 million. In 1962, before the sale of its traction and telephone utilities, Brazilian had 45,017 employees. In 1966, this figure was 25,138, including 72 who lived outside Brazil. It is the largest employer in Brazil. Brazilian shares are listed on stock exchanges in Canada, the United States, London,

1. By supplementary letters patent, dated June 23, 1969, the company's name was changed to Brascan Limited.

Brussels, and Paris. Directorships reflect its international ownership, with board members from North America, Europe, and Brazil.

Since its formation, Brazilian has been engaged at one time or another, in almost all of Brazil's public utility sectors, including tramways, gas, electricity, and telephones. Recently, the company has withdrawn from tramways and telephones, and is disengaging from gas. As a consequence of these latter developments, its former name, Brazilian Traction, Light and Power Company, Limited, was changed to Brazilian Light and Power Company Limited by supplementary letters patent dated July 4, 1966.

ELECTRIC UTILITIES

The principal present-day operations of the company are its electrical utilities, which serve a population of over 15 million in the areas of Rio de Janeiro, Sao Paulo, and Santos. It is the sole distributor of electric power in these areas. At the end of 1966, it had 2,403,000 customers, who purchased almost 13 billion kilowatt-hours at a total cost of $218,942,000, representing more than 90 percent of the operating revenues of the company, and almost 100 percent of the net operating income.

In 1967, the two chief electric subsidiaries of the company, Rio Light S.A. and Sao Paulo Light S.A. (owned 85 and 82 percent respectively by the company, with remaining ownership in local individuals) were consolidated into Light-Servicos de Eletricidade, to increase efficiency and ease of management.

The company's generating capacity is 2,150,000 kilowatts, all of which is produced by hydro power, except for 450,000 kilowatts of oil-fired thermal production. Since 1957, there have been no increments in company-owned generating facilities because of government policy that all new generation should be owned by authorities of the state and federal governments. Brazilian, however, remains responsible for distribution of electricity, and purchases for sale through its interconnected systems all the power generated by the nationally-owned plants. In 1966, such purchases reached 4,150 million kilowatt-hours, or 32 percent of the power sold by the company that year.

Consumption of electricity is expanding at about 7 percent per year in Brazil. To meet these needs, the company entered into a three year program in 1965 under which it intends to spend $122 million for improvement and extension of distribution facilities. Of this sum, $40 million is being financed through a loan from the United States Agency for International Development. This was the first loan extended by the AID to a private institution.

Rate Schedules. The key to profitable operations of utilities in Brazil is the rates permitted by the public authorities. Until 1965, the basic rates, exclusive of surcharges, had not been revised since 1955 and 1956. Brazilian's 1963 Annual Report summarized that the "combination of frozen rates and severe inflation has virtually eliminated the return on the equity investment in these (electric) subsidiaries. Moreover, it has become impossible for the electric companies to obtain from any source the financial resources required to expand their distribution systems to meet new demands."

In March, 1965, under the government of President Humberto Castello Branco, new electric rates were set that permitted supply on a "service at cost" basis. Under this system, basic rates are fixed for a three-year period. To the basic rates are added surcharges that automatically enable interim adjustments to cope with inflation, such as collective wage increases and higher prices for fuel oil and purchased power. Other components of the "service at cost" formula are depreciation, reversion, and remuneration, all of which are related to "plant in service". The "plant in service," for all purposes connected with rate-making, is the cost to the companies in historic cruzeiros of the fixed assets used in providing electric service. This cost has been determined by a government commission. Then each year, this cost is written up according to a government-determined coefficient of monetary correction that reflects the decline in value of the cruzeiro.

Depreciation allowed in the "service at cost" is presently at a high 5 percent of the corrected historic cruzeiro cost. This high rate is temporary and is designed primarily to allow extra cash generation for expanding distribution facilities. Reversion is set at 3 percent of the corrected historic cruzeiro cost. Reversion moneys are intended to be paid to shareholders of the electric utilities in partial amortization of their investment in anticipation of the fixed assets of the utilities reverting to the conceding authorities at the termination of the concessions. To date, however, the authorities have directed that reversion funds be used to expand distribution systems. The final element in the "service at cost" is remuneration of 10 percent computed on the corrected historic cruzeiro cost, plus working capital, less reserves for depreciation and reversion.

Introduction of this new rate system in 1965 raised immediately the selling price of electricity by 50 percent. Surcharges and monetary corrections have allowed further increases, and for the first time, the company has begun to earn what it considers a fair rate of return on its investment. As mentioned, the electric subsidiaries are the only profitable utility operations of Brazilian.

GAS UTILITIES

Until 1966, Brazilian subsidiaries supplied gas in three cities, Rio de Janeiro, Sao Paulo, and Santos. For the previous fifteen years, sales had remained constant at between ten and twelve million cubic feet per year. As the following table demonstrates, capital investment in gas utilities did not constitute a large percentage of the total.

Book Value of Shareholders' Equity,
December, 1965

Gas Utilities	$ 15,000,000
Electric Utilities	384,000,000
Telephone Utilities	96,000,000
Nonutility investments	5,000,000
	$500,000,000

As with its other utilities, operations are carried out under concession contracts entered into with the state authorities. Brazilian was anxious to obtain long-term concessions that would ensure reasonable profits before undertaking modernization of its gas-producing facilities. Heavy capital costs would have been necessary to convert its coal-burning to petroleum-fired plants, but conversion would have resulted in long-term economies. Without these changes, gas was a marginal operation, and produced no net income. Accordingly capital expenditures were held in abeyance.

In 1966, the company decided to discontinue gas services in Santos, and shut down its operations there in January, 1967, after an explosion crippled the plant. In April, 1967, the company notified the municipal authorities of Sao Paulo that it wished to withdraw from the manufacture and sale of gas in that city because of its inability to negotiate a satisfactory concession to replace the one that had expired in 1960. Since 1967, the city has taken over operation of this utility. Compensation to the company has not yet been determined, although the courts have been asked to make an appraisal. In Rio de Janeiro, the gas operating subsidiary was converted in 1966 from a

Belgian company into a Brazilian company, Sociedade Anonima do Gas do Rio de Janeiro, and was the last of the operating utility subsidiaries to become a Brazilian company. This company continues to operate in Rio, but without modernization and a favorable concession, its future remains uncertain. It is not likely that Brazilian will continue its operation for a long time.

TRACTION UTILITIES

At the end of 1962, Brazilian subsidiaries held concessions for the operation of electric tramways in Rio de Janeiro. Spiraling inflation and decreasing passenger usage meant that each year of operations produced greater operating deficits. State of Guanabara authorities refused to grant rate increases and the company sued for damages for prior years' losses and for rescission of the existing concession contracts, which obligated the company to continue tramway operations. Although Brazilian won in the court of first instance, the actions were finally settled out of court. Under the settlement dated December 30, 1963, the State of Guanabara acquired all the assets of the traction subsidiary, along with 6 billion cruzeiros (about $10,-000,000 at the time). Brazilian was relieved of all its future operating obligations under two concession contracts, one of which terminated in 1965 and the other in 1970.

TELEPHONE UTILITIES

On March 26, 1966, Brazilian sold all its telephone utilities in Brazil to the federal government. The events preceeding the sale, and the terms of the sale typify many of the problems of private ownership of public utilities in developing nations.

Brazilian's subsidiary, Companhia Telefonica Brasileira, was faced with much the same problems as the traction, gas, and electric utilities. Inadequate rates and increasing costs of operation and construction, with the concomitant impossibility of raising capital, resulted in a great telephone shortage throughout the areas it serviced. At the end of 1964, there were 862,648 telephones in service in the company's networks (over 80 percent of the telephones in Brazil), but the number of unfilled applications totalled 578,000.

Discussions had begun in the late 1950's with municipal, state, and federal authorities. In 1960, Mr. Carlos Lacerda, Governor of the new State of Guanabara (formerly the Federal District of Rio de Janeiro) appointed a commission to study the shortages. President

Quadros followed this in 1961 by appointing a work group to make recommendations on a national telephone policy, with a view to safe-guarding national security in the installation, maintenance, and ex-pansion of an integrated telephone system throughout Brazil. Quad-ros retired in August, 1961, and the company continued discussions with President João Goulart's government.

On March 2, 1962, Goulart issued a federal government decree deeming telephones to be a basic industry because their shortage was restricting security, economic development, and the conduct of busi-ness. Brazil's National Economic Development Bank, the Banco Na-cional do Desenvolvimento Economico (BNDE) was authorized to make whatever financial arrangements were necessary for the devel-opment of the telephone industry. By decree, the State of Guanabara precluded any sales of telephone property in that state without its prior consent. Then on March 23, 1962, at the American Chamber of Commerce in Rio de Janeiro, President Goulart outlined the prob-lems that utilities in Brazil were experiencing, and concluded that it would be his government's policy to evolve a plan under which own-ership of all public utility companies could be transferred, with just compensation, into the hands of Brazilians. He also mentioned that it would not be difficult to have this capital transferred into other activ-ities in Brazil where it could continue to assist in the nation's devel-opment.

This declaration of intention was followed four days later by a de-cree for the regulation of interstate telephone services in Brazil. It precluded the breaking up, even through expropriation by local con-ceding authorities, of the property, services, or assets of any telecom-munication company that had operations in more than one state without authorization of the federal Ministry of Public Works. One of the stated purposes of the decree was to assure a continuity and regularity of telephone services, especially interstate communications and those with the country's capital, by keeping them intact.

Three days later, Governor Lacerda issued with federal consent a decree that commenced proceedings for expropriation of Brazilian's telephone assets in the State of Guanabara. Assets in Sao Paulo were not affected by this latter decree. At this time, the telephone utilities had about 18,000 employees, less than 20 of whom were recruited from outside Brazil. Its book value was set at $135 million, a conser-vative estimate according to Brazilian. About 45 percent of these as-sets were in the State of Guanabara.

Negotiations between the company and Guanabara State were undertaken, but broken off in June, 1963. In November, 1963, a new contract was entered into for telephone services in Sao Paulo. It provided for rate surcharges and contributions by new subscribers that would encourage expansion of facilities, allow the company a fair return, and provide for the eventual amortization of Brazilian's capital investment. In Guanabara, rates were increased to adjust only for increased labor costs. The arrangements made with San Paulo, and similar ones negotiated in 1964 with Rio de Janeiro failed, however, to achieve the approval of CONTEL, the federal communications agency. The 1964 Annual Report of Brazilian, nevertheless, stated that "the prospects for securing more adequate rates in the coming year are considerably improved." Much of this optimism resulted from the approach adopted by Brazil's new President, Humberto Castello Branco, toward foreign capital. His promises of nondiscriminatory treatment of foreign investment, and reasonable rights to repatriate capital and remit earnings, encouraged fresh inflows of foreign capital. He also announced that public utilities would receive "just remuneration by way of adequate tariffs". But Brazilian still recognized that the likelihood of nationalization of the telephones was high because of declared government policy, the inadequacy of existing telephone services, and their national importance.

In early 1966, Brazilian and Branco's government consummated negotiations for the sale to Empresa Brazileira de Telecomunicacoes (Embratel), an agency of the federal government of Brazil, of all of Brazilian's telephone utilities.

The Telephone Sale Agreement. The sale, effective as of December 31, 1965, was completed on March 26, 1966, and accorded registration by the Federal Accounting Tribunal. Direction of the utility was turned over to Embratel in June, 1966.

The selling price of all of the telephone assets was $96,315,787, payable over a twenty-year period. Outstanding balances are secured by a 6 percent serial bond from Embratel, and guaranteed by the federal government. Quarterly instalments are calculated to result in payment of $10 million on principal, plus all accrued interest in the first thirty months. The remaining $86,315,787 with interest thereon was made payable in 80 quarterly instalments. Both series of instalments commenced as of January 1, 1966. Brazilian is obligated to reinvest in other enterprises in Brazil 75 percent of the $86,315,787 (about $65 million) as it is received, over the 20 year pay-out period. This means that Brazilian is able to repatriate, without further tax or penalty, principal of $10 million, all of the interest on the $96 million, and the 25 percent of the $86 million principal that is not slated for reinvestment. Accordingly, total proceeds of principal and interest over the twenty year period will work out to about $158,-060,210, all of which can be repatriated except for about $65 million.

The price of $96,315,787 was $18,815,426 less than the adjusted book value of the telephone assets. This deficiency was charged up in 1965 to consolidated earned surplus. Under terms of the sale agreement, a Swedish engineering firm was appointed to value the assets sold, and provision was made for downward, but not upward, adjustment of the price. This appraisal was completed in January 1967, and showed that the price was reasonable.

This sale has improved Brazilian's financial picture. In the first half of 1965, telephone operations had resulted in a new operating loss of $1,278,000 but in the first half of 1966, income from proceeds of the sale were $2,837,000. The total interest proceeds for all of 1966 were over $5.5 million.

Reinvestment Program. Guidelines were laid down in the telephone sale agreement for reinvestment by Brazilian of the $65 million. Unless authorized by the BNDE, reinvestment may be made only in industrial, agricultural and cattle raising, and financial undertakings, or in companies that have as their object the organization of, and participation in, such undertakings.

The company also laid down its own guidelines, which are:

1. The enterprise invested in should be in a productive activity, contributing to the development of Brazil. Export industries are specially attractive.

2. Investment should be to expand productive capacity, not to buy out existing proprietors.

3. Investment should be within the sale agreement guidelines, and

4. Investment should be as a minority shareholder only.

5. Because Brazilian has no management or technical know-how apart from the utility field, it laid down additional guidelines for its initial investment of the telephone proceeds. As mentioned, it will not purchase a controlling interest in any of the companies it chooses for investment. Furthermore, no investments are made in a company that does not already possess the technical know-how necessary to carry out its operations. Consequently, after buying into a company, Brazilian does not upset the existing management structure.

Each year, Brazilian must report its investments to the BNDE. Although there is no prior authorization required for investments that are within the sale agreement guidelines, the company consults informally with BNDE officials before undertaking any.

Prior to the sale of the telephone operations, Brazilian and its subsidiaries showed "other investments" on the consolidated balance sheet that were outside the utility field, of about $5 million. These were managed by a separate investment subsidiary. With the advent of the telephone funds, this subsidiary was converted in 1966 into an investment and development bank, a new type of institution authorized by Brazilian legislation. It is named Banco de Desenvolvimento e Investimento Brascan S.A. (Banco), and coordinates all of the investment activities of the Brazilian group.

Banco owns all the shares of two other investment subsidiaries, Organizacao e Empreedimentos Gerais S.A. (OEG) and Empresa Tecnica de Organizacao e Participacoes S.A. (TOP). OEG existed before the telephone sale, and acted as a holding company for a number of the Brazilian subsidiaries. As investments of the telephone company proceeds were made, OEG became the holding company for five of the companies in which Brazilian had acquired a minority interest by the end of 1967. TOP was incorporated under Brazilian law in 1966. Its charter corresponds to the terms of the telephone sale agreement, in that it is considered to be a "financial institution" in which telephone sale proceeds can be invested, and the reinvestment obligations will be met. By this arrangement, if other suitable investment opportunities can not be found, the proceeds can be invested immediately in TOP. TOP can undertake a wide range of financial activities, including purchases of equities and making loans. Unlike OEG it can also trade in treasury bills. At the end of 1967, it owned the shares of two of the joint ventures. Its loans are of an interim nature, on a short term basis, to earn a return on funds that are awaiting investment in equities.

Brazilian feels that it can contribute two things to the joint ventures in which it participates through OEG and TOP, capital and financial know-how. Banco has an investment supervisory team of six individuals, four of whom are chartered accountants. This team manages all Brazilian's investments in joint ventures, which job includes the review of potential investments, and the provision to the joint ventures of continuing advice on accounting, financial control, and management policies that involve these areas. This team also works out a joint venture agreement with each company in which it decides to invest. By registration of the agreements, their terms can be judicially enforced. An integral part of every joint venture agreement is that the company must adopt North American accounting practices. This requirement serves to protect Brazilian's investment, and it also assists the joint venture in establishing sound financial controls. Brazilian attempts to set up an accounting system for each joint venture that will provide management with the precise information it requires to make business decisions, without at the same time encumbering it with too much paper work. Consequently, an accounting system is tailor-made for each company.

It has been Brazilian's experience to date that it can make its greatest contribution to the joint ventures through this financial supervision. There are very few qualified accountants and auditors in Brazil. The government appreciates the need for more sophistication in this area, because of its desire to attract foreign investment into the private sectors of the economy. It also wants to establish a public market for securities of local companies in Brazil, for which uniform and sound accounting procedures are a necessity.

Common to all the joint venture agreements is that Brazilian obtains the right to have its nominees appointed as directors of each of the companies. The ordinary Brazilian corporation, the "sociedade anonima", has two governing boards, the "conselho fiscal" and the "conselho consultativo". The conselho fiscal is the official governing body of the company, with responsibility for *pro forma* functions such as signing the books. The conselho consultativo, like a North American Board of Directors, determines policy for the company, but in addition, its members participate in the daily operations and management. As stated, however, Brazilian's representative on each of these boards restricts his management functions to financial matters, and questions of personnel, production, and marketing are determined by the local partners. The team of six from Banco fill these positions on the boards as representatives of Brazilian.

The Joint Ventures

By the end of 1967, Brazilian had invested or committed over $8 million (out of its reinvestment obligation of $65 million) to purchasing minority ownership in seven joint ventures in Brazil. Briefly outlined, the joint ventures are as follows:

Fabrica Nacional de Vagoes S.A. (*Vagoes*). Vagoes is a "sociedade anonima" or S.A. form of limited liability corporation, engaged in the manufacture of railroad cars and accessories, truck chassis frames and wheels, earth-moving equipment, and farm implements. Through OEG, Brazilian owns approximately 25 percent of its capital. Formed in 1943, it is now the largest builder of railroad cars in Brazil. Its main customer for railroad cars to date has been the Brazilian Government and the state railroad company in Sao Paulo. Under a recently concluded licensing agreement with Allis Chalmers, it has commenced production of construction and farm implements in Brazil.

Before Brazilian bought into this company in March, 1966, its capital was about $4.5 million. A majority of the shares were owned by three members of the founding family, who also managed the company. The minority shares were scattered amongst a number of other owners. When Brazilian entered into the joint venture, through its investment subsidiary OEG, the authorized capital of the company was increased from 9 to 16 billion cruzeiros, partly through a revaluation of assets, and partly through the purchase by OEG of newly authorized shares. The total authorized capital consists of 12,000,000 common shares, 8,319,233 Preference A shares, and 3,680,767 Preference B shares. Both the Preference A and B shares are 6 percent, noncumulative, and nonvoting, unless no dividends are paid for three consecutive years. Of these, OEG owns 1,000,191 common shares (approximately 8%), 467,981 Preference A shares, and all 3,680,767 of the Preference B shares.

Vagoes was anxious to have Brazilian's participation, because of its need for increased capital to expand its production facilities to produce the Allis Chalmers earth-moving and farm equipment. Because of the sound organization of this company, Brazilian has had a limited role to play in directing its operations, although it has participated in all management decisions affecting financing. Brazilian's main concern is to secure a continuing income on its preference shares, since they constitute its main holdings.

The financial results of Vagoes have been good. Its total sales in 1966 were 22,400,000 new cruzeiros, in spite of severe credit restrictions that prevailed in Brazil. By September of 1967, sales for that year had already surpassed total sales for 1966. Regular yearly dividends have been paid on the preference shares.

Industrias Alimenticias Carlos de Britto (*Peixe*). Peixe is an "ordinary company" engaged in the food growing and processing business. Through TOP, Brazilian owns about 28 percent of its capital stock. The head office of Peixe is at Recife, and its plants and farms are situated at Recife, Pesqueira, Sao Paulo, and Mogi Mirim. Peixe was founded in 1899 as a family company by the grandparents of the present six local owners. The company began by manufacturing tomato paste in the north of Brazil. Since then, it has become Brazil's second largest canning company, producing jams, jellies, preserves, ketchup, and related products.

Before Brazilian acquired its interest in Peixe in November, 1966, through TOP, the company's total capitalization was 9 billion cruzeiros, consisting of 9 million common shares of Cr. 1,000 par value each. For the entry of TOP, the authorized capital was increased to Cr. 12.5 billion, through the creation of 3.5 million, 10 percent noncumulative, nonvoting preference shares with par value of Cr. 1,000 each. In the event that dividends are not paid for three consecutive years, the shares become entitled to one vote each. Brazilian's investment amounts to $1,590,909.

The present head of Peixe is Carlos de Britto, who is a grandchild of the company's original founder. Along with five other of the grandchildren, he has continued to carry on the business, and is its present manager. Since its formation, the company has never become a "limitada" or "sociedade anonima", but has been run as an ordinary company whose common shareholders are subject to unlimited liability. Brazilian insisted on acquiring preference shares so that its liability would be limited. In spite of its large position in the canning industry, Brazilian found that Peixe had been suffering from a lack of financial and accounting controls, and from poor internal organization. Carlos de Britto was anxious, apart from acquiring the additional capital, to implement the types of controls and organization necessary for a company of its size. Under direction from Brazilian, these controls are being implemented. As part of the reorganization plans, it is anticipated that Peixe will become a limited liability company in the near future. The local partners have been delighted with the contributions made by Brazilian in financial and organizational matters. In return, Brazilian's investment subsidiary TOP, has received its yearly 10 percent dividend without interruption.

Eucatex S.A.—Industria e Comercio (Eucatex). Eucatex is a "sociedade anonima" (limited liability) form of corporation engaged in the manufacture of wallboard, accoustical tiles, and related building materials. Through OEG, Brazilian owns approximately 20 percent of its capital. The head office of Eucatex is in Sao Paulo, and its factory and sawmill are located at Salto de Itu, 110 miles from Sao Paulo. The business was started in 1951 by two brothers who were financed initially by their mother. Eucalyptus trees, which grow to maturity in five years, are cut and chipped, and then cooked and pressed into the tiles or wallboard in much the same way that paper is made. The company has about two hundred employees.

Brazilian acquired its interest in Eucatex in October, 1966. Before Brazilian's entry, the share capital consisted of 7,500 common shares with par value of Cr. 1,000 each. With the entry of Brazilian, the authorized capital was increased to Cr. 11,990 million, consisting of 7,990,000 common shares with par value of Cr. 1,000 each: 10,-000 noncumulative, nonvoting, 10 percent Preference A shares, with par value of Cr. 100,000 each: and the 2,000,000 noncumulative, nonvoting 10 percent Preference B shares with par value of Cr. 1,000 each. The Preference A and B shares become entitled to one vote each in the event that dividends are not paid for three consecutive years. Brazilian subscribed for all of the Preference B shares and 200,000 common shares, making its total capital contribution Cr. 2.2 billion (approximately $1 million), or about 20 percent of the capital of Eucatex.

The participation of Brazilian had been sought to provide funds for improvements to the factory at Salto de Itu and to acquire its fiscal and cost accounting expertise. As of October, 1968, Eucatex was the only one of Brazilian's joint ventures that had undertaken export operations. It has shipped to the United States and the United Kingdom. Brazilian has received its 10 percent dividend each year on the Preference B shares, but to date, no dividends have been declared on the common shares.

Empresa Industrial Garcia S.A. (Garcia). Garcia is a "sociedade anonima" textile corporation with limited shareholder liability engaged in spinning and the weaving of towels, bed and table linen, and other related products. Through OEG, Brazilian owns 25.9 percent of its capital. The head office and plant of Garcia are at Blumenan, in the State of Santa Catherina in the south of Brazil. The business was started in 1883, and has been continued by the founder's descendants as a family enterprise since that date. It has grown from a one-man operation to a plant that has 242 automatic and 110 mechanical looms.

The authorized capital of the company is Cr. 8,280 million, consisting of 8,280,000 common shares of Cr. 1,000 par value each. Fifty percent of these were issued and owned equally by the two active partners, one of whom is the general manager. The company was in need of additional capital to finance the purchase of additional looms, and to convert mechanical ones to automatic. For the entry of Brazilian, it was arranged that Brazilian would subscribe for 2,-145,900 shares for Cr. 1,866 million ($848,182), and the remaining 24.1 percent of the shares were sold to a number of other individuals. The general manager was not interested in having Brazilian acquire any more than 25.9 percent of the shares, but wanted it to subscribe for that many so that combined with his 25 percent, he and Brazilian together would have majority control of the company. There has been no shareholders' agreement, but since Brazilian's entry in September, 1966, it has always voted with the general manager as agreed.

Brazilian found that, apart from the need for additional capital, the biggest problem of Garcia was inventory control. Brazilian arranged for a complete new accounting system for the company, and introduced a method of inventory control that has eliminated duplication and the accumulation of dead stock. Since then, the financial results have been good, and Brazilian has received a dividend regularly on its common shares. The company expects to commence export operations in the near future.

Farloc do Brazil S.A.—Industria e Comercio (Farloc). Farloc is a "sociedade anonima" engaged in the production and sale of brake and radiator parts for automobiles. Through OEG, Brazilian owns 41.6 percent of its capital stock. The head office is located in Rio de Janeiro, and its plant is on the outskirts of Rio. It presently has about 250 employees.

Farloc was founded in 1956 by Wagner Electric Corporation of St. Louis and Robert Webber, a Brazilian of Swiss origin, to supply brake cylinders and brake fluid to automobile manufacturers in Brazil. Wagner Electric is one of the main suppliers of Ford in the United States, and has provided Farloc with technical know-how under a license agreement. In Brazil, Farloc supplies Ford, and has just received a contract to provide Volkswagen with master and slave cylinders for hydraulic brakes, brake fluid, the rubber brake connections, and radiator hoses and connections. The company purchases the moulds for the brake cylinders from the United States. The rubber hoses for radiators are purchased, and the company attaches connections of its own manufacture before selling them. About one-half of Farloc's production is supplied under contract to Ford and Volkswagen for incorporation into new cars. The remaining 50 percent is sold for replacement parts. It also acts as a distributor of brake linings, which it sells to replacement parts retailers.

Participation by Brazilian had been sought because of the need for more capital to expand its production to meet the needs of Volkswagen and the growing needs of its other customers. Farloc had no internally-generated capital resources, because during four of its first six years of operations it had suffered large losses. From 1963 to 1965, it had been making only very small profits. In 1966, a good profit had been anticipated, but it failed to materialize when the government exercised tight controls on credit and price increases to combat inflation. The extra capital made available by Brazilian helped it to overcome this problem. With the entry of Brazilian, 1,-350,000 new 10 percent noncumulative, nonvoting, convertible preference shares of Cr. 1,000 par value each were created for issue to OEG. Along with these were also created 1,350,000 additional common shares of Cr. 1,000 each. OEG subscribed for the convertible preference shares in 1966, and shortly thereafter converted them to common shares on a one for one basis. The present capital of the company is Cr. 3,238,110,000, consisting of 3,238,110 common shares of Cr. 1,000 par value each. Brazilian is the largest shareholder with 41.6 percent (1,350,000 shares); Wagner Electric is next with 30.4 percent (981,440 shares); and Robert Webber owns the remaining 28 percent (906,670 shares). Brazilian's total contribution was Cr. 1,350 million, which amounted to $613,636.

Brazilian was not anxious to keep its original 10 percent convertible preference shares because at the time of its entry in 1966 there was no prospect that the dividends would be paid for several years. It chose rather to convert the shares to common, and thereby participate to a much fuller extent in the expected growth. Brazilian looks on its position as the largest single shareholder not as a means of exercising control, which it does not want, but only as an investment in a company that finds itself in a turn-around situation. As of the end of 1967, no dividends had been declared on the common shares. New car production had increased considerably and was expected to continue its growth. Brazilian expects that it will achieve a good appreciation on its investment.

Brink's S.A. Transportes de Valores (Brink's). Brink's is a "sociedade anonima" engaged in the armored car transportation of cash and securities. It was incorporated in 1966 with its head office at Sao Paulo. Through OEG, Brazilian owns 49 percent (588,000 shares) of the share capital and Brink's Corporation Limited of the United States owns the remaining 51 percent. The authorized capital is Cr. 1,200 million, consisting of 1.2 million common shares of Cr. 1,000 par value each. Brazilian's investment of Cr. 588 million represents $267,273.

Brink's Corporation Limited of the United States approached Brazilian in 1966 when it was considering expanding into Brazil. It wanted a local partner who was familiar with conducting business in Brazil, and who would be able to supply some of the risk capital necessary to become established. Brazilian considered the idea sound, and agreed to enter as a minority partner. As with all of its joint ventures, Brazilian does not assume any role in the day-to-day management of the company, but with its knowledge of local conditions and its business reputation in Brazil, it has been of great assistance in the establishment of Brink's and in finding customers. With the establishment of Brink's operations in the major commercial centres of Brazil, it will be able to service Brazilian's many companies. Both Brazilian and its United States partner expect that their returns will come from dividends, but as of the end of 1967 none had been declared.

Celfibras-Fibras Quimicas do Brazil Limitada (Celfibras). Celfibras is a "sociedade de responsabilidade limitada par quotas" ("limitada") or a private limited company formed in 1966 for the purpose of manufacturing nylon yarn in Brazil. In 1966, Celanese Corporation of New York approached Brazilian with the concept of establishing this company. A joint venture agreement was entered, specifying that the company to be formed would have an authorized capital of Cr. 13,200 million, consisting of 13.2 million common shares with a par value of Cr. 1,000 each. Celanese was to subscribe for 55 percent and Brazilian 45 percent of these shares. A purchase-sale clause was inserted in the agreement, giving to either party the right to buy the other out should it wish. Although capital contributions were in the ratio of 55 to 45, it was also agreed that no dividends would be paid for three years, and thereafter, earnings would be paid out equally to each partner.

In 1966, the "limitada" was formed and each partner subscribed for its shares. The limitada form of corporate entity was utilized because it allows for greater flexibility among the participants *inter se* than does a S.A. corporation. The deed spells out that profit distributions are to be on a 50-50 basis, while voting rights are on a 55-45 basis. Most of the other terms of the joint venture agreement are spelled out in the deed as well, providing at the same time, limited liability for the members. The deed also specifies that Celanese is charged with the administrative powers of Celfibras. This in line with Brazilian's policy of not participating in the day-to-day management of the companies in which it invests, and the advantage of the limitada is that its deed, minutes, and financial statements are not public documents.

The head office and plant of Celfibras are situated at Sao Bernardo in the State of Sao Paulo in southern Brazil. Through TOP, Brazilian has subscribed for 5,940,000 shares, for a total investment of Cr. 5,940 million ($2,700,000). It represents Brazilian's largest investment in a joint venture company up to the end of 1967. Returns on this investment are not anticipated before 1972, since it is not expected that the plant will be completed and commence production before the end of 1969. Details of the plant's capacity have been kept confidential to date.

PROBLEMS OF DOING BUSINESS IN BRAZIL

Brazilian has faced two major problems in conducting its business in Brazil, both of which are somewhat interrelated: lack of a firm government policy towards the operation and conduct of public utilities, and runaway inflation. Brazilian possessed a virtual monopoly for many years on the traction, gas, telephone, and electric utilities in Brazil. As a privately-owned company, Brazilian could not operate without a fair return on its investment. To achieve this, it required long-term concessions from the government, and a pricing structure that would allow not only a reasonable return on investment, but the generation of sufficient reserves to continually expand the services, and upgrade their quality. In the case of the traction and telephone utilities, the government did not permit a sufficient increase of prices to make operations profitable, and Brazilian could not eventually supply adequate services in either. In the case of the gas utilities, Brazilian was not granted a long-term concession that would have permitted a switching from coal to petroleum power in the production of gas. Only in 1965 was Brazilian able to obtain the "service at cost" pricing basis that allowed an adequate return to the electric utilities.

A succession of governments from the mid 1950's until 1965 was responsible for this position. Not until President Goulart announced in 1962 an intention to nationalize all public utilities did a definite government policy concerning public utility ownership emerge. The reason may well have been the magnitude of the financial burden involved in the taking over of Brazilian's assets.

In all its utility operations, Brazilian has been in a squeeze situation. The government sets rates, leaving Brazilian in the position of either continuing to operate at a loss, or abandoning the unprofitable operations. The latter course was followed for the tramways, and Brazilian had to give up all of its traction assets plus $10,000,000 to be relieved of the remainder of its operating obligations. Brazilian's only bargaining position in this type of situation has been that the country needs utilities, and the government must either take the operations over itself, or set rate schedules that permit Brazilian to supply the services needed. The government's problem has been that rate increases exacerbate the inflation problem and are politically unpopular.

Before this dilemma for both Brazilian and the government can be resolved, inflation must be controlled. Between 1963 and 1966, the value of the cruzeiro declined from about Cr. 550 per $1.00 to Cr. 2200 per $1.00. Inflation such as this makes business difficult. Retained earnings and accounts receivable decline in value from month to month. To meet this, complicated escalation clauses would have to be made applicable to accounts receivable. To cope with the problem of attrition of working capital, companies can deduct the attrition as a cost of doing business. But to become eligible for this deduction, the company can make only limited price increases. This had been Farloc's problem in 1966. To be able to take the deduction, it was not able to increase prices sufficiently to show a profit. Another means of mitigating the effects of inflation is the permission to write up the value of assets for capital cost allowances. Brazilian has found, however, that there was always the time lag between the time when the value of assets can be written up, and the time when their value has actually declined. The biggest contribution of President Branco's government has been to curb somewhat this runaway inflation, which has allowed more realistic rate schedules for Brazilian's remaining utility operations. One of the methods used to curb it has been control of prices and wages. During 1966, for example, the cost of living in Brazil increased by 44 percent, but wages were allowed to rise by only 31 percent. Such hard political measures have been successful, however, because in 1967, the cost of living increase was only 25 percent, a significant improvement over 1964, when it was 86 percent.

In the utility companies and in the joint ventures, inflation has caused the price of labor to spiral. Wages have to be adjusted regularly to cope with the increased costs of living. These adjustments are made through negotiations with employee representatives, and are conducted within the guidelines laid down by the government to combat inflation.

As mentioned, one of the chief problems of Brazilian had been to generate enough profits for internal financing of expanded and improved utility services. Outside help has been necessary and has come from the United States Agency for International Development, and the International Bank for Reconstruction and Development (World Bank). Loan agreements made with AID and coming into force in June 1966, provided $40 million to help finance the three-year $122 million expansion program for electrical distribution facilities in Rio de Janeiro and Sao Paulo. The loans were at 5½ percent for 15 years with a 3-year grace period. Interest was payable in cruzeiros. In addition, as of December, 1967, Brazilian had borrowed a total of $120,390,000 from the World Bank, and had repaid $68,-849,000. Most of the new capital equipment for the electric companies has been financed through the AID loans, which have been tied to purchases of equipment in the United States. This tying has applied even in the case of rewindings for generators.

While Brazilian has received considerable help from the United States and from the World Bank, the Export Credit Insurance Corporation of Canada has not assisted. In the past, it has provided financing for sales by other Canadian companies to Brazil, but a recent application for export assistance to purchase generating equipment from Canadian General Electric was refused. In the past, Latin American countries have not been large beneficiaries under any of Canada's external aid programs. Recent developments, however, suggest that this policy will be changed.

EVALUATION OF JOINT VENTURES

In a typical joint venture in a developing country between a local partner and a foreign partner, the foreign partner's contributions are technical know-how and capital, and the local partner's contributions are labor, land, and knowledge of local conditions. Viewed in terms of this definition, it cannot be said that any of the seven companies in which Brazilian has invested is a typical joint venture in Brazil between local and foreign partners. In the first place, Brazilian is not the *de jure* foreign partner in any of the joint ventures; its wholly-owned Brazilian investment subsidiaries, OEG and TOP, are. Moreover, in three of the companies, there is a foreign partner who fills the typical role of providing know-how and capital. These are Celfibras, owned 55 percent by Celanese Corporation of the United States; Brink's, owned 51 percent by the American parent; and Farloc, owned 30.4 percent by Wagner Electric of the United States. In both Celfibras and Brink's, Brazilian is acting as a typical local partner, in that it is supplying, along with capital, an intimate knowledge of local governmental and market conditions and it is this local expertise that has led to Brazilian being chosen as the local partner.

A second way in which these joint ventures differ from the norm is the method through which Brazilian has become involved. Foreign investors wishing to establish an enterprise in a developing country will often form a joint venture with local partners in order to secure favorable tax and other concessions, or because local laws prohibit outright foreign control. Neither of these reasons applied to Brazilian; it had $65 million of blocked telephone sale proceeds that it was obligated to invest in specified industries in Brazil. Brazilian's main aim, then, has not been that of a foreign developer-operator bringing funds into Brazil, but that of an investor who is forced to protect the value of blocked funds by finding suitable investments.

A third way in which these operations are not typical joint ventures is that Brazilian does not participate in the day-to-day management of any of them. This is because Brazilian does not profess to have any expertise in the operations of the joint ventures. Rather, Brazilian has limited its role to providing capital, and to assuring that proper fiscal and cost accounting standards are followed. For this latter purpose, Brazilian has secured representation on the "Conselho Fiscal" and "Conselho Consultativo" of the "sociedade anonima" corporations, which are Vagoes, Eucatex, Farloc, Garcia, and Brink's. With respect to Peixe, the shareholders' agreement specifies that Brazilian is to have a veto in all matters dealing with financial controls and accounting. The same is true for Celfibras, a "limitada" corporation, where this right is included in the Deed of Constitution of the company.

One further way in which Brazilian has not adopted the role of a typical foreign partner in a joint venture is that Brazilian has adopted a firm policy of not acquiring a majority or controlling position in any of the joint ventures. It does not even own any common voting shares in Peixe. In Vagoes and Eucatex, most of its holdings are in preference shares. In Brink's, Celfibras, Garcia, and Farloc, it owns only a minority of the common shares, and except for the informal voting arrangement with the General Manager of Garcia, is not in a position to determine control of the joint ventures. Besides the fact that control would entail responsibilities for management from day to day, Brazilian has avoided acquiring a majority holding in any of the joint ventures because of its concern for the maintenance of good relations with the government. Although all the investments are made through OEG and TOP, Brazilian can still be regarded as a foreign company whose loyalties lie with foreign shareholders. By limiting foreign ownership in the joint ventures to a minority position, the risk of nationalization is decreased. It also places the joint ventures in a better position to obtain government approval for measures to counter the effects of inflation, such as price increases and tax rulings. Because there is some sensitivity towards foreign investment, and because government policy can so directly determine the profitability of both the joint ventures and the utility companies, Brazilian has wisely restricted its investment to a minority position.

These justifications for being only a minority partner would not apply necessarily to Brink's and Celfibras, which have no local partner except for OEG and TOP respectively. In the same vein, Farloc is not majority-owned by nationals, since Wagner Electric and Brazilian have a combined holding of 72 percent of the capital stock. On the other hand, in companies such as Farloc, Brink's, and Celfibras, Brazilian can very much claim to be a local partner. It has been conducting operations in Brazil since 1899, and has worked closely with the government since that time. Its investments are made through companies incorporated locally, and except for about 70 head office personnel in Canada, all its employees are resident in Brazil. It has extensive connections through the business community, and is certainly the best known of all enterprises in Brazil. These factors, combined with the fact that it has a lot of capital to invest, make Brazilian a highly desirable partner for foreign investors such as Brink's and Celanese. Brazilian is also a highly desirable partner for existing local enterprises such as Vagoes, Peixe, Eucatex, and Garcia. Apart from the capital, Brazilian has been able to contribute North American techniques and standards of accounting and fiscal control that have increased their operating efficiency.

It can be seen then that Brazilian has been able to act without self-contradiction, as both a local partner and as a foreign investor with respect to joint ventures in Brazil, and has made highly significant contributions in each capacity. As developing countries continue to nationalize public utilities, but wish to avoid the disruption engendered by a sudden repatriation of capital, they might well follow the example of Brazil, by blocking a total repatriation, and laying down certain guidelines for its reinvestment. From the point of view of a foreign owner of public utilities, this can be a more attractive alternative than continuing operation of utilities at a loss. Shareholders of Brazilian have certainly benefited from this course of action with quarterly dividends of 25 cents having been resumed, and the stock selling at an all-time high of more than $18.00. It has been satisfied with the investments of more than $9,000,000 it has made in joint ventures. For its part, Brazilian has deliberately chosen to reinvest the telephone proceeds in the joint ventures as a minority partner, even though no legal constraints or incentives dictated this business decision. It intends to follow the investment pattern and guidelines adopted so far with respect to investment of the remaining $56 million.

XVIII: STUDY OF ATTITUDES TOWARDS JOINT VENTURES IN A CAPITAL IMPORTING COUNTRY (INDIA)

The Indian Economy

Economic Planning. Although the scope and modalities of planning have been adapted to changing circumstances, India has persisted in its basic policy of planned economic development through a succession of Five-Year Plans. The Planning Commission has played an important role in the formation of Indian plans. Founded in 1950, the commission is not a ministry or a department but acts as an independent advisory body. Whereas the Prime Minister is *ex-officio* chairman of the commission, the day-to-day work is executed by the deputy chairman and by four members. The Planning Commission gives its advice on all aspects of Indian economic life, with the exception of defense requirements, and establishes national priorities. However, the final decisions are taken by the government, which also considers the suggestions submitted by various ministries. These can sometimes be conflicting: on the problem of exports for instance, the Ministry of Finance, the Ministry of Commerce, and the Planning Commission may have divergent opinions.

The Planning Commission is represented in the Foreign Investment Board, which has to examine the joint venture proposals. The role of the commission's representative is to judge whether the proposal is in conformity with the needs of the economy and the priorities established in the plan. A proposal may exceptionally be submitted to the Planning Commission for a thorough examination.

The Five-Year Plans, which are highly flexible, are complemented by annual plans that are more specific about the precise allocation of money. The degree of success of each plan is of course a matter for debate. According to Mr. K. S. Sundara Rajan, however, the First Plan (1951–1952 to 1955–1956) was a success and the targets of the Second Plan (1956–1957 to 1960–1961) were almost reached, whereas the Third Plan (1961–1962 to 1965–1966) fell far short of its targets.[1]

The goal of the Fourth Five-Year Plan (1969–1970 to 1973–1974) is the self-reliance of the Indian economy.[2] This means reducing the level of foreign aid, reducing imports, and increasing exports. All efforts toward self-reliance will be fruitless, however, if the birth rate is not checked and if agriculture is not substantially developed.

Family Planning. Mainly because of improved health and medical services and great success in checking diseases like malaria, the population increased from 363 million in 1950–1951 to 524 million in 1968.[3] This large increase has counteracted many of the gains achieved in industrial and agricultural production.

Although the Indian Government, in 1950, became the first government in the world to adopt an officially-sponsored family planning program, for many years these efforts were not very successful. Only a limited number of people in the upper income groups and urban areas seem to have benefited from the program.

The government is now determined to intensify its efforts. Family planning is being introduced to both the town-dweller and the villager through a variety of communications media such as the radio, the cinema, the press, the mail, wall posters, as well as exhibitions and audiovisual vans. A large number of medical personnel and para-medical personnel have been trained in family planning methods and task forces have been set up. Although probably fewer babies were born in 1967 than in 1966, the population growth rate is still about 2.5 percent a year. The government is determined to halve this rate between now and 1975.

1. Former Minister (Economic), Embassy of India in U.S.A. and now Chairman, Central Board of Direct Taxes. See: *The Indian Economy: Recent Developments and Future Prospects,* New Delhi, Indian Investment Centre, p. 5 (1967). In India, the financial year begins on April 1 and ends on March 31.

2. *Fourth Five-Year Plan 1969–1974—Draft,* Delhi, Planning Commission, 357 pp. (1969).

3. Mid-year estimate.

Emphasis on Agriculture. In 1965 it was decided henceforth to give the highest priority to agriculture. Agricultural yields have traditionally been low as compared with the yields in technologically advanced countries. Moreover, it has taken time for the agricultural scientists and research workers in India to experiment with the new seeds that would improve these yields.

When new seeds responsive to intensive application of fertilizers became available in 1965, the government decided upon a new agricultural strategy that mainly consisted in the exploitation of the new high-yielding varieties of seeds for rice, millet, and wheat, in areas where water was not lacking. This has been carried out on a progressively increasing scale with heavy doses of fertilizers, plant protection materials, and appropriate volumes of farm credit. The farmers readily came forward not only to try the new seed varieties and use large amounts of fertilizers, but they were also willing to make supplementary investments in wells, pumping sets, and the like.

In order to encourage both foreign and Indian private investments in fertilizers, the government announced a series of measures in December 1965, removing all distribution and price controls on fertilizers for a period of seven years from the commencement of commercial production. Foreign investors can choose to enter into partnership with private Indian parties or with the government.

The Role of Foreign Investment. The reasons that induce foreign corporations to invest in developing countries in general and in India in particular, have been the object of much debate. A popular argument is that foreign investors can expect higher profits on the Indian market than on their home markets. Although the situation varies from one industry to another, it is widely admitted that profits have generally been higher in India than abroad. This trend, however, was reversed some time before the devaluation of June 6, 1966, after which profits in India remained lower than in developed countries till 1968.

Even under normal circumstances, it is doubtful whether foreign investors are primarily attracted to India by the expectation of higher profits. Other reasons are probably more decisive. First, the foreign markets of developed countries are becoming saturated, while India has still a very large potential market. Second, India protects investors by imposing restrictions on competing imports, a practice that induces the formation of "tariff factories." Third, if a large corporation neglects the investment opportunities of India, its direct competitors may seize them. Moreover, the investing firm is often able to export machinery or components to India. Furthermore, to produce in India is sometimes a means of securing raw materials. All these factors are, in fact, as important as returns on capital.

During the first three Five-Year Plans, foreign public aid and foreign private capital made a substantial contribution in carrying out various development programs. The total inflow of private foreign capitals of Rs. 625 crores during the three Plans constituted about 25 percent of the total private sector investment in the industrial field.[4] Most of the investment of foreign private capital has been in the form of direct investment.

Foreign investors were so eager to enter the Indian market that some influential circles warned of the danger of possible foreign economic domination. Actually, in recent years, several events have contributed to alarm the foreign investors already present on the market and have discouraged many newcomers. The Sino-Indian conflict of 1962 and the Pakistano-Indian war of 1965 have drained a not negligible proportion of the limited national resources. Moreover, the severe droughts of 1965–1966 and 1966–1967 have greatly reduced the impact of the efforts made by Indian agronomists and farmers. Since the agricultural sector accounts for 50 percent of the national income, a setback in this sector naturally reduces the buying power of the rural population. Furthermore, inflationary prices in 1966–1968 strongly influenced industrial costs. Also, political instability was felt in some states and this has constituted a relative deterrent to foreign investment for the first time since independence. Finally, some foreign countries (especially the U.S.A. and the U.K.), have lately been preoccupied by balance-of-payments considerations and have consequently restricted their investments abroad.

Fortunately, the economic situation is now slowly improving. With the monsoon rains, the new seed strains have permitted bumper crops in 1967–1968 and 1968–1969. The capital market has also shown signs of revival; new issues in 1968 were well below the level of previous years, but some, like that of Nestlé, were heavily oversubscribed. The rise in equity prices of over 6 percent was another hopeful sign.

If the favorable evolution of the agricultural sector and of the capital market were to persist, it would probably be accompanied by a revival of industrial activity. In particular, the increased income gen-

4. One crore = 10 million rupees. One dollar = 7.5 rupees.

erated in the agricultural sector is expected to provide the market for a wide variety of consumer goods and agro-industries. Nevertheless, the government faces a difficult alternative concerning the industrial sector: as the Fourth Five-Year Plan aims at the self-reliance of the economy, imports ought to be reduced; on the other hand, India cannot stimulate economic growth without providing for larger imports of machinery, components, and raw materials that cannot be obtained in India.

The government has made an attempt to solve this problem by adopting a selective, liberalized import policy. Fifty-nine priority industries accounting for over 80 percent of industrial production have been selected. These industries are allowed to import the raw materials, components, and spare parts necessary to maintain production at full capacity.

Even so, imports are bound to remain considerable. India has engaged in a vigorous and consistent effort toward self-reliance, but the country will still be in need of a good deal of foreign aid and substantial foreign private investments over a long period.

Technical Collaboration

Indian Research Effort. India has certainly made a vigorous effort to reach self-reliance in technology, at least in certain fields. For instance, the government has made remarkable progress in nuclear energy research. Because the government does not approve of technical agreements with foreign firms for periods greater than ten years (subject to possible extension), and because tax incentives are provided for research and development, the private sector has tried to develop its own research facilities.

Tata has devoted long and costly efforts to reach self-sufficiency in its chemical activities and has been largely successful in its endeavor. A Tata officer recognized, however, that such an effort was only possible because the company had qualified personnel for undertaking chemical research. In the field of engineering, on the other hand, Tata initially had to rely heavily on collaboration agreements concluded with foreign partners, but as a result of continuous and intensive training of local personnel, it is now almost self-reliant in this field.

A highly-placed Birla executive admitted that the research efforts of the company have brought about appreciable results, but only in certain fields. He cited the discovery of a staple fiber made from bamboo and used in cloth: there is only one plant in Asia, it seems, producing this fiber.

Generally speaking, Indian businessmen seem realistic in their appraisal of national research. Mr. G.L. Mehta, former Ambassador of India to the United States and currently Chairman of the Industrial Credit and Investment Corporation of India (ICICI), has emphasized the need for external assistance in technology:

While I wholeheartedly support the principle that we should make full use of the technological advances and skills developed within the country, there are many areas in which we still need to import technology for many years to come. . . . While appreciable progress has been made in manufacture of capital equipment in the country, progress in respect of design, engineering and research has not been encouraging.[5]

As it is often more economical to borrow a technique and develop it to function in Indian conditions, many technical agreements have been concluded with foreign partners.

Advantages and Disadvantages of Technical Collaboration. By "technical collaboration" we mean the collaboration agreements that are concluded without the assumption of an equity participation by the foreign partner.[6] A Tata economist pointed out that India should now adopt the policy followed by Japan, which attracts foreign know-how and tends to discourage the entry of foreign capital. More than 2,500 technical agreements have been hitherto approved by the Government of India. Until now, there has been a greater diversity of technology-supplying countries than of capital-supplying countries.

After a thorough review of the policy relating to foreign private investment and foreign technical collaboration, the government decided in 1968 to take a number of practical steps designed to speed up the process of deciding on proposals. Consequently, the government has drawn up lists of industries (a) where foreign investment may be permitted with or without technical collaboration; (b) where foreign technical collaboration may be permitted but not foreign investment and (c) where no foreign collaboration (financial or technical) is considered necessary. The cases where foreign investment—

5. *Development and Foreign Collaboration,* New Delhi, Indian Investment Centre, p. 17 (1968).
6. The total number of foreign collaboration agreements (that is, technical collaboration and equity joint ventures) in India from 1957 to 1967 was 2,743. A large majority of them were technical collaboration agreements.

usually as part of a joint venture—may be allowed will be dealt with below.

With regard to the cases that involve only technical collaboration, it was decided that the final decision should be left to the administrative ministries. These ministries deal only with cases involving payment in cash of royalty or fees for technical know-how up to the ceiling rates proposed by the Ministry of Industrial Development, Internal Trade and Company Affairs, in consultation with the administrative ministries and the Ministry of Finance. Normally, technical collaboration agreements are permitted for a period ranging from 5 to 10 years, the duration depending upon the product and the technological skill involved in its production. Extension of these agreements beyond this specific period is subject to a review by the government of the progress and performance of production. As the government aims at the development of indigenous know-how, foreign technical agreements cannot be prolonged indefinitely. Some foreign investors have pointed out that excessive severity towards the renewal of these agreements could nullify all the other attempts now being made to encourage increased foreign investment.

Finally, the government requires that whenever an Indian consultant is available, he should be used exclusively, and where a foreign consultant is also required, he should be hired only with an Indian consultant as the primary contractor.

Mr. Bharat Ram, the head of the large Delhi Cloth and General Mills Co. Ltd. and of other Indian enterprises, has until now concluded only technical agreements. As part of the agreements, the Delhi Cloth personnel is usually trained in foreign plants. Generally speaking, the royalties are based on sales and the products are sold under Delhi Cloth's name. In the experience of Mr. Ram, these collaborations have on the whole been satisfactory. Other Indian businessmen, however, emphasized that an equity participation is sometimes necessary to induce the foreign partner to take an active interest in the success of the enterprise.

Actually, the choice between a mere technical agreement and an equity joint venture depends greatly on the type of product. Although technical collaboration is sufficient for products which involve relatively simple technological skills, equity joint ventures are often preferable in the case of sophisticated products, because the continuing influx of new techniques from the foreign partner is thus more readily available to the local partner.

As a rule, foreign corporations agree to the use of their brand name only if they hold an equity participation in the enterprise. Accordingly, technical agreements may be used in the case of products where the brand name is not too important: this is true, for instance, of many engineering goods for which the design is more important than the brand name. Equity joint ventures tend to be preferred, on the other hand, in the case of certain consumer goods where the brand name is especially important.

Foreign exchange requirements are another relevant factor. When most of the capital, components, and raw materials can be found in India, mere technical agreements are often sufficient. On the other hand, if the construction of the plant and the operation of the enterprise require substantial imports from abroad, the foreign partner might be offered an equity participation for which he would pay in foreign exchange. Moreover, foreign financial institutions often agree to grant loans in foreign currency only if the foreign partner has at least some equity participation in the enterprise.

For a long time the government feared that the royalties relating to the technical agreements would be very high and thus constitute an unbearable burden for the balance of payments. This danger seems to have been greatly reduced by the fact that the level of royalties remitted abroad is now subject to strict government control. The lists of industries in which technical collaborations are permitted indicate the range of royalty that is allowed in each industry. Royalty payments for such collaboration are usually in the range of 3 to 5 percent based on the net sale value of the production. It is important to note that exceptions to the usual rules are permissible. As will be seen below, these royalties are subject to Indian taxes. In a few but important cases (e.g. fertilizers, offshore oil exploration), no royalties are allowed.[7]

Turn-key Contracts. In a "turn-key contract" the construction and engineering aspects of a project are usually executed entirely by a foreign corporation or, more often, by a foreign consortium. These contracts are generally concluded for the realization of large projects, such as a dam, a steel factory, or an oil refinery. Upon completion of the project, the plant or the dam is remitted to a local entrepreneur.

---

7. In cases where no royalty is allowed, a lump sum fee is another method of payment for technical services. In some cases, if the know-how is already available indigenously, government may not allow any payments at all for know-how.

In India, turn-key jobs have been executed in both the public and private sectors. Following a number of unfortunate experiences, turn-key contracts as a whole have been much criticized in the country.

Previously, many turn-key jobs were handed over to foreign consortia. Even today, there are several Indian economists who recognize that these contracts have been useful in the early stages of Indian industrialization. More recently, however, the atmosphere turned against this form of investment. It was felt that contracts of this kind did not permit a sufficient training in design and engineering for the Indians. More often than not, the local entrepreneur remained practically out of the picture until he took possession of the completed project. Furthermore, turn-key contracts tended to be regarded as too costly for India because they involved considerable imports of capital goods that had not always been purchased with great cost consciousness. Because of this, many Indians began to wonder whether the additional cost was justified by any specific advantage. Since India has already developed fabricating and designing capacities in various fields, turn-key contracts for the construction of plants by foreign-led consortia are no longer wanted, whenever engineering and consulting services are available within the country.

An Indian economist observed that the true objection is not to the turn-key jobs as such, but to the fact that the choice of the foreign builder is often poor. He added that Indian firms should now, more than in the past, be able to combine in a consortium and to execute jobs with a "systems approach." Many important contracts were granted to foreign consortia merely because otherwise the Indian customer would have been obliged to conclude several separate contracts with various Indian firms. If local corporations were better able to form consortia for the execution of specific jobs, this would also mean that a larger part of the equipment would be purchased in India.

Technical Collaboration with Eastern European Enterprises

Advantages. In recent years, there has been a significant increase in the number of collaboration agreements concluded between Eastern European enterprises and private or public Indian corporations. Most of these agreements have been confined to technical collaboration. As the Eastern European countries do not readily permit the investment of money abroad, until recently only a handful of equity joint ventures have been formed. As compared with the technical agreements concluded between Indian and Western firms, the collaboration agreements with Eastern European enterprises have their distinctive features, their advantages, and their limitations.

The proliferation of these collaboration agreements was due, in part, to the relative reluctance shown by Western companies to enter the Indian market between 1966 and 1968. For instance, the Indian Government contacted the American firm Kodak, but no agreement was reached. As a result, the government turned towards the East German firm Agfa; yet these negotiations proved no more successful. Finally, an agreement was concluded with a French firm which was subsequently taken over by a U.S. corporation.

It is likely that the increase in the number of collaboration agreements concluded with Eastern European enterprises was also due to other factors. First, many products from Eastern Europe are quite as good as Western products for the Indian market. The cement machinery and the tractors of Czechoslovakia may be cited as outstanding examples of high quality. Second, the terms offered by Eastern European enterprises are attractive because they usually ask for a lump sum payment, which the debtor executes in two or three installments. These agreements generally do not involve the payment of royalties, which makes the Indian entrepreneur financially more independent.[8] Third, Eastern Europeans are often less concerned than Westerners about the protection of know-how and the Indian entrepreneur is usually free to adapt the designs to Indian conditions. Fourth, Eastern Europeans do not ask for restrictive clauses on exports, which is not unimportant today in view of the present government drive to expand exports.

The Delhi firm, Escorts Limited, has been one of the Indian companies to conclude agreements along these lines. In 1962, Escorts concluded a technical agreement with the Polish enterprise Cekop (Warsaw), relating to the manufacturing of motorcycles; Cekop received a lump sum in exchange for drawings, technical data, information, and technical assistance over a period of 10 years. In 1963, Escorts and Motoimports (Warsaw), signed a technical agreement relating to the manufacture of tractors, and Escorts again made a

---

8. Nevertheless, it has been contended in India that as long as technical agreements are tied with large imports of components, foreign entrepreneurs may tend to raise artificially the prices of such components in order to provide for hidden royalties.

lump sum payment. Neither agreement provided for any royalties. According to a senior Escorts executive, these agreements have hitherto worked satisfactorily.

Disadvantages. On the other hand, cooperation with Eastern Europeans has certain disadvantages. In a number of cases, it has been found that the quality of the equipment sold to the Indian company as part of the agreement was not up to standard. Moreover, Eastern Europeans often do not make as vigorous a research effort as Western corporations. As a result, their products sometimes become obsolete. Although this might not be a decisive handicap for relatively simple products, it can be very detrimental in the case of sophisticated products. Furthermore, as India has bilateral, commercial barter agreements with Eastern European countries, technical agreements cannot be concluded freely.

Prospects. Recently there has been an interesting evolution in the business methods of Eastern European enterprises: they are becoming increasingly businesslike, and they now enjoy greater autonomy in negotiations. And whereas previously they were interested primarily in exports of technical know-how and skills, they now show interest in investing. Moreover, whereas previously they generally asked for lump sum payments, they now often require the payment of royalties.

Nevertheless, the future of these technical collaboration arrangements seems rather limited, especially if Western corporations show a revived interest in the Indian market. The prospects will vary according to the type of industry. The increasing demand for tractors in India, for example, will provide Eastern European enterprises with interesting opportunities. However, although they produce good metallurgical products, they will probably not conclude many more collaboration agreements in this field, because the productive capacity in India is already quite substantial. At present, petrochemicals are one of India's most promising industries, but many Eastern European enterprises have not yet reached the degree of sophistication attained by Western enterprises in this field.

The Government and the Formation of Joint Ventures

As has already been mentioned, Indian entrepreneurs realize that equity joint ventures are sometimes preferable to mere technical agreements.[9] A senior Tata officer observed that his company would deliberately favor an equity joint venture when considerable foreign exchange was needed, because the foreign partner could provide it or help to find available sources. A highly-placed Birla officer asserted that without an equity participation the foreign partner may not be sufficiently interested in the success of the enterprise and may not send his best technicians to India. Similarly, a former ambassador, who is now advising a U.S. company, affirmed that equity joint ventures often involve more cooperative effort than mere technical collaboration.

The Indian Government's policy is a decisive factor in the ways of doing business in the country. As the government has a positive attitude towards foreign capital and technology, it has granted tax concessions and provided various tax incentives to attract foreign private investment. From a national point of view, however, the desirability of foreign capital varies with each industry. Consequently, the government has adopted a selective approach towards foreign investment, which is thus submitted to a thorough screening.

Screening of Foreign Investment. The procedures involved in establishing any new industrial undertaking in India require a number of favorable decisions by the government. First, it is necessary to obtain approval by the government for the basic proposal for the joint venture. In addition, it is necessary to obtain:

1. An industrial license under the Industries (Development and Regulation) Act of 1951;
2. Approval with reference to the foreign exchange implications of the proposed investment under the Foreign Exchange Regulations Act of 1947;
3. A license for the import of capital equipment and machinery under the Imports and Exports (Control) Act of 1947;
4. Consent for the issue of capital stock under the Capital Issues (Continuance of Control) Act of 1947; and
5. A certificate of incorporation under the Indian Companies Act of 1956.

The basic decision on a joint venture proposal is made by the Foreign Investment Board. Previously, it had been taken by one of two special government bodies: the Foreign Agreements Committee or

9. For detailed information on equity joint ventures and technical agreements in India, see *Directory of Foreign Collaborations in India,* Delhi, De Indiana Overseas Publications, 2 vols., 900 and 1080 pp. (1969).

the Foreign Investment Committee. Although a large number of joint venture proposals had materialized, under this system, to the mutual satisfaction of all parties involved, procedural delays were often a source of frustration.

Administrative Delays. Foreign investors generally, and Americans especially, have often complained about the complexity of procedures and the "red tape" in India that impede the rapid realization of their projects. Actually, many joint venture negotiations have indeed broken off because the foreign investor was not able to wait any longer or because the economic conditions surrounding the project had changed in the course of negotiations.

On this subject, government officers answered that the screening procedure cannot always be expeditious, because the proposals are numerous and have to be submitted to several authorities. Moreover, it was contended that too often foreign investors are themselves slow in answering the official demands for clarification concerning their joint venture proposals. Furthermore, it was asserted that many foreign negotiators—those for U.S. corporations in particular—continually have to refer to their home headquarters, which is a further cause of delay.[10]

A government official cited as an example of an efficient handling of negotiations, the procedure that was followed to gain approval for a fertilizer project presented by Indian Explosives Limited, which is a joint venture between Imperial Chemical Industries Limited (ICI), the government, the International Finance Corporation of Washington, and the public. To begin with, ICI executives and government officials had informal discussions on the project. As a result, most of the essential points were settled before the formal proposal was submitted to the government. The procedure was also accelerated by the fact that the Chairman of ICI of India had appropriate authority to agree personally and immediately on basic decisions.

Although foreign investors have their share of responsibility for administrative delays, the government does not deny that too often

10. In connection with this problem of procedural delays and with the difficulty of matching partnership, the Indian Investment Centre is in a position to assist local and foreign investors efficiently. This organization was born out of a conscious need for an active and objective agency, with which investors could confer freely and frankly and secure an understanding of the lines on which a proposal may be made or accepted. The Indian Investment Centre has its head office in Delhi and branch offices in New York and Düsseldorf. It has issued a number of excellent publications.

"red tape" and "bottlenecks" slow down the normal functioning of Indian administration. After careful examination of the whole screening procedure, the government decided in 1968 to take a number of practical steps designed to reduce administrative delays.[11]

The Foreign Investment Board. To curb undue delay in the disposal of the basic proposals for joint ventures, the government established, in 1968, the Foreign Investment Board. It must, as far as possible, dispose of any application within three months. The Chairman of the Board is a secretary in the Ministry of Finance and other members are the secretaries of the economic ministries principally concerned with foreign investment and joint ventures.[12]

All cases of foreign investment fall within the jurisdiction of the board. Accordingly, the applications for joint ventures are received centrally in the Secretariat of the Board, which is located in the Department of Industrial Development of the Ministry of Industrial Development, Internal Trade and Company Affairs. The board normally meets once a fortnight. In order to ensure the speedy disposal of cases, the board delegates adequate authority to the administrative ministries who are primarily responsible for the prompt disposal of applications falling within their particular field in accordance with certain specific guidelines laid down for this purpose.

The Foreign Investment Board deals with the majority of all joint venture proposals. Some cases are dealt with by a subcommittee of the board,[13] and others are examined by the Central Cabinet Com-

11. Press Note issued by the Government of India on July 20, 1968; Announcement of the Government of India, November 27, 1968. These documents have been published in *Foreign Investment and Collaboration— Guidelines,* New Delhi, New York, and Düsseldorf, Indian Investment Centre, 26 pp. (1968).

12. The composition of the Foreign Investment Board is as follows: Chairman: Secretary, Ministry of Finance. Members: 1. Secretary, Department of Industrial Development. 2. Secretary, Ministry of Petroleum and Chemicals. 3. Secretary, Department of Company Affairs. 4. Secretary, Ministry of Foreign Trade. 5. Secretary, Planning Commission. 6. Secretary of the administrative ministry concerned. 7. Director-General, Council of Scientific and Industrial Research. 8. Director-General, Technical Development. 9. Member-Secretary, to be provided by the Department of Industrial Development. The Executive Director of the Indian Investment Centre is an invitee to the meetings of the Board.

13. The composition of the Subcommittee of the Foreign Investment Board is as follows (at the level of Joint Secretaries): *Chairman:* Department of Industrial Development. *Members:* 1. Department of Economic Affairs.

mittee.[14] The subcommittee deals with cases involving foreign participation up to 25 percent where total investment does not exceed Rs. 10 million. Cases of technical collaboration where know-how fees are payable in shares are treated as cases involving foreign investment. The cases that require clearance of the Central Cabinet Committee are those where total investment exceeds Rs. 20 million of equity capital, those where the foreign investment exceeds 40 percent of the issued equity capital, and cases of importance involving any special point on which the Foreign Investment Board may desire guidance from the Cabinet Committee.[15]

Although important changes have been introduced, the new organization does not represent a fundamental departure from the previous system.

The Scope for Joint Ventures. Until 1968, the rules that applied to the disposal of joint venture proposals were developed largely on a case-by-case basis. In order to facilitate the work of the newly-established Foreign Investment Board and thus speed up the disposal of applications, the government decided in 1968 to draw up lists in consultation with the administrative ministries and other departments. As has been mentioned previously, the lists distinguish the cases (a) where foreign investment may be permitted with or without technical collaboration; (b) where foreign technical collaboration may be permitted but not foreign investment and (c) where no foreign collaboration (financial or technical) is allowed. These lists also indicate the range of royalty payments that are permissible. They are published and reviewed at least once a year. To a large extent, these lists represent a written version of the rules that had previously developed as on a case-by-case basis. Although the rules that apply to the entry of

2. Department of Company Affairs. 3. Ministry of Foreign Trade. 4. Ministry of Petroleum and Chemicals. 5. Department of the administrative ministry concerned. 6. A representative of the Planning Commission. 7. A representative of the Directorate-General of Technical Development. 8. A representative of the Council of Scientific and Industrial Research. 9. Member-Secretary to be provided by the Department of Industrial Development.

14. The composition of the Central Cabinet Committee would depend on the nature of the industry it is to deal with for purposes of foreign collaboration. Basically, it would comprise representatives of economic ministries like Finance (Economic Affairs), Industrial Development, Foreign Trade, Petroleum and Chemicals, and the Planning Commission.

15. The Rs. 20 million ceiling refers to the equity capital only and not to loans. Issue of shares in exchange for capitalized technical know-how is to be included in the calculation.

foreign capital are not static, by and large the lists faithfully respect the principles that have been applied consistently in recent years.

It should be noted at the outset that the foreign companies that remain in India on a wholly-owned basis—either with a branch or with a subsidiary—are largely historical exceptions. When such companies wish to undertake an expansion, the government usually asks them to proceed with a public issue of shares, as was the case for the U.S. firm Pfizer, for instance. Until now, IBM has consistently refused to sell shares to the Indian public, but it may experience difficulties when asking for a major expansion.

As a rule, the government does not permit the entry of foreign capital in fields that have a strategic importance, nor in those that are by now well-established and adequately handled by Indian managerial talent and with local technical skills.[16] Thus, joint ventures are not allowed in distribution, banking, and insurance. Similarly, marketing is generally regarded as a nontechnical field, although the success of any productive effort is closely dependent upon scientific marketing—which in many cases could be adequately provided by foreign investors. The main traditional industries in which foreign interests are no longer needed are cotton textiles, cement, paper, sugar, tea, certain engineering items, and some basic chemicals. Foreign financial collaboration may sometimes be permitted even for a traditional product, when a new process or a special technique is involved; a foreign company may thus associate with a local partner for the manufacture of instant tea.

On the other hand, the government encourages the formation of equity joint ventures in those advanced fields in which considerable foreign exchange and sophisticated techniques are needed: petrochemicals, fertilizers, pesticides, electronics, specialized kinds of steel, metals, machine tools and machinery, earth-moving equipment, and shipbuilding. In the course of the next few years, petrochemicals, fertilizers, and electronics will be especially attractive fields for joint ventures in India.

The case of electronics is somewhat special. Curiously enough, all electronics (radios, television sets, as well as professional computers) are handled by the Ministry of Defense. Prior to 1966, this sector was the responsibility of the Ministry of Industrial Development, which has to deal with a wide range of problems. A considerable in-

16. Except (as will be shown more in detail *infra*) if the business is to have a strong export orientation.

crease in the production of electronics is expected over the next few years. As a special coordinated effort was required to deal with this development, it was decided in 1966 to place all electronics under the single responsibility of the Ministry of Defense, because defense is the main purchaser of electronic equipment. A great many joint ventures have already been concluded in this field with firms of several foreign countries such as France, Germany, Italy, Japan, the U.K., and the U.S.A.; U.S. corporations have been especially eager to take an early lead in the Indian electronics market.

Criteria of Appraisal. Even if a joint venture proposal relates to an industry that is included in the list of cases where foreign investment is welcome, this does not necessarily mean that the proposal will be accepted. Although to a certain extent each case is judged on its own merits, all joint venture proposals are examined according to more or less the same criteria. It is true, however, that the importance of any criterion may vary from time to time. For instance, some steel ventures that had been undertaken with foreign assistance proved to be premature. Because of this, the government decided that the needs for foreign investment and collaboration should no longer be assessed mainly in terms of technological improvements, but equally in view of the country's real needs. Upon examination of the targets established by the Planning Commission in any particular field, the Foreign Investment Board must decide whether there is need for additional capacity in that sector.

After examination of the country's needs, the essential criteria that are taken into consideration are the following:

the foreign exchange requirements, the import saving and export earning of the project (in view of the foreign exchange difficulties of India, this criterion is especially important);

the degree of voting and managerial control to be awarded to the foreign investor;

the extent of development of indigenous technology in the industry under consideration, the technical contribution of the foreign partner (especially in advanced fields and sophisticated industries), and the level of royalties to be given in exchange for his services;

the extent of employment opportunities to be created by the realization of the project and the possibilities of access by Indians to qualified jobs and managerial posts.

The export potential of a project is an increasingly important factor that is now being taken into consideration, but on the whole it has not yet become a primary criterion in the refusal or the acceptance of a joint venture proposal. Many joint ventures can hardly supply even a significant part of the Indian market. In the field of fertilizers in particular, it would be irrational to insist on exports as long as internal demand is so acute. An important new development, however, is the recent liberalization in the government's policy, according to which foreign collaboration is now permitted even in low-priority and nonessential industries and also for trading activities if these are export-oriented.[17]

Another recent development that may influence the approval or refusal of specific joint venture proposals is the determination of the government to ensure equality of opportunities for industrial development in all regions and areas of India. The central and state governments are interested in encouraging industrial schemes designed for location in the underdeveloped areas of the country. The government feels that foreign collaboration has a role to play in accomplishing this objective.

No one criterion can be singled out as having a decisive influence in the disposal of a proposal. The decision taken by the Foreign Investment Board—or the Cabinet Committee, as the case may be—is based on an overall consideration of all relevant criteria.

The Need for Flexibility. The practical steps that have been taken may well be effective in reducing administrative delays. At the same time, however, it is to be feared that the establishment of definite categories of industries where foreign investment is not permitted may introduce a certain rigidity in the treatment of foreign capital.

In 1968, after thorough examination of all aspects relating to foreign private investment and technical collaboration, the government concluded that no significant change in the broad policy followed previously on these subjects was called for and that it was not necessary to issue any formal resolution on the subject. It is to be hoped that these conclusions may be interpreted as the government's determination to maintain, in the handling of joint venture proposals, the flexibility which in the past has proved so useful for all parties concerned.

17. See below, "Joint Ventures and Exports," at pp. 351–55.

Financing of Joint Ventures

Financial Needs and Sources. Various requirements of the government and the nature of the Indian economy pose a number of problems for a firm that needs capital. The rupee requirements of joint ventures are generally substantial. First, the partners often try to maximize the purchase of Indian equipment, as they have committed themselves vis-à-vis the government. Second, they have to provide for the working capital requirements of the enterprise. Sometimes, the local partner provides at least part of the rupee financing out of its own funds. More often, the partners have to solicit the capital market or specialized local financial institutions. The extent of the demands on these institutions is indirectly dependent upon the state of the general capital market.

The foreign exchange requirements of an enterprise in India can be considerable, especially when costly machinery and equipment have to be imported during the construction period. Even in the period of operation, components and raw materials may have to be imported in bulk, at least initially. The importation of cash capital by foreign investors has been relatively small; imports of machinery and equipment have constituted the majority of their contribution. Quite frequently, however, these purchases have been financed by foreign currency loans from Indian, foreign, or international financial institutions.

Normally, the "equity" of a company is required to be less than one half of its "debt," but exceptions are permissible, with specific government consent.[18] Some leftist circles contend, however, that the financing of enterprises should rely only on loan capital because, in the long run, the equity capital brings about a greater outflow of foreign exchange. On the other hand, it should be noted that most of the time, foreign loans are tied to equipment purchases in the lending country, which may also be regarded as a disadvantage from an Indian national point of view. Moreover, many foreign investors aim at

18. "Debt" includes all borrowings, repayable not earlier than five years from the date of borrowing (whether debentures, loans, or deferred payments including interest thereon, for the purchase of capital equipment), and preference shares redeemable not later than twelve years from the date of issue. "Equity" includes paid-up equity share capital, share premium, free reserves, irredeemable preference shares, and preference shares redeemable not earlier than twelve years from the date of issue.

growth and plow back profits, while the conclusion of new loans cannot be ensured in advance. Actually, equity capital and loan capital are generally complementary.

Control of the Issue of Securities. The financial and foreign exchange aspects of joint ventures have always been a matter of particular concern for the Indian Government. The Capital Issues (Continuance of Control) Act of 1947 provides the government with the means to control the issue of equity and debt securities, with a view to ensuring that investments are channeled into productive enterprises to meet the economic and industrial needs of the country and to ensuring also that the capital structures of companies are sound and are in the public interest.[19]

The broad policy of the union government in considering a proposal for a capital issue is that it should be based on reasonable estimates and provide adequate long-term capital from the beginning; also, that undue dependence on loans from intermediate sources or on the earning of large profits in the future should be avoided. Where the capital issue is for a particular industrial project, the amount of the issue should be such that the company does not have to approach the capital market a second time before the project is completed.

Indian law permits payment for shares other than by cash. Shares can be issued in consideration of transfer of property, tangible or otherwise, and for rendering services. Thus, shares can be issued against the supply of plant and machinery, technical know-how, patent rights, or engineering services. The value of shares to be issued in such cases and its proportion to the total paid-up capital are subject to negotiation between the parties and to the final approval of the government.

Once the terms of investment and collaboration have been approved, there are no restrictions on the outward remittance of divi-

19. In this respect, government regulations are very liberal. The issue of capital, other than bonus shares, in an amount not in excess of Rs. 2.5 million at a time by any company, does not require the specific prior consent of the Controller of Capital Issues. Even in the case of a public company, proposing to raise capital other than through bonus shares, in an amount exceeding Rs. 2.5 million, no prior consent is necessary if the proposal conforms to certain prescribed criteria. In such a case it would suffice that the company files a statement of its proposal for the issue of capital with requisite particulars with the Controller of Capital Issues, who will advise the company within a period of 30 days as to whether the proposal qualifies for the exemption from specific prior consent.

dends, interest on loans, fees, royalties, and other similar accounts. Such remittances are freely allowed, in accordance with the terms of approval. Similarly, the repatriation of foreign capital invested in India, together with any capital appreciation, is permitted by the Reserve Bank of India on application. In view of the continuous difficulties experienced by India with regard to foreign exchange, the excellence of its record in the free repatriation of capital and dividends is praiseworthy.

Public Issues of Shares. A cornerstone of government policy has been the determination to create an active capital market, to educate the public in investing habits, and thus to bring about a broad ownership of the securities in circulation. Some critics of government policy have asserted that the public issue of shares does not really benefit the national economy; because public ownership has not often involved participation by Indian investors in the operation of a firm, there is no transfer of skills to Indian hands. In some cases however, the government has indicated that it was not satisfied with a mere public issue and that it required the presence of an Indian promoter in the venture. A government official also observed that even when a powerful Indian concern is in partnership with foreign interests, this does not necessarily bring about a transfer of technological skills.

Most Indian entrepreneurs are accustomed to seek financial resources in the capital market. According to a highly-placed official of the Reserve Bank of India, local investors are frequently eager to buy shares when they know that a foreign corporation is a partner in the offering company. Local investors have also proved to be very selective and sophisticated in their investment decisions. Although the capital market was depressed between 1966 and 1968, some capital issues were oversubscribed even during this period. On the other hand, the capital market has shown a revival since 1968, but this has not precluded the failure of some capital issues. At present, electronics, fertilizers, and the food industry are generally popular industrial sectors, but the selectivity of the investing public is also leading it to discriminate between different companies in the same industry.

Specialized Financial Institutions. The process of industrial growth requires, among other factors, a well-developed capital market with financial intermediaries, i.e. banks, insurance companies, underwriting agencies, investment trusts, and finance corporations that can channel the demand for loan funds into industrial investment. In India, commercial banks have generally catered to the short-term requirements of trade and industry. Therefore, specialized financial institutions had to be established in order to meet the growing needs of the expanding industrial sector, in general, and of the increasingly numerous joint ventures, in particular, for medium and long-term finance.

India has several specialized financial institutions: the Industrial Development Bank of India, the Industrial Finance Corporation of India, the Industrial Credit and Investment Corporation of India Limited (ICICI), the State Financial Corporations,[20] the National Small Industries Corporation Ltd., the Life Insurance Corporation of India (LIC), and the Unit Trust of India (UTI). Among these institutions, those capable of drawing on the genuine savings of the people are mainly two, i.e. LIC and UTI. In many respects, however, the most interesting institution is ICICI, which has manifold impacts on investments made in India.

The Industrial Credit and Investment Corporation of India (ICICI), set up in 1955 as a joint stock company, provides long-term financial assistance to the private sector. Financial assistance in the form of foreign currency loans constitutes a substantial part of its lending operations. Thirty percent of ICICI's total share capital of Rs. 75 million has been subscribed by institutional investors in the Federal Republic of Germany, France, Japan, U.K., and the U.S.A. Moreover, it has obtained several lines of credit from the World Bank, the U.S. Agency for International Development, and the German Kreditanstalt für Wiederaufbau.

ICICI gives financial assistance to industrial concerns in various forms, such as long- and medium-term loans, equity participation, underwriting of new shares and debentures, and guaranteed loans raised from other private investment sources. No proposal for financial assistance can be too large for ICICI, since it is able to consider it in collaboration with other financial institutions both Indian and foreign, such as the International Finance Corporation of Washington, the Industrial Development Bank of India, and the Commonwealth Development Finance Company Ltd. of London. In addition, the various Indian financial institutions have adopted a consortium approach in order to ensure that no economically viable project is held up for lack of funds.

Investment is considered by ICICI a cooperative effort in which the entrepreneur is helped by the financial institutions to carry out the

20. Each Indian State has a separate state financial corporation established under the enabling central act of Parliament, i.e. the State Financial Corporations Act of 1951.

project. From the time of conception to completion, a project may undergo various changes and developments, as thought is devoted to its various aspects. ICICI has often required changes in the financial structure, in the strengthening of collaboration arrangements, and assurances regarding raw material and power supply.

ICICI has fulfilled the very important role of "catalyst" for other sources of funds: the institution claims that every rupee that has been sanctioned by it has made possible a total investment of five times that amount. Not only has ICICI acted as an active coordinator between various sources of funds, but its mere presence in a project has often brought about a positive decision from potential investors. However, ICICI's main contribution has been to assist new entrepreneurs and to encourage the development by the public of the investment habit. An investment company is effective only to the extent that entrepreneurs come forward to set up industries and investors to take up industrial securities.

The Life Insurance Corporation of India (LIC) came into being in 1956 when the government nationalized all the life insurance companies in the private sector. With a paid-up capital of Rs. 50 million, it is now the only life insurance organization in India. LIC plays an important role in the capital market of India and, at present, is by far the largest institutional investor in India. With a view to diversifying its investments, LIC invests in shares of promising industrial enterprises, grants loans on property mortgages, and underwrites new issues (apart from making traditional investments in government securities). It also maintains close contact with other financial institutions.

The Unit Trust of India (UTI) was set up in 1964 mainly with a view to mobilizing the savings of small investors. It channels the savings into productive investments by subscribing to, and underwriting, the shares and debentures of industrial undertakings. UTI has an initial share capital of Rs. 50 million subscribed mainly by the Reserve Bank of India, LIC, and the State Bank of India. It acquired capital of Rs. 187.3 million through sales of "units," a type of security of which the first Rs. 1,000 is exempt from taxation.

Taxation of Joint Ventures

A Narrow Tax Base. The purpose of this section is not to review extensively the Indian fiscal laws and practices, but to indicate the basic principles that apply to the taxation of joint ventures. We shall also try to answer a question that is the object of much debate between foreign investors and the Indian authorities, that is, whether India's taxation constitutes an incentive or a deterrent for foreign investors.

Allegedly high rates of taxation are often stated to be the major cause of India's failure to attract more foreign investment. Nevertheless, government officers have pointed out that the tax burden, in the aggregate, is not heavy and that it still accounts for less than 15 percent of national income. The real difficulty stems from a narrow tax base, at least as far as direct personal and corporate taxation is concerned. In a country where agriculture is still predominant, no central taxes are levied upon agricultural income.[21] As a result, rates are inevitably high and are likely to remain so in the foreseeable future. Consequently, for the time being the gross return on investment in India has to be considerably greater than in many other developing countries if net returns in India are to be similar to those in other countries.

In the long run, the tax structure will have to be revised. The difficulty lies in finding ways in which the tax base can be widened, so as to reduce the heavy burden imposed on a relatively small sector of the economy. The widening of the tax base will involve higher taxation of agricultural income, which may have serious social and political consequences. It is to be hoped that agricultural income will continue to rise so as to permit this fundamental and necessary change.

The Principles of Indian Corporate Taxation. Taxation in the case of a company depends upon whether it is a domestic or a foreign one, whether it is a closely-held company (i.e., a company with a limited number of shareholders), or a widely-held company (i.e., one in which the public is substantially interested), and whether it is an industrial, an investment, or a trading company.

Foreign companies (i.e., those that do not make the prescribed arrangements for the declaration and payment of dividends in India) are taxed at somewhat higher rates than domestic companies. The object of this is to compensate for the loss of revenue from the non-resident shareholders who would not be subject to Indian tax on divi-

21. On the other hand, all state governments have levied taxes on agricultural incomes. The main complaint in some circles has been that the rates are too low, or that there is a lack of integration with other sources of income.

dends declared by such companies outside India out of the profits earned in India.

In the category of domestic companies, widely-held companies pay income tax at lower rates than those applicable to closely-held ones. Among the closely-held domestic companies, industrial companies are treated favorably as compared to investment and trading companies. Among the industrial companies generally, the smaller ones with income up to Rs. 1 million get the benefit of paying income tax at a lower rate.

An examination of the basic tax rates would seem to indicate that the Indian tax burden is quite heavy. However, the fiscal burden is very heavy only for the long-standing enterprises that do not expand. New enterprises (especially in the field of priority industries), and business expansions benefit from tax incentives (e.g. tax holiday, development rebate) that are substantial. Consequently, the effective tax rates are not burdensome for the newcomers and the well-established, expanding enterprises. Therefore, it cannot be asserted that the level of taxation has acted as a real deterrent to foreign investment in India.

Basic Tax Liability of Joint Venture Companies. The tax liability that a foreign investor has to bear on various types of income derived by him from his investment in India depends to some extent on the size of the profits of the company that manages the joint enterprise set up by him and the Indian entrepreneur. Normally, such a joint venture company will be a domestic industrial one and the rate of taxation will vary, depending upon whether it is a widely- or a closely-held company. In the former case, the rate of tax is 45 percent if the total income does not exceed Rs. 50,000, but 55 percent when it exceeds this sum. In the latter case, the rate of tax is 55 percent on the first Rs. 1 million and 60 percent on the balance. If the closely-held joint venture is an investment company or a trading company, the rate of tax is 65 percent, irrespective of the size of its profits.

A company has also to pay a surtax at the rate of 35 percent of the profits exceeding Rs. 200,000 or a sum equal to ten percent of its capital, whichever is greater.

Incentives and Effective Tax Rates. The effective rate of tax is generally lower than the rates stated above, as a result of the numerous deductions allowed from profits as tax incentives. Domestic companies engaged in "priority" industries are allowed a deduction of a sum equal to 8 percent of the profits from manufacture. Deduction for depreciation allowance is increased in the case of factories working extra shifts. In addition to depreciation, a special deduction is allowed by way of development rebate at a certain percentage of the cost of new plant and machinery, which may be as high as 35 percent in the case of a "priority" industry, and 20 percent in the other cases.

There are a number of other reliefs, such as deductions for revenue and capital expenditure on scientific research, and amortization of the cost of patent rights and copyrights. There was previously a tax incentive for exports, but after the devaluation of June 6, 1966, it was replaced by a cash subsidy. Tax concessions are available for market research abroad or competition in bidding for international tenders.

New industrial undertakings enjoy a tax holiday under which income up to 6 percent of the capital employed is deducted in the first five years. If the taxable profits in any of these five years are less than 6 percent of the capital employed, the deficiency may be carried forward and deducted from the profits of the succeeding years, but this advantage is only available for a period of three years in addition to the five years of the tax holiday.

Tax Liability of Foreign Investors. Intercorporate dividends are taxed at a lower rate than other kinds of income. If the investor is a foreign company, the dividends received by it are reduced by a straight deduction, so that the effective rate of taxation is lowered. After deduction, a tax rate of 14 percent applies to dividends received by a foreign company from a closely-held Indian company mainly engaged in "priority" industries. A tax rate of 24.5 percent applies to dividends, after the appropriate deductions, received by a foreign company from any other type of domestic company. From a fiscal point of view, there is no discrimination between a foreign majority participation and a foreign minority participation. If the foreign investor is not a company, the dividend income will be part of the Indian income and will be taxed at the appropriate rates.

The foreign investor also has to pay taxes on the fees for technical services rendered to the joint venture and on the royalties received for the use by the joint venture of patents, copyrights, and trademarks. If the recipient of fees for technical services is a foreign company and the agreement has been entered into after February 29, 1964, the fees are taxed at a concessional rate of 50 percent. Similarly, if the recipient of royalties is a company and the collaboration agreement has been made after April 1, 1961, the concessional rate of 50 percent is applicable.

Interest received by a foreign investor, whether a company or an individual, from an industrial undertaking in India, on money borrowed or on a debt incurred by the Indian firm in a foreign country, for purchase of capital plant and machinery or raw materials from abroad, is exempt from taxes to the extent of the approved rate. It might be thought that this would induce the foreign investor to seek a high ratio of loan capital to equity capital in the financing of the joint venture. Actually, the Controller of Capital Issues is careful to avoid any disequilibrium in this ratio.[22] Even from the foreign investor's point of view, several other, perhaps more important, factors have to be taken into consideration when determining the capital structure of the joint venture.

Double Taxation Relief or Avoidance. Double taxation may leave little for the investor if the burden is not reduced, and it may, in the process, discourage the flow of foreign capital into developing countries. To avoid double taxation, India has entered into bilateral agreements with a number of countries such as Austria, Ceylon, Denmark, the Federal Republic of Germany, Finland, Greece, Japan, Norway, Pakistan, and Sweden. Agreements with Belgium, France, Italy, Lebanon, Rumania, the U.A.R., the U.K., and the U.S.A. are under negotiation.

In the case of countries with which India does not have a reciprocal arrangement, the Indian tax laws grant unilateral relief to a resident in India, limited to the lower of the two taxes on the doubly taxed income. Similar unilateral relief is provided by many other countries, such as the U.K. and the U.S.A., to their residents in order to avoid the onus of double taxation with regard to the same income.

Control of Joint Ventures

Foreign Investors' Attitudes. Many foreign investors today still consider that voting and managerial control of a joint venture is essential for the satisfactory operation of the enterprise. The intensity of this resolve is of course dependent upon many factors: generally, foreign investors will be more insistent on control in the case of so-

22. See *supra*, pp. 329–30.

phisticated industries; by and large, U.S. corporations will be less inclined than others to make concessions on the degree of participation they will hold in joint ventures; sometimes, the foreign industrial company insists on the control of the joint venture because a foreign or international financial institution would not, otherwise, grant a loan.

A significant example of this policy is the case of Imperial Chemical Industries Ltd. (ICI), which, throughout the world, has shown a strong and constant preference for majority participation in its joint ventures. This clear policy caused some difficulties when the Indian Government and ICI decided to undertake a fertilizer project at Kanpur: if a new company had been created, it might have been difficult for the government to agree on a foreign majority participation. At that time, however, ICI had a 70 percent participation in an existing company, Indian Explosives Ltd. (IEL).[23] At first sight, explosives and fertilizers may seem unrelated products, but they both require the use of ammonia in their manufacture. Consequently, it was thought possible to place the manufacture of both products with the same company. Although, then, it is not easy for the government to agree on a foreign majority participation in the case of a new company, it may more easily be prepared to leave the control in foreign hands in the case of a well-established enterprise, even if the business expands. Therefore, ICI was allowed to maintain a 51 percent participation in IEL. The International Finance Corporation of Washington also became a shareholder when the Kanpur fertilizer project was set up.[24]

Nevertheless, foreign investors will have to make increasing concessions on this problem of control in the future. Competition among foreign investors for entry into Indian markets is bound to increase, especially in the more promising fields. In many instances, the government may be naturally tempted to give its preference to the company that shows maximum flexibility as to the financial and control arrangements.

Indian Entrepreneurs' Attitudes. Until a few years ago, and much to the displeasure of the government, many Indian entrepreneurs had

23. The registered office of the company is in Calcutta, while the site of explosives manufacture is at Gomia in Bihar.
24. The total equity capital is held in the following proportion: President of India: 12.75 percent; Imperial Chemical Industries (U.K.): 51.02 percent; the public: 26.22 percent; International Finance Corp. (U.S.A.):10.01 percent.

been more than willing to leave control in the hands of foreign partners because they were not prepared to assume management responsibilities. Even today, a number of Indian industrialists are without the technical and managerial skills that would enable them to control and operate efficiently a joint venture.

Nevertheless, the situation has changed markedly in the last few years. The Birlas, the Mafatlals, the Mahindras, the Rams, the Tatas, and other local entrepreneurs are able to assume the control of joint ventures in an increasing number of fields. Consequently, in their negotiations with foreign investors, they all tend to be more demanding than in the past concerning the financial and control arrangements, some following a stricter policy than others in this respect.

A senior Tata executive emphasized that, as a rule, his company now aims at a voting majority and the management control of the joint ventures in which it becomes a partner and also observed that this pattern is favored by the government. Mr. Bharat Ram, Chairman of Delhi Cloth, explained that, generally speaking, he aims to assume management responsibility, and that what he requires from the foreign partner is principally know-how and foreign exchange. Mr. Arvind Mafatlal, Chairman of the Mafatlal Group, also showed preference for a voting majority and management control.

Mr. K. K. Birla, a director of Birla Brothers Private Ltd., was of the opinion that the choice of the foreign partner is very important, but that control has not necessarily to be in Indian hands. Advice from and agreement with the foreign partner are always sought. In principle, Mr. K. K. Birla has no objection toward foreign majority participations or 50-50 joint ventures. Nevertheless, the Birla Group assumes control whenever the foreign partner asks it to do so, which is more frequent than might be expected. Thus, Birla has control of Hindustan Aluminium, a successful joint venture with the U.S. firm Kaiser Aluminum & Chemicals Corporation, which has only a 26 percent participation.

The increasing desire of Indian entrepreneurs to obtain and retain control of joint ventures is beginning to produce control fights that are somewhat similar to the proxy fights current in developed countries. Hindustan Pilkington, a tile-producing company, is a joint venture between an Indian partner and Pilkington, a U.K. company. Initially, the Indian partner held a relative majority of the shares and Pilkington a substantial minority, while there were a few other investors in addition. A right of first refusal had been provided only between the two main partners. After some time, Pilkington bought from two smaller shareholders (two U.K. companies) shares representing 2 percent of the capital and thus acquired control of the joint venture. The Indian partner was understandably displeased by this reversal of control, but there was nothing in the law, nor in the contract, that could alter the situation.[25]

With the increasing development of the Indian capital market, fights for control will inevitably become more numerous. The government may of course enact legislation regulating such fights, but a severe restriction would seem inconsistent with the announced policy to encourage the formation of a broad and active capital market.

The Principle of Government Policy. In a statement to Parliament in 1949, the Prime Minister announced that as a rule, the financial majority of joint venture enterprises ought to lie in Indian hands.

The principle of local financial majority was inspired by both broad policy considerations and by the exigencies of specific situations. It is difficult to assert with any degree of certainty which consideration was of primary importance in determining this policy. Historically, however, there was a definite fear that an excessive inflow of foreign capital might influence political decisions and bring about foreign economic interference in national affairs. After all, India has been independent for less than a quarter of a century. Then, as the Indian economy made substantial progress, the government decided that Indian entrepreneurs should assume their share of responsibility in local enterprises, another argument against foreign majority participations. More recently, the government further resolved to stimulate the investing habits of the public in order to create a broad and active capital market and also, probably, to discourage any excessive concentration of economic power. Consequently, the government views favorably at present those companies in which an Indian partner, a foreign partner, the public, and financial institutions have each a share of the capital: e.g. Voltas, a well-established trading company, which has now also branched out into the field of manufacture.[26]

There are also special circumstances that reinforce the application

---

25. According to a private source, the government could have, with its administrative powers, objected to Pilkington acquiring majority shares. Apparently, the Pilkington proposal was approved due to a misunderstanding, which the officials concerned later regretted.

26. For the case of Voltas, see pp. 151–66.

of the general principle of Indian majority participation in joint ventures. To begin with, when the joint venture proposal relates to an industry in which the profits can be expected to be high, the government is especially insistent on a local majority in order to avoid an excessive drain on foreign exchange. Moreover, because the newcomers have to go through the screening process, the government generally takes this convenient opportunity of requiring them to associate with a local partner and to make a public issue of shares, which will often leave the foreign partner with only a minority participation. Furthermore, the government has noticed that in the course of negotiations some foreign applicants adopt a rigid attitude against accepting a minority participation in a joint venture, although they had agreed to leave control in local hands in other countries. The government of course uses this argument in its negotiations with the foreign investor.

Exceptions to the Principle. Until now the application of this principle has been flexible because the government was aware that the developed countries and many developing countries offer competing investment opportunities. Especially with regard to new industries, which at present are officially encouraged as part of Indian planning, it is doubtful whether certain foreign investors would come to India at all without the guarantee of voting and managerial control of the joint ventures to be created.

Economic necessities thus bring about exceptions to the general principle, which may extend to a whole industry. When the government decided in 1965 to give high priority to the development of fertilizers, it announced that henceforth foreign majority could be the rule in this field.[27] This important exception to general policy was motivated by the fact that considerable financial resources would be needed, and that frequently foreign loans could be obtained only if the foreign industrialist was allowed to obtain a voting majority or management control. The government also took into consideration the fact that specialized technical expertise and experienced managerial skills would be needed in the development of this product.

Individual exceptions are even permitted in more traditional fields. The government has consistently avoided compelling the foreign majority partner of a well-established enterprise to transfer its control to

27. In particular, nitrogenous fertilizers is a field which has been specifically indicated by the government as open for foreign majority capital participation.

local hands. When an enterprise has for a long time complied with general government policy (for instance, by an extensive "Indianization" of its personnel), it is more or less considered as an Indian enterprise, which is regarded as more important than the exact degree of participation held by the foreign partner. This is the case, for instance, of Union Carbide of India, which was one of the first foreign enterprises to make a public issue of shares (40 percent). In the case of a major expansion, it is likely that the government would ask Union Carbide of the U.S.A. to decrease its participation from 60 percent to 51 percent, but the U.S. corporation does not expect to lose voting control in the near future.

Special circumstances sometimes induce the government to agree to a foreign majority participation in a specific case. Firstly, the government is anxious to avoid any form of discrimination. The question arose in 1958 when the government favored the formation of a 50-50 joint venture between Merck Sharp and Dohme of the U.S.A. and a governmental corporation. The U.S. pharmaceutical corporation made a counter-proposal for a 60-40 joint venture with a private Indian concern. The government had previously agreed to similar proposals in the same economic sector, so in order to avoid any discrimination, it agreed to the MSD proposal, though this was contrary to its expressed wishes.

Even in economic sectors where local majority is the rule, the government has sometimes made an exception when a very specialized process was required. For instance, there are very few foreign companies that are technically capable of manufacturing paints for ships. Because no substitute can be used in place of these special paints, the government allowed the formation of a joint venture with a foreign majority participation.

Even where, in the government's judgment, a specific joint venture should be controlled by Indians, a compromise arrangement is sometimes adopted. In a few cases (in electronics, for instance), the government has agreed that management control be given to the foreign investor for a limited period of time, after which the managerial responsibility will be transferred to the Indian partner, who had a majority participation from the start.

A Sensitive Problem. The problem of control in joint ventures is not only of real importance to the foreign investor, his local partner, and the government of the recipient country, but it has also political and psychological aspects that do not facilitate the search for a workable compromise. In India, a number of joint venture negotiations were actually broken off because no agreement could be reached on this sensitive problem.

This kind of difficulty arose for instance in the negotiations between the government and three U.S. companies for a large petrochemical project. It was agreed that the government would have 51 percent of the capital, and the three U.S. corporations would share the remaining 49 percent. A large part of the financing was to be provided by long-term loans concluded with U.S. banks. The foreign companies agreed to an Indian majority on the Board of Directors. Nevertheless, at the express demand of U.S. banks, they insisted on the control of the Executive Committee, which was to be entrusted with the day-to-day management of the enterprise.

Although agreement had been reached on many points, the negotiations ultimately failed to reach any satisfactory conclusion. A government official asserted that disagreement on the foreign sources from which raw materials would be imported had been a major cause of the failure. It is more likely, however, that the main cause was rather the problem of control. As the foreign control of the Executive Committee was regarded as an essential condition by the U.S. banks, the U.S. corporations were not ready to compromise on this point. Nor was the government inclined to do so, as the political opposition was expected to react violently to concessions on this matter. Even more important, the principle of Indian majority in joint ventures tolerates only rare exceptions, when the government is to be the local partner in the proposed venture.

Although the government and the foreign investors all had valid reasons for their firmness, it seems fair to say that, with a little more flexibility from both sides, an acceptable compromise might have been found.

A Deterrent or an Alibi? Although the "51 percent principle" may still appear as a cornerstone of official philosophy, the government fortunately has generally shown flexibility in its handling of the problem of control in joint ventures. To a certain extent, each case has been dealt with on its own merits. A highly-placed government official has accurately described government policy as developing by a case-by-case process. Indian company law alone would provide a first argument against any absolute interpretation of the "51 percent principle." Although 51 percent participation in principle bestows on its holder the control of the joint venture, Indian company law has made this assumption somewhat questionable. Under the Companies Act of 1956, important matters (such as the consent to the company commencing new lines of business, or the alteration of or addition to the articles of association) have to be decided by special resolution of the members of the company.[28] The articles of association of the company may, in addition, provide that other specified matters shall be decided only by special resolution. As a special resolution requires a three-fourths majority, substantial minority holders can, by resorting to this arrangement in drafting the articles, ensure that important matters relating to their interest in the company cannot be decided without their consent. Consequently, the government should, in a way, be as concerned about a 26 percent foreign minority as about a 51 percent foreign majority. Similarly, a foreign investor might not unreasonably attach as much importance to the acquisition of a "safety" 26 percent minority participation as to the financial majority. It is also obvious that the government should be more concerned about a 76 percent foreign majority than about a 51 percent majority.

There are other more important elements, however, which limit the significance of voting control. The relative strength of each partner is at least as important as its voting power. For instance, Birla, with its financial resources, managerial skills, and technical expertise, would have much more power in a joint venture with only a 40 percent participation than a smaller Indian corporation with a 70 percent participation. Moreover, some Indian industrialists believe that the government should always pay the closest attention to the division of managerial responsibilities in a joint venture proposal, as these are often just as important as voting control. Furthermore, as a few cases in India have painfully illustrated, the choice of the partner and the mutual confidence existing between the partners carry an essential significance.

The Government of India has certainly not been indifferent to the fact that the real control of a joint venture is influenced by a number of factors and that this control cannot be entirely determined in advance by formal arrangements. Partially on the basis of such considerations, the government has rightly adopted a realistic and flexible approach in the handling of the control problem.

28. See Art. 189.

Today, however, the case-by-case process is under sharp criticism. Opposition parties especially—but not exclusively—have denounced the "inconsistencies" of government policy and have warned against the risks of foreign economic interference. While, at the end of 1968, the government defined the industries in which foreign investment or foreign collaborations are welcome, it did not allude to the problem of voting control in a joint venture. As has already been mentioned, after a thorough examination of all aspects pertaining to foreign private investment and foreign technical collaboration, the government decided that no significant change in the broad policy followed on these subjects in the past was called for and that no formal resolution would be issued on these matters. As the government has established the above-mentioned categories,[29] however, it may well also decide in the next few years to codify the rules applying to the problem of majority control.

Mr. R. K. Hazari, an Indian economist, believes that the government should establish precise categories of industries, for instance: (1) cases in which the foreign investor could not obtain more than 10 percent of the capital; (2) cases in which he could not obtain more than 25 percent; and so on. In his view, a precise classification would be advantageous for all parties concerned, as it would eliminate uncertainty and shorten the length of negotiations.

In view of past experience in India, the arguments of Mr. Hazari carry an undeniable weight. Nevertheless, the disadvantages of a precise classification might well outweigh its advantages. Many successful joint ventures in India were compromise solutions following hard bargaining. The government has at its disposal sufficient means of control to counteract a joint venture which could present the threat of economic interference. The foreign investor, on the other hand, is usually powerful enough to be adequately protected against arbitrary decisions. The negotiators of both sides should normally be granted maximum freedom, as this would allow them from the start to adapt the legal and financial structure of the joint venture to the specific realities of the case.

At present, the government could rightly claim that the "51 percent rule" is perhaps an "alibi," but certainly not a deterrent to foreign investment. It is to be feared that greater rigidity in the handling of the control problem could transform the "alibi" into a real and effective deterrent.

29. See *supra*, p. 324.

Management of Joint Ventures

The Importance of Brand Names. A characteristic of the Indian market is the general stability of consumers' tastes. As Mr. Khanna put it:

From morning till bed-time the life of every well-to-do Indian is dominated by foreign brand names. More likely than not he wakes up with a cup of Brooke Bond or Lipton's tea, cleans his teeth with Colgate or Forhan's toothpaste, has his bath with Pear's or Lifebuoy soap, breakfasts on Britannia bread and Nescafé, goes to office in a Standard-Herald car and is borne to his fourth floor office in an Otis lift.[30]

The majority of Indian consumers are not attracted by promotional gadgets and have definite brand preferences. Because of this, newcomers are often at a disadvantage, while enterprises long established in India are able to maintain the success of their brands. For example, Singer has been absent from India for many years, but the consumers still recall its name and, according to a government official, would favorably respond to the reappearance of the company's products. Indian entrepreneurs have sought collaboration with foreign partners not only to obtain foreign exchange, technical expertises or managerial skills, but also to benefit from the advantage of a famous brand name.

Unified Day-to-day Management. In a great number of cases, the day-to-day management is under the sole responsibility of the foreign partner. An Imperial Chemical Industries Ltd. (ICI) official observed that for practical purposes, the company manages Indian Explosives Limited (IEL) like a wholly-owned subsidiary. Contrary to many foreign corporations, the ICI Group in India has at its constant disposal a great number of employees who can be transferred at any given time from one joint venture to another. For instance, the construction of the new IEL fertilizer plant in Kanpur necessitated the presence of 200 supervisory employees who came from the ICI companies in other parts of India. This great mobility of staff favors the implementation by ICI of its day-to-day management responsibilities.

Many foreign corporations are not ready or able to send numerous employees to India on a permanent basis. Consequently, management

30. K. C. Khanna: "Foreign Collaboration—Concern Over High Costs," *Times of India,* May 24, 1968.

responsibilities are in the hands of a limited number of people. In Coromandel, for instance, the managing director and the deputy managing director (both U.S. citizens) have extensive powers, although the important marketing function has been left with Parry's, the Indian partner.

From an over-all point of view, the "Indianization" of senior personnel is advisable but this cannot be realized overnight, especially in technical posts. It has been suggested that as early as the time of negotiation, prospective partners should agree in advance on the transfer of management to local hands after a given period of time. In practice, however, it would seem preferable not to fix any predetermined schedule and to allow the partners to take the initiative of the transfer whenever such a fundamental change becomes clearly advisable and feasible.

In the past, few joint ventures were under a unified Indian management. According to an Indian financier, too many local entrepreneurs were only too happy to benefit financially from a brand name and leave the problem of management to the foreign investor. Fortunately, India now has a number of industrialists who are ready, and even eager, to assume management responsibilities. A notable case is Mahindra and Mahindra Ltd., an enterprise which is less than a quarter of a century old and which is engaged principally in the manufacture of electrical and engineering products. From the beginning, the company has endeavored to obtain from abroad the most sophisticated techniques, almost always on a joint venture basis. Sometimes the company holds a majority participation in the capital of the joint venture, sometimes only a minority participation (e.g., 30%, as in Otis Elevators), but it always aims to assume the management of the enterprise. Mr. Keshub Mahindra emphasized that although the company does need technical expertise from abroad, it should as a rule know more about management in India than its foreign partners. He felt that joint day-to-day management is usually not a workable solution. He also observed that the claim of Mahindra and Mahindra for management responsibilities has never been opposed in any negotiation with a foreign investor. The Mahindras, however, are reluctant to engage in the manufacture of products that imply entirely new techniques and technological skills. The main reason for this voluntary limitation is that the company's contribution to a joint venture with a foreign partner is not its ability to provide finance, but its capacity to assimilate techniques and apply them under Indian conditions.

Joint Day-to-day Management. Although many Indian entrepreneurs and foreign investors stress the dangers of joint day-to-day management, in fact the responsibilities are shared in a not insignificant number of joint ventures.

Upon completion, the National Organic Chemical Industries Ltd. (NOCIL) will be the largest petrochemical enterprise in India. NOCIL is a joint venture between the Mafatlal Group (one third of the capital), the Royal Dutch/Shell Group (one third of the capital), and financial institutions and the public (also one third of the capital). The management responsibilities are shared between a technical managing director from Royal Dutch/Shell and an administrative managing director from Mafatlal. Mr. Arvind N. Mafatlal recognized that in the beginning cooperation between these two senior executives was not without its problems. As Chairman of NOCIL, however, Mr. Mafatlal is in a position to coordinate the technical and administrative wings of the company.

In India, like everywhere else, joint day-to-day management has proved to be workable only when the respective managerial responsibilities are clearly defined and delimited, and when the senior executives in charge of these operating responsibilities are able to get along together satisfactorily.

Friction Between Partners. The sophistication of the prominent Indian entrepreneurs has substantially eased the solution of the problems that so often affect relations between joint venture partners. Although in many developing countries the local investors have the reputation of aiming at quick profits, the large and medium-sized Indian enterprises have, as a rule, followed a policy of long-range growth and reinvestment. Profit policy has not, therefore, been a major source of conflict with foreign partners.

The lack of industrial background has proved to be a more important source of difficulties. In 1958, Parsons and Whittemore Inc. (a U.S. company) and two Indian brothers formed, in the State of Mysore, the Mandya National Paper Mills Ltd., a joint venture for the manufacture of paper.[31] The enterprise did not operate satisfactorily,

31. Parsons and Whittemore Inc. are also a partner in another joint venture, the Seshasayee Paper Board Ltd. (Madras), which was formed in 1960 and which is a successful enterprise.

because the Indian partner lacked sufficient technical knowledge to handle this kind of product, and the factory had to be closed down. The plant has since been reopened, mainly as a result of the efforts of the Mysore Government to revive the venture by injecting further money into it.

Other joint ventures have experienced difficulties because the machinery and equipment imported by the foreign partner were not suited to Indian conditions, were too expensive, or were simply not in good working order. Such difficulties often affect seriously the relations between the partners, and sometimes cause the failure of the joint venture.

The Industrial Credit and Investment Corporation of India (ICICI) is in a unique position to prevent such difficulties, as its officers can point out to prospective partners the necessity for a sound financial and industrial basis. When conflicts come out into the open, ICICI can also act as a conciliator between the partners. It remains true, however, that it is primarily the partners themselves who must try to circumvent any such conflicts or difficulties.

The Managing Agency System and the New Trends in Management Organization. Management of firms in India has traditionally been carried out by managing agencies. The system involves a long-term arrangement, under which an individual, a partnership firm, or a corporation undertakes to manage another company. The services that managing agency houses were in a position to supply included not only managerial and marketing functions, but also promotional and financing activities. The assumption of these various functions by a single business organization ensured full and unified responsibility. This system, therefore, played a significant role in the expansion of trade and industry in the country.

Unfortunately, the opportunity and the power to indulge in unfair practices were inherent in the system. Often, the managing agents did not have a direct or substantial financial stake in the managed company. Their financial return derived from the managing agency remuneration, commissions on sales and purchases, and office allowances and appointments. At the same time, they were in a special position to exercise control and authority over all aspects of management and operations, as well as over the funds of the company. Unfair practices and the misuse of power caused increasing damage to the companies that were being managed and to their shareholders. The government has therefore reacted vigorously and taken severe measures to check abuses by managing agents, and to protect shareholders.

Apart from this, there has been in recent years a growing feeling that the managing agency system has outlived its usefulness and is no longer adequate to modern economic conditions. The wider diffusion of managerial skills, the broadening of the capital and securities markets, and the expansion of banking facilities and specialized financial institutions have combined to render the system largely superfluous. Accordingly, the Parliament adopted in May 1969 the Companies (Amendment) Bill. The main feature of this bill is to do away with the traditional system of management of companies by managing agents. The date for the effective abolition of the system was fixed as April 3, 1970, because the government wanted to give the managing agents time to wind up their affairs.

Other modes of management, including the employment of professional and full-time managerial executives, provide effective alternatives that are more in tune with modern trends in corporate management. In particular, it has been suggested that in the wake of the disappearance of the managing agency system, it might be advisable to provide in Indian company law for a modified pattern of the management system as used in Germany. German company law provides for two management organs, namely, the supervisory board (*Aufsichtsrat*), which deals with the general policy of the company, and the management board (*Vorstand*), which handles the day-to-day operations.

It has been further suggested that in the Indian context, a proper adaptation of the German system would be to provide for a supervisory board consisting of shareholders' representatives, senior and middle management, the workers, and the public. Its functions would be limited to those matters that are now the concern of composite boards consisting of internal as well as external directors [32] under the Indian system of management. The management board, on the other hand, would be an executive committee consisting wholly of internal employee-directors. The managerial problems created by the disappearance of the managing agency system in this country would, it has been finally suggested, call for a network of consultative, advisory, and financial institutions.

If these changes in Indian Company Law were indeed to material-

32. "Internal" directors are full-time employees of a company. "External" directors are persons of high standing or special knowledge who have more of an advisory function.

ize, they would have significant consequences for prospective joint venturers. In some cases, they might give practical solutions to the sensitive problem of management control in a joint venture: for example, control of the supervisory board would be entrusted to the Indian partner, while the foreign enterprise would, for at least some time, retain control of the management board and day-to-day operations. The separation of general control and day-to-day management responsibilities is already being applied in some cases, but this solution would more easily present itself if it were formally provided for in the company law.

Labor Problems and Relations With Personnel. As unemployment is widespread in India, it is understandable that the government is devoting close and constant attention to labor problems. It is, therefore, all the more remarkable that no special laws or regulations have been passed for limiting the employment of foreign personnel in any business enterprise in the country. The government has not stipulated, even administratively, any fixed minimum proportion of Indian nationals to be employed in Indian enterprises. It has, however, indicated that it will encourage employment of Indians wherever possible.

It is the general policy of the government to facilitate the employment of foreign technical personnel wherever needed. However, it does review the proposals of prospective investors for the employment of foreign technical personnel in order to ensure that provision is made for training Indian nationals to occupy responsible positions in the enterprise over a reasonable period of time. In this respect, a government official observed that to a limited extent, "Indianization" of personnel is also a means of ensuring the transfer of foreign technology into Indian hands.

A highly-placed government official observed that the "Indianization" of personnel is still a sensitive political subject. He recognized, however, that by and large foreign investors in India have implemented a substantial degree of "Indianization." Unfortunately, investigation has shown that salaries accorded to nationals and foreigners in equal positions are still unequal in many cases. The social contribution of foreign investors is otherwise regarded as generally satisfactory.

For a long time, foreign entrepreneurs have been accustomed to deal with labor relations in their own countries: consequently, they are usually ready to tackle labor relations in India in a pragmatic way. According to the same above-mentioned highly-placed government official, difficulties arise in joint ventures, somewhat paradoxically, because the Indian partner sometimes does not agree with the salary increases or social advantages that the foreign partner has recognized by experience as a necessary concession to the personnel.

Another problem arises from the fact that by tradition most Indian entrepreneurs are not used to delegating substantial powers to their subordinates. As job opportunities are very limited when compared with the magnitude of the labor force, a number of Indian employees feel that their best chance to retain their job is to fulfill scrupulously the duties formally attached to it, and to avoid, as a rule, taking initiatives. This attitude is perfectly understandable in view of the realities of the country, but, as a result, the operation of an enterprise is often dependent on a very limited number of top executives. Partnerships between foreign and local interests can be very useful in the solution of this difficult social problem, because the experience of dealing with personnel acquired by the foreign executive in his own country often enables him to give valid advice to his Indian counterpart.

For the time being, however, many entrepreneurs have to deal with more immediate problems, as labor unrest brings about frequent strikes in some parts of the country. The economic recession of 1966–1968, the inflation, and the food shortage, have increased the frustrations of a labor force that aspires to better social conditions. Political considerations have also influenced strikes in a country where the four central trade unions have each a different political orientation. It is to be hoped that the present revival of the Indian economy will progressively reduce these serious social stresses.

Joint Ventures and Exports

The Government Drive. The official drive to promote Indian exports is relatively recent. It stems from the conviction that in the long run the balance-of-payments problems and foreign exchange difficulties of the country can only be solved by a substantial and sustained increase in exports. It is true that the two traditional remedies —internal deflation or a devaluation of the rupee—have not been sufficient to correct the deficit of the balance of trade. On the other hand, since the balance of payments also depends to a large extent on the movement of capital and services, there may be a slight overemphasis in India today on the importance of the export remedy. In a broader context, development of exports—as well as import substitution—is one means of reaching the primary goal set out by the Planning Commission: the self-reliance of the Indian economy.

In any case, the present drive has two main consequences for Indian and foreign investors. First, the liberalized import policy has been fashioned in such a way as to favor industries that export. Secondly, in the screening of a joint venture proposal, the export potential is becoming a more important factor than it has been hitherto.

After the devaluation of June 6, 1966, a liberal import policy was adopted to enable priority industries to meet their full requirements of imported raw materials, components, and spare parts, after taking into account indigenous availability. In February 1968, the government decided that the liberalized import policy should become more selective so as to favor the export-orientated enterprises. Since then, the nonpriority industries are also entitled to be granted the necessary permits for their full import requirements provided that they develop their exports. Moreover, enterprises that have a good export performance—whether in priority or in nonpriority industries—are permitted to import their requirements from whichever foreign source they wish. In addition, their applications for the expansion of productive capacity and for imports needed to effect such expansion are considered favorably. On the other hand, if the industries, which in the government's judgment have a good export potential, show a poor export performance, they may be penalized by cuts in their import allocations.[33] The principle of linkage between imports and exports is continually respected, but the modalities of application may vary from one year to another.

The second consequence of the government drive is that the export potential of an industry has now become a more important criterion of appraisal in the screening of a joint venture proposal than it was in the past. In January 1969, the Ministry of Industrial Development, Internal Trade and Company Affairs took a series of measures which accentuated the relevance of export potential to prospective Indian and foreign partners. Whereas as a rule joint ventures are encouraged primarily in priority sectors, foreign (technical or financial)

33. See a Press Note on Import Policy, issued by the Ministry of Commerce on April 1, 1968, at p. 2, point IV. This specific measure has been criticized in India on the ground that reduction in import allocations would mean lower activity in manufacturing units, which may cause retrenchments in the personnel of these enterprises.

collaboration proposals may also be considered favorably in low-priority or nonessential industries if the collaborator agrees to devote a major share of the production to export. Moreover, although foreign collaboration is frankly discouraged in trading activities, it may nevertheless be permitted if such collaboration is exclusively aimed at increasing exports. Furthermore, the Ministry of Industrial Development, Internal Trade and Company Affairs has confirmed and elaborated a policy measure that had been adopted in February 1968, in connection with the selective liberalized import policy: those enterprises with substantial export performance to their credit are allowed, on the merits of the case, to expand their production capacity so as to be able to step up their exports.

In addition to these basic measures, the government has at its disposal many other means of encouraging exports. As has already been mentioned, since the last devaluation the fiscal rebates and credits for exports no longer exist, but the enterprises that effect market surveys or send commercial teams abroad can claim a tax deduction for their development of foreign markets. Moreover, cash assistance is available for exports of nontraditional industries, such as engineering and chemical goods. The government can also act through the intermediary of the Reserve Bank of India, which influences the credit policy of commercial banks.

The Obstacles to Exports. The obstacles to a sustained development of exports are considerable. They are to be found both in India and in foreign markets.

The size of the Indian market does not favor the development of exports, because internal demand is often so large that it absorbs the entire local supply. Obviously, it would be irrational to export fertilizers from India as long as a substantial quantity has still to be imported to satisfy local needs.

There are obstacles to exports on the production side as well. Production costs in India are often high when compared with costs in other countries. Because of this, the economist R. K. Hazari, without denying the importance of the measures adopted by the government, asserted that the long-term solution to export problems lies with productivity increases and reduction in production costs. As Western and Japanese interests have a quasi-monopoly in shipping, transportation costs significantly increase final sale prices abroad. In some cases, the inferior quality of the products also impedes the development of exports.

Multinational corporations that have selling agencies or manufacturing subsidiaries nearly all over the world are anxious to avoid any competition between the products made or sold by their affiliated companies. Because of this, in the past many joint venture agreements contained a clause that restricted the exports of the joint venture so as to avoid any competitive conflict. The Indian Government now closely examines the restrictive clause of each new joint venture proposal and does not permit substantial limitations. As many well-established enterprises seek to obtain the various benefits that now derive from a good export performance, in many joint ventures of long standing the management tries to negotiate with the foreign partner for the elimination or the modification of the restrictive clause. The agreement of the foreign partner is often dependent upon some kind of compensation.

Nor are the obstacles encountered in foreign markets by any means negligible. Although it may vary considerably from one product to another, most developing countries have built up a severe general tariff and quota protection against external products.[34] Unfortunately, developing countries have not yet succeeded in implementing an international specialization of labor among themselves. However, Indian products are not rejected by artificial barriers alone. After all, Japanese products—with extremely competitive prices, it is true—have succeeded in overcoming these barriers. Actually, Indian enterprises are probably even more handicapped by their lack of knowledge of foreign markets. Mr. Keshub Mahindra, who welcomes all the latest government measures in favor of exports, asserted that private initiative was essential in the creation and development of foreign markets for Indian products. With this purpose in mind he has sent abroad a commercial team on a permanent basis whose specific task is to carry out market research and discover sales opportunities.

In this respect, by their extensive knowledge of international markets, the foreign partners in Indian joint ventures might well be able to offer efficient assistance to their local counterparts over the next few years, thus making a significant contribution to India's development.

Prospects. Although the obstacles to the development of exports are considerable, along with the record agricultural output one of the most significant economic achievements of 1968 was the remarkable rise recorded in overseas sales. If the trend is continued, it should not be difficult to attain the target growth rate of 7 percent in exports

34. It goes without saying that developed countries have also adopted this defensive attitude, and in no less a degree.

as set by the Planning Commission. A noticeable feature of the export performance was the higher percentage of nontraditional exports, such as engineering goods. Whether the increase was a late consequence of devaluation, or the result of government measures, or of private initiative is not known for certain.

In any case, with its intermediate technology and substantial industrial experience, India does hope to become a natural "launching pad" for the development and manufacture of industrial products especially adapted to the needs of the developing world.

The 1968 increase in exports should not be overestimated, because the comparative basis of the previous years is relatively low. The government measures will certainly continue to have a beneficial effect on the growth of exports. In the long run, however, it is likely that the creation and the development of foreign markets will be primarily dependent upon the ability of the enterprises established in India to reduce their costs gradually and to launch vigorously their own direct commercial campaigns abroad.

Indian Joint Ventures Abroad

Purpose. Paradoxically, the Indian market is small in some respects, because the average income is low. Because of this limitation, some Indian entrepreneurs are now seeking to create joint manufacturing ventures in foreign countries, especially in those fields where developed techniques have been assimilated or created sufficiently, such as in engineering and textiles. Some developing countries are now at a stage of development comparable to that of India as many as fifteen years ago.

For the time being, this new trend is primarily a technique of export promotion. By the creation of joint manufacturing ventures in foreign countries, these Indian entrepreneurs hope to sell machinery, equipment, components, and raw materials. The technical assistance that they provide is also an important source of various incomes: royalties, received in exchange for know-how; fees, received in exchange for managerial and commercial services; and salaries, as payment of engineers or other experts. The export opportunity created by the formation of the joint venture may vary considerably from one case to another: for instance, a local corporation may seek the technical assistance of a foreign partner, but buy the machinery from another foreign corporation.

The government supports the trend towards the formation of Indian joint ventures abroad, because it considers them as a means of increasing exports and to a lesser extent, contributing to Indian goodwill generally. The Finance Bill of 1966 provides a special concessional tax rate of 25 percent on dividends, royalties, and other income received by an Indian company from a foreign company. The government is aware that India is not the only country trying to capture these promising foreign markets and that it has to take some practical steps in order to place Indian enterprises in a good competitive position. The development of exports is thus dependent upon a complex combination of financial and technical measures that are being taken both by the government and by the exporter. As the Planning Commission pointed out,

trade with developing countries would require provision of technical and financial assistance along with engineering goods. Very often, turn-key projects are sought and consultancy services become paramount for the sale of machinery and equipment. Faced, as these countries are, with adverse trade balances and with alternate sources of supply on a deferred payment basis, it would be possible to step up our exports of engineering goods to developing countries only within the framework of comparable deferred payment arrangements on exports. Given these facilities, the scope for expanding the export of engineering goods is large and growing.[35]

A Selective Process. Until now, Indian joint ventures abroad have, curiously enough, concentrated on a limited number of developing countries, mainly Ceylon, Ethiopia, Iran, Malaysia, and Nigeria. Several considerations may explain this selective process.

The concentration on Ethiopia, Malaysia, and Nigeria may be partially explained by the presence in these countries of large Indian colonies. Moreover, as India follows in foreign affairs a policy of nonalignment, it is normal for the government to favor the formation of joint ventures in countries that are neutralist or nonaligned, such as Ceylon or Iran. From the point of view of these governments, the collaboration of Indian entrepreneurs might likewise present fewer risks of economic interference than the cooperation proposed by other countries. In this connection, a parallel may be drawn with international organizations, the civil servants of which are often chosen from among Indians, precisely because India is a nonaligned country.

35. *Approach to the Fourth Five-Year Plan,* New Delhi, Planning Commission, pp. 3–4 (1968).

Finally, Indian entrepreneurs have probably also considered the political or monetary stability of some of these countries, e.g. Iran.

In addition, some Indian joint ventures have been established in other countries for what seem to be purely economic reasons, such as in Canada and Northern Ireland.

As the trend towards the formation of Indian joint ventures abroad is relatively recent and is only now gathering momentum, the concentration on a few countries may all the same be a temporary phenomenon. Nevertheless, although Indian joint ventures are likely to spread over a great number of countries, the special incentives that have encouraged concentration on a few countries will continue to be effective.

The Pattern of Investment. As India is a capital-importing country, it can afford to export capital only to a limited extent. It is, therefore, essential that the formation of joint ventures abroad does not engender balance-of-payments problems or foreign exchange difficulties. Consequently, as a rule the government does not permit the Indian participation in foreign equity joint ventures to be paid in cash. Usually, the Indian enterprise receives a share in the capital in exchange for the export of machinery, equipment, know-how, or other services.

As Indian managerial talent is not overabundant, Indian enterprises venturing abroad are already confronted with a relative shortage of managerial personnel. Mahindra and Mahindra, who along with the Birlas have been especially audacious in venturing abroad, thus manage in Iran a joint venture for automotive products, although they are in the position of minority partners. Nevertheless, a transfer of management to local hands would certainly not be out of the question if it became feasible. Similarly, Delhi Cloth now manages an equity joint venture in Ceylon for the manufacture of sewing machines, but again, the management might well be transferred later to local hands. In both cases, the relative scarcity of Indian managerial talent led to the training by Indians of the local partner for management responsibilities.

Indian entrepreneurs in joint venturing abroad will have to face the same kind of difficulties as have been experienced by foreign investors in their joint ventures in India. As an indirect consequence, they may acquire a better understanding of the sometimes divergent opinions defended by their foreign partners in joint ventures in India.

Indian joint ventures abroad seem destined for a bright future, especially in developing countries. Although the government's reluctance towards cash remittances abroad is perfectly understandable, it is nevertheless to be hoped that the policy on this matter will become more flexible. Too much rigidity might deprive Indian entrepreneurs of excellent opportunities, especially if competitors from other countries are only too ready to bring in the cash funds required. Moreover, although cash remittances represent for India a net outflow of capital at the time when they are effected, in many cases these investments will in the long run engender a substantial capital inflow.

Joint Ventures and Local Savings

The Traditional Uses of Money. To a large extent, the traditional uses of money were based on the structure of Indian society, which, among other essential features, is characterized by the predominance of agriculture, vast unemployment and underemployment, and the low standard of living of the majority of the population.

Investing habits have concentrated on fixed assets such as land, houses, and gold. This preference for fixed assets was generally not motivated by the hope of quick and high profits through speculation, but by the deep feeling that land or gold represent something real, something safe. Conversely, shares and bonds were not often regarded as much better than a piece of paper. In addition, as most industries were basically family affairs, only in few cases was money sought from the public. Therefore, circulation of equities was limited both on the side of demand and on the side of supply. Furthermore, Indians have never shown much inclination to deposit their money abroad, in Swiss or U.S. banks.[36]

Lending habits have similarly derived from social patterns. Shopkeepers, dealers, farmers have always been accustomed to lending money, but the loans were made by one friend to another, or by one member of the family to another. Nothing was ever written down in any contract. The idea was to lend only to someone with whom one was well acquainted, someone one could trust.

At present, it is illegal to buy gold, and the considerable expenses incurred in ritualistic marriage ceremonies are slowly declining.

36. It is known, however, that some foreign banks doing business in India have drawn large local deposits. Moreover, a high proportion of the foreigners in India have been doing their banking business in this country only through foreign bankers.

These are minor changes, however, when compared with a much more fundamental evolution: although there is still a strong and persistent preference for fixed assets, the habit of investing in shares and bonds is slowly taking root in Indian society.

The Growth of Institutional Finance. Some financial institutions have played an essential role in the formation and encouragement of saving and investing habits. Life Insurance Corporation (LIC) and Unit Trust of India (UTI) are the two government-owned financial institutions that draw on the genuine savings of the Indian public. They allocate the funds available to them over a large number of investments. Whereas LIC's funds derive directly from insurance transactions, UTI endeavors to develop the investment habits of small investors. As most of these investors aim primarily at investing safely, they are satisfied with the reasonable return offered by UTI. Moreover, the dividends paid by UTI on its "units" are taxed only on amounts over Rs. 1,000.

Although the Industrial Credit and Investment Corporation of India Ltd. (ICICI) has received considerable resources from the Government of India, the World Bank, the U.S. Agency for International Development, and the German Kreditanstalt für Wiederaufbau, it also draws funds from the capital market by selling its own holdings or issuing debentures when market conditions warrant. ICICI is in a unique position to act as an active intermediary between investors and entrepreneurs from India and abroad.

Prospects in Urban Areas. Although deposits and investments have developed on a large scale only in a relatively recent past, they have been an accepted source of finance in India ever since large-scale plants and factories were set up. For such large projects, Indian industry has relied from the beginning on these deposits for supplying a proportion of its needs. Traditionally, the bulk of savers and investors came from the cities. Even today, a large proportion of them are to be found in urban areas. Between 1965 and 1967, the recession, inflation, and taxes have been detrimental to savings and investments generally. As from 1968, the public's ability and inclination to save and invest have again been increasing.

Indian investors in the cities are now becoming very sophisticated and selective. They tend to invest primarily in industries that have a promising future in India, such as electronics and petrochemicals. Whenever a "good share" is offered on the market, the public issue is oversubscribed several times. On the other hand, when doubts are raised about the future of an industry, the corresponding issue of shares may be unsuccessful and the underwriters—that is, financial institutions—have to take a major share of the issue.

An original development has opened up a new outlet for investment. Due to temporary credit restrictions, a number of companies —e.g. Delhi Cloth—have accepted direct deposits from savers and granted an interest rate that is somewhat higher than that granted by banks. These deposits are legal and appear in the balance sheets. Savers are also very selective regarding the companies in which they make deposits. Whether these direct deposits are linked to the temporary restrictive measures imposed by the government or whether they are a more durable phenomenon, remains to be seen.

Prospects in Rural Areas. Although most landlords have no savings to speak of, a growing middle class of farmers has now risen beyond the mere subsistence level. During the recession, the income of the farmers was affected by bad crops, but on the other hand inflation was not felt to the same extent as in the cities. In 1968 agricultural output reached a record level, thus opening up new possibilities for savings.

Although substantial savings are made in rural areas and are growing remarkably at present, industrialists seeking funds are facing a major publicity problem. Previously, only four products, which were produced and distributed mainly by British-controlled companies, reached the villages: tea, tobacco, kerosene (oil), and soap. Today the farmers want to know and appreciate a product before the manufacturing company can propose shares to them. Moreover, the expected return has to be quite attractive.

After ICI and the Government of India had agreed on a new fertilizer plant to be established in Kanpur (Uttar Pradesh), ICI marketers were unwilling to confine their contacts to officials of the Uttar Pradesh and Punjab State Governments. They, therefore, decided to go to the areas where the production would be distributed, systematically visiting the farmers and explaining to them the qualities and the methods of utilization of these products. Only later did they offer shares to the peasants, who subscribed in large numbers. The offer was successful, because ICI's reputation was well-known to the farmers; the fact that by then they were acquainted with the product to be distributed in their areas and also the prospect of an attractive dividend were further incentives to buy the shares.

Both in the cities and in the country, prospective joint venturers will find increasing opportunities for associating the public in new enterprises. A great publicity effort will be required to exploit these opportunities successfully. The government favors this evolution as a means of broadening the capital market and ensuring an Indian majority in enterprises. Foreign investors also find definite advantages in the participation of the public, especially as small investors usually take no part in the operation of the enterprise as such.

Evaluation and Prospects

The future of joint ventures in India has to be evaluated in relation to the drive of the Indian economy towards self-reliance. The Planning Commission thus emphasized that

foreign collaboration and the import of foreign know-how is connected with the question of foreign aid. The general approach to both these has to be the same as that in relation to foreign aid and import substitution, i.e., we must make every effort to attain self-reliance even in this respect. Foreign collaboration must, therefore, be looked upon as something which may be resorted to only for meeting a critical gap.[37]

This statement, which may not seem very encouraging to foreign investors, has certainly the merit of being unambiguous. Whereas self-reliance in itself is a natural aspiration for an independent country, the basic question is to know whether this goal should be reached primarily by restrictive measures or rather by positive steps. At present, the Government of India is trying to achieve the goal by combining both attitudes in its policy.

Since foreign collaboration has been a reality in India for more than two decades, it is not premature to seek to strike an economic balance of joint ventures in this country. It is true that a few notable failures have raised doubts as to the usefulness of joint ventures as a whole. Neither can it be denied that a number of joint ventures have not been as successful as anticipated. Moreover, the need for foreign collaboration has been progressively decreasing in most traditional economic sectors.

Nevertheless, joint ventures have on the whole been beneficial to the economic development of India. Some outstanding successes have

37. Planning Commission, *op. cit. supra* note 35, p. 7.

underlined the practicability and the usefulness of close partnerships between Indian and foreign partners. Many enterprises would not have come into existence or would have taken many years to expand without the financial resources, managerial ability, and technological skills of foreign partners. These assets are still needed in most priority industries in general, and in the most advanced fields in particular. The government is likely to be increasingly selective in its approval of joint venture proposals. As foreign investors are going to be increasingly selective themselves, it is to be hoped that enough flexibility will be maintained on both sides. It is also to be hoped that when a joint venture proposal is once accepted, the foreign partner may be reasonably certain as to the duration of the collaboration. Even after a technique has been assimilated by the Indian partner, a lasting association is sometimes justified by the ability of the partners to achieve a fruitful cooperation.

Moreover, the self-reliance of India's economy cannot be achieved simply by the rejection of joint venture proposals or by other restrictions on the import of foreign financial and technical resources. A most natural means of achieving self-reliance consists in taking positive measures to develop local techniques and skills and to encourage the formation of local managerial talents. Although the government has made energetic and persistent efforts in this direction, these endeavors have not always been very successful. In particular, indigenous research remains inadequate in a number of industries.

Whereas purely economic considerations do not seem to warrant excessive restrictions on foreign capital, the question of foreign investment has also to be examined in the context of Indian economic independence. Actually, the screening procedure enables the government to establish a balance between local and foreign investment, and also between the various sources of foreign capital. Thus, no foreign country, nor any foreign corporation is allowed to take a dominant position in any economic sector. Even during the period of operation of a joint venture, the government has at its disposal sufficient means of control so as to restrain any foreign firm from adopting measures or policies detrimental to national interests. The mere presence of government power is usually a sufficient deterrent against any unfair activity. It may therefore be concluded that at the present time, foreign investment does not present a serious risk of economic interference in Indian national affairs. Consequently, considerations of national independence do not justify excessive restrictions against foreign capital.

In discussions pertaining to foreign investment in India, it has often been apparent that government officials tend to concentrate on the possible "contribution" of foreign investment to the economic development of the country. On the other hand, foreign investors often insist on the "guarantees" available to them, sometimes forgetting the vastness of the problems that have to be solved by the government. Moreover, serious divergences of opinion between the partners have often appeared during the operation of joint ventures. Notwithstanding the natural differences between public and private goals and the frequent disagreements between local and foreign partners, however, joint ventures in India have on the whole proved to be a valid means of bridging the gap between this developing country and its industrialized counterparts.

XIX: THE CONTROL OF JOINT VENTURES

The Problem of Control [1]

Most large multinational corporations are tending increasingly to undertake joint ventures in developing countries.[2] In so doing, they are confronted with a variety of difficult problems. Among these, the problem of control appears to be especially intricate and significant.[3]

1. The evaluation of companies' policies is the sole responsibility of the author and does not necessarily reflect the views of the companies' executives. On the other hand, the factual information given in this study has, as a rule, been obtained directly from corporate executives. In a few cases, and at the express demand of the corporate executives concerned, the name of the company is not mentioned. The information relating to India has been obtained through a study conducted in the field.

2. Although no precise and generally-accepted definition of the "multinational corporation" exists as yet, it would seem inappropriate to qualify as "multinational" a corporation which would not have affiliated companies in several countries. Unless otherwise indicated (see especially the last sub-section, pp. 412–18) this chapter deals with equity joint ventures, i.e., companies in which shareholders are investors from both developed and developing countries, who share the risks and the profits of a common venture.

3. See W. G. Friedmann and G. Kalmanoff (eds.), *Joint International Business Ventures,* New York and London, Columbia University Press, pp. 155–67 and pp. 266–68 (1961); J. N. Behrman, "Foreign Associates and their Financing," in R. F. Mikesell (ed.), *U.S. Private and Government Investment Abroad,* Eugene, University of Oregon, pp. 77–113 (1962); L. N. Cutler, "Joint Ventures with Foreign Business Associates, Investors and Governments," *Institute on Private Investments Abroad,* New York, Matthew Bender, pp. 265–72 (1959); C. E. Maw, "Joint Ventures Abroad: Forms and Methods," in *Negotiating and Drafting International Commercial Contracts,* New York, Matthew Bender, pp. 176–81 (1966); P. Kuin, *Frank Exchange of Views on*

When a foreign corporation sets out to form a joint venture in a developing country, it tries to obtain, or is obliged to accept, a definite percentage in the equity capital of the company.[4] Therefore, the first important question is to know whether it is more advantageous for the foreign investor to hold a majority, an equal, or a minority participation in the equity capital. In this respect, it should be noted at the outset that comparison is extremely difficult. For example, Unilever is a majority partner in one equity joint venture (soap industry) in Ghana and a minority partner in another (textile industry) in the same country. Until now, management problems have probably been more serious in the joint venture in which Unilever is in a minority position. However, this difference is not necessarily due to the degree of participation but is, rather, inherent in the nature of the two enterprises.

To what extent majority participation ensures real control of a joint venture is an open question. Its answer is dependent upon the evaluation of the other constituent elements of control. It should be noted that the difficulties and length of negotiations between prospective joint venturers on the control problem have often resulted in the failure of such negotiations. Thus the collapse a few years ago of some important petrochemical negotiations between three large U.S. corporations and the Indian Government. This was probably due to a disagreement over this matter.

Finally, it is equally important to consider to what extent control by the foreign corporation will contribute to the overall success of a joint venture. Other factors, perhaps, are as significant in contributing to this success as control.

Majority Participation

At the present time, it is far more usual for foreign corporations to hold majority than minority participations in equity joint ventures

the Economic Development by the Increase of the Flow of International Private Investments, Document of the International Chamber of Commerce (I.C.C.) No 550/48, pp. 21–25 (1960); J. C. Ramaer, *International Joint Business Ventures,* Document I.C.C. 111/174, p. 12 (1968). This report of Dr. Ramaer (Financial Department, Philips, Netherlands) was the result of extensive inquiries with business leaders.

4. In this study, the term "foreign" relates to investors from developed countries, while the term "local" relates to investors from developing countries.

in developing countries.[5] Very often, foreign investors hold large majority participations, the number of majority participations progressively decreasing as the percentage approaches 50 percent. A few foreign corporations have a strong preference for majority participation: this is the case, for instance, with the British chemical firm, Imperial Chemical Industries Ltd., and with the U.S. pharmaceutical company, Merck & Co., Inc.

GOVERNMENT POLICIES

Some foreign investors wrongly imagine that under no circumstances could they acquire a majority participation in any enterprise in a given country. India has been cited as a case in point. It is true that India has adopted the principle of local control in joint ventures, but in fact the government permits a large number of exceptions. Government officials know that attractive investment opportunities exist in other developing countries, and even more so in developed countries. Moreover, to a large extent, Indian policy toward foreign investment is determined by the requirements of economic planning. Thus, because the development of the priority sector of fertilizers required considerable foreign exchange, specialized technical expertise, and experienced managerial skills, the government decided in 1965 that foreign financial and management control could be the rule in this sector.

In actual fact, the majority of developing countries allow foreign majority participation in most economic sectors, while local control is the rule only in public utilities and in a few strategic or essential industries. A significant case of flexibility is provided by Indonesia's Foreign Investment Law of December 24, 1966.[6] This law permits

5. Sources of statistics in this important matter, are rare and incomplete. See, however, S. Pizer and F. Cutler, *U.S. Business Investments in Foreign Countries*, Washington D.C., U.S. Department of Commerce, 147 pp. (1960). See also the statistics and comments on U.S. investment abroad which regularly appear in the monthly *Survey of Current Business*, Washington D.C., U.S. Department of Commerce, Office of Business Economics.

6. See *International Legal Materials*, Washington D.C., A.S.I.L., pp. 203–225 (1967): Law Concerning Investment of Foreign Capital (p. 203); Executive Directives for the Policy on Foreign Capital (p. 215); Decree Returning Foreign Enterprises to Former Owners (p. 221); Decree Ending Governmental Control of Foreign Oil Companies (p. 223). See also Soedjutmoko, "Foreign Private Investments in a Developing Nation: An Indonesian Perspective," in *Problems and Solutions in International Business in 1969*, New York, Matthew Bender, pp. 305–29 (1969).

direct foreign investment in all fields except the defense industries. In fields vital to the public welfare, however, such as transportation, telecommunications, and electricity, the law specifies that foreign capital may not exercise "full control." [7] Although the government is, moreover, entitled to declare certain fields closed to foreign capital, the general trend and spirit of the law are clearly to avoid any unnecessary restrictions.

Most governments of developing countries are flexible in their attitude toward foreign participations in joint ventures, because they know that often local interests—whether private or public—have insufficient financial resources, technical expertise, and managerial skills to finance and manage a joint venture themselves. Naturally, the ability of local entrepreneurs to take a leading role in joint ventures varies considerably according to the country's stage of development. For example, many Indian entrepreneurs have traditionally been more than willing to leave control in the hands of foreign partners, because they were not prepared to face management difficulties themselves. In the last few years, however, the situation has markedly changed and today, the Birlas, the Mafatlals, the Mahindras, the Rams, the Tatas, and other local entrepreneurs are able to assume the control of joint ventures in an increasing number of fields.

THE REQUIREMENTS OF MANAGEMENT

The possession of a majority of shares generally confers on its holder the majority of votes in the company's organs, but this is not necessarily always the case. While the French aluminum company Pechiney is only a minority shareholder in the multinational joint mining venture Fria in Guinea, it nevertheless holds a majority of votes through a device of "decuple-vote shares": each share owned by Pechiney is entitled to ten votes, whereas each other share is entitled to only one vote.

Many foreign investors request voting control in joint ventures as a necessary condition for management control. The executives of the German steel company Mannesmann feel that only if they have a decisive say in the management of the joint venture are they able to apply their own technological skills. In the experience of Mannesmann, a company without the voting control of a venture is too easily subject to constant interference from the other partner or party

7. This means that in these fields, foreign investors are not entitled to form wholly-owned subsidiaries.

involved. Sometimes, this may also be true of joint ventures with governments, as is shown by the preference of the British trading and manufacturing firm, the United Africa Company, for voting and/or managerial control.[8] When that company's and the government's representatives on the board of a joint venture have agreed on a basic decision, this decision can be more expeditiously implemented afterwards.

When the production involves a complex technology, management control appears to be even more necessary. This partially explains why at the present time the U.S. computer firm International Business Machines (IBM) has control over all its foreign ventures. According to a highly-developed specialization process, each unit has the task of producing a certain component module. All these various elements contributed by different manufacturing units have to be properly assembled. As the manufacture of component modules and the implementation of the assembly process require extreme precision, production has to be carefully coordinated on a uniform basis. In the experience of IBM, wholly-owned subsidiaries have proved to be proper instruments to satisfy these production requirements.

In addition to these everyday management requirements, a specific determination to protect patents and know-how and to preserve technical secrets may reinforce a firm's preference for majority participation. This is especially true for a number of chemical and pharmaceutical companies. For example, Merck & Co., Inc. was anxious for the patents and know-how granted to its Indian joint venture to be adequately protected, which they were, in effect, through majority ownership.[9]

Quite often, foreign and international financial institutions grant loans only on the condition that the financial and management control of the joint venture is given to the foreign corporation. This condition is a significant example of the growing role assumed by fi-

8. When the United Africa Company is unable to obtain voting control in a joint venture, it generally tries to have at least the day-to-day management of the enterprise. U.A.C. is a subsidiary of Unilever Ltd. It has engaged in a large number of joint ventures with African governments. See *supra,* at pp. 273–80.

9. The local partner in Merck Sharp and Dohme of India Ltd. is the large Tata concern. See the case study, *supra* at pp. 235–44. On the link between majority ownership and the protection of patents and know-how, see *Panel on Foreign Investment in Developing Countries,* Amsterdam Meeting of February 16–20, 1969, Department of Social and Economic Affairs, New York, United Nations, p. 19 (1969).

nancial institutions in international business transactions with developing countries.[10] Allusion has been made above to the important petrochemical negotiations that were held a few years ago between the Indian Government and three U.S. corporations. On that occasion, it had been agreed that the government would have a majority participation in the capital and a majority of the seats on the Board of Directors. At the express demand of the U.S. banks that were to provide long-term loans for the venture, however, the U.S. companies insisted on the control of the Executive Committee, which was to deal with day-to-day management. The resulting disagreement over this issue was probably the major cause for the ultimate failure of the negotiations.

Even when the foreign investor enjoys the voting control of the joint venture, the local partner is often entrusted with specific management responsibilities. For instance, in the joint Turkish steel venture, Mannesmann-Sümerbank Boru Endüstrisi T.A.S., the local partner has the responsibility for commercial and administrative matters. In other cases, the desire of the foreign investor to obtain a majority participation in order to satisfy managerial requirements is restricted to certain aspects of business operations. In Chile, the French automotive firms, Renault and Peugeot are minority partners in a joint venture that manufactures gearboxes, while they are majority partners in a joint venture that deals with assembly operations. Here, the foreign companies felt that in the first case they would be satisfied with an adequate quality control, whereas in the second case the need for the unity of voting and operational control was underlined by the requirements of an assembly process characterized by delicate and complex technical operations.

THE COORDINATION OF MULTINATIONAL OPERATIONS

For a large multinational group, a powerful incentive in seeking voting control of its foreign joint ventures lies in the need to coordinate its activities around the world. As the following examples would indicate, the requirements of this multinational coordination can easily conflict with local interests.

Majority participation may be considered by the foreign group as a means to obtain the greater benefit in the transactions between the parent corporation, or its affiliated companies, and the joint venture. For example, if the foreign group is to sell machinery, parts, compo-

10. See also *infra,* pp. 401–403.

nents, and even raw materials to the joint venture, it may be tempted to use its majority position in order to obtain high prices for the goods provided. To a certain extent, this attitude is understandable from a purely commercial point of view. Unfortunately, some foreign corporations have abused their position of power by asking prices that were excessive. These abuses have provoked great resentment in some host countries, such as India, especially since the governments concerned experience some difficulty in controlling these "intracorporate" transactions. Consequently, local interests have often required that these transactions between a foreign group and a joint venture be negotiated "at arm's length." [11] Ideally, the individuals negotiating for the foreign group should not be too closely associated with the joint venture. However, although the idea of negotiating "at arm's length" would seem to be sound, its implementation is difficult in practice.

Multinational corporations with selling agencies or manufacturing subsidiaries scattered throughout the world are anxious to avoid any competition between the products made or sold by their affiliated companies. Because of this, many joint venture agreements in the past contained a clause that restricted the exports of the joint venture so as to avoid any competitive conflict. Consequently, foreign groups sometimes consider majority participation the means necessary to obtain the restrictive clause, at which they are aiming, and to enable them to subsequently oppose any sudden and far-reaching modification of the clause. Nevertheless, as a developing country is especially anxious to develop its exports for balance-of-payments reasons, governments at present are using pressure on foreign corporations in order to obtain the revision or the suppression of these restrictive clauses. A long-term solution to this difficult problem may be found in the international specialization of manufacturing activities, which is now undertaken by an ever-increasing number of multinational groups.

In several developed countries, such as the U.S.A. or the U.K., a majority participation classifies the company (i.e. the joint venture) as a subsidiary, which, therefore, can be consolidated in the balance sheet of the parent corporation. Some foreign corporations, such as the United Africa Company, see in this a further argument in favor of a majority participation. Generally speaking, the consolidation of

11. This expression, which is used mainly in the U.S.A. means that the negotiators bargain as if the foreign group and the joint venture were independent entities.

the considerable assets of numerous subsidiaries in the balance sheet of the parent corporation may influence directly the evolution of companies' ratings on stock exchanges.

THE POLITICAL MEANING OF
MAJORITY PARTICIPATION

Majority participation presents undeniable advantages to the foreign investor as far as management is concerned. It remains to be seen, however, whether such control does not involve certain political or psychological risks for the multinational group, especially since developing countries are understandably anxious to avoid any form of foreign economic domination.

It is especially difficult to answer this question, because comparisons drawn from concrete cases may easily be misinterpreted. In cases where a government treats a joint venture with foreign majority participation unfavorably, it is always extremely difficult to ascertain whether this attitude is caused by foreign majority control as such or by some other factor, such as the general attitude of the joint venture's management.

Nevertheless, the experience of the Société Industrielle et Agricole du Niari (Sian, which was created by the Grands Moulins de Paris) in several African countries gives some useful indication as to the answer. In partnership with governments, the Sian Group has initiated a number of joint ventures, mainly for the production of sugar and flour. Although foreign interests are in a majority position in each of these ventures, they have never been accused of neo-colonialism and have maintained excellent relations with African governments. This may seem especially surprising in Congo (Brazzaville), which is a socialist-inclined country, and in Cameroon, which ranks among the countries most concerned about their economic independence. The Sian Group seems to be respected for several reasons: economic success of the group, good relations between the group and the African governments, presence of the governments as shareholders in all ventures (with one exception), and local employment opportunities offered by the group.

When a developing country is subject to a wave of nationalism, nationalization or other governmental measures are likely to hit all foreign interests in the same way, without discrimination against majority participations. On the other hand, in normal times, majority participation as such does not usually seem to present significant political risks for the foreign investor.

Equal Participation

Although for a long time 50-50 joint ventures have been relatively rare, in recent years their number has significantly increased.[12] Some governments of developing countries favor this form of partnership with foreign interests. There are some foreign investors, however, who feel that equal participation is the worst possible formula. For example, during negotiations with the Chilean Government, the executives of the U.S. copper firm, Kennecott, did at first consider the possibility of engaging in a 50-50 joint mining venture; but feeling that such a split could easily cause trouble, they subsequently decided on a minority position.[13] On the other hand, other foreign investors are of the opinion that equality in the equity capital would lend a special feeling of partnership to the two parties.

FORMATION

The governments of some developing countries regard 50-50 joint ventures as a symbol of equality and partnership between their country and foreign interests. Shortly after President Tubman of Liberia was first elected to the Presidency in 1944, foreign capitalists were invited to invest in that country on a partnership or joint-participation basis with the government. An important application of the "Tubman formula" was the creation, in the fifties, of the Liberian American-Swedish Minerals Company (Lamco), a 50-50 joint venture between the government and foreign interests, mainly Swedish.[14]

Other developing countries take a slightly different approach and consider 50 percent foreign participation as the maximum compatible with national economic independence. Yugoslavia does not yet permit the formation of equity joint ventures, but favors the conclusion of contractual joint ventures.[15] A law of July 11, 1967, which came into force on July 27, stipulates that foreign participation in in-

12. See *supra*, note 5 at p. 366.

13. See *infra* at pp. 386–87, 394, and *supra* at pp. 82–85, 96–98.

14. Lamco was incorporated in Liberia in 1953, but the important agreements between the government and the company were concluded in 1960. The large company Grängesberg—as the delegate of a consortium of Swedish corporations —is employed as manager for all operations. See *supra*, p. 55–76.

15. W. G. Friedmann and L. Mates (eds.), *Joint Business Ventures of Yugoslav Enterprises and Foreign Firms,* Belgrade, Columbia University and the Institute of International Politics and Economy, 192 pp. (1968).

vestments and costs necessitated by these joint undertakings should not exceed 50 percent.[16] Moreover, the government is entitled to limit the total amount of foreign investments according to what appears to be the maximum capital-import capacity of the country. In Iran, the formation in 1957 of the Société Irano-Italienne des Pétroles (Sirip), a 50-50 joint stock company between Assienda Generale Italiana Petroli (Agip) a subsidiary of the Italian state-owned holding company, Ente Nazionali Idrocarburi, (ENI), and the National Iranian Oil Company (Nioc), represented an important step in the evolution of Middle Eastern oil agreements.[17] The old system of concessions issued against a 50-50 sharing of the profits gave way to the system of a joint stock company in which the country is an equal partner in terms of financial contribution and representation on the Board of Directors, the profits being split 75-25 in favor of the host country. To the government's way of thinking, however, the permanent sovereignty of Iran over its oil resources can be realized only by a long-term and gradual policy. Therefore, even though the 50-50 joint stock company can rightly be regarded as a true symbol of equality between the government and foreign interests, subsequent developments in Iranian oil agreements demonstrate that this formula was only one step in a constant and consistent evolution.

Equal participation sometimes represents the only permissible exception to the general policy of those multinational groups that normally have a strong preference for a majority participation in foreign joint ventures. For example, Imperial Chemical Industries Ltd. (ICI) has formed a 50-50 joint venture in India (Atic Industries Ltd.), because the local partner was apparently not ready to accept a minority participation.[18] In Pakistan, ICI purchased the holding of a U.S.

16. See a document of the Economic Commission for Europe, *Industrial Cooperation,* E/ECE/730, Add. 1. pp. 12–13 (1969).

17. The text of the agreement, between NIOC and Agip (August 3, 1957) as well as the text of the Iranian Petroleum Law (July 31, 1957) may be found in *Middle East Basic Oil Laws and Concession Contracts,* New York, Petroleum Legislation, Vol. I (1959). See also J. Logie, "Les contrats pétroliers iraniens," *Revue Belge de Droit International,* pp. 392–428 (1965); E. H. Wall, "The Iranian-Italian Oil Agreement of 1957," *International and Comparative Law Quarterly,* pp. 736–52 (1968); and H. Cattan, "Present Trends in Middle Eastern Oil Concessions and Agreements," in *Problems and Solutions in International Business in 1969,* New York, Matthew Bender, pp. 135–73 (1969).

18. The initial agreement was signed by Kasturbhai Lalbhai, Atul Products Ltd., Imperial Chemical Industries India Ltd., and Imperial Chemical Industries Ltd., London. The signing occurred on August 4, 1955.

company in an existing paint company, Paintex Ltd. ICI would have liked to have had more than 50 percent of the equity in Paintex, but this was not possible because the Pakistan Government permission involved in the original creation of Paintex prohibited it. As a result, an increase in foreign participation was out of the question. Merck & Co., Inc. has a single case of 50-50 joint venture, in Japan, which it had to accept because the government is very strict toward foreign participations. These exceptions to general policy have all been accepted because of the special attraction offered by these markets.

MANAGEMENT

Today, the pressure of international competition is so demanding that the management of a multinational corporation has to be able to take swift and unencumbered decisions. Therefore, the partners in a 50-50 joint venture have to decide who is the actual holder of management responsibilities. Although the partners would not normally question their equality at general meeting or board level, they often try to agree on a unified day-to-day management organization in order to avoid delays in the operation of the enterprise.

The solutions to this specific problem of the 50-50 joint venture may vary. While the Liberian Government and foreign interests have equal votes in Lamco's General Assembly, the latter have a majority of six to five on the Board of Directors and are entrusted with the day-to-day management responsibilities. Nioc and Agip have each three seats on the Board of Directors of Sirip, but the approval of four directors is necessary for the validity of the board's decision: as the representatives of any party are most likely to present a common front in discussions, this means in effect that the board's decisions require the unanimity of the directors; however, because it would be difficult to expect unanimity in day-to-day management, the partners have agreed to let Agip designate the managing director.

DEADLOCK

Agreement on a practical solution for day-to-day management does not eliminate the possibility of conflict at the level of the general meeting of shareholders or of the board of directors. When such a conflict is serious and lasting, it can be considered a deadlock.[19]

19. "Stoppage or standstill resulting from the action of equal and opposed forces": *Webster's New World Dictionary of the American Language,* Cleveland and New York, World Publishing Company, p. 377 (1966). "A position in which it is impossible to proceed or act": *The Shorter Oxford English Dictionary,* Oxford, Clarendon Press, p. 458 (1964).

Business and corporate lawyers generally regard the deadlock as the most serious problem with which the 50-50 joint venture may have to contend. Apart from the antitrust considerations involved in the case, the long and arduous legal battle between the U.S. air transport company, Pan American, and the U.S. manufacturing and transport company, W. R. Grace, concerning their 50-50 joint venture, Panagra, was a most striking example of deadlock and of its grave consequences.[20] The collapse of Panagra is likely to have been one of the factors that induced Grace to revise its global attitude toward joint ventures.

When a 50-50 joint venture encounters policy conflicts, it is difficult to ascertain to what extent compromise is rendered more difficult by equal participation. For example, a few years ago ICI had to face some problems with Paintex Ltd., its 50-50 joint venture in Pakistan. It seems that the primary cause of the trouble was the profound difference in business philosophy between the foreign and the local partners. From ICI's point of view, however, the situation was rendered more difficult by the fact that the company was a 50-50 joint venture and by the ensuing deadlock. With a 50 percent-plus-one-share majority participation, it would have been possible for ICI to put an end to the management responsibilities of the local partner. Eventually, the initial local partner sold his shareholding to another Pakistani investor. The joint venture has functioned satisfactorily ever since.

In view of the serious difficulties arising from any impasse, it would seem natural that prospective partners in a 50-50 joint venture would be very anxious to provide for a deadlock-breaking procedure. Curiously enough, a great number of 50-50 joint venture agreements do not include such a clause. This reluctance to tackle the risk of deadlock in advance was explained by a study group from the Harvard Law School in the following way:

The conceptual and verbal difficulties of devising a deadlock-breaking procedure consonant with the needs and business understanding of most corporate joint venturers have made most of them unwilling to risk having a decision imposed upon them in circumstances that they cannot anticipate. Instead, they accept without qualification the principle of joint action and joint agreement on all questions, relying entirely on their abil-

---

20. *United States v. Pan American World Airways Inc.,* 193 F Supp. 18 (S.D.N.Y. 1961), decision reversed, *Pan American World Airways Inc.* v. *United States,* 371 U.S. 196 (1963).

ity to choose a compatible partner who will always maintain an attitude of good faith and co-operation. . . . From the standpoint of the business lawyer, calculated ambiguity and calculated uncertainty can themselves be important drafting techniques.[21]

Nevertheless, a number of prospective joint venturers prefer not to take any chances and agree on one of the numerous deadlock-breaking procedures. In Atic Industries Ltd., the Chairman of the Board has a casting vote and there is an alternate chairmanship of the board between the two partners every three years. It may seem at first as if this device might endanger the continuity of management, but actually it is more likely that the chairman, aware of being replaced at the end of three years, will make every effort to achieve constant agreement and compromise with representatives of the other party.

Prospective joint venturers may also elect a "swingman" director, that is, a personality independent from both the local and the foreign corporation; but they may have some difficulty in finding a person with the required qualifications and, in addition, they may feel some reluctance in handing over a leading role and full knowledge of the company's affairs to a third party.

A different system consists in giving, not to a director, but to a trustee, the deadlock-breaking vote. Nioc on the one side, Agip, Phillips, and the Oil and Natural Gas Commission of India on the other, are partners to a contractual joint venture, which was formed by the Agreement of January 17, 1965. The partners thereupon incorporated the Iranian Marine International Oil Company (Iminoco), a 50-50 joint stock company, which is a nonprofit operating corporation. The statutes of Iminoco provide that each shareholder deposit in a designated Swiss bank a number of shares equal to 1 percent of the capital.[22] By virtue of a mandate, in case of deadlock the bank can intervene in the General Assembly of Shareholders. The decision of the bank becomes the irrevocable decision of Iminoco. A similar system had previously been provided in Sirip's statutes. The device is interesting because the bank is entitled to intervene only in case of deadlock, which leaves the normal operation of the enterprise exclusively in the hands of the main partners. It remains to be seen how

21. "Joint Venture Corporations: Drafting the Corporate Papers," *Harvard Law Review*, pp. 405–406 (1964). A Harvard team sent a questionnaire on 50-50 joint ventures to 250 foreign corporations. 61 of them answered, with information concerning 35 concrete cases.

22. This clause is fully consistent with Article 12 of the Iranian Petroleum Law (July 31, 1957): "In order to ensure that a majority is attained at the or-

this system would function were an actual deadlock to occur. The principle of "voting balance" has been widely adopted by the privately held Industrial Mining and Development Bank of Iran (IMDBI) and the state-owned Industrial Development and Renovation Organization (IDRO). Thus, in a joint venture between the Iranian Government and Siemens of Germany for the construction of a telephone equipment plant, in which the Government and Siemens each hold 40 percent, IMDRI holds the balance of 20 percent. (*The Economist,* October 31, 1970, p. xxxii.)

In addition to these devices specifically designed for the solution of a deadlock in a 50-50 joint venture, the partners may also use the procedures that can be provided in any joint venture agreement: conciliation or arbitration between the partners, purchase by one partner of the other partner's shares, dissolution, and liquidation.

Despite a few cases of deadlock, one should not overlook the fact that a majority of 50-50 joint ventures (e.g. Sirip) appear to have operated so far without any impasse at all. The risk of deadlock itself acts as a powerful incentive to the partners, encouraging them to go to any lengths to find a solution to any disagreement by discussion and compromise.

THE EQUILIBRIUM OF THE 50-50 JOINT VENTURE

The specific difficulties arising from equal participation are undeniable, but they should not be overestimated. In any situation and with any kind of joint venture there is a risk of some kind of policy conflict between the partners. As a rule, a realistic approach would take into account the power of the partners as well as the shares or the seats they hold. Thus, although foreign interests hold a majority of the seats on Lamco's Board of Directors, they are not ready to take a long-term position against the Liberian Government. Besides, any serious conflict, for instance on Lamco's profit policy, would most likely be solved by bargaining and compromise rather than by a unilateral move from one or the other partner.

The study of specific cases suggests that the difficulties experienced

---

dinary and extraordinary general meetings of mixed companies, in which the parties have equal shares, each of the parties to the agreement shall assign the voting right of one of its shares to a third person to be nominated by mutual agreement." It may be noted that the Petroleum Law does not specify that that third person shall be a national of a third country.

in some 50-50 joint ventures do not mainly stem from equal participation as such, but rather from differences in business philosophy or
from an inappropriate choice of partner.

Minority Participation

The total number of minority participations that multinational
groups hold in foreign joint ventures is less than the total number of
majority participations.[23] Nevertheless, foreign corporations at present tend to acquire more minority than majority participations.
However, this significant and fairly recent tendency is to be found
more in business transactions between developed countries than in
investments from developed to developing countries.

While most foreign corporations have several cases of majority
participation, the pattern relating to minority participation is more
variable: some foreign corporations still retain majority control in all
their affiliated companies, others have one exceptional case of minority participation in only one joint venture, others now have minority
participation in several of their joint ventures.

A distinction has sometimes been drawn between "voluntary," "induced," and "compelled" minority participations. In fact, the distinction is not clear-cut and the final decision of the foreign corporation
is often the result of a number of considerations.

THE REQUIREMENTS OF LOCAL LAW
OR GOVERNMENT POLICY

Developing countries may adopt restrictions on foreign participation by different legal means: a clause in the constitution, specific
laws, or government policy.[24]

23. See *supra,* test and note 5, pp. 365–66.
24. On such limitations in the field of extractive industries, see: "I. The Status of Permanent Sovereignty over Natural Wealth and Resources.—II. Report of the Commission on Permanent Sovereignty over Natural Resources,"
New York, United Nations, pp. 30–36 (1962); M. A. Mughraby, *Permanent
Sovereignty over Oil Resources,* Beirut, The Middle East Research and Publishing Center, 233 pp. (1966); J. N. Hyde, "Permanent Sovereignty over Natural Wealth and Resources", *American Journal of International Law,* pp. 854–
67 (1956); G. Fisher, "La souveraineté sur les resources nationales". *Annuaire
Français de Droit International,* pp. 516–28 (1962); K. N. Gess, "U.N. Resolution on Permanent Sovereignty over Natural Resources", *International and
Comparative Law Quarterly,* pp. 398–450 (1964).

The Constitution of the Philippines provides in Article XIII, Section I, that the percentage of foreign participation in companies exploiting natural resources may not exceed 40 percent. This provision for domestic control of all natural resources exploitation has been buttressed by a large number of provisions in laws dealing with particular resources.[25] United States citizens are exempted from this limitation by terms of the Parity Amendment approved by plebiscite on March 11, 1947, if they invest through corporations organized under the laws of the Philippines and at least 60 percent U.S. owned.[26]

In Mexico the restrictions on foreign majority participation derive mainly from specific laws and to a lesser degree from government policy.[27] The Presidential Decree of 1944 (which dealt with some public utilities and a few other sectors), the Petrochemical Law of 1959, and the Mining Law of 1961 required that companies operating in these sectors be at least 51 percent domestically-owned. Government policy plays a significant role in the application of these laws, especially where borderline cases are concerned.

Until now, restrictions in India on foreign majority control have derived exclusively from government policy. In a policy statement on Foreign Capital of April 6, 1949, the Prime Minister announced that the majority control of joint venture enterprises should, as a rule, be in Indian hands.[28] As has already been mentioned, the application of

25. As to Philippines policy toward foreign investment, see Administrative Order No. 21, setting forth the Philippines policy on domestic and foreign investments, issued September 6, 1966, *International Legal Materials,* Washington, D.C., A.S.I.L., pp. 1090–93 (1966); Philippines Investment Incentives and Guarantees Act, approved September 16, 1967, *International Legal Materials,* Washington, D.C., A.S.I.L., pp. 1174–93 (1967).

26. See also the Laurel/Langley Agreement of December 15, 1954, Art. VI. The Parity Amendment expires in 1974. On the preparation of the new agreement, see "The Philippines and United States: Report on the Philippines—U.S. Economic Relations (Principles of Agreement to Replace Laurel-Langley Trade Agreement)," *International Legal Materials,* Washington, D.C., A.S.I.L., pp. 87–104 (1968).

27. F. B. Loretta, "Joint Ventures in Mexico," in *Doing Business in Mexico,* New York, American Management Association, pp. 13–17 (1964).

28. On this statement and its implications, see M. J. Kust, *Foreign Enterprise in India: Laws and Policies,* Chapel Hill, University of North Carolina Press, pp. 63–74 and pp. 141–55 (1964). On joint ventures in India generally, see G. L. Mehta, *Development and Foreign Collaboration,* New Delhi, New York, and Düsseldorf, Indian Investment Centre, 22 pp. (1968). Mr. Mehta is a former Ambassador to the United States. He is now Chairman of the Indian

the rule has hitherto been flexible.[29] A number of exceptions have been permitted, especially when they have proved necessary in national planning. At the end of 1968, after a thorough examination of all aspects pertaining to foreign private investment and foreign technical collaboration, the government decided that no significant change in the broad policy hitherto followed in this field was called for and that no formal resolution would be issued on these matters.[30] It is to be hoped that the government will not yield to the temptation of codifying the rules applying to foreign participation and consequently endanger the flexibility that has, in the past, proved to be so useful to all parties concerned.

Various reasons motivate the legal and administrative restrictions to foreign majority participation in certain sectors. As the colonial period has but recently come to an end, the main reason for these restrictions probably continues to be the fear of foreign economic domination.[31] In many cases, however, governments of developing countries are also determined to have local entrepreneurs increasingly assume financial and management responsibilities. It is obvious that

Investment Centre and of the Industrial Credit and Investment Corporation of India Ltd. (ICICI). And see *supra*, pp. 331–32, 348.

29. For a critical view of this flexibility, see M. Kidron, *Foreign Investments in India*, London, Oxford University Press, pp. 285–96 (1965).

30. Press Note issued by the Government of India on July 20, 1968. Announcement of the Government of India, November 17, 1968. See the text of these official documents in *Foreign Investment and Collaboration: Guidelines*, New Delhi, New York, and Düsseldorf, Indian Investment Centre, 26 pp. (1968).

31. Even developed countries such as Canada show concern about this risk. The Government of Canada commissioned a group of experts (the "Task Force") to undertake a study on the degree and influence of foreign ownership in Canadian industry. This study was presented on January 12, 1968, and published under the auspices of the Privy Council Office: *Foreign Ownership and the Structure of Canadian Industry*, Ottawa, Privy Council Office, 427 pp. (1968). The conclusions of the Task Force are worth noting (see p. 345): "Foreign direct investment tends to shift the locus of decision-making outside of Canada and risks reducing the capacity of the Canadian Government to implement its decisions in the public interest. Increasing the Canadian private presence in the decision-making of foreign-controlled subsidiaries would facilitate the expression of Canadian points of view and provide a vehicle for the Canadian Government for the exercise of its policy. More generally, the Canadian public interest would be directly served by new national policies which recognize the need for a stronger government presence to countervail the power of multinational firms and, on occasion, foreign government power exercised over these firms."

in order to reach this goal, governments have to combine positive incentives to local entrepreneurs with the restrictive measures taken against foreign investors. Furthermore, as most governments are deeply concerned about balance-of-payments difficulties and foreign exchange shortages, they sometimes discourage foreign majority participation in the enterprises where profits are expected to be particularly high.

On the whole, not many developing countries have adopted general restrictions on foreign majority participation in many economic sectors.[32] On the other hand, every government has the means to lay down the terms of approval of a foreign investment, including the requirement of a local majority participation for any specific venture.

THE ADVANTAGES OF MINORITY PARTICIPATION

Even when local law or government policy does not require a local majority participation, the foreign investor may, for various reasons, ask for a minority participation.

A number of developing countries present certain political and economic risks, such as nationalization, devaluation or foreign exchange blockage, and excessive taxation. Therefore foreign investors are often willing to accept a minority participation in order to reduce the financial risk involved in the investment. The French automotive firm, Renault, which has traditionally been export-orientated, has in a few countries been confronted with significant risks, especially that of the impossibility of transferring capital and profits. In accordance with host government policy, however, Renault has had to undertake local manufacture and to participate financially in the manufacturing company in order to obtain the right to export to these countries machinery, parts, or vehicles of another category. The natural compromise between government rules and Renault's desire to limit its risks was minority participation. Other foreign investors feel that with a minority participation it is easier to withdraw from a joint venture before some foreseen trouble actually occurs.

Even large multinational groups have certain limitations in terms of financial resources and management personnel. Consequently, some of them appreciate a local partner who is able to take a major-

32. On the generally sensitive sectors of the economy in developing countries, see D. U. Stikker, *The Role of Private Enterprise in Investment and Promotion of Exports in Developing Countries,* UNCTAD, New York, United Nations, pp. 224–29, 241–43, and 287–94 (1968).

ity participation and to assume management control of a joint venture. Hindustan Aluminium Corporation Ltd. (Hindalco) is a successful joint venture between the U.S. firm, Kaiser Aluminum & Chemical Corporation, and the Indian company, Birla.[33] Kaiser was not prepared to provide a large proportion of the capital, nor to send many employees to India on a permanent basis. The U.S. firm had moreover full confidence in Birla's capacity to manage the enterprise efficiently. Consequently, it assumed only a minority participation in the capital (26 percent), but provided the joint venture with all the necessary know-how, technical assistance, and training. Part of Kaiser's share was obtained against cash payment, and the remainder was acquired in exchange for its know-how and technical assistance. Although Birla has the leading role in the venture, Hindalco is the result of close cooperation between the foreign and the local partners.

Some foreign investors are more willing to accept only a minority position, when they think that the local partner's voting control will cause him to feel a greater sense of responsibility for the success of the enterprise. This is one of the reasons which induced a large Dutch chemical and food company to be satisfied with a minority position in a project of agricultural industrialization in Tunisia. The local partner received a 55 percent participation in exchange for the land. He has taken a personal and active interest in the management and in the success of the project, but has nevertheless constantly needed practical assistance from the Dutch company. It should be noted, however, that many foreign investors are not ready to accept a minority participation on that specific ground.

THE DISADVANTAGES OF
MINORITY PARTICIPATION

Foreign investors have experienced a variety of disadvantages in minority participation.

For some foreign investors, minority participation is a serious impediment to adequate control over the business policy of the joint venture. In Mexico, a foreign textile company is a minority partner in one of the country's largest joint ventures. The government required and obtained a major expansion of the enterprise, thanks to the influence it exercises on the banking interests that are the local majority partners in the joint venture. The management of the for-

33. The negotiations were held in the late 1950's.

eign corporation was not in favor of this expansion. It was contended that resistance to government pressure would have been easier if the foreign corporation had been in a majority position. This point is arguable, because a government usually has sufficient means of control with which to put effective pressure on foreign as well as on local partners, and on majority as well as on minority investors. It is true, however, that the intensity of government pressure may vary from one case to another.

Most multinational corporations develop a planned and global strategy in their foreign operations. Consequently, coordination between the numerous subsidiaries and affiliated companies is often of the utmost importance to the group. The coordination requirements are one of the main reasons for the reluctance shown by many foreign investors toward minority participation. It should be noted, however, that the need for coordination is not felt to the same extent by all multinational corporations and that divergences of opinion exist as to the best means of implementing this coordination.

A major cause for such differences would appear to be the nature of the product. For instance, it is certain that the need for coordination is not felt to the same extent in the food industry as in the electronics industry. The Unilever Group mainly manufactures consumer products, such as edible fats, foods and detergents. As a rule, Unilever's production in a developing country is destined, for economic reasons, to supply the requirements of that country. In many cases the transactions between Unilever's subsidiaries and affiliated companies are therefore relatively limited. Consequently, joint ventures and minority participation usually do not in themselves constitute a problem as far as the coordination of Unilever's multinational operations is concerned.

As compared with the food industry, the electronics industry involves a very complex and ever-changing technology. A final electronic product is generally distributed in the various national markets with only minor changes from one country to the other. On the other hand, production of electronic commodities is often highly specialized. Accordingly, the affiliated companies established in various countries are frequently concerned with the manufacture of only part of the product. It is therefore obvious that as a rule, the need for the coordination of international operations is felt to a greater extent in the electronics industry than in the food industry. Nevertheless, inside the electronics industry, the various companies have different business philosophies in general, and divergent opinions as to the best means of satisfying the requirements of international coordination in particular. The following comparison between the Philips and IBM cases tends to confirm this observation.

Philips has traditionally concentrated on entertainment electronics, but it is now entering the field of computers. The company's executives feel that even in the very sophisticated fields of electronics, the formal matter of voting control is not a necessary condition for an efficient coordination of the group's multinational activities. Philips considers it essential to grant a large degree of autonomy to managements abroad. Given this general philosophy, the most essential precondition for cooperation in a joint venture is that partners be persuasive. Philips feels that it has the arguments and the knowledge necessary to convince its partners.

As compared with Philips' policy, that of IBM presents both similarities and dissimilarities. Like the Dutch concern, the U.S. group delegates major operational responsibility to each country's manager. Within the framework of centrally coordinated policy, the manager responsible in each country for the company's operations has full responsibility with regard to personnel programs, marketing, and customer service. Contrary to Philips, however, full control over foreign companies has until now been, in IBM's experience, a constant corollary of international coordination between the relatively numerous and highly-specialized manufacturing units.[34] On the other hand, although the need for foreign partners has not until now been felt, it should be emphasized that IBM's executives are ready to consider any joint venture if this would be the best course in reaching an objective. They nevertheless observe that, with time, all computer companies arrive at a common organizational approach to the special problems that this particular industry poses. This similarity of pattern is reinforced by the rapidity of technological change, which requires great adaptability from the manufacturing companies. In the next few years, it will be interesting to observe whether Philips management, which is consciously fostering the growth of the company's computer department, will apply a policy similar to that of IBM, at least as far as this activity is concerned.

34. "Full control" here means that IBM's history does not include a single case of equity joint venture with an industrial partner. On the other hand, IBM shares are listed on principal stock exchanges in Europe. On IBM's policy, see also *supra*, pp. 218–21.

Generally speaking, it can be concluded as to this aspect of the subject that the nature of the product is an important factor in the determination of a company's policy toward the degree of participation in a joint venture, although the business philosophy of the company has also a strong impact on policy decisions. For the time being, a number of foreign corporations consider minority participation an obstacle to the coordination of their multinational activities and they are more likely to take this view when the technology of their production is highly sophisticated.

THE POLITICAL MEANING OF MINORITY PARTICIPATION

It remains to be seen whether the absence of voting control and its disadvantages for the foreign corporation may be compensated by sufficient political and psychological advantages. In other words, it is important to know whether a foreign minority participation might give a truly local identity to a joint venture and if this would entail significant rewards for foreign interests. In this respect, it should be noted that as a rule the circumspect or hostile attitudes that some developing countries have at times adopted toward foreign economic interests, have been directed toward foreign investment in general and without discrimination. The nationalizations in Cuba and the expropriations in Egypt have not spared the joint ventures in which foreign interests were in a minority position. Generally speaking, government decisions affecting foreign interests or properties are not primarily based upon the importance of foreign holdings.

SPECIAL AGREEMENTS AND *De Facto* CONTROL

Once a foreign corporation has sought or accepted a minority participation, it often tries to compensate for the absence of voting control by concluding special agreements with the local majority partner and/or by exercising a *de facto* control on the enterprise.

Some foreign investors feel that their technical superiority represents a sufficient influence by which to prevent the local majority partner from abusing its voting control. The President of an Italian textile company thus asserted that technical control was much more important than voting control. E. R. Barlow, who has studied joint ventures between U.S. and Mexican interests, observed on this matter:

Although the loosest control over the subsidiaries in Mexico was found among those companies with only a minority interest in the subsidiary, one concern managed to maintain a considerable amount of control over the local subsidiaries despite its minority interest. The company was an industry where technical change was rapid and vital. Thus the technical agreement to supply information that would permit the subsidiary to keep up to date with all the improvements and new discoveries was at least as important as the name, skill and know-how supplied initially. Therefore, as part of the technical contract the company was able to require that the general manager, treasurer, sales manager, and production manager should either be supplied by the United States company or should be persons who were satisfactory to it.[35]

Yet other foreign investors feel that technical control without majority participation is illusory. More than thirty years ago, a British tire-manufacturing firm took a minority participation in a joint venture in a developing country and concluded a know-how and technical assistance agreement with this company. As the royalties paid to the foreign partner had been a fixed amount and as prices in general had been inflating, they represented a real value far inferior to that of thirty years ago. Consequently, the British firm asked for renegotiation of the agreement, but being in a minority position was not strong enough to obtain a significant increase in the royalties. Nevertheless, although a number of foreign investors likewise feel that voting and technical control should always be linked, a majority of them consider their technical superiority an adequate means of exercising a lasting *de facto* control over the foreign joint ventures where they are in a minority position.

In other cases, foreign investors rely on a management contract or on their managerial skills for acquiring a substantial degree of control in a joint venture. In particular, it is relatively frequent to have the foreign minority corporation responsible for day-to-day management. In the Sociedad Minera El Teniente, which is a joint venture between Kennecott and the Chilean Government, the U.S. company has obtained the technical management of the enterprise through a management contract. Although foreign technical assistance appears to be necessary for the satisfactory operation of the venture, the possibility of a conflict between the government-controlled Board of Directors and Kennecott's managers cannot be excluded. In this re-

35. E. R. Barlow: *Management of Foreign Manufacturing Subsidiaries,* Boston, Harvard University, pp. 144–45 (1953).

spect, however, Kennecott has accepted a calculated risk by agreeing to the transfer of 51 percent of its shares to the Chilean Government.[36]

It is more difficult to evaluate the degree of foreign control in Coromandel Fertilizers Ltd., a joint venture between two U.S. companies (Chevron Chemical Company of San Francisco and International Minerals & Chemical Corporation of Skokie), an Indian company (EID–Parry Ltd. of Madras), local financial institutions, and the public. On the one hand, Indians hold a majority of the shares and Parry's has an important role in the everyday operations through its position as principal sales agent and marketing advisor. On the other hand, Chevron and IMC, which are two powerful groups, hold half of the seats on the Board of Directors and indirectly play an essential role in day-to-day management through the managers whom they loan to Coromandel.

The danger of a conflict between a foreign minority partner who has the day-to-day management or at least some management responsibilities and the locally-controlled Board of Directors should neither be underestimated nor exaggerated. In order to eliminate or reduce such risks, the managerial responsibilities have to be clearly defined and delimited, and, of course, the managers have to be able to get along with one another and with the directors. Because the operation of a joint venture is determined not only by the formal dispositions that have been taken on this matter, but also by the respective power and managerial skills of each partner, it is often difficult to evaluate with precision the degree of control a foreign corporation exercises on the enterprise through management.

THE RIGHTS AND PROTECTION OF FOREIGN MINORITY SHAREHOLDERS

For the same reason, it is sometimes difficult to state with exactitude where the *de facto* control over the joint venture ends and where the protection of minority shareholders begins. In other words, a careful combination of several effective measures of protection may well in fact give the actual control of the joint venture to the minority shareholder.

Somewhat paradoxically, an officer from the publishing company, Business International, argued that a foreign investor may be better protected with a 49 percent participation and certain defined rights

36. See also *supra*, pp. 82–85, 96–98 and *infra*, p. 394.

than with a 51 percent participation. The possible advantage for the foreign investor was seen in the fact that, in such a situation, the local majority partner will from the start have expressly accepted a few important and clearly defined rights of the foreign investor, such as management fees and royalties. Although there may be some truth in this paradox, most foreign investors do not seem willing to admit it.

At any rate, once foreign corporations have sought or accepted a minority participation, they usually have the choice of a variety of protective devices.[37] Some of these are specifically provided for in the local company law, while others have to be stipulated in the joint venture company's statutes. The right of veto and representation in management bodies are two of the most effective and most frequently used protective devices.

The right of veto is often regarded as the safest means of protecting the fundamental interests of a minority partner. The foreign investor who has yielded voting control to the local partner, often endeavors to obtain at least the percentage of votes which, according to local company law, is sufficient to impose a veto on fundamental decisions. Under the Indian Companies Act of 1956, certain matters have to be decided by a special resolution of the members of the company.[38] The articles of association of the company may, in addition, provide that other specified matters may be decided only by special resolution. As such decisions require a three-quarter majority, substantial minority holders can, by resorting to this arrangement in drafting the articles, ensure that important matters relating to their interest in the company may not be decided without their consent. It can be seen, therefore, that Kaiser's participation in the capital of

37. F. de Sola Canizares, "The Rights of Shareholders," *International and Comparative Law Quarterly,* pp. 564–78 (1953). M. R. Sonnenreich, "Protecting the United States Minority Shareholder in Joint International Business Ventures in Latin America," *Virginia Journal of International Law,* pp. 1–35 (1964). D. Schmidt, *Les droits de la minorité dans la société anonyme,* Paris, Sirey, 265 pp. (1970).

38. See Art. 189. Matters for the consideration of a general meeting are expressed in the form of resolutions. They are of two types, ordinary and special. A bare majority of votes of members present, either personally or through proxies, is sufficient for passing an ordinary resolution. A special resolution has to be approved by at least a three-fourth majority of members voting personally or through proxies.

Hindalco, i.e. 26 percent, constitutes a share sufficient to give a right to veto to its holder.[39]

Prospective partners may also provide for a specific right of veto or something equivalent in the statutes and adapt it to the requirements of the situation. Compañía Centroamericana de Productos Lácteos S.A. (Prolacsa) is a multinational joint venture for the manufacture of powdered milk in Nicaragua and its distribution in the Central American Common Market.[40] The equity financing was provided by the Swiss company, Nestlé, and shareholders from all the Common Market countries. No single stockholder was given a majority participation in the company's capital, nor a majority of the seats on the Board of Directors. All decisions of the board have to be approved by a majority of four votes out of five. Although no formal and general right of veto was provided for in the statutes, Nestlé has in fact, with two seats on the board, the power to veto any decision which would be contrary to its interests. Apart from this, Nestlé was of the opinion that since Prolacsa would have numerous passive shareholders, they would normally prefer to take any available profits as cash dividends. Accordingly, a statutory provision stipulates that any formation of voluntary reserves has to be accepted by a majority of shareholders in each series of shares, which means in fact that each important shareholder has a right of veto in this matter. These various provisions may at first seem somewhat complex, but they do adequately take into account Nestlé's desire to exercise a substantial but not an overriding degree of management control over Prolacsa.

According to the National Industrial Conference Board, which carried out an enquiry on joint ventures with a number of foreign corporations, representation on the board of directors or in the key operating management posts is "the most frequently mentioned safeguard for a minority shareholder." [41] In the Ghana Textile Printing Company Ltd., a joint venture between a foreign consortium and the

39. See *supra*, p. 343. It is obvious that the bare minimum would be 25 percent plus one share.

40. Production started in the second half of 1969. See also *infra*, pp. 126–39. On joint international business ventures in the CACM, see M. W. Gordon, "Joint Business Ventures in the Central American Common Market," *Vanderbilt Law Review*, pp. 315–38 (1968).

41. K. K. Bivens and E. N. Lovell: *Joint Ventures with Foreign Partners*, New York, National Industrial Conference Board, International Survey of Business Opinion and Experience, p. 43 (1966).

government, the consortium (which only has a minority participation), nominates two out of the board's five members and also designates the managing director and the technical manager.[42] The consortium, therefore, succeeds in making itself heard in a company which had previously been wholly-owned by the government.

Although the principle of the minority shareholder's protection is basically sound, its application should nevertheless respect some limits. If the conception of the minority shareholders rights is excessively "democratic," it is likely to run counter to the interests of the company itself. In some cases, abuse of the right of veto may thus unduly obstruct the normal operation of the enterprise.

In addition to the protection provided for by local company law or stipulated in the statutes, the foreign investor may try to obtain some external measures of protection. Australia, Denmark, Germany, Japan, Norway, and the United States have governmental systems of guarantees against noncommercial investment risks, which may apply to minority participations in joint ventures formed in developing countries. In an Amsterdam meeting arranged by the United Nations in February 1969 between business and government representatives from developed as well as developing countries, Dr. Pieter Kuin, of Unilever, proposed the elaboration of an insurance scheme run by an international board, in which small as well as large countries could take part.

At present, if the political risk materializes, the foreign minority shareholder may be confronted with the difficult problem of the diplomatic protection of shareholders as such.[43] In the future, it is likely

42. The United Africa Company has a leading role in the consortium. On U.A.C.'s policy, see *supra,* pp. 279–80, 368, 370–71.

43. On February 5, 1970, the International Court of Justice rejected the demand that had been introduced in 1962 by Belgium on behalf of the Belgian controlling shareholders in the Canadian-incorporated Barcelona Traction Light and Power Company. Nevertheless, some of the judges wondered whether international law does not present a lacuna as far as the diplomatic protection of shareholders as such is concerned. *Barcelona Traction Case, I.C.J. Reports,* 1970. This important problem has been the subject of considerable analysis. See, among others, Ch. de Visscher, "De la protection diplomatique des actionnaires," *Revue de Droit International et de Législation Comparée,* pp. 624–51 (1934), and "La technique de la personnalité juridique en droit international public et en droit international privé," id., pp. 475–87 (1936); S. Bastid et al., *La personnalité morale et ses limites,* Paris, L.G.D.J., 286 pp. (1960); D. Bindschedler-Robert, "La protection diplomatique des sociétés et des actionnaires," *Revue de la Société des Juristes Bernois,* pp. 141–

that the proliferation of national systems of guarantee against investment risks, the possible adoption of a multinational insurance system, and even more important, the increasing use by foreign investors and developing countries of the Convention on the Settlement of Investment Disputes [44] will somewhat reduce the practical significance of this difficult problem.

Changes in Participation

It should be noted at the outset that a proposal to change the degree of participation to an extent that involves a transfer of voting control during the operation of the enterprise often meets with serious obstacles. For any investor, it is one thing to go from 100 percent to 75 percent, and it is quite another thing to pass from 50 percent plus one share to 50 percent less one share. For example, a local group may often be very reluctant to permit any decrease of its participation, because it feels vulnerable vis-a-vis the foreign multinational corporation. Changes in participation are obviously especially delicate in the case of 50-50 joint ventures, which have often been organized that way simply because no prospective partner was ready to accept a minority participation at the time of negotiating.

Nevertheless, the failure to adapt the joint venture to changing circumstances can be most detrimental. A French gas-producing company that has a joint venture in Spain had difficulty to undertake the necessary expansion of the enterprise, because the local investors refused to accept Spanish banks as new partners and thereby run the

---

89 (1964); J.-P. de Hochepied, *La protection diplomatique des sociétés et des actionnaires*, Paris, A. Pédone, 276 pp. (1965).

44. The World Bank Convention was signed on March 18, 1965 and came into force on October 14, 1966. See the "Report of the Executive Directors of the I.B.R.D. and Convention on the Settlement of Investment Disputes Between States and Nationals of Other States," *International Legal Materials*, Washington D.C., A.S.I.L., pp. 524–44 (1965).

On the jurisdiction of the center regarding juridical persons, Article 25(2)b), see G. Delaume, "La convention pour le règlement des différends relatifs aux investissements entre états et ressortissants d'autres états," *Journal du Droit International (Clunet)*, pp. 33–34 (1966); M. Amadio, "Le contentieux international de l'investissement privé et la Convention de la Banque Mondiale du 18 mars 1965," Paris, L.G.D.J., pp. 116–17 (1967); *Investissements Étrangers et Arbitrage entre États et Personnes Privées, La Convention B.I.R.D. du 18 mars 1965*, Paris, A. Pédone, 196 pp. (1969); articles by P. Reuter (pp. 20–22), and R. Kovar (pp. 43–47).

risk of diluting their voting power. However, the partners agreed in 1969 on a public issue of shares as a convenient means of new financing.

In most cases of joint ventures, the partners are similarly conscious of the fact that a joint venture cannot be a rigid structure and that at times changes of participation are necessary. For instance, in 1962 the French equipment manufacturing company, Fives Lille-Cail (FLC), entered a joint venture agreement with a group of Spanish entrepreneurs and investors for the manufacture of cement on the island of Mallorca: Portland de Mallorca S.A. Because the Mallorcan cement market has developed very rapidly ever since, in the mid-sixties it became obvious that the company's production would have to be expanded significantly. Consequently, a new partner was sought, and the U.S. company, American Cement Corporation, agreed to become a shareholder in Portland de Mallorca, on the condition that its participation would be at least 50 percent. Out of economic necessity FLC agreed to this change in the capital structure, although the control exercised by the U.S. corporation has left little initiative to the other industrial partners in the venture.

FROM A MINORITY TO A MAJORITY PARTICIPATION

A foreign minority investor may acquire a majority participation either because the financial requirements of a needed expansion induce him to do so, or because he has previously planned to do so.

In cases of expansion, individuals, local companies, or governmental corporations sometimes have difficulty in providing their share of the capital increase.[45] In order to continue a joint venture's development, Nestlé has sometimes had to provide for the necessary additional funds and consequently, to increase its participation. Difficulties in the operation of the enterprise may also induce investors to take over the financial and management control of the joint venture.

The attitude of Philips can be considered to lie somewhere between the unavoidable and the planned changes of participation.[46] The Dutch company often starts with a minority or equal participation, but this does not mean that it will always remain in such a position. Quite frequently, Philips later proceeds to a majority position.

45. We refer here to the cases where debt financing of the expansion would not be advisable, or feasible.

46. On Philips' policy, see *supra*, pp. 250–52, 384.

This step is not usually provided for from the start; but the company seizes the opportunity whenever it arises.

A certain large U.S. company that manufactures a wide range of products pursues a planned policy regarding changes in participation. Quite often it acquires from the start a majority participation in a foreign joint venture and later tries to retain its majority control of the venture. In other cases, however, such as in Greece, this U.S. company may not be well acquainted with the country of investment or the prospective local partner and, consequently, may prefer to participate in the venture with only a minority investment and a technical assistance agreement. If it subsequently proves worthwhile to develop and diversify the business, then the company tries to obtain a majority control of the joint venture. It is reasonable to assume that the implementation of this policy, which shows a somewhat cautious approach to investment in certain developing countries, requires at least the tacit anterior approval of the government and of the local partner. Otherwise, frictions are, of course, bound to arise at the time when the U.S. company begins to show its real intentions.

FROM A MAJORITY TO A MINORITY PARTICIPATION

Some authors, such as Suy and Navadan, favor the "spontaneous naturalization" of foreign interests.[47] By that they mean that an early agreement providing for the release of certain portions of foreign shares to local interests according to predetermined schedules should be an adequate antidote to any danger of outright confiscation. It is, however, difficult to find cases where this procedure has been applied. Large multinational groups that pursue an expansionist policy take a dim view of the idea of entering a foreign market with the knowledge that they will have to withdraw gradually.[48] Moreover, it is not advisable to adopt a predetermined and rigid schedule that may not fit in well with economic realities.

It is more frequent that a foreign investor relinquishes the majority control of a joint venture without any prior arrangement and under

47. E. Suy, "La protection des investissements étrangers," *Industrie*, p. 591 (1963). S. Navadan, *Ways to Minimize Obstacles Confronting Joint Ventures in the Region: the Attitudes of the Partners*, Doc. N. 520–XIV/103, C.A.F.E.A.–I.C.C., p. 3 (1966).

48. See *Foreign Investment in Developing Countries*, Department of Social and Economic Affairs, New York, United Nations, §56 (1968).

government inducement or pressure. In Chile, in the early sixties, Kennecott decided to undertake a major expansion of the El Teniente mine and consequently requested fiscal and foreign exchange guarantees from the government. Although the negotiations with the Alessandri Government did not succeed, Kennecott and the Frei Government concluded an agreement in December 1964. In becoming co-owner with the Chilean Government and in giving to this government the satisfaction of being a majority partner, Kennecott's management obtained the indispensable guarantees it needed for expansion.[49] It must not be forgotten that the evolution of the uncertain political situation in Chile could bring about drastic steps with respect to all U.S. copper interests in the country.[50] It must be recognized, however, that Kennecott's release of majority control to the government is an audacious step which contrasts with the more circumspect attitude observed by a number of other foreign corporations in developing countries.

THE RIGHT OF FIRST REFUSAL AND THE TRANSFER-APPROVAL CLAUSE

Most of the time, joint ventures are the result of negotiations and cooperation between a limited number of senior executives from the participating companies. Consequently, a joint venture is usually the result of personal contacts and the personal element often remains significant during the entire operation of the enterprise. In such cases, prospective joint venturers tend to insert limitations on the transfer of shares in the basic agreement or in the company's statutes.[51]

Many negotiators, who are not prepared to adopt excessive limitations on the transfer of shares, consider a right of first refusal to be

49. Decree of the Ministry of Economy, Development and Reconstruction of March 20, 1967. See *International Legal Materials,* Washington D.C., A.S.I.L., pp. 1151–61 (1967).

50. On June 26, 1969, the government and the U.S. firm Anaconda agreed on a "long-term nationalization" of the Chuquicamata and El Salvador mines. The chosen status is a middle way between a gradual "Chileanization" and an outright expropriation. The parties to the agreement decided that the first step would be the creation of mixed companies in which the government would be a majority shareholder from the outset; the remaining shares owned by Anaconda will be gradually transferred to the government.

51. On the extent to which such restrictions are valid, see H. W. Ballantine, *Ballantine on Corporations,* Chicago, Callaghan, pp. 775–76 (1946).

adequate protection.[52] Should one of the partners be willing to retire from the venture, the other participants have an option to buy his share during a limited period of time. If at the expiration of this period the option has not been exercised, the retiring partner is then entitled to sell his share to a third party. Usually the right of first refusal may be exercised by any of the company's shareholders, but in some cases it is available to only a few of them. For instance, in a large Indian joint venture that groups three industrial companies, some financial institutions, and the public, the right of first refusal has only been provided for the three main partners.

The procedure of the right of first refusal is especially useful when one of the partners intends to retire and the other prefers to continue the business alone. Philips has thus been known to buy out the share of the partner when the quality of its products was at stake. The Dutch company, which is highly dependent on foreign markets, has always regarded its reputation as a very important asset vis-à-vis the public, the government, and business circles in the countries of investment.

Sometimes the partners do not consider the right of first refusal as adequate protection against intruders. In such cases, they may adopt a "transfer-approval" clause,[53] which conditions the right to transfer shares on the approval of the board of directors or the general assembly of shareholders. In 1964, the Kaiser Aluminum & Chemical Corporation (U.S.A.), Alcan Aluminium Ltd. (Canada), Compagnie Pechiney (France), and Conzinc Riotinto of Australia Ltd. (85 percent British-controlled), concluded an agreement for the construction and operation of an alumina plant at Gladstone, Queensland, in Australia. The partners formed an operating company, the Queensland Alumina Ltd. (QAL).[54] They decided that no party had the right to transfer or assign its rights or obligations in the agreements to which it is a party, the shares of QAL owned by it, or any indebtedness of

52. On the right of first refusal ("droit de préemption"), see G. Ripert, *Traité Élémentaire de Droit Commercial,* Tome I, pp. 572–75 (1963). On the basis of French law, Ripert thoroughly analyzes the nature and functioning of this specific right.

53. See G. Ripert, *ibid.*

54. QAL is not a mining company: the participants purchase bauxite, and QAL converts the mined product to alumina. For the time being, QAL is a profit company, because there are certain tax incentives to being a profit-seeking company in the early years. Nevertheless, when these incentives run out, QAL will become a nonprofit company.

QAL held by it to any other corporation, unless all parties first consented to such transfer or assignment.[55] This strict regulation was motivated by the magnitude of the investment and the considerable assistance obtained from financial institutions. The lenders were anxious to prevent the replacement of any debtor partner by an unknown third party. Nevertheless, this right of veto over the transfer of rights, obligations, and shares is not absolute. According to the basic agreement:

> it is understood that no party shall withhold its consent arbitrarily, but each party may, in giving or withholding consent, consider any legitimate business reason, particularly in consideration of the magnitude of the project, the length of its term, the financial obligations of the parties hereto, and the large degree of managerial discretion given to each party hereto in the management and control of the project.[56]

The statutes of Sirip, the joint venture between Nioc and Agip, provide for both a right of first refusal and a transfer-approval clause. In any event, where the option is not exercised, the seller may not transfer his share to third parties without the unanimous consent of the Board of Directors. In the Agreement of January 17, 1965, between Nioc (First Party) and Agip/Phillips/Oil and Natural Gas Commission of India (Second Party), the partners decided that the latter may not transfer its interest in the "joint structure" without the prior written approval of Nioc. Meanwhile, the Agreement of 1965 does not in any way restrict Nioc's right of transfer, which was perhaps a way by which Iran asserted its permanent sovereignty over its oil resources. The restrictions to the right of transfer are stricter in the case of Sirip and of the 1965 agreement than in the case of QAL. In these oil agreements, the consent or opposition to a transfer of shares, rights, and obligations does not need to be justified. The personal character of these joint ventures is thus strongly accentuated.[57]

55. Participants Agreement of July 31, 1964, Article 30 (D).
56. *Ibid.*
57. In a somewhat different context, the system of "bound" registered shares, which can be used in some countries, would raise a similar observation. See, for instance, Art. 686, par. 1 and 2, of the Swiss *Code des Obligations* (French version): "La société a le droit de refuser l'inscription sur le registre des actions pour les motifs que prévoient les statuts. Les statuts peuvent disposer aussi qu'il est permis de refuser l'inscription sans indication de motifs." These paragraphs may be translated as follows: "The company is entitled to refuse the entry on the register of shares for the reasons that are pro-

WITHDRAWAL

The withdrawal of a partner may cause a number of difficulties. To begin with, the partners may not easily agree on the price of the shares to be sold. Prospective partners, however, may try to forestall this kind of difficulty. The U.S. firm, Litton Industries, is a partner in a 50-50 joint venture in Spain for the manufacture of steel furniture. The partners have inserted a buy-and-sell clause in the basic agreement. A dissatisfied partner can fix a price at which the other can buy the former's share in the company's capital. If the latter declines the offer, then the former can buy the share of the other at the same price. Obviously a dissatisfied partner can only use this clause efficiently if he has substantial financial resources.

Withdrawal may also entail serious economic and psychological consequences for the retiring partner. As a rule, Nestlé endeavors to include in any joint venture agreement a right of first refusal in anticipation of a partner's withdrawal. Nestlé itself has seldom withdrawn from any venture. Not only is the company convinced that in developing countries, withdrawal from an enterprise would create bitterness and that Nestlé's reputation would consequently suffer; it further believes that even if a particular business seems to be temporarily on the decline, this is no reason to justify a withdrawal. Large multinational corporations also have to examine carefully the effects that a withdrawal would have on the attitude of actual or potential competitors.

It remains true, however, that the withdrawal of one of the shareholders is sometimes unavoidable. For instance, Brazilian Light and Power Company, a Canadian holding and management company for utility subsidiaries, was compelled by strong political pressures to sell its telephone and telegraph operations to the Brazilian Government and to invest most of the proceeds in small manufacturing ventures as a minority shareholder. To take another example, for years International Telephone & Telegraph (ITT), a large U.S. company, operated the public telephone system in Lima, Peru. Customers' tariffs were the cause of constant friction between the government and the Compañía Peruana de Teléfonos (CPT).[58] ITT owned 69.11 per-

vided in the charter. The charter may also stipulate that it is allowed to refuse the entry without indication of any reason."

58. Therefore, these frictions were anterior to the difficulties between the Peruvian and U.S. Governments that partially resulted from the expropriation of the International Petroleum Company in October 1968.

cent of CPT's capital; the remaining 30.89 percent was scattered among many local private investors. In the mid-sixties, the government repeatedly expressed its determination to acquire effective control of this essential public utility, in the interest of furthering national policy on local telecommunications.[59]

On August 11, 1967, the government, CPT, and ITT concluded two contracts by which three important decisions were taken: [60]

1. As in the past, CPT would continue to operate the public telephone system in the provinces of Lima and Callao.

2. CPT would be involved in the expansion plans of the public telephone system.

3. At any time between 1967 and 1971, the government would be entitled to purchase the shares of CPT held by ITT and thus become a majority shareholder of the company. The government was to acquire at least a 51 percent participation (but possibly even more), at the time of purchase. The "Peruvianization" of the company's capital was to be financed at least partially by the telephone subscribers.

At the end of July 1969, the government announced its decision to nationalize all telecommunication companies operating in Peru, expressly mentioning that the decision would be implemented in a gradual manner. At that time, the modalities and dates of the effective measures affecting the various companies were not announced.

Lengthy negotiations between the government and ITT resulted in an agreement that was signed on October 29, 1969.[61] The agreement called for Peru to acquire ITT's 69.11 percent interest in CPT, nationalize the company, and assume the effective control of it. In exchange for ITT's interest in CPT, the government agreed to pay a compensation of $17.9 million.

The U.S. corporation took the commitment of reinvesting $8.2 million in Peru, which will finance the construction of an ITT-Sheraton hotel in Lima and of a telephone equipment factory. The hotel

59. On Peruvian policy towards foreign investments during that period, see D. U. Stikker, *op. cit. supra* note 39, §§300, 321 and 329.

60. The text of the contracts was published in El Peruana, the official newspaper of the Peruvian Government, on August 12, 1967.

61. "International Telephone and Telegraph Corporation—Peru: Agreement on the basic Conditions for Nationalizing the Peruvian Telephone Company," in *International Legal Materials,* Washington, D.C., A.S.I.L., pp. 80–98 (1970). "Peru: Decree-Law Approving the Agreement with International Telephone and Telegraph Corporation on the Nationalization of the Peruvian Telephone Company," *ibid.,* at pp. 186–91 (1970).

will be operated by an ITT wholly-owned subsidiary. The telephone equipment company will be 60 percent ITT owned, whereas the government will hold the remaining 40 percent; after a period of eight years, the company may become, at the demand of the government, a 50-50 joint venture.

It is interesting to note that in the three cases of Anaconda in Chile, of Brazilian Light and Power in Brazil, and of ITT in Peru, the government has preferred a negotiated nationalization to an outright confiscation, even though negotiations have been lengthy and difficult. Both the Brazilian and ITT cases demonstrate that telecommunications are an extremely sensitive industry from the national point of view. Nevertheless, in neither case has the withdrawal of the foreign corporation been complete, and in either case at least part of the compensation proceeds have been reinvested in less sensitive industries.

Degree of Participation and Control

The foregoing analysis has shown that, although the general attitude of foreign investors is becoming more flexible, they still generally show a strong preference for majority participation. In many cases, the multinational corporation is justified in seeking a majority participation in its foreign joint ventures, but the advantages of such participation are in no way absolute.

Another basic and complementary question is to ascertain, from an objective point of view, the relative importance of the degree of participation in the control of a joint venture.

DISCREPANCIES BETWEEN
FORMAL ARRANGEMENTS AND
EFFECTIVE CONTROL

The control of a joint venture depends not only on formal arrangements but also, and perhaps to a greater extent, on the way these agreements are applied. The actual equilibrium of a joint venture takes shape by the manner in which the enterprise is operated and by the partners' day-to-day relations.

Professor Kindleberger of the Massachusetts Institute of Technology has accurately analyzed the relative character of control:

To lawyers, a business is or is not controlled abroad by virtue of its 100, 51, 48, or some such numerical percentage of foreign ownership in a cohesive voting bloc. To a student of industrial management, control is not an either-or proposition, but a question of infinite degrees of divisibility, depending upon the nature of the decision-making process and the division of authority between the head office and the foreign unit. This control may cover any or all of a variety of separate functions—hiring and firing, investment programming, research and development, pricing, dividend remittances, marketing, and so on. A company can control all phases of a subsidiary's operations with merely 25 percent of the equity, on the one hand, or it may passively receive dividends without interfering in any of the affairs of its 100 percent-owned foreign operation. In the latter case, it is in effect merely a portfolio owner.[62]

Kindleberger's analysis is confirmed by the case studies contained in this book. In a number of Nestlé investments, a local majority partner is constantly kept informed about the operation of the enterprise by the Swiss company, which has the management control of the joint venture. Tata has a leading role in Voltas, although it only holds an 18 percent participation in this joint trading and manufacturing venture with Volkart, Life Insurance Corporation, Unit Trust of India, and the public; to a large extent, Voltas' evolution has been determined by the power and influence of the large Indian concern. The relative "strength" of each partner is often at least as important as its participation in the capital and voting power in corporate organs.

At the present time, multinational joint ventures—that is, joint ventures with several partners from different countries—are proliferating. It should be noted that the problem of control in multinational joint ventures cannot be examined with exactly the same approach as that adopted for the study of joint ventures with only two partners. In a dual joint venture, with only few exceptions one of the partners has a leading role. It can also happen in a multinational joint venture that one of the partners has a leading role: for example, in Queensland Alumina Ltd. (Australia),[63] Kaiser Aluminum & Chemical Corporation initially acquired a 52 percent majority participation (mainly for tax purposes, it is true) and exercised important responsibilities for day-to-day operations.[64]

62. C. P. Kindleberger: *International Economics,* 3rd edition, Homewood, Ill., R. D. Irwin Inc., p. 404 (1963).

63. See *supra,* pp. 395–96.

64. In particular, the Kaiser organization had substantial responsibilities for the design and construction of the plant. Furthermore, in the early days of its operations the general manager and the chief financial officers of QAL, among

In a number of multinational joint ventures, however, the partners were not willing or not able to concede a leading role to any particular partner. As Prolacsa was to have a truly regional character and to be financed by shareholders from all the Central American Common Market countries, it would have been inappropriate for any single shareholder to have a majority participation and the control of the board.[65] As in such multinational joint ventures no one shareholder is given an overrriding role, each shareholder tries to obtain the statutory measures that he regards as indispensable in protecting his own basic interests. As far as the interests of the joint venture itself are concerned, the main problem perhaps consists in finding a working arrangement in order to ensure the unified day-to-day management policy of the enterprise.

In conclusion, although the degree of participation is usually a significant element of control, it is not often a decisive one.

THE ROLE OF FINANCIAL INSTITUTIONS
IN JOINT VENTURES

In recent years, one of the most important developments in international business transactions with developing countries has been the increasing role and influence of financial institutions, either local (e.g. the Industrial Credit and Investment Corporation of India Ltd.), foreign (e.g. the Commonwealth Development Finance Company Ltd., U.K., or the Compagnie Financière pour l'Outre-mer, Cofimer, France), or international (which may be public as is the International Finance Corporation of Washington D.C. or private as is Adela of Luxembourg).[66]

---

others, were supplied by Kaiser. However, the formal arrangement always provided that QAL would be managed by its own officers and employees. As time has passed and the plant has been successfully operating, this has become true in fact, as well as in principle, with most of the QAL personnel now being Australian. Moreover, it was decided in 1969 that upon completion of the plant's second expansion, Kaiser's share in QAL's capital would be decreased from 52 to 43 percent.

65. It seems that Nestlé has been the first multinational corporation to seek the creation, in a developing country, of a regional enterprise with shareholders coming from all the region's countries. On the means to stimulate the formation of joint ventures inside a regional market, see *Trade Expansion and Economic Integration Among Developing Countries,* UNCTAD, New York, United Nations, §§ 54–58 (1967).

66. For an extensive review of the financing of international business transactions, see W. S. Surrey and C. Shaw (eds.), *A Lawyer's Guide to Interna-*

Their role and influence vary considerably with the importance of the investment and the nature of the industry. In Africa, the Société Industrielle et Agricole du Niari (Sian) is certainly an important agro-industrial enterprise, but its need for equity and loan capital is relatively limited. Consequently, ventures such as Sian are not too dependent on financial institutions for loans or investments. The situation is different in joint mining ventures, which usually require considerable investments. Because of this, the ratio of loan capital to equity capital can be quite high, as is shown by the case of Lamco in Liberia; at the end of 1968, Lamco's long-term debt amounted to about $152 million, while the equity capital (capital stock, capital obligation and reserves) amounted to about $28 million. It should be noted, however, that as the loans are gradually repaid, the ratio of loan capital to equity capital becomes more balanced.

It does not happen often that financial institutions take an active role in the management of a joint venture. Nevertheless, they often have specific demands for the protection of their loan at the time of formation of the joint venture and also require means of supervision for the period of operating the enterprise. Before granting its loan to El Teniente in Chile, the Export-Import Bank of Washington, D.C., did not require that any structural change be made in the enterprise, but asked merely that the operations be run by Kennecott (Braden) and that the equipment necessary for expansion be bought in the United States ("tied loan").[67] The Eximbank's rights are not only stipulated in the loan agreement, they are also indirectly guaranteed by a government decree.[68] Hindalco in India also benefits from a large loan from Eximbank, which in this case obtained control of dividend pay-out policy. This means that until a certain proportion of the loan is repaid, the rate of dividend is fixed in advance in accordance with the bank's requests. In itself, this right may seem a strict

---

tional Business Transactions, Philadelphia, A.L.I. and A.B.A., pp. 387–616 (1963). For IFC and Adela, see also *infra,* pp. 405–407. One should also mention the important role played by the Inter-American Development Bank. See T. G. Upton, "The Inter-American Development Bank and Private Investments in Latin America," in *Problems and Solutions in International Business in 1969,* New York, Matthew Bender, pp. 111–35 (1969).

67. The Export-Import Bank is an independent agency of the U.S. Government. It is run by five directors appointed by the President. It makes dollar loans repayable in dollars, and local currency loans repayable in local currency.

68. See *supra* p. 88 and note 49, at p. 394.

control measure on the company's operations, but in actual fact it does not exclude flexibility in its application. In 1967, the dividend was limited in principle to 7.5 percent, but Eximbank agreed to a dividend of 10 percent because of the good performance realized by Hindalco that year.

THE NEED FOR FLEXIBILITY

We have just seen that the degree of participation is only of relative importance in determining control in a joint venture. This is a forceful argument in favor of flexibility in the negotiations between foreign investors, local entrepreneurs, and governments of developing countries.

General restrictions on foreign participation are often unnecessary and counteractive. A government usually has enough means of control and of pressure to neutralize a foreign corporation that may be tempted to misuse its majority position in a way contrary to national interest. In this respect, the generally flexible approach adopted by the Indonesian Government is noteworthy.[69] Philips was permitted to take a majority participation in the joint venture that it formed with the government, P. T. Philips Ralin Electronics Ltd. The Dutch concern's executives are fully aware of the fact that they have to move cautiously in a country where the memory of colonial domination is still fresh. As Indonesia urgently needs the financial, managerial, and technical resources of Philips, the partners are determined to solve any disagreement which may arise by discussion and compromise.

At present, investors from developed countries are much tempted by the extremely attractive investment opportunities that exist in other industrialized countries. Consequently, in order to obtain a balanced growth, developing countries generally, and semi-industrialized countries such as Mexico or India especially, have an interest in avoiding restrictive measures toward foreign participations in local enterprises, and in providing positive encouragement to local entrepreneurs and incentives for local savings.

Similarly, the executives of multinational groups should not exclude *a priori* minority participation in foreign joint ventures. As a rule, the need for foreign investors is sufficiently great to enable them

69. This observation relates to the period following the adoption of the Foreign Investment Law (1966). See *supra,* pp. 255–58, 366–67.

to resist efficiently the local (whether public or private) partner who might be tempted to abuse his voting control in a joint venture.

The requirements of foreign markets and the pressure of international competition constitute powerful incentives to induce multinational groups to make exceptions to established policy regarding the degree of participation and control. In the IBM group, the parent company has until now not yielded up any part of its control over its foreign subsidiaries in developing countries. Nevertheless, as has already been mentioned, IBM's executives insist on the fact that they are ready to consider any form of investment, including joint ventures. IBM might well have the opportunity in the near future to show its flexibility in certain developing countries that are at present endeavoring to attract foreign computer companies and that at the same time favor some kind of local participation in industry.

Although the planning requirements of the country of investment always have to be taken into account in joint venture negotiations, each joint venture proposal should as far as possible be dealt with on its own merits. The negotiators representing the prospective partners and the government should normally be granted maximum freedom and a sufficient delegation of power, as such credentials would allow them to adapt the legal and financial structure of the joint venture to the specific realities of the case.

The Control and Success of a Joint Venture

A lawyer from the Commonwealth Development Corporation (CDC) [70] observed that in their foreign ventures, British economic interests under the Empire and U.S. economic interests at present tended to rely excessively on pressure and voting power. As this opinion is not unfounded, it is important to stress some of the factors that may contribute to the success of a joint venture.

Actually, due to economic diversity and human contingencies, no one formula can comprise all the conditions for the success of a joint

70. CDC was established in 1948 by an Act of the United Kingdom Parliament as a statutory corporation with commercial terms of reference. Its purpose is to assist the economic development of the British dependent territories, and of those self-governing territories which have achieved independence within the Commonwealth since 1948. CDC operates on commercial lines and has a statutory obligation to pay its way, taking one year with another.

venture. Nevertheless, certain elements can no doubt contribute to success in many cases.

PUBLIC ISSUES OF SHARES

A number of developing countries are endeavoring to foster the development of a broad and active capital market. Governments try to induce the public to invest in industrial securities, to refrain from investing excessively in real estate or in more speculative securities, and to abstain from exporting funds to foreign banks. Some of them also feel that a broad ownership of the securities in circulation can contribute to the social equilibrium of the country and that it is in the long run an adquate means of counterbalancing the excessive power of local monopolies. In addition, governments feel that their nationals have to be provided with the opportunity of sharing in the benefits of profitable enterprises. The Government of India has certainly been one of the most persistent in its determination to promote a broad and active capital market.

A public issue of shares may be a convenient means for enabling the foreign investor to give a local identity to his enterprise in the country. Such a move is most likely to be appreciated by the national government. Moreover, the issue may be an indirect way of making the products known to the public, which is especially important for the companies manufacturing widely-distributed consumer products. Most of the time, however, a great publicity effort is required to exploit successfully the increasing opportunities for associating the public in new enterprises. In India, the ICI marketers for the production of a new fertilizer plant in Kanpur (Uttar Pradesh) considered this aspect so important that they systematically visited the farmers in the areas where the production was to be distributed. After having explained the qualities and the utilization methods of these products, they offered shares to the farmers who subscribed in large numbers. In this case, the main reason for the special effort made by ICI to encourage the participation of farmers related to a general exercise in public relations, useful both in the local and national fields.

For foreign investors, the public issue of shares represents an advantageous form of local participation, because the public usually takes no part in the management of the enterprise as such and even tends to be absent from, or passive in, the general assembly of shareholders. Even if a majority of the shares were in the hands of the public, this would generally not present a great risk for the foreign investor who may keep a minority participation of control vis-à-vis a majority of shares scattered among many local investors. Moreover, the relative lack of sophistication of capital markets in developing countries makes it difficult for an ambitious minority group to organize a proxy fight in order to gain control of a company.[71]

Nevertheless, the foreign investor has not always the practical possibility of effecting a public issue of shares, because in a number of developing countries the capital market is still in an early stage of development. The public issues of shares offered by some U.S. corporations in Latin American countries have at times been quite unsuccessful.[72] In many developing countries local savings are very limited, and often local investors prefer to invest in speculative ventures rather than in industrial securities.[73] Fortunately, even though a public issue of shares may not have been feasible at the time of the formation of a joint venture, certain financial institutions, such as the International Finance Corporation [74] of Washington, D.C. (a subsidiary of the World Bank) or the Atlantic Community Development Group for Latin America (Adela) of Luxembourg, do in some cases resell part or all of their investments to local investors when the conditions of the capital market are favorable.[75] Adela [76] is a multinational private investment company (incorporated in 1964), which seeks to encourage and support the formation of joint international

71. This does not imply that it is easy to organize a proxy fight in a developed country.

72. On this difficulty of attracting local savings in industrial investment, see the remarks made by the late T. E. Monaghan (Standard Oil Company of New Jersey) at the conference on legal problems of trade and investment in Latin America: *United States Trade and Investment in Latin America,* New York, Columbia Society of International Law, p. 185 (1963).

73. When it is feasible, they may also prefer to invest in foreign securities.

74. M. M. Rosen, "The International Finance Corporation and Private Investment for Economic Development," in *Problems and Solutions in International Business in 1968,* New York, Matthew Bender, pp. 29–39 (1968).

75. Local development banks also play sometimes an essential role in this redistribution of stock ownership. See the collective book edited by the Institut d'Etudes Bancaires et Financières: *Les banques de développement dans le monde,* Paris, Dunod, 2 vols. (1965).

76. See J. H. Allan, "Adela Sets Latin Targets," *The New York Times,* March 10, 1968; W. D. Falcon (ed.), *Financing International Operations; a Guide to Sources and Methods,* New York, American Management Association, pp. 149–52 (1965).

business ventures in Latin America and to contribute to the implementation of economic integration in this region. Adela does not seek financial control or management responsibilities in enterprises in which it invests. It prefers to leave control and management in the hands of the local participants in each country. Where the capital requirements for a project cannot be met locally, Adela may own a majority interest. In such cases Adela may grant options to local shareholders and to management. Later, it may sell its investments, preferably to local investors or by public offers on the capital markets, when the business conditions of the enterprise concerned warrant it and when it can do so on favorable terms.

In conclusion, although the public issue of shares is not feasible or even advisable in all cases, it has in many instances positive results for the country of investment and also for the partners to the joint venture.[77]

THE EXTENSIVE EMPLOYMENT OF NATIONALS

Although all developing countries endeavor to promote the employment of nationals in partially or wholly foreign-owned companies, some of them are especially insistent on this point. Congo (Brazzaville) tries to ensure the "Congolization" of personnel by a number of means: in 1968, for example, a decree stated that administrative jobs in companies would have to be filled by Congolese. This concern of developing countries is understandable and sound, but these requests are reasonable only if adequate programs are established for the training of local personnel. In India, the creation of management institutes and the extensive studies undertaken by the National Commission on Labour have played a useful role in this respect.

Almost all executives from foreign corporations pursue a policy of extensive employment of nationals (whether in wholly-owned subsidiaries or in joint ventures). However, this policy is not always fully applied in developing countries with regard to senior management posts because of insufficient determination or actual impossibility. Large multinational groups are usually more systematic than smaller

---

77. The desirability of such public issues of shares was underlined in the report that the Commission on International Development prepared for the World Bank. See L. B. Pearson, *Partners in Development,* London, Pall Mall Press, pp. 112–13 (1969).

foreign corporations in the application of this policy, because they tend to develop an "internationalization" of their staff that is intended to be consistent with corporate loyalty. A senior executive from the Italian firm Olivetti thus expressed the hope that in the near future, more foreign executives might work in the company's Italian headquarters.

The extensive employment of nationals is advantageous to the foreign investor for both economic and psychological reasons. As many foreign corporations suffer from a relative shortage of management personnel, they are only too pleased when they can avoid sending executives abroad on a permanent basis. Moreover, even a wholly foreign-owned or foreign-controlled enterprise is sometimes regarded as national when management and personnel are essentially local. Comalco Industries Pty. Ltd. is the largest Australian integrated aluminum producer (bauxite, alumina, primary aluminum, and aluminum fabricated products). It is a 50-50 joint venture between the U.S. firm, Kaiser Aluminum & Chemical Corporation, and Conzinc Riotinto of Australia Ltd., which is an 85 percent-owned subsidiary of the British Rio Tinto-Zinc Corporation Ltd. The role and proportion of Australian nationals in Comalco's management are predominant; notably, the senior executives and the general manager are Australians. Because of this, Comalco is largely regarded as an Australian company, even though it is almost wholly foreign-owned. This local identity of Comalco is not unimportant in a country where public opinion and the press tend to criticize the considerable weight of foreign economic interests in the national economy.[78]

78. According to an article by E. Shirley in _Fortune,_ April 1969, pp. 59 and 62, Prime Minister Gorton expressed concern about the small Australian share (less than 1 percent) in Queensland Alumina Ltd., which is, as has already been mentioned, a joint venture between Kaiser Aluminum & Chemical Corporation, Alcan Aluminium Ltd., Compagnie Pechiney, and Conzinc Rinotinto of Australia Ltd. See _supra,_ pp. 395–96 and 400. To a large extent, QAL is now operated and staffed by Australians also. However, because of the nature of its business, it is unlikely to be accepted as Australian in the way that Comalco is. Public opinion in Australia is especially sensitive to the possibility of foreign domination in the extraction of natural resources and in primary processing: whereas Comalco is an integrated aluminum producer, QAL deals with the transformation of bauxite into alumina. The general question has therefore caused QAL to redouble its public relations effort to show the benefits that the project has brought to Australia. See also the Australian reaction to the General Motors Holden venture, Friedmann and Kalmanoff, _op. cit. supra_ note 3, at p. 134.

As a result of such experiences, the extensive employment of nationals at all levels is often considered a more effective way to promote a local identity for the joint venture than the renunciation of majority control by foreign interests. This sensible policy, however, should not be used as an excuse for a rigid attitude toward the degree of local participation. It should also be remembered that this policy has often to be applied in a gradual manner. Finally, the continual presence of a few foreign executives and the fruitful cooperation at management level in most cases seem necessary in order to transform the joint venture into a true partnership.

THE CHOICE OF THE PARTNER

Personal elements are usually important not only at the time of the formation of the joint venture, but also during the entire existence of the enterprise. Coromandel Fertilizers Ltd. is an excellent case in point. In 1965–1966, the two U.S. companies, Chevron and International Minerals and Chemical Corporation on the one hand, and the Indian company, Parry's, on the other, disagreed on the question of product distribution. By their persistent efforts the executives from the three companies succeeded in finding a solution to a conflict that could have endangered the joint venture.

Naturally, the capacity of persons to get along together is important not only at board level, but also at all operating levels. In the initial period of Atic Industries Ltd., British technicians from Imperial Chemical Industries Ltd. (ICI) and Indian personnel had some difficulty in working and getting along together. After some of the British technicians had been replaced, the relationships between local and foreign personnel improved noticeably, and they have remained on good terms ever since. It should be noted that ICI's general experience of labor relations in India has been excellent. The difficulties that affected the initial operation of Atic Industries Ltd. are not representative of ICI's experience and record in India.

At first, it would seem that the basic choice facing the foreign investor is between a public and a private local partner. A large majority of foreign corporations still have a marked preference for private local partners. For example, in Unilever's experience, private interests can generally be expected to take a more business-like view of the enterprise than state or para-state corporations. Moreover, in case of disagreement, a partnership with other corporations can be dissolved and new partners can be sought, whereas the unwinding of a business partnership with a government would have obvious complications.

In actual fact, the experience of Unilever and of its large subsidiary, the United Africa Company, as well as that of many other foreign corporations, shows that there is often no choice but to associate with a government or a government corporation. Sometimes the foreign investor is unable to find a private partner with adequate financial resources. Moreover, the government of a developing country tends to assume a far-reaching role in all sectors of the country's economic life. In addition, as far as natural resources are concerned, the governments of many developing countries find that joint ventures are an efficient means of asserting their permanent sovereignty over their resources as well as of taking an active and ever-increasing part in their exploitation.

One of the main difficulties in the choice of partner is that, because the political, economic and social situation of the host country may evolve quite rapidly in unforeseen directions, the right partner today is not necessarily going to represent a judicious choice tomorrow. Whatever his own preferences and wishes, the foreign investor seeking the formation of a joint venture in a Latin American country has often no choice but to associate with the local ruling and wealthy oligarchy. He cannot be sure, however, that the slowly growing middle class will not assume a prominent role in a few years from now, which may result in the social effacement or even the flight abroad of his partner. Although any forecast as to the internal evolution of a developing country is to some extent hazardous, no multinational group can completely ignore this kind of prospective enquiry. For foreign senior executives, the choice of partner often entails a difficult debate on the short-term interests and the long-term goals of the multinational corporation, as viewed against the background of developing countries' evolution.

The judicious introduction of a local investor to a foreign investor has been at the origin of some well-known successful joint ventures. Mr. George Woods, the former president of the World Bank, had been a personal friend of the Birlas and a financial advisor for Kaiser.[79] Thinking that an association between the Indian concern and the U.S. firm could be fruitful, he introduced Mr. Edgar Kaiser to

79. As regards the views of G. Woods on economic development, see: *Finance for Developing Countries: A Time for Decision*, New York, Columbia University, 18 pp. (1967).

the Birla family. In 1958–1959, the formation of Hindalco was the result of the negotiations conducted at top level. Although the Birlas did not have any previous experience in the aluminum industry, the enterprise is very successful. A highly-placed government official cited it as an example of successful Indian-foreign cooperation. Conversely, the unhappy partnership of certain local investors with certain foreign investors has provoked the most striking failures of joint ventures. In India, for example, there have been a few cases in which the local partner's lack of industrial background and/or the foreign partner's infringements on professional ethics, have led to the complete collapse of the joint venture.

When all partners have a good reputation and are able to cooperate smoothly, voting control does not need to be more than a means of last resort. In such a situation, decisions should naturally arise from an objective consideration of the facts and open discussion between the partners. Whereas decisions made in opposition to a minority partner through the exercise of voting power may often prove to be Pyrrhic victories, in the long run decisions reached by discussion and compromise are more likely to lead to the success of a joint venture.

DIVERSITY AND COMPLEXITY OF
LEGAL AND FINANCIAL STRUCTURES

An increasing number of joint ventures, especially in the extraction of natural resources, require considerable investments and the participation of several partners. In such cases, the legal and financial structure of the joint venture is sometimes quite complex, as it is drawn up so as to fit in with the wishes and needs of the various partners, whether public or private, foreign or local.

A combination of two equity joint ventures was adopted for the exploitation of the Boké bauxite mine in Guinea. The Compagnie des Bauxites de Guinée is an equity joint venture between the Guinean Government (49 percent) and an international consortium, Halco (Mining) Inc. (51 percent). Halco is itself an operating joint venture between several foreign corporations.[80]

The combination of a contractual joint venture with a nonprofit,

80. Halco's shareholders are: Alcan Aluminium Ltd. of Canada (27 percent); Aluminum Company of America (27 percent); Harvey Aluminum Inc. (20 percent); Pechiney-Ugine-Kuhlmann (10 percent); Vereinigte Aluminiumwerke A.G. (10 percent); Montecatini-Edison (6 percent).

equity joint venture was chosen as the structure best fitted for the exploitation of oil in District No. 1 of the Persian Gulf in Iran. The Agreement of January 17, 1965,[81] created a "joint structure" between two equal parties (Nioc on the one hand, Agip, Phillips, and the Oil and Natural Gas Commission of India on the other). The partners also formed Iminoco, a nonprofit, operating joint stock company that is purely instrumental and subordinate to the contractual joint venture.

The combination of a contractual joint venture with a profit-seeking, equity joint venture was chosen as the most convenient structure for the exploitation of the Nimba iron ore mine in Liberia. The contractual joint venture between Lamco and Bethlehem Steel is the titular owner of the mining concession. Lamco itself is a 50-50 equity joint venture between the government and foreign interests (notably the Swedish company, Grängesberg, which acts as manager for all operations). The power and influence of this equity joint venture far exceed those of a mere nonprofit operating company such as Iminoco.

Policy goals and local requirements determine in each case the general structure and different modalities of the joint venture, which is a flexible device. They also determine in each case whether the equity or the contractual joint venture (or a combination of both) is to be chosen as the best way to perform the joint undertaking.

The Problem of Control in Contractual Joint Ventures

THE PROLIFERATION OF CONTRACTUAL JOINT VENTURES

In recent years, contractual joint ventures (a term used here in its broad meaning, that is, covering various kinds of nonequity joint ventures) have been resorted to with increasing frequency in international business transactions generally and, more specifically, in industrial cooperation with developing countries. Technical agreements, engineering and construction jobs, turn-key contracts, service contracts, and similar forms of collaboration have proliferated nearly all over the world.[82] Business lawyers and economists have devel-

81. See *supra,* pp. 39–51, 376–77.
82. Ph. Kahn, "Problèmes juridiques de l'investissement dans les pays de l'ancienne Afrique française," *Journal du Droit International (Clunet),* p. 349 (1965): "Ce type de rapport constitue vraisemblablement la formule de l'avenir," (this type of relation is likely to constitute the formula of the future).

oped diverse forms of cooperation, which have not until now been the object of comprehensive theoretical study. The legal construct of the "contractual joint venture" or of the "engineering contract" still remains to be worked out.[83]

The determined assertion by one developing country after another of its permanent sovereignty over its natural resources, and its fear of foreign economic domination, have strongly stimulated the formation of contractual joint ventures. In this perspective, contractual relations are sometimes regarded by the governments of developing countries as the proper substitute for ownership relations.[84]

After the Government of Congo (Kinshasa) had nationalized the Union Minière du Haut-Katanga (a large subsidiary of the sizeable Société Générale de Belgique) and its properties, a technical cooperation agreement was concluded in 1967 between a government corporation and another subsidiary of the Société Générale de Belgique.[85]

In a more gradual way, oil-producing countries are tending to substitute the service contract formula for the previous concession relationship. In the Agreement of March 3, 1969, signed between Nioc and five Western European firms for the exploration and exploitation of oil in South Iran (near the Persian Gulf), no oil conces-

83. Lawyers and economists, however, have discussed this problem in conferences or special reports. See L. Kopelmanas, *Rapport sur les questions de responsabilité,* Paris, Ecole pratique des hautes études, VIth Section, mimeo., 22 pp. (1964); C. D. Marmol and L. Dabin, "L'apport des juristes à la solution des problèmes de la gestion des affaires," Liège, *Annales de la Faculté de Droit,* p. 89 (1964); C. Schmitthoff (ed.), *The Sources of the Law of International Trade,* London, Stevens, p. 281 (1964). See a more comprehensive analysis in a collective book, *Contrats d'engineering,* Commission droit et vie des affaires, Liège, Faculté de Droit de l'Université de Liège, 224 pp. (1964).

84. In the same perspective, purely contractual relations entail specific advantages, but specific risks as well, for the foreign investor. See Ph. Kahn, *op. cit. supra* note 82. "This formula eliminates the direct ownership of the foreigner on the enterprise and, therefore, avoids the accusation of colonialism, as well as the risk of nationalization. However, the risk of nonpayment does exist, either because of the debtor's insolvence, or for reasons that are not relevant to the debtor (exchange control, political troubles)." (author's translation).

85. Convention of Technical Cooperation, with Protocol, of February 15, 1967, between the Générale Congolaise des Minerais (Gécomin) and the Société Générale des Minerais S.A., Brussels, (S.G.M.). See the text of the Convention in *International Legal Materials,* Washington, D.C., A.S.I.L., pp. 909–14 (1967). See also R. Kovar, "La congolisation de l'Union Minière du Haut-Katanga," *Annuaire Français de Droit International,* pp. 742–81 (1967).

sion was granted to the foreign companies, which operate as mere contractors for Nioc.[86]

For different reasons, investors from Western countries have formed a number of contractual joint ventures in certain Eastern European countries,[87] notably in Yugoslavia which, for the past two decades, has pursued an economic philosophy of its own.[88] The governments of these countries have not yet permitted the formation of equity joint ventures, which have been regarded as incompatible with the socialist organization of the economy and as dangerous for national independence. It is to be hoped that in the future, foreign investors and Eastern European governments may also find a mutually acceptable way of forming equity joint ventures.

ADVANTAGES AND DISADVANTAGES OF CONTRACTUAL JOINT VENTURES

Although many foreign investors have a marked preference for the equity joint venture, an increasing number among them now seem prepared to consider the advantages of the contractual joint venture. The latter is usually a more flexible form of cooperation than the former. Almost any rule can be adopted in the contract at the parties' will, the ties with the local legal system being looser. For example, the partners to a contractual joint venture do not need to comply with corporate formalities relating to profit sharing. They benefit immediately from the result of productive and commercial operations. An Agip executive emphasized that in the experience of his company, this flexibility has proved to be of great value.

As has been mentioned above, "contractual joint venture" may be used as a broad term covering various forms of cooperation between

86. For details of the contract, see *supra,* pp. 52–53. The foreign firms are: France's ERAP, Italy's Agip, Spain's Espanoil, Belgium's Petrofina, and Austria's OMW.

87. See *Industrial Cooperation,* a document, already cited *supra,* note 16, of the Economic Commission for Europe, E/ECE/730 (1969), which deals with industrial cooperation between Western investors and Eastern European enterprises. See also D. V. Petroni, "Doing Business in Eastern European Countries," in *Private Investors Abroad: Structures and Safeguards,* New York, Matthew Bender, pp. 261–327 (1966); I. Shapiro, "Obstacles to Trade with, and Investment in the Soviet Union and Eastern Europe," in *Problems and Solutions in International Business in 1969,* New York, Matthew Bender, pp. 173–91 (1969).

88. W. G. Friedmann and L. Mates, *op. cit. supra* note 15, pp. 20–24 and 39–40. See also *supra,* pp. 372–73.

local and foreign entrepreneurs. Some foreign companies (notably, some Italian engineering and construction firms) have experienced a specific form of joint international business venture that in several respects is analogous to the joint venture that U.S. jurisprudence [89] gradually developed as a *sui generis* type of association.[90] In this kind of joint international business venture, there is no corporation or equity capital. Each expense is divided between the joint venturers according to a fixed percentage. As a rule, a local corporation (often, a governmental agency) is the sponsor of the project. The sponsor has sole responsibility towards third parties. Once these obligations are executed, the sponsor can turn back to his partner for the reimbursement of the share of expenses corresponding to the fixed percentage assumed by this partner. The absence of any heavy corporate organization certainly provides the valuable flexibility that has been described above. Moreover, because the sponsor tends to be a government agency, these foreign companies hope that the government of the developing country will be less subject to the fear of foreign economic domination, and therefore, less tempted to take measures adversely affecting foreign interests.

Nevertheless, the contractual form of partnership may raise some difficult problems of cooperation between foreign interests and developing countries.[91] An illustration is the experiment of Litton Indus-

89. The definition of the joint venture in this specific meaning may be found in a number of law cases, for instance in *Tompkins v. Commissioner of Internal Revenue,* 97 F. 2d 396, 398–99 (4th Cir. 1938): "It is a special combination of two or more persons, where, in some specific venture, a profit is jointly sought without any actual partnership or corporate designation."

90. For an articulate analysis of the joint venture in this strict sense, see W. H. E. Jaeger, "Joint Ventures: Origin, Nature and Development," *American University Law Review,* pp. 1–23 (1960); "Joint Ventures: Membership, Types and Termination," *American University Law Review,* pp. 111–29 (1960); "Joint Ventures: Recent Developments," *Washburn Law Journal,* pp. 9–44 (1964). The analogous type of joint venture that is used in international business transactions, has been analyzed by A. G. Raymond, "Tax Aspects of Joint Ventures and Oil Operations in Latin America," *Institute on Private Investments Abroad,* New York, Matthew Bender, pp. 77–78 (1962). Raymond observes that the joint international business venture in this sense is contractual in character.

91. Litton Industries, a U.S. company, was created in 1954. It has been one of the fastest-growing and most rapidly diversifying U.S. corporations. In 1968, Litton was a multinational corporation with more than 100,000 employees in 26 countries, including the United States. An excellent management, a determination to engage in new and highly technological fields, and an auda-

tries in its venture with the Greek Government. On May 15, 1967, Litton signed an agreement with the Greek Government.[92] The agreement designated Litton as a general promoter, supervisor, and coordinator for the economic development of Crete and of Western Peloponnesus. The overall aim of the program was to improve living standards and increase per capita income in the two regions. With the concurrence and assistance of the government, Litton was to define the problems and opportunities, set goals, weigh various alternative approaches, establish coordinated performance, and implement the plans. In Crete, the company's plan provided for increased tourism, the irrigation of thousands of acres of farmland, and the development of natural resources and industry in order to increase employment. In the Western Peloponnesus, provision was made for new hotel facilities, new airports, industrial centers, and harbors. The initial phase of the program was to cover three and a half years, during which Litton would implement projects for a total value of $240 million to be raised from international investment sources. The company also employed outside contractors for the implementation of specific projects. It was probably the first time that a multinational corporation attempted to use systems analysis in planning the economic development of two large areas in a developing country.

In October 1969, the Greek Government cancelled the contract.[93] After two years of efforts, Litton had made investment proposals for only $50.7 million. Out of that amount, only $11.5 million had been approved by the Greek Government. It seems that the reasons for the failure have been several. Whenever Litton started to plan the construction of a plant in a certain area, the proposal immediately provoked an active speculation on the land of that area. Moreover, a number of local industrialists did not consider favorably the coming of the "foreign invaders." Furthermore, the U.S. company experienced some difficulties in the relations with local labor and with the

cious policy of mergers and take-overs appear to be the main reasons for this rapid growth.

92. Greece-Litton Industries: Agreement for the Development of Crete and the Western Pelopponesus. See the text in *International Legal Materials,* Washington D.C., A.S.I.L., pp. 18–30 (1969). The history of the negotiations is related in a Preliminary Note (p. 18), which was prepared by A. A. Fatouros, Professor of Law, Indiana University.

93. *The New York Times,* October 15, 1969, p. 61. "End of the Affair," *The Economist,* October 18, 1969, pp. 75 and 78.

administration. Abroad, because of the political situation in Greece the Litton project was not always considered favorably.

The failure of the Litton experiment in Greece does not mean that a similar project would be unsuccessful in other countries. The basic plan of the U.S. company was imaginative. In the future, it will be interesting to see if the government of a developing country and a multinational corporation can succeed in participating jointly in the economic development of a whole geographical area.

CONTROL AND COORDINATION IN CONTRACTUAL JOINT VENTURES

The corporate form of doing business provides an adequate frame for an integrated managerial organization. One can therefore speculate whether (compared to equity joint ventures) contractual joint ventures or analogous forms of association are not hampered in their activities by the difficulty of reconciling a flexible legal structure with a strong and efficient management. As a contractual joint venture has neither a general assembly of shareholders nor a board of directors, the promoter or the main partner is unable to impose a decision by exercising its voting power. In the absence of formal control, it is important to find out whether cooperation between the partners may be ensured by other means.

Some foreign engineering and construction firms recognize that, in their experience, it has been somewhat difficult to establish satisfactory cooperation in a contractual joint venture. In the absence of an autonomous corporate entity and of a formal managerial organization, the partners feel sometimes hampered from taking the swift initiatives required by the evolution of the economic and political situation. Moreover, a complex system of contracting and subcontracting may cause serious difficulties in the execution of contractual obligations and raise awkward problems of contractual responsibility. Furthermore, foreign experts and technicians are sometimes tempted, especially in engineering and turn-key contracts, to hasten their work unduly in order to start a new task elsewhere as quickly as possible.[94] It should be noted, however, that the difficulties experienced in con-

94. Because of this, certain forms of contractual joint ventures are viewed unfavorably in some developing countries. In fact, criticisms seem to be directed rather against certain corporations or persons than against definite types of contractual cooperation.

tractual joint ventures have, in a number of cases, resulted from professional inability or unethical conduct.

Quite to the contrary, other foreign investors (notably in the oil industry) stress the fact that, in their experience, cooperation between partners has not been any more difficult to achieve in contractual joint ventures than in equity joint ventures. In the basic agreement, the partners have every latitude to provide one or several executives with extensive powers and with the means of using these powers. The senior executive in the contractual joint venture may thus be granted powers as extensive as those of a managing director in an equity joint venture. Moreover, the senior executive has to be provided with the financial means of applying these powers. In principle, the management in a contractual joint venture cannot exceed the precise budgetary limits that have been agreed to by the partners in any given year. In practice, however, the budget may be planned so as to leave a sufficient margin of financial freedom to the senior executive. Moreover, the rules of the agency contract would, generally speaking, seem applicable in cases of emergency. It can therefore be concluded that the flexibility inherent in a contractual joint venture is far from being necessarily an obstacle to the cooperation between the partners and to the efficiency of management.

It would be wrong to assume a general superiority of the contractual joint venture over the equity joint venture. The reverse would be an equally improper generalization. Nevertheless, developing countries have not forgotten the excesses of the colonial period and they are constantly on guard against a form of neo-colonialism that would take the form of domineering foreign ownership in national enterprises. Therefore, it is likely that they will favor increasingly the development of cooperation with foreign investors based merely on contractual obligations.

GENERAL BIBLIOGRAPHY ON JOINT VENTURES

A. Documents and Sources of Information

ANTITRUST PROBLEMS

Attorney General's National Committee to Study the Antitrust Laws, Washington, D.C., U.S. Government Printing Office, 393 pp., esp. pp. 1–114 (1955).

International Aspects of Antitrust, Hearings before the Subcommittee on Antitrust and Monopoly of the Committee on the Judiciary, U.S. Senate, 89th Congress, 2nd Session, Part 2, Appendix, pp. 647–1356, esp. pp. 1035–1157 and 1255–1307 (1967).

CANADA

Foreign Ownership and the Structure of Canadian Industry, Task Force on the Structure of Canadian Industry, Ottawa, Privy Council Office, 427 pp. (1968).

CAPITAL NEEDS OF DEVELOPING COUNTRIES

Trade Prospects and Capital Needs of Developing Countries, UNCTAD, New York, United Nations, 614 pp., esp. pp. 34–48 (1968).

CHILE

"Decree of the Ministry of Economy, Development and Reconstruction (March 20, 1967), authorizing the Sociedad Minera El Teniente S.A. to invest U.S. dollars 230.241.000 in the El Teniente mine and complementary installations," *International Legal Materials,* Washington D.C., American Society of International Law, (hereafter cited as *I.L.M.*), pp. 1151–61 (1967).

"President's Statement on Negotiations for Government Acquisition of Anaconda Company Properties (June 26, 1969)," *I.L.M.,* pp. 1073–78 (1969).

CONGO (KINSHASA)

"Convention of Technical Cooperation, with Protocol, of February 15, 1967, between the Générale Congolaise des Minerais (Gécomin) and the Société Générale des Minerais S.A., Brussels (S.G.M.)," *I.L.M.*, pp. 909–14 (1967).

EASTERN EUROPEAN COUNTRIES

Industrial Cooperation (Between Western Investors and Eastern European Enterprises), Geneva, Economic Commission for Europe, Doc. E/E.C.C./730, Add. 1, 16 pp. (1969).

ECONOMIC INTEGRATION

Trade Expansion and Economic Integration Among Developing Countries, UNCTAD, New York, United Nations, 106 pp., esp. §§ 54–58 (1967).

FOREIGN INVESTMENT

Foreign Investment in Developing Countries, Department of Economic and Social Affairs, New York, United Nations, 61 pp., esp. §§ 52–68, (1968).

Multilateral Investment Insurance: A Staff Report, Washington, D.C., International Bank for Reconstruction and Development, 51 pp. (1962).

"Report of the Executive Directors of the I.B.R.D. and Convention on the Settlement of Investment Disputes Between States and Nationals of Other States," *I.L.M.*, pp. 524–44 (1965).

FOREIGN INTERESTS, POLICY AS REGARDS OWNERSHIP BY

"Key Investment Factors in Foreign Operations," in W.S. Surrey and C. Shaw, *A Lawyer's Guide to International Business Transactions*, Philadelphia, American Law Institute and American Bar Association, pp. 288–98 (1963).

GREECE

"Greece–Litton Industries: Agreement for the Development of Crete and the Western Pelopponesus," with a Preliminary Note (p. 18) prepared by A.A. Fatouros, *I.L.M.*, pp. 18–30 (1969).

INDIA

Approach to the Fourth Five Year Plan, Planning Commission of the Government of India, Publications Division, 38 pp. (1968).

Foreign Investment and Collaboration: Guidelines, Indian Government statements, New Delhi, Indian Investment Centre, 26 pp. (1968).

INDONESIA

"Foreign Investment Law of December 24, 1966," *I.L.M.*, pp. 203–25 (1967):

Law Concerning Investment of Foreign Capital (p. 203);

Executive Directives for the Policy on Foreign Capital (p. 215);

Decree Returning Foreign Enterprises to Former Owners (p. 221);

Decree Ending Governmental Control of Foreign Oil Companies (p. 223).

INTERCOLLEGIATE CASE CLEARING HOUSE

Business schools in the United States and abroad produce a considerable amount of case material, which is centralized in the Harvard Business School. Copies of the cases dealing with joint ventures problems may be obtained from the I.C.C.H. (Harvard University, Graduate School of Business Administration, Soldiers Field Post Office, Boston, Massachussets 02163).

INTERNATIONAL FLOW OF LONG-TERM CAPITAL

The External Financing of Economic Development: International Flow of Long-term Capital and Official Donations, 1963–1967, Department of Economic and Social Affairs, New York, United Nations, 126 pp., esp. §§ 223–24 (1969).

INVESTMENT LAWS

Foreign Investment Laws and Regulations of the Countries of Asia and the Far East, Economic Commission for Asia and the Far East (E.C.A.F.E.), New York, United Nations, 88 pp. (1951).

Investment Laws and Regulations in Africa, Economic Commission for Africa (E.C.A.), New York, United Nations, 79 pp. (1965).

A number of new investment laws are published in the *International Legal Materials.*

IRAN

"Agreement Between the National Iranian Oil Company (N.I.O.C.) and the Assienda Generale Italiana Petroli (A.G.I.P.) of August 3, 1957," and "Iranian Petroleum Law of July 31, 1957," See the text of these documents in *Middle East, Basic Oil Laws and Concession Contracts,* New York, Petroleum Legislation, Vol. I (1959).

MULTINATIONAL CORPORATIONS AND DEVELOPING COUNTRIES

The International Corporation, XXIInd Congress of the International Chamber of Commerce (ICC) (Istanbul, May 31–June 7, 1969), Paris, ICC, 202 pp., esp. pp. 29–47 and 119–40 (1969).

NATURAL RESOURCES, PERMANENT SOVEREIGNTY OVER

I. The Status of Permanent Sovereignty over Natural Wealth and Resources; Study by the Secretariat. II. Report of the Commission on Permanent Sovereignty over Natural Resources, New York, United Nations, 245 pp. (1962).

Natural Resources—Restrictions, Regulations, Agreements; Oil, Land, Minerals, New York, U.N. International Review Service, 98 pp. (1964).

OVERSEAS BUSINESS REPORTS

Overseas Business Reports is a publication of the U.S. Department of Commerce, Bureau of International Commerce, Washington D.C., published irregularly. Frequently contains information on doing business in foreign countries generally, and on joint international business ventures more specifically.

PANAGRA CASE

United States v. Pan American World Airways Inc., 193 F. Supp. 18 (S.D.N.Y. 1961). Decision reversed in *Pan American World Airways Inc. v. United States,* 371 U.S. 196 (1963).

PERU

"International Telephone and Telegraph Corporation—Peru: Agreement on the Basic Conditions for Nationalizing the Peruvian Telephone Company," *I.L.M.,* pp. 80–98 (1970). "Peru: Decree-Law Approving the Agreement with International Telephone and Telegraph Corporation on the Nationalization of the Peruvian Telephone Company," *I.L.M.,* pp. 186–91 (1970).

PETROLEUM EXPORTING COUNTRIES, ORGANIZATION OF THE

"Declaratory Statement of Petroleum Policy in Member Countries," OPEC Sixteenth Conference (Vienna, June 24–25, 1968), *I.L.M.,* pp. 1183–86 (1968).

THE PHILIPPINES

Philippines policy towards foreign investment:

"Administrative Order No. 21 setting forth the Philippines policy on domestic and foreign investments, issued September 6, 1966," *I.L.M.,* pp. 1090–93 (1966).

"Philippines: Investment incentives and guarantees act, approved September 16, 1967," *I.L.M.,* pp. 1174–93 (1967).

"The Philippines and United States: Report on the Philippines–U.S. Economic Relations (principles of agreement to replace Laurel-Langley Trade Agreement)", *I.L.M.,* pp. 87–104 (1968).

SAUDI ARABIA
"Accord entre l'Ente Nazionali Idrocarburi (E.N.I.) et l'Arabie Séoudite: un nouvel accroc au régime traditionnel des concessions," 1099 *Revue pétrolière,* p. 39 (1968).

SURVEY OF CURRENT BUSINESS
Survey of Current Business is a monthly periodical, issued in Washington D.C. by the U.S. Department of Commerce, Office of Business Economics. Contains statistics and comments on U.S. private investments abroad.

TRANSFER OF TECHNOLOGY
The Role of Patents in the Transfer of Technology to Developing Countries; Report of the Secretary General, Department of Economic and Social Affairs, New York, United Nations, 95 pp. (1964).

UNITED NATIONS AMSTERDAM PANEL
"Panel on Foreign Investment in Developing Countries," Amsterdam Meeting of February 16–20, 1969, Department of Economic and Social Affairs, New York, United Nations, 57 pp. (1969).

UNITED STATES PRIVATE INVESTMENTS
Involvement of U.S. Private Enterprise in Developing Countries, U.S. Congress, House of Representatives, Committee on Foreign Affairs, Washington D.C., Government Printing Office, 364 pp. (1968).

B. *Books*

Aitken, T., *A Foreign Policy for American Business,* New York, Harper and Bros., 159 pp., esp. pp. 72–74, 101, 105–106, 133, and 139 (1962).

Amadio, M., *Le contentieux international de l'investissement privé et la Convention de la Banque Mondiale du 18 mars 1965,* Paris, L.G.D.J., 276 pp., esp. pp. 110–17 (1967).

Ballantine, H.W., *Ballantine on Corporations,* Chicago, Callaghan, 992 pp., esp. pp. 775–76 (1946).

Ballon, R.J., *Joint Ventures and Japan,* Tokyo, Sophia University, 138 pp. (1967).

Baranson, J., *Manufacturing Problems in India: the Cummins Diesel Experience,* Syracuse, Syracuse University Press, 146 pp. (1967).

Baranson J., *Automotive Industries in Developing Countries,* I.B.R.D., Baltimore, John Hopkins Press, 106 pp. (1969).

Barlow, E.R., *Management of Foreign Manufacturing Subsidiaries*, Graduate School of Business Administration, Boston, Harvard University, 223 pp., esp. pp. 114–47 (1953).

Barlow, E.R., and I.T. Wender, *Foreign Investment and Taxation*, Englewood Cliffs, N.J., Prentice-Hall, 481 pp., esp. pp. 204–205 (1955).

Bastid, S., et. al., *La personnalité morale et ses limites*, Paris, L.G.D.J., 286 pp., esp. pp. 159–269 (1960).

Berle, A.A., *Latin America—Diplomacy and Reality*, New York, Harper and Row, 144 pp., esp. pp. 31–48 (1962).

Bivens, K.K., and E.B. Lovell, *Joint Ventures with Foreign Partners*, New York, National Industrial Conference Board, 92 pp. (1966).

Brandeburg, F., *The Development of Latin-American Private Enterprise*, Washington D.C., National Planning Association, 136 pp., esp. pp. 50–100 (1964).

Brewster, K., *Antitrust and American Business Abroad*, New York, McGraw-Hill, 509 pp., esp. pp. 86 and 200–25 (1958).

Bugnion, J. R., *La politique d'investissement et de financement des entreprises internationales: un essai sur la théorie du budget de capital*, Geneva, Médecine et Hygiène, 314 pp., esp. pp. 155–65 and 209–26 (1967).

Cattan, H., *The Evolution of Oil Concessions in the Middle East and North Africa*, Dobbs Ferry, N.Y., Oceana Publications, 173 pp. (1967).

Centre de recherche sur le droit des marchés et des investissements internationaux de Dijon, *Investissements étrangers et arbitrage entre états et personnes privées. La Convention du 18 mars 1965*, Paris, Pédone, 196 pp., esp. pp. 20–22 and 43–47 (1969).

Clarke, W.M., *Private Enterprise in Developing Countries*, Oxford, Pergamon Press, 59 pp. (1966).

Commission droit et vie des affaires de Liège, *Contrats d'engineering*, Liège, Faculté de Droit de l'Université de Liège, 224 pp. (1964).

Elbialy, F., *La Société Financière Internationale*, Geneva, Droz, 323 pp., esp. pp. 266–307 (1963).

El-Sayed, M., *L'organisation des pays exportateurs de pétrole*, Geneva, Imprimerie Nationale, 219 pp., esp. pp. 60–68 (1967).

Falcon, W.D., *Financing International Operations: a Guide to Sources and Methods*, New York, American Management Association, 192 pp., esp. pp. 149–52 (1965).

Fatouros, A.A., *Government Guarantees to Foreign Investors*, New York, Columbia University Press, 411 pp., esp. 1–59, 339–58 (1962).

Fayerweather, J., *Management of International Operations: Text and Cases*, New York, McGraw-Hill, 604 pp. (see Index: Capital) (1960).

Fenn. D.H., *Management Guide to Overseas Operations*, New York, McGraw-Hill, 308 pp., esp. pp. 93–116 (1957).

Friedmann, W. G., *The Changing Structure of International Law*, London, Stevens, 410 pp., esp. pp. 27–29 and 150 (1964).

Friedmann, W.G., and G. Kalmanoff, *Joint International Business Ventures*, New York, Columbia University Press, 558 pp. (1961).

Friedmann, W.G., and L. Mates, *Joint Business Ventures of Yugoslav Enterprises and Foreign Firms*, Belgrade, Columbia University and the Institute of International Politics and Economy, 192 pp. (1968).

Friedmann, W.G., and R.C. Pugh, *Legal Aspects of Foreign Investment*, London, Stevens, 812 pp., esp. pp. 751–52, 760, and 772–83 (1959).

Fugate, W.L., *Foreign Commerce and the Antitrust Laws*, Boston, Little, Brown and Co., 384 pp., esp. pp. 235–41, and 276–78 (1958).

Fulbright, J.W., *The Arrogance of Power*, New York, Vintage Books, 264 pp., esp. pp. 209–10 (1966).

Graham, A., *Report on Prospects for Private Investment in India, with Particular Reference to Joint Collaboration Ventures*, London, Economic and Development Research Ltd., 42 pp. (1964).

Hilten, H.W. van, *Joint Ventures*, Deventer, Kluwer, 183 pp. (1968).

Hochepied, J.-P. de, *La protection diplomatique des sociétés et des actionnaires*, Paris, Pédone, 276 pp., esp. pp. 143–90 (1965).

Institut d'Etudes Bancaires et Financières, *Les banques de développement dans le monde*, Paris, Dunod, 2 vols., 504 pp. and 500 pp., (1965).

Islam, N., *Foreign Capital and Economic Development: Japan, India and Canada; Studies in Some Aspects of Absorption of Foreign Capital*, Rutland, Tuttle, 251 pp., esp. pp. 164–66 (1962).

Kidron, M., *Foreign Investments in India*, London, Oxford University Press, 368 pp., esp. pp. 258–96 (1965).

Kindleberger, C.P., *International Economics*, Homewood, Irwin, 686 pp., esp. pp. 404–25 (1963).

Kindleberger, C.P., *American Investment Abroad: Six Lectures on Direct Investment*, New Haven, Yale University Press, 225 pp., esp. pp. 145–78 (1969).

Kopelmanas, L., *Rapport sur les questions des responsabilités*, Paris, Ecole pratique des hautes études, VIth Section, mimeo, 22 pp. (1964).

Kuin, P., *La coopération internationale, clef du progrès économique*, Paris, Chambre de Commerce Internationale, 47 pp. (1965).

Kust, M.J., *Foreign Enterprise in India: Laws and Policies*, Chapel Hill, University of North Carolina Press, 498 pp., esp. pp. 63–74 and 141–55 (1964).

McLaughlin, R.U., *Foreign Investment and Development in Liberia*, New York, Praeger, 217 pp., esp. pp. 45–64 (1966).

Marmol, C.D., and L. Dabin, *L'apport des juristes à la solution des problèmes de la gestion des affaires*, Liège, Faculté de Droit de l'Université de Liège, 120 pp., esp. p. 89 (1963).

Mehta, G.L., *Development and Foreign Collaboration*, New Delhi, Indian Investment Centre, 22 pp. (1968).

Morgan, D.J., *British Private Investment in East Africa: Report of a Survey and a Conference*, London, Overseas Development Institute, 63 pp. (1965).

Mughraby, M.A., *Permanent Sovereignty over Natural Resources*, Beirut, The Middle East Research and Publishing Center, 233 pp. (1966).

Navadan, S., *Ways to Minimize Obstacles Confronting Joint Ventures in the Region: The Attitude of the Partners*, International Chamber of Commerce, Doc. No. 520-XIV/103, 5 pp. (1966).

Nwogugu, E.I., *The Legal Problems of Foreign Investment in Developing Countries*, Manchester, Manchester University Press, 320 pp., esp. pp. 1–6 and 11–12 (1965).

Pearson, L.B., *Partners in Development*, I.B.R.D., London, Pall Mall Press, 399 pp., esp. pp. 112–13 (1969).

Penrose, E.T., *The International Oil Industry in the Middle East*, Cairo, National Bank of Egypt, 35 pp. (1968).

Penrose, E.T., *The Large International Firm in Developing Countries: The International Petroleum Industry*, London, George Allen and Unwin, 311 pp., esp. pp. 211–16, 235, 288–92 (1968).

Pizer, S., and F. Cutler, *U.S. Business Investments in Foreign Countries*, Washington D.C., U.S. Department of Commerce, 147 pp. (1960).

Preiswerk, R., *La protection des investissements dans les traités bilatéraux*, Zurich, Ed. polygraphiques, 242 pp., esp. pp. 78–81 (1963).

Proehl, P.O., *Foreign Enterprise in Nigeria—Laws and Policies*, Chapel Hill, University of North Carolina Press, 250 pp., esp. pp. 170–73 (1965).

Ramaer, J.C., *International Joint Ventures in Developing Countries*, International Chamber of Commerce Commission on International Investment and Economic Development, Doc. III/174, 16 pp. (1968).

Ripert, G., *Traité élémentaire de droit commercial*, 5th edition by R. Roblot, Paris, L.G.D.J., 2 vols., 975 pp. and 791 pp., esp. Vol. 1, pp. 417–25 and 572–75 (1963–1964).

Schmidt, D., *Les droits de la minorité dans la société anonyme*, Paris, Sirey, 265 pp. (1970).

Schmitthoff, C.M., *The Sources of the Law of International Trade, with Special Reference to East-West Trade*, New York, Praeger, 292 pp., esp. p. 281 (1964).

Schwarzenberger, G., *Foreign Investments and International Law*, London, Stevens, 237 pp., esp. pp. 135–81 and 189 (1969).

Stikker, D.U., *The Role of Private Enterprise in Investment and Promotion of Exports in Developing Countries*, New York, United Nations, 112 pp., esp. §§83–90, 224–29, 241–43, 287–94 (1968).

Suckow, S., "Nigerian Law and Foreign Investment," Paris, Mouton, 225 pp., esp. pp. 136–41, and 200–202 (1966).

Surrey, W.S., and C. Shaw *A Lawyers Guide to International Business Transactions,* Philadelphia, A.L.I. and A.B.A., 1071 pp., esp. pp. 196–200, 387–616, 630, and 806–12 (1963).

Tomlinson, *The Joint Venture Process in International Business,* Cambridge, Mass. and London, The M.I.T. Press, 227 pp. (1970).

Tunc, A., R. Gendarme, et al., *Les aspects juridiques du développement économique,* Paris, Dalloz, 206 pp., esp. pp. 11–12, and 44–46 (1966).

Walinsky, L.J., *Economic Development in Burma, 1951–1960,* New York, The Twentieth Century Fund, 680 pp., esp. pp. 301, 315, 349–51, 496, and 514–15 (1962).

Wurfel, S.W., *Foreign Enterprise in Columbia: Laws and Policies,* Chapel Hill, University of North Carolina Press, 563 pp., esp. pp. 81–82 and 334–35 (1965).

C. Articles

Abi-Saab, G., "The Role of Law in the Process of Development, with Special Reference to the Transfer of Technology to Underdeveloped Countries," in C. Nader and A.B. Zahlan, *Science and Technology in Developing Countries,* Cambridge, Cambridge University Press, pp. 493–519 (1969).

Adkins, L.D., R.L. Gilpatric, and R.E. Abraham, "Corporate Joint Ventures in Operation," *Business Lawyer,* pp. 285–308 (1959).

Afterman, A.B., "Directors' Duties in Joint-Venture and Parent–Subsidiary Companies," *Australian Law Journal,* pp. 168–75 and 216–24 (1968).

Ahooja, K., "Development Legislation in Africa," *Journal of Development Studies,* pp. 297–322 (1966).

Alyea, E.D., "Subsidiary Corporations under the Civil and Common Law," *Harvard Law Review,* pp. 1227–37 (1953).

Angers, F.-A., "Les effets de l'entrée de la firme à capital extérieur sur la structure et le comportement de l'économie canadienne," in: *La politique industrielle de l'Europe intégrée et l'apport des capitaux extérieurs,* Paris, P.U.F., pp. 131–49 (1968).

Austin, E.T., "Protection of Private Property and Investments of Foreigners Abroad: Foreign Investment Laws of Newly Emerging Nations," *Howard Law Journal,* pp. 270–84 (1966).

Baade, H.W., "Permanent Sovereignty over Natural Wealth and Resources," in: R.S. Miller and R.J. Stanger, *Essays on Expropriation,* Columbus, Ohio State University, pp. 3–40 (1967).

Balog, N., "Legal Relations Concerning Foreign Investment in Yugoslav Economic Organizations," *New Yugoslav Law,* pp. 20–40 (1968).

Baranson, J., "Transfer of Technical Knowledge by International Corporations to Developing Countries," *American Economic Review*, pp. 259–267 (1966).

Barre, R., "L'indépendance à l'épreuve des réalités économiques," in J.-B. Duroselle et J. Meyriat, *Les nouveaux Etats dans les relations internationales*, Paris, Colin, pp. 195–235 (1962).

Behrman, J.N., "Foreign Associates and their Financing," in R.F. Mikesell, *U.S. Private and Government Investment Abroad*, Eugene, Oregon, University of Oregon, pp. 77–113 (1962).

Behrman, J.N., "Foreign Investment and the Transfer of Knowledge and Skills," in R.F. Mikesell, *U.S. Private and Government Investment Abroad*, Eugene, Oregon, University of Oregon, pp. 114–36 (1962).

Berlowitz, A.J., "Doing Business in Liberia," *Columbia Journal of Transnational Law*, pp. 258–72 (1967).

Berman, R.S., "Natural Resources: State Ownership and Control Based on Article 130 of the Revised (Ethiopian) Constitution," *Journal of Ethiopian Law*, pp. 551 *et seq.* (1966).

Bertin, G.Y., "Les rapports entre l'Etat national et l'entreprise étrangère," *Analyse et Prévision*, pp. 459–73 (1968).

Bindschedler-Robert, D., "La protection diplomatique des sociétés et des actionnaires," *Revue de la Société des Juristes Bernois*, pp. 141–89 (1964).

Bloch, H.S., "Financial Strategy for Developing Nations: Afterthoughts to the Amsterdam Panel," *Columbia Law Review*, pp. 797–806 (1969).

Blough, R., "Joint International Business Ventures in Less Developed Countries," in *Institute on Private Investments Abroad*, New York, Matthew Bender, pp. 513–26 (1960).

Bonin, B., "Observations sur les effets de l'entrée de la firme à capital extérieur sur la structure et le comportement de l'économie canadienne," in *La politique industrielle de l'Europe intégrée et l'apport des capitaux extérieurs*, Paris, P.U.F., pp. 150–59 (1968).

Bradshaw, C.J., "Joint Ventures in Japan," *Washington Law Review*, pp. 58–104 (1963).

Broches, A., "Le financement du développement économique: Aspects politiques, juridiques, et économiques," *Chronique de Politique Etrangère*, pp. 401–17 (1967).

Byé, M., "Vers l'association à la production et au développement mondial. Un exemple: les accords franco-algériens," in *Les investissements et le développement économique des pays du tiers monde*, Paris, Pédone, pp. 348–91 (1968).

Canizares, F. de Sola, "The Rights of Shareholders," *International and Comparative Law Quarterly*, pp. 564–78 (1953).

Cardinale, J.S., "Local Capital Participation v. the Wholly-owned Company. Legal Factors and Implications," in *Increasing Profits from Foreign Operations*, New York, International Management Association, pp. 108–17 (1957).

Carl, B.M., "Incentives for Private Investment in Brazil," *Columbia Journal of Transnational Law*, pp. 190–257 (1967).

Cassoni, G., "I contratti di concessione stipulati fra stati o enti pubblici statali e societa' commerciali straniere," *Diritto Internazionale*, pp. 235–61 (1965).

Cattan, H., "Present Trends in Middle Eastern Oil Concessions and Agreements," in *Problems and Solutions in International Business 1969*, New York, Matthew Bender, pp. 135–73 (1969).

Chi-Ming Hou, "The Oppression Argument on Foreign Investment in China, 1895–1937," *Journal of Asian Studies*, pp. 435–48 (1961).

Cohen, M., "Mergers and Joint Ventures: a Canadian-American Perspective and Comparison," A.B.A., *Antitrust Law Journal*, pp. 188–214 (1966).

Collado, E.G., "Economic Development through Private Enterprise," *Foreign Affairs*, pp. 708–20 (1963).

Coret, A., "Les institutions financières internationales à vocation universelle et les investissements en Afrique," *Pénant* (No. 690) pp. 45–56 (1962).

Corthésy, J.-C., "Certains aspects économiques et industriels de l'Amérique latine," *Revue économique et sociale*, (special issue) pp. 132–45, esp. pp. 141–42, Feb. (1962).

Cutler, L.N., "Joint Ventures with Foreign Business Associates, Investors and Governments," in *Institute on Private Investments Abroad*, New York, Matthew Bender, pp. 261–84 (1959).

Delaume, G., "La convention pour le règlement des différends relatifs aux investissements entre états et ressortissants d'autres états," *Journal du Droit International (Clunet)*, pp. 26–49 (1966).

Ely, N., "Legislative Choices in the Development of Mineral Resources," in *Science, Technology, and Development. II. Natural Resources*, Washington, D.C., U.S. Government Printing Office, pp. 33–44 (1963).

Evangelista, R.E., "Republic Act No. 1180 and Foreign Investments in the Philippines: a Dilemma of Economic Nationalism," *Journal of Law and Economic Development*, pp. 60–88 (1968).

Fatouros, A.A., "International Economic Development and the Illusion of Legal Certainty," *American Society of International Law Proceedings*, pp. 117–26 (1963).

Fisher, G., "La souveraineté sur les ressources nationales," *Annuaire Français de Droit International*, pp. 516–28 (1962).

Frei Montalva, E., "Urgencies in Latin America: the Alliance that Lost its Way," *Foreign Affairs*, pp. 437–48 (1967).

Friedmann, W.G., "Antitrust Law and Joint International Business Ventures in Economically Under-developed Countries," *Columbia Law Review*, pp. 780–91 (1960).

Friedmann, W.G., "Relevance of International Law to the Development

Process: a Panel," *American Society of International Law Proceedings,* pp. 8–15, esp. pp. 13–15 (1966).

Führer, H., "Le rôle des investissements privés étrangers dans le développement économique," in *L'Observateur de l'O.C.D.E.,* (special issue on development aid) pp. 43–50, September (1966).

Gaitskell, A., "Joint Capital Structure," in *Investment and Development: the Role of Private Investment in Developing Countries,* London, Overseas Development Institute, pp. 51–57 (1965).

Gess, K.N., "U.N. Resolution on Permanent Sovereignty over Natural Resources," *International and Comparative Law Quarterly,* pp. 398–450 (1964).

Golbert, A.S., "Legal Incentives and Realities of Private Foreign Investment in Turkey," *American Journal of Comparative Law,* pp. 351–60 (1967).

Gordon, M.W., "Joint Business Ventures in the Central American Common Market," *Vanderbilt Law Review,* pp. 315–38 (1968).

Haight, G.W., "The Sherman Act, Foreign Operations and International Law," in C. Shaw, *Legal Problems in International Trade and Investment,*" New York, Oceana Publications, pp. 89–109, esp. pp. 92–96 (1962).

Haight, G.W., "Some Aspects of United States Antitrust Laws and Foreign Commerce," in H. Landau, *Doing Business Abroad,* New York, Practicing Law Institute, pp. 266–84, esp., pp. 271–76 (1962).

Henderson, D.F., "Contract Problems in United States–Japanese Joint Ventures," *Washington Law Review,* pp. 479–515 (1964).

Hyde, J.N., "Permanent Sovereignty over Natural Wealth and Resources," *American Journal of International Law,* pp. 854–67 (1956).

Hyde, J.N., "Economic Development Agreements," 105 *Hague Recueil de Cours,* pp. 271–374, esp. pp. 271–87, 332–55 (1962).

"International Joint Ventures Corporations: the Drafting of Control Arrangements," *Duke Law Journal,* pp. 516–30 (1963).

Jaeger, W.H.E., "Joint Ventures: Origin, Nature and Development," *American University Law Review,* pp. 1–23 (1960).

Jaeger, W.H.E., "Joint Ventures: Membership, Types and Termination," *American University Law Review,* pp. 111–29 (1960).

Jaeger, W.H.E., "Joint Ventures: Recent Developments," *Washburn Law Journal,* pp. 9–44 (1964).

Jennings, R.Y., "Extraterritorial Jurisdiction and U.S. Antitrust Laws," *British Year Book of International Law,* pp. 146–75 (1957).

Johnson, J.G., "Problems of Organization for Overseas Operations," in C. Shaw, *Legal Problems in International Trade and Investment,* Dobbs Ferry, N.Y., Oceana Publications, pp. 27–44, esp. pp. 35–39 (1962).

"Joint Venture Corporations: Drafting the Corporate Papers," *Harvard Law Review,* pp. 393–425 (1964).

Kahn, Ph., "Problèmes juridiques de l'investissement dans les pays de l'ancienne Afrique française," *Journal du Droit International (Clunet)*, pp. 338–90 (1965).

Kahn, Ph., "Problèmes juridiques des investissements étrangers dans les pays en voie de développement," *International Law Association Conference Report*, pp. 835–60 (1966).

Kopelmanas, L., "Le régime juridique des investissements étrangers dans les pays en voie de développement," Milan, Università, Instituto di Diritto Internazionale e Straniero, Communicazioni e Studi, pp. 1–20 (1966).

Kovar, R., "La congolisation de l'Union Minière du Haut-Katanga," *Annuaire Français de Droit International*, pp. 742–81 (1967).

Kozyris, P.J., "Equal Joint Venture Corporations in France: Problems of Control and Resolution of Deadlocks," *American Journal of Comparative Law*, pp. 503–28 (1969).

Krause, H.D., "The Multi-Corporate International Business Under Section 1 of the Sherman Act—Intra-Enterprise Conspiracy Revisited," *Business Lawyer*, pp. 912–38 (1962).

Kurk, N.M., "Foreign Collaboration Agreement: Policy as Law," *Journal of the Indian Law Institute*, pp. 1–70 (1967).

Kust, M.J., "Minority Ownership in the Context of Sound Finance for Developing Countries," in J.F. McDaniels, ed., *International Financing and Investment*, Dobbs Ferry, N.Y., Oceana Publications, pp. 503–13 (1964).

Lachmann, K.E., G. Swope, Jr., S.V. Goekjian, and S. Sherwood, "Role of International Business in the Transfer of Technology to Developing Countries," *American Society of International Law Proceedings*, pp. 31–57 (1966).

Lagos, G., "Socio-economic, Legal and Institutional Aspects of Multinational Enterprises," in *Multinational Investment, Public and Private, in the Economic Development and Integration of Latin America*, Bogota, Inter-American Development Bank, pp. 199–231 (1968).

Laughran H.S., and J.V. Foster, Jr., "Foreign Investment in Mexico: the Emergency Decree of 1944," *Tulane Law Review*, pp. 538–57 (1965).

Legoux, P., "De quelques codes d'investissement," *Revue Juridique et Politique—Indépendance et Coopération*, pp. 939–86 (1968).

Logie, J., "Les contrats pétroliers iraniens." *Revue Belge de Droit International*, pp. 392–428 (1965).

Loretta, F.B., "Joint Ventures in Mexico," in *Doing Business in Mexico*, New York, American Management Association, pp. 13–17 (1964).

McDonald, R.J., "Controlled Foreign Corporations," *Institute on Private Investments Abroad*, New York, Matthew Bender, pp. 5–58 (1963).

Malia, G.A., "Jointly-owned Companies Operating Abroad: a Problem in Antitrust Policy," *Georgetown Law Journal*, pp. 125–42 (1958).

Martin, E.M. Jr., "Multilateral Investment Insurance: The O.E.C.D. Proposal," *Harvard International Law Journal,* pp. 280–338 (1967).

Maw, C.E., "Joint Ventures Abroad—Forms and Methods," in *Negotiating and Drafting International Commercial Contracts,* New York, Matthew Bender, pp. 171–98 (1966).

Meek, M.R., and I.R. Feltham, "Foreign Sales, Distribution, Licensing and Joint Venture Agreements," *De Paul Law Review,* pp. 46–76 (1967).

Meynen, J., W.G. Friedmann, and K. Weg, "Joint Ventures Revisited," *Columbia Journal of World Business,* pp. 19–31 (1966).

Michida, S., "Capital Liberalization as a Treaty Question and Offensive and Defensive Strategy Concerning Foreign Capital," *Law in Japan,* pp. 1–44 (1968).

Mikesell, R.F., "Some Conclusions for Public Policy in the Light of Current Developments," in R.F. Mikesell, *U.S. Private and Government Investment Abroad,* esp. pp. 541–88 (1962).

Moon, F.F., "Administrative and Legal Controls: How and Who?," in *Private Investors Abroad: Structures and Safeguards,* New York, Matthew Bender, pp. 1–21 (1966).

Nitschke, R.A., "Some Antitrust Aspects of Doing Business Abroad," *Institute on Private Investments Abroad,* New York, Matthew Bender, pp. 559–83, esp. pp. 570–72 (1959).

Paillère, M., "Le contrat d'investissement dans les pays en voie de développement," in *Les investissements et le développement économique des pays du tiers monde,* Paris, Pédone, pp. 118–57 (1968).

Parsons, R.W., "Tax Problems Relating to a U.K. Business Operating in Australia," *British Tax Review,* pp. 177–96 (1968).

Pedler, F.J., "The Problem in East and West Africa," in *The Encouragement and Protection of Investment in Developing Countries, International and Comparative Law Quarterly,* Supple. 3, pp. 63–77, esp. pp. 72–77 (1962).

Penard, M., "Les contrats de licence," *Revue économique et sociale,* pp. 9–22 (1964).

Penrose, E.T., "Foreign Investment and the Growth of the Firm," *Economic Journal,* pp. 220–35 (1956).

Penrose, E.T., "Monopoly and Competition in Petroleum Industry," *Year Book of World Affairs,* pp. 150–78 (1964).

Perroux, F., and M. Byé, et al., "Firmes plurinationales," *Economies et sociétiés,* Geneva, Droz, pp. 1701–1867, esp. pp. 1725–45, 1829–67 (1968).

Pešelj, B.M., "Yugoslav Laws on Foreign Investments," *International Lawyer,* pp. 499–518 (1968).

Petroni, D.V., "Doing Business in Eastern European Countries," in *Pri-*

vate Investors Abroad-Structures and Safeguards, New York, Matthew Bender, pp. 261–326 (1966).

Pitofsky, R., "Joint Ventures under the Antitrust Laws: Some Reflections on the Significance of Penn-Olin," *Harvard Law Review,* pp. 1007–63 (1969).

Proehl, P.O., "Private Investments Abroad," *Journal of Public Law,* pp. 362–73 (1960).

"Pros and Cons of Joint Ventures Abroad," New York, *Business International,* 22 pp. (1963).

Raymond, A.G., "Tax Aspects of Joint Ventures and Oil Operations in Latin America," *Institute on Private Investments Abroad,* New York, Matthew Bender, pp. 63–109, esp. pp. 77–78 (1962).

"Rights of Private Investors in, and Legal Nature of Joint Ventures," *United States Trade and Investment in Latin America,* Conference on Legal Problems of Trade and Investment in Latin America, New York, Columbia Society of International Law, pp. 173–98 (1963).

Rogers, P.N., "Private Investment in Developing Areas: a Private View and a Private Experience," in *Methods of Industrial Development,* Paris, O.E.C.D., pp. 287–98 esp. pp. 292–94 (1962).

Rosen, M.M., "The International Finance Corporation and Private Investment for Economic Development," in *Problems and Solutions in International Business in 1968,* New York, Matthew Bender, pp. 29–39 (1968).

Rosenstein-Rodan, P.N., "Multinational Investment in the Framework of Latin-American Integration," in *Multinational Investment, Public and Private, in the Economic Development and Integration of Latin America,* Bogota, I.D.B., pp. 21–87, esp. pp. 52–87 (1968).

Ross, W.R., "The Foreign Joint Venture Corporation: Some Legal and Business Considerations," *Denver Law Journal,* pp. 4–19 (1968).

Samuelson, A., "Les investissements directs américains dans une économie engagée dans le développement: le cas du Mexique," *Revue de Science Financière,* pp. 896–954 (1968).

Sanchez, J.D., "Benefits and Contributions of Foreign Banks to Developing Nations," Washington D.C., Mexico–United States Committee, 5 pp. (1967).

Scace, A.R.A., "Degree of Canadian Ownership: an Exercise in Futility?" *Osgoode Hall Law Journal,* pp. 295–315 (1965).

Schwarzenberger, G., "The Principles and Standards of International Economic Law," 117 *Hague Recueil de Cours,* pp. 5–98, esp. pp. 29–33 (1966).

Schwarzenberger, G., "An International Insurance Agency?", *Year Book of World Affairs,* pp. 172–84 (1969).

Scott, J.C., and S.K. Yablonski, "Transnational Mergers and Joint Ventures Affecting American Exports," *Antitrust Bulletin*, pp. 1–36 (1969).

Shapiro, I., "Obstacles to Trade with, and Investment in the Soviet Union and Eastern Europe," in *Problems and Solutions in International Business in 1969*, New York, Matthew Bender, pp. 173–91 (1969).

Sherwood, R.E., "Antitrust Considerations in Negotiating and Drafting International Commercial Contracts," in *Negotiating and Drafting International Commercial Contracts*, New York, Matthew Bender, pp. 81–101 (1966).

Soedjatmoko, "Foreign Private Investments in a Developing Nation: An Indonesian Perspective," in *Problems and Solutions in International Business in 1969*, New York, Matthew Bender, pp. 305–29 (1969).

Soemitro, R., "Investment of Foreign Capital in Indonesia," *Bulletin for International Fiscal Documentation*, pp. 496–510 (1968).

Sonnenreich, M.R., "Protecting the United States Minority Shareholder in Joint International Business Ventures in Latin America," *Virginia Journal of International Law*, pp. 1–35 (1964).

Sproul, R.G., Jr., "United States Antitrust Laws and Foreign Joint Ventures," *American Bar Association Journal*, pp. 889–95 (1968).

Stunzi, J.R., "Local Capital Participation v. the Wholly-owned Company —Advantages and Disadvantages of the Two Approaches," in *Increasing Profits from Foreign Operations*, New York, International Management Association, pp. 101–107 (1957).

Suy, E., "La protection des investissements étrangers," *Industrie*, pp. 584–97, esp. p. 591 (1963).

Thompson, A.R., "Sovereignty and Natural Ressources—A Study of Canadian Petroleum Legislation," *Valparaiso University Law Review*, pp. 284–319 (1967).

Upton, T.G., "The Inter-American Development Bank and Private Investments in Latin America," in *Problems and Solutions in International Business in 1969*, New York, Matthew Bender, pp. 111–35 (1969).

Vagts, D., "The Multinational Enterprise: A New Challenge For Transnational Law," *Harvard Law Review*, pp. 739–92 (1970).

Vernon, R., "Multinational Corporate Planning," *Harvard Business Review*, pp. 156–72 (1967).

Vernon, R., "Conflict and Resolution between Foreign Direct Investors and Less Developed Countries," *Public Policy*, pp. 333–54 (1968).

Vernon, R., "Economic Sovereignty at Bay," *Foreign Affairs*, pp. 110–22 (1968).

Visscher, Ch. de, "De la protection diplomatique des actionnaires," *Revue de Droit International et de Législation Comparée*, pp. 624–51 (1934).

Visscher, Ch. de, "La technique de la personnalité juridique en droit international public et en droit international privé," *Revue de Droit International et de Législation Comparée*, pp. 475–87 (1936).

Wall, E.H., "The Iranian-Italian Oil Agreement of 1957," *International and Comparative Law Quarterly*, pp. 736–52 (1958).

West, M.W., Jr., "Thinking Ahead: The Jointly Owned Subsidiary," *Harvard Business Review*, pp. 31–32, 34, 165, 166, 168–70, and 172 (1959).

Woods, G., "Finance for Developing Countries: A Time for Decision," New York, Columbia University, 18 pp. (1967).

INDEX